RELUCTANT ACTIVIST

OTHER BOOKS BY ROBERT BONAZZI

Author

Awakened by Surprise: Selected Fictions
Outside the Margins: Literary Commentaries
Man in the Mirror: The Story of Black Like Me
The Scribbling Cure: Poems & Prose Poems
Maestro of Solitude: Poems & Poetics
Perpetual Texts: Poetic Sequences
Fictive Music: Prose Poems
Living the Borrowed Life: Poems

Editor

(Books by John Howard Griffin)

Black Like Me: 50th Anniversary Edition
Follow the Ecstasy: Thomas Merton's Hermitage Years
Scattered Shadows: A Memoir of Blindness and Vision
Available Light: Exile in Mexico
Prison of Culture: Beyond *Black Like Me*
Encounters with the Other, Essays
Street of the Seven Angels, Novel
The Devil Rides Outside, Novel
Nuni, Novel
Pilgrimage, Fiction

RELUCTANT ACTIVIST

The Spiritual Life and Art of John Howard Griffin

AN AUTHORIZED BIOGRAPHY

Robert Bonazzi

TCU Press
FORT WORTH, TEXAS

Library of Congress Cataloging-in-Publication Data

Names: Bonazzi, Robert, author.
Title: Reluctant activist : the spiritual life and art of John Howard Griffin / Robert Bonazzi.
Description: Fort Worth, Texas : TCU Press, [2018] | Includes bibliographical references.
Identifiers: LCCN 2017017818 (print) | LCCN 2017021835 (ebook) | ISBN 9780875656793 | ISBN 9780875656663 | ISBN 9780875656663?q(alk. paper)
Subjects: LCSH: Griffin, John Howard, 1920-1980. | Authors, American—20th century—Biography. | Civil rights workers—United States—Biography. | Catholic converts—United States—Biography.
Classification: LCC PS3557.R489 (ebook) | LCC PS3557.R489 Z57 2017 (print) | DDC 813/.54--dc23
LC record available at https://urldefense.proofpoint.com/v2/url?u=https-3A__lccn.loc.gov_2017017818&d=DwIFAg&c=7Q-FWLBTAxn3T_E3HWrzGYJrC4RvUoWDrz-TlitGRH_A&r=O2eiy819IcwTGuw-vrBGiVdmhQxMh2yxeggw9qlTUDE&m=7gPT-v5aScP5Mp36xwlIPwa4Rdw4aJpViFD7rmoE-uYg&s=f_61MTerf5ak9DUY7cuLorrQlyK-CIKvwQsC8VIHmzWQ&e=

TCU Press
TCU Box 298300
Fort Worth, Texas 76129
817.257.7822
www.prs.tcu.edu
To order books: 1.800.826.8911

Cover and Text Design by Preston Thomas

Cover photo by Gregory Parker Griffin

To Paul Christensen—
always in the dialogue.

In Memoriam for
John Howard Griffin
Elizabeth Griffin-Bonazzi
Gregory Parker Griffin
Lawrence Bonazzi
Daniel L. Robertson
Russell Hardin

CONTENTS

PART IV

INTRODUCTORY

Real genius is nothing else but the supernatural virtue of humility in the domain of thought.

—SIMONE WEIL (1909-1943)

But in the fund of the Spirit what matters most is not what we do but what is done to us.

Pious people are apt to be rather inhuman; holy people never.

—GERALD VANN (1906-1963)

Before the cliff top is reached the artist creates art for his people; when it is reached, the artist expresses his great and violent vertigo of discovery—and this is usually and rightfully of a realism that many call obscene—and finally, when he plunges into the transfigured world of mysticism, his art must become dedicated to the essence of his love, which is God, and secondarily and subsidiarily to man.

The three levels of time: The plane of inertia, the plane of moral taboo, and the belief not become faith. The crucial, critical time-lapse when the artist is given a vision of the Eternal and a simultaneous vision of the status quo; when the artist realizes the vast divergence between the dead motives of credibility and the living realism of Faith as reflected in society and as reflected in God.

—JOHN HOWARD GRIFFIN (1920-1980)

John Howard Griffin

Strange, even prophetic, reads the liturgy for Griffin's birth date of June 16, 1920. He observes in the *Journal* on February 21, 1977:

> I was reading through today's Mass, and then looking up once again the liturgy that was being celebrated for January 31, 1915, the day Thomas Merton was born. The readings that day are almost prophetic of the man he became. Then I decided to look up the liturgy that was being celebrated the morning I was born. Checked it both in the English Missal and in an antique French Missal—and they coincided. I was simply astonished. It was as though all my problems, all my vocation in life were formed by the liturgy of that day.
>
> The versicle of the Gradual reads: "Lord, deliver me from treacherous lips, the perjured tongue." Always the most difficult part of my life has been the attempts to character-assassinate me, to ruin our name. And the Gospel, dealing with the rich man who gave the dinner party, and when his guests found excuses not to come, sent out for the poor, the crippled, the blind, and the lame.

Griffin was *not* being merely rhetorical in identifying with that list of guests, for he had lived through a decade of blindness, endured paralysis during the mid-1950s, and periods of immobility due to diabetes and heart disease in the late 1970s. His intense faith began with a conversion to Roman Catholicism in 1951, even as he struggled with a sense of unworthiness. "My strength of soul is so insulated with weakness, love of luxury, lust, and jealousy that it deadens me, and now, since I will never

Gregory Parker Griffin (at age ten) took this photo of his father in 1966, when the author was forty-six, in Fort Worth, Texas. The portrait was the dust jacket for *The John Howard Griffin Reader* (Houghton Mifflin, 1967).

become a monk, I begin to make the private attempt to live like one during certain hours of the day, offering all my work to God."

His daring genius inhabited a secular cell, keeping his secrets in the intimate *Journal*. As with Albert Camus, a writer he admired enough to make a rough translation of *The Stranger*, Griffin strived for a vision beyond the absurd, to "remain lucid in ecstasy," as Camus writes. And like his fellow outsider in France, Griffin understood that art and suffering were necessary counterpoints, sensing the truth in Camus's metaphor: "Illness is a convent which has its rule, its austerity, its silences, and its inspirations."[1]

Born Howard Griffin in Dallas, and always called "Howard" by family and old friends, his name went through various permutations. While a student at the Lycée Descartes boy's school in Tours, traveling to France in 1936 several months before he turned sixteen, he adopted his father's name of "John" ("Jean" in French), because teachers and classmates mispronounced Howard as "Ho-vard," and that would not do for a budding Francophile. After escaping the Gestapo in 1939 and joining the Army Air Force in 1941, Griffin pretended to be a Frenchman among fellow soldiers. But his war buddies were *not* impressed and called him "Griff"—a name that stuck throughout 39 months of service in the South Pacific.

Early on during blindness, Griffin used "Lou Smollett" as a pseudonym (a play on Scottish poet and picaresque novelist Tobias Smollett) when his first short story, "The Big-Time Stockman," appeared in *Farm and Ranch-Southern Agriculturist* in 1952. He was pleased because his family and their neighbors read the magazine, and he was proud to have earned his first small paycheck as an author.

When Griffin's first novel, *The Devil Rides Outside*, was also to be published that year, he preferred to remain anonymous.[2] But the local first-time publisher hoped to capitalize on his notoriety as "a blind war hero"—a promotional strategy he could not abide. It was the *only* book ever published by the Smith brothers of Fort Worth, Texas. Finally they all settled on "John H. Griffin" (copyright reads "John Howard Griffin"). When Houghton Mifflin published *Nuni*, he became John Howard Griffin on the title page, and the issue was resolved.

But what's in a name? The Griffin, that mythical creature formed of a lion's body and the head and wings of an eagle, was an apt symbol for his character. He had the ethical courage and purity of heart attributed to the lion. He also had the qualities symbolized by the eagle—speed of flight in the sense of imaginative leaps, and an inner vision to match the keen acuity of that airborne hunter.

The word *Griffin* also refers to an Occidental recently arrived in the Orient—an equivalent for a stranger in a strange land. He knew the predicament of the *outsider* in foreign countries, as well as being a *stranger* in the mirror in *Black Like Me*. Also the term *griffe* in the dialect of the Deep South meant a child born of Negro or mulatto parentage. Irony of ironies.

In the 1966 portrait on the dust jacket of *The John Howard Griffin Reader*, we see him at age 46, in a photograph taken by younger son Gregory Parker Griffin. The author wore dark glasses to shield his eyes that were highly sensitive to sunlight, after recovering sight in January of 1957. But in this portrait he has no glasses, pictured at the apex of fame and at the height of his powers, appearing deceptively healthy and peering intently into the camera.

Griffin had high rounded cheeks and a strong cleft chin. Handsome proportions distinguished his mature visage—a nose with a slender ridge above thin lips. A prominent forehead revealed furrows when he stared with deeply set hazel eyes. Thick, straight brown hair was parted on the left, neatly trimmed, graying at the temples. In later years he went entirely gray and wore several differently shaped beards. When he stood to his full height (six feet, two inches), he projected a formidable presence, but never a threatening one. While not possessed of athletic grace, he moved smoothly for a large man, then about 220 pounds. He was capable of nimble dexterity when handling a camera, playing a piano, using a typewriter, and lighting one cigarette after another.

One would *not* have presumed Griffin to be an artist, until he began to speak. In a rich tenor, he softly enunciated words with a distinctive accent that carried a hint of French. He was also a good mimic and could produce a convincing Southern or Texan accent. Griffin's natural tenor was resonant and confident, although it turned nasal and agitated when he was engaged in a heated discourse. This was clear in his first radio interview with Studs Terkel in 1960, when he spoke rapidly, with his pitch rising sharply.[3] His lectures were studded with sophisticated arguments and vivid anecdotes that he delivered calmly and without notes.

When among family and friends, Griffin never tried to impress anyone with his erudition. He told a story with suspense, set a scene in precise detail, and drew laughter with his dry wit. He was quick to smile and to laugh in a funny *staccato* giggle that belied his physical stature. He was sweet-natured, gracious, and courteous; one sensed in him an air of gentility. Griffin was capable of dominating a conversation, yet rarely did so, because he was also an intent listener. In dialogues with family and friends he was immersed in the immediate conversation and nothing else seemed to matter except that human moment of communion. This does not include all his moods, for Griffin was an extraordinarily complex and sensitive person who could display a wider range of emotions in private situations. We have his widow's witness and Griffin's naked *Journal* to substantiate this more comprehensive portrait.

Writing in several genres, Griffin's natural approach was to be as truthful as possible—most obviously in the *Journal*, in personal essays, and in texts on racism. His novels echoed classical music forms, and while he said his characters were fictional, some were based on people he had encountered. Only in rare instances did he allow anyone except an editor to read manuscripts before publication. This attitude was born of a brooding insecurity about everything he wrote, which can be traced back to having begun writing when he was nearly thirty and already blind. He was unselfconscious while writing, but extremely self-conscious about publication. When he wondered if his books were good enough, he was asking if they were *true to the experience or the vision of the work*. Once any writing was published, however he never looked back over his shoulder to admire it. The goal was always to be writing the next work.

After the publication of *Black Like Me*, everything Griffin said or wrote about racism came under the deepest self-scrutiny. He never avoided the implications of prejudice, and his ethical and moral views demanded that he encounter, understand, and strive to transcend his own racism. These questions were at the root of his solitary struggle, but since he would become a public figure, his queries about sincerity and privacy of conscience became part of the political debate on racism. He succeeded with seeming effortlessness in the public arena, keeping his focus and everyone's attention on the central issues. If he thought he had found a solution to the problem, he expressed it, but if he was uncertain or did not know, he said so. His sincerity and humility were genuine, but by his own account, he was grossly imperfect. He knew he was a sinner who could fall into anger or despair, because he was all too human. But without this deep sense of justice for humanity and genuine self-criticism, his work would have been irrelevant.

Intelligence and ethics controlled his viewpoint in nonfiction works. He approached and analyzed cultural phenomena but was always compelled by human essences. Griffin was *not* a saint, although he strived for sanctity in humility, but never expected to reach such stratospheres. He was in awe of the Desert Fathers, St. Thomas Aquinas, and St. John of the Cross—and considered the theologians and philosophers he knew to be spiritual guides. Often he praised writers outside the Catholic tradition—Heraclites, Chuang Tzu, Montaigne, G.B. Shaw, Viktor Frankl, James Baldwin, Malcolm X, Lillian Smith, Ernest Becker, Jonathan Kozol, and many others.

Griffin's vow of obedience in offering his work to God reads more nakedly than conventional tact might decree. But his vows were kept secret in the private pages of the *Journal* and personal letters. He believed that it was no one's business, and he never paraded his spiritual vision for public scrutiny.

His approach to photography was different from the writing he slaved over. Often he developed photographs in the darkroom the day they were shot, sharing the images immediately. Classical music was also a spontaneous experience, and his delight or disapproval in a performance was apparent. Griffin grew up in the early modern period that seems quaint now, when a middle-class family might have a piano in the parlor, before they owned a phonograph. It was an era when painting meant using oils and easels, when cumbersome cameras shot black and white film that was loaded from canisters, and writing was done in handwritten notebooks. He did not learn to type until his first attempt to write fiction. He matured during the time of typewritten manuscripts and never saw a personal computer or a digital camera.

Griffin's photography advanced once he regained sight in 1957, but he had no darkroom until moving to Mexico in 1960. His sophisticated cameras (a Swiss Alpa and several Leicas) were loaded with black-and-white film. He used color film for family photos, which were printed commercially. Before regaining sight, he played the radio in the barn studio—not always with happy results—as popular programming assaulted his musicologist's ear. After regaining sight, he listened to classical music on an impressive collection of long-playing records. Later he embraced the advantage of taping the LPs to cassette tapes for a portable recorder.

Everything Griffin published opened a divide between supporters and detractors. Those who criticized him were offended by his uncompromising vision and because he was a person they could *not* imagine being. The artists and thinkers who supported him recognized that exposing the truth would always be controversial. The voice is clearly his in all the work, the same voice heard during our visits, over the phone, and in taped interviews. His published work reached the world and touched the depths of shared human experience beyond cultural prejudices. He was a universal writer because his words went to the heart of the human condition. He was a "radical"—but only one for equal justice for all people.

Nonetheless it is *Black Like Me* that most readers know, if they know of Griffin's name and books at all. The case was never made for *Black Like Me* as the very first "nonfiction novel" before that term was coined, when Norman Mailer and Tom Wolf were publishing their "non fiction novels" to popular acclaim. Griffin integrated all of the novelistic techniques in *Black Like Me*, although never thinking about inventing a new form. Griffin read few novels, because he did not want to be influenced by popular or even literary fiction. Perhaps now we can read *Black Like Me*, containing beautiful lyricism and ethical empathy, and be moved by the fine writing, and by its humane, spiritual perceptions.

Strangers in the Mirror

There are several key passages about peering into the mirror in *Black Like Me*, used as a framing device throughout the book, including when Griffin first examines his disguise as a black man on November 7, 1959. "In the flood of light against white tile, the face and shoulders of a stranger—a fierce, bald, very dark Negro—glared at me from the glass. He in no way resembled me."

Years before *Black Like Me*, when Griffin was blind and never expected to regain sight, he muses in the *Journal* on August 10, 1954.

> I wonder how I should feel if I could suddenly see my face in a mirror after these long years of blindness. What did I look like? I remember no face in any mirror, but I do remember my face in photographs. Would I be shocked by the change? I know that my hair is graying, that my face perhaps has deeper wrinkles, but what of the expression? Would I look anything like I think I look—but then it occurs to me that I have no thoughts whatsoever of how I look. This must have been the concept man had before the invention of mirrors.

Ending with "the invention of mirrors" recalls the words of John Harper, the first-person narrator of *Nuni*, conjuring "aboriginal" man looking into a calm pool in the jungle. Griffin composed all of his novels during a decade of blindness, basing *Nuni* on his year among the native people of the Solomon Islands during World War II. In this scene, the American professor who reached the island after a plane crash sees a reflection of himself for the first time since the plane crashed weeks before.

> For an instant I see the unruffled picture of an old man, his sparse hair awry, his bearded features sketched in with peculiar softness, his eyes hollow and deeply sunk beneath the silvered outcroppings of his eyebrows, his face given fullness by the down pull of gravity. The image overwhelms me with its newness.
>
> It is the first time I have seen myself since the crash, and I am seeing here a stranger, coarsened and aged beyond all recognition, but also strengthened in traits with a thick vein I have never before noticed tracing itself down the side of my temple. Beyond treetops in the water, clouds march majestically across the heavens, full-bulked and somber, until a drop of sweat from my nose detaches itself and ripples the vision.

After Griffin regained eyesight in January of 1957, he notes in the *Journal*, "By noon—and it was that way every day—I was exhausted from nothing more than the intense excitement of seeing new things. This day had marked one week since regaining sight. Then it struck me that I had not yet looked in the mirror. I saw the face of a stranger, a man now graying and lined. It never occurred to me that a decade would make such a difference in my appearance."

In the initial mirror encounter in *Black Like Me*, in the scene from *Nuni*, and on first seeing his reflection after sight recovery, Griffin spies a stranger in the mirror. In all of these scenes he does *not* recognize himself—in *Black Like Me* because disguised, in *Nuni* because the narrator has no mirror, and in the *Journal* entry, because he had been blind for a decade. The resemblances in these reflections, written close in time between 1954 and 1959, are consistent in their perplexity about extrinsic identity and concern for the person hidden under layers of social conditioning. The physical changes and the loss of his image reservoir are metaphors for perceiving humanity stripped of cultural veneer. Griffin learned to see in a fresh way.

More than fifty years ago, Griffin embarked on his 1959 journey through the South disguised as a Negro, a bold risk based on a simple, provocative premise—to experience daily life as a black laborer and to keep a journal with absolute truthfulness, even if his discoveries proved to be prejudicial, embarrassing, or naïve. Rather than explain personal motivations for *Black Like Me*, he offered an "official" explanation, explaining that he was researching the escalation of black male suicides in the South.

He documents this in *A Time to Be Human* (1997), his final book on racism, providing detailed information about the premise and data.[4] He began by mailing questionnaires to whites and blacks in the traditional mode of sociology. But the replies soon convinced him this basic "objective" approach was not useful. While many opinions were gathered, the data revealed no truths. The replies received from whites were usually the same—they did not believe that black people committed suicide. "They are just naturally happy-go-lucky people," opined one white man. "When something troubles a Negro," said another, "he goes out and finds a shady spot under a tree and sleeps it off."

Griffin recognized two obvious fallacies in these replies. "First, I could not question the sincerity of these people. We have been brought up to believe these myths about blacks. Second, it was evident that no matter how distinguished a person might be, or how much the vast majority accepted such myths, the myths were untrue. The history of suicides among black people and other minorities in this land is, and has always been, appalling. To suggest that black people, by racial characteristic, never commit suicide is simply to lie in the face of fact and history."

The responses of black people were entirely different. Griffin was "astonished" that their questionnaires contained no answers. "The few that were returned blank were accompanied by explanatory letters. These said, in essence, 'We don't answer this kind of questionnaire anymore. We have answered them in the past but we will not answer them in the future.' For the first time one black man used the term I had never heard before, but I found it accurate and illuminating. He said, 'You probably can't help it, but you think white.' A black sociologist wrote: 'We don't believe it's possible for a white man, even one trained in the sciences, to interpret his findings without *thinking white* and thereby falsifying the truth.'"

Griffin took his cue from what the unnamed black people had said. "It seemed to me that if I could take on the skin of a black man, live whatever might happen and then share that experience with others, perhaps at the level of shared experience we might come to some understanding that was not possible at the level of pure reason." He attempted to communicate experience at the level of human understanding, rather than merely *thinking* white or black.

He gave a more personal answer in *A Time to Be Human.* "I think it finally boiled down to the fact that I had children. I knew without a doubt that my own formation, no matter how benevolent, had filled me with prejudices at deep levels that had probably handicapped me for life. And I did not want my children, or the children of any person (of any color), to grow up in a climate of permissive suppression of fellow human beings, if I could do anything to prevent it. In other words, my deepest motive was simply to preserve my children and the children of others from the dehumanizing poison of racism."

Earlier in a 1966 interview, Griffin echoed this response and added something else. "I tell people simply that I don't want my children to become racists. And that's a good enough answer, even though it is not the real answer." Why was it not the real answer? "In the first place, it was nobody's damned business what my motives were. It's true that I don't want any child growing up being a nasty little klansman with distorted views of what fellow human beings are. But the very idea of anyone probing the privacy of another man's conscience, it seems to me, is the greatest obscenity we know today. I utterly refuse to judge a man's motives, because I don't think you can know a man's motives. And I think this is a frightful, obscene thing to do, and it is also highly dubious."[5]

The integrity of the act was significant for Griffin. Any attempt to affix a motive to a particular action, to psychoanalyze, or to judge from a distance, was appalling to him. He believed that the fascinating questions emerged from examining the cultural formations of prejudice. If there were real answers, they would be discoverable in the learned behavioral patterns of a society, since we are conditioned by the same clichés and the same system of unconscious values that society consciously reinforces. The real question must be why is America a racist society and *not* why did Griffin disguise himself as a Negro. Any "motivations" for the experiment are illuminated by the events and influences that led up to that bold encounter.

Griffin's southern background had taught him the "whole mythology of race." He knew the essential importance of understanding cultural conditioning, believing firmly that real knowledge emerged from direct experience, self-criticism, and evolving insight. He had learned from direct experience about blindness and suffering, about racism and war. Black experience could never be understood from the vantages of academic armchairs and psychoanalytic couches, or from *thinking white*. These racist myths were exposed with deepening understanding in his subsequent lectures, articles, interviews, monographs, and books. Yet Griffin felt no necessity to explain his reasons in the search for justice any more than he needed to explain his creative process in the quest for art.

From the outset of Griffin's lecture tours and network appearances in 1960, he made it clear that he was speaking only about his experiential encounters with racism. "I don't stand up here and represent myself as a spokesman for black people," he told audiences, repeating this critical point in articles. "This is a personal book," he writes in *A Time to Be Human*. "I will simply talk about my own experiences with racism; first as a white child growing up in Texas, then as a black man in the South in 1959, and since then as a white man once again in the ghettos of most of our major cities and in many other countries."

Unlike his friends in solidarity—Martin Luther King, Medgar Evers, and the unsung troops in the Civil Rights Movement—Griffin was not murdered. But he did suffer a brutal beating in Mississippi in 1964. The Ku Klux Klan members left him for dead, but he survived the injuries and never spoke of it publically.

In a 1975 interview with Studs Terkel, Griffin explains. "I have become far less visible as a public figure involved in racial reconciliation. Once a few whites had to speak out for justice and interracial dialogue at a time when whites would not listen to blacks and few blacks would listen to whites. But those days are over and it is absurd for a white man to presume to speak for black people when they have superlative voices of their own."[6] He agreed with black leaders who suggested that white activists needed to focus on educating their own communities.

Throughout his public career, from 1960 to 1975, Griffin addressed mostly white student audiences because Dr. Martin Luther King and Roy Wilkins encouraged him to enlighten white America, since African Americans knew segregation intimately. Griffin viewed his role as "a bridge to reconcile the tremendous duality of information and viewpoint which whites and blacks have and on which they make judgments—as well as the kind of misinformation whites believe that leads them to make judgments that are ethnic rather than human." He was an effective voice for equal justice because of the unique perspective of *Black Like Me* and his involvement in the human rights movements and crises of the 1960s and 1970s. But he was effective also due to his communicative gifts and compelling qualities as a man. He functioned as a bridge of dialogue, because he had "access to and experience in both black and white cultures." It was "not a vocation that is specifically black and white," but "a vocation for the reconciliation of humanity." He held no heroic illusions about himself or what he did, realizing that it was "not the kind of work which produces statistical or measurable results." He did not expect to end racism or to see equal justice in his lifetime, but he continued the struggle even though it went against his deepest inclinations.

"It isn't my nature to be an activist," Griffin tells Studs Terkel in their final conversation in 1978, "but your vocation doesn't necessarily conform to your nature."[7] The public life cut against the grain of his deepest desires for family intimacy, solitary writing, and spiritual contemplation. Yet Griffin obeyed a greater will that demanded merciful acts in a merciless world, and "if you get the calls you can't say no." He went on tour when he was quite ill or recovering from various surgeries, and even when his mobility was reduced to crutches or a wheelchair.

Always the reluctant activist, Griffin hesitated in 1959 before departing on his six-week journey through the Deep South. He was not fearless—and fear had to be overcome. Even as he faced the stranger in the mirror that first time in New Orleans, he wondered what to do, how to do it, and where he would find the courage. On several occasions in *Black Like Me* he retreats—from fear and doubt, despair and exhaustion—to seek refuge and replenishment in the homes of friends, in a Trappist monastery, or by withdrawing into the solitude of a shanty room. Yet Griffin returned to the journey in order to test his ethical convictions, to search for a deeper understanding, and to follow his avowed faith in "the reconciliation of humanity."

Text of the Body

John Howard Griffin lived a long dying that he contemplated in his last years as a double reality. He viewed the pain and physical disintegration as only one level of truth to be accepted simply as what was and as what must be.

"If all this is my reality," Griffin points out in the 1978 *Journal*, "there is another reality that makes mine also slightly different." That other reality, not separate but coupled in an embrace of wholeness, was perceived "in the fact that God has sent me a great richness of friends so that the emptiness of trying to live is mitigated by the fullness of that love, which seems a direct and real expression of God's love." Griffin believed "because of the blessings, this is a time of the most powerful richness and the most terrible wretchedness of my life. The fact that they happen to coincide is the greatest blessing of all."

The spiritual realm did not erase the pain, emotional stress, or mental anguish, but provided the courage to transcend the trap of meaninglessness. Griffin glimpsed this when facing oncoming blindness in 1946, while making a monastic retreat in Paris. Focusing on sunlight bathing the snow-covered trees, he observes in *Scattered Shadows*: "It rarified the atmosphere within my cell, gave a hitherto unnoticed detail and dimension to the walls, the furniture, and to my senses. 'This must always be,' I told myself. If this ever vanishes into the other, then it will all be delusion. The body must not become my enemy."[8]

Griffin realized the incongruity of his situation. Even if he were *not* blind, he had been formed intellectually by a classical education, and his emotions were impassioned by the ancient spirituality of Gregorian Chant that lifted his spirit to realms he did not yet dare to know. Later he would feel out of place in rural Texas, and out of time during the placid 1950s, yet it would become the space of remote solitude he needed. Griffin knew the world of silence to be eternal, if he could but hear it. Soon he would be blind and it would take years to adapt to the modalities of sightlessness. But he would not feel it necessary to dread the future. This earlier intuition held true in his magnificent essay, "The Terrain of Physical Pain," and reasserted its wisdom during his final years. The dying body did not become his enemy, but the instrument for enlightenment, even as its limitations could not be escaped.

Griffin's prose illuminates poetic texts of the body. He became a connoisseur of the other senses that were greatly enhanced and refined—judging livestock by feel, hearing tones in the voices he had missed while sighted, and developing the senses of smell and taste as a gourmet cook of French cuisine.

When enduring paralysis during 1954, he views his body as "a different species, as legitimate and normal as that other animal whom I resemble in some ways. I am an eyeless and legless man in whom pain is the norm—"

> a completely different entity, completely normal to the potentialities and drawbacks of my state (I do not say *condition*). It would be as ridiculous to mourn the fact that I have no eyes and legs as it would be for another to mourn that he has not four eyes and six legs.
>
> He is a two-legged, two-eyed type and I am a no-legged, no-eyed type, and I know, although he would find it difficult to believe, that what I am and what he thinks I am are two different things entirely, for he is incapable of judging me except from his own standards. So he grieves my loss, whereas I can feel no loss at all, but only confidence that God made me this way because He wants me this way. . . .
>
> We are the lucky ones, for what God takes away, He replaces, and we get a great intimacy with God without doing anything voluntarily ourselves.[9]

Griffin turned out to be right in saying that what is taken away is returned, for the paralysis was lifted and eyesight returned. He refined sight beyond its previous level of acuity, making this apparent in visionary photography. Encased in the time-bound wound rose a spirit to the threshold of liberation, lifting the ravaged body beyond inertia and pain, beyond doubt and fear—to a realm of second innocence. The body endured the discord of temporality, as he transcended toward the eternal embrace.

"I don't know how other people work on faith," Griffin says in a 1977 interview with Thurston Smith, "but for me it was an almost existential choice. There was no other way to go. I tried to do the will of God as well as I could, and the first thing I discovered was that this didn't automatically make me a lover of God." His reference was to blindness, when he had experienced spiritual crises that were resolved only by immersion in writing as a gift to God. "The second thing I discovered is that most often people interpret the will of God through their own desires. I found that never really worked for me; the will of God rarely coincided with any desire of mine!" His allusion was to the ardent desire for artistic solitude and family intimacy against the deep loathing for the public life that *Black Like Me* had demanded. Yet he obeyed the call of justice, accepting the inevitable attacks.

Then Griffin speaks of a most recent discovery. "Toward the end, I've come to the realization that all that I believed was right and all of it was truth. That I was right about the reality of faith. That's been an extraordinary revelation."[10] The rightness had come with his first "yes" to God, uttered cautiously in 1946, while he was studying Gregorian Chant at the Abbey of Solesmes, shortly before his eyesight was entirely gone. That was when he began the journey along a solitary path, even though many crises would obscure it and violent crossroads would seem to obliterate it. He had not perceived it then, because his inner path would be revealed only in the darkness of his spiritual struggles during blindness.

Griffin's resistance to conversion is reflected in *The Devil Rides Outside*.[11] The unnamed narrator of his first novel, an American student of musicology researching the chants in a French monastery, does *not* make the great leap of faith. In *Scattered Shadows*, the autobiographical text that covers his actual stay at Solesmes, Griffin made it clear that he did say "yes" there and then, but admitted that his affirmation had been whispered with great fear and trembling.

Griffin made his commitment "official" in 1951, when he was converted to Roman Catholicism. But even after marriage in 1953, he agonized over his unworthiness, doubting not God but himself. That period of agony is reflected in his second novel, *Nuni*, when he was paralyzed by spinal malaria. "I am aware perhaps that I am putting the problems of my life into the lap of Professor Harper and I am desperate for him to solve them," he admits in the *Journal.*

> I am stripping him of everything that men generally consider necessary to a man's ability to function at the human level—family, friends, even clothing, and plunging him into a world he is ill fit to live in. With me, the prospect is similar, though I never mention it aloud. First my blindness, then this paralysis and loss of mobility, the uncertainty of the prognosis. It must drive us to turning into vegetables of frustration or it must drive us to God or an equivalent thing above and beyond us, to abandon ourselves finally, after all the self-delusions of seeming abandonment, to the great "yes" (as the French call it), to the *fiat*, and only after passing through it can we begin to live again as functioning human beings.

Professor John Harper must find faith in a silent God, while stripped of identity and stranded on an unknown island. The narrator becomes immersed in that reality, releasing delusions of self-interest and preconceptions of a "superior" civilization that had conditioned him. Harper goes deeper into the spiritual realm than the anonymous narrator of the first novel. The professor risks everything to save an innocent native girl-child, whereas the musicologist in *The Devil Rides Outside* is unable to transcend his egocentric predicament, denying the selfless love that the professor embraces. Each narrator reflects, in artistic terms, the reality of the author's personal struggles, and each novel maps in fiction the inner path that Griffin followed toward spiritual liberation. While *The Devil Rides Outside* builds a bridge toward illumination for the narrator and eventual conversion for its author, *Nuni* maps paths of pain, emotional loss, and spiritual crisis for both Harper and Griffin.

Black Like Me traces a textual map of Griffin's journey, viewing a series of mirror images that reflect his real struggle. The stripping-away process—as he slowly lets go of self-interest and the stereotypes of white supremacy and privilege—allows him to be immersed in transformative experience, while simultaneously observing his evolving behavior toward absolute justice. *Black Like Me* is at once the externalized body of a new text and the interior vision of flawed humanity.

The dramatic risk of "becoming a Negro," which tends to be the aspect that impresses most readers, was secondary to dismantling his unconscious prejudice. Writing the book was the first stage. By allowing it to be published, he offered to the public shameful disclosures in print and later in lectures. Certainly the bold experiment took courage, but retelling his story took greater courage.

Peeling away layers of ego, Griffin's artistic credo of "selfless self-awareness" held a disciplined focus on the good of the work. As essential as his ethical responsibility to fight injustice, his spiritual solitude was equally essential. Thurston Smith evoked the risk of *Black Like Me* in the interview.

> Smith: Well, you've made some fantastic gambles in your life. The obvious one was putting that drug into yourself and changing the color of your skin. That is a risk unparalleled.
>
> Griffin: But what people don't really know is that a long time before this, I took another great gamble—what the French call simply *le grand oui*, 'the great yes.' The gamble was for God. That means leaping off that cliff and never knowing where you're going to land, but you have the faith that you are going to land somewhere.
>
> Smith: What are you referring to?
>
> Griffin: My conversion. But it was more than that for me. I took the initial gamble, but it's not the one that lasts. I go through reconversion every day.

By "reconversion," Griffin meant saying "yes" to God and offering everything in faithful adoration. Earlier it had meant his works of art and acts of social conscience, and all along his path it included contemplation, prayer, and the suffering of physical pain. Near the end of life, with only a small residue of energy remaining, he offered what was left—the very wretchedness of his dying.

The once robust man had been reduced to a helpless invalid. The last journals reflect the vision of a dying man nurturing an undying faith, a naked mercy, and the wisdom of second innocence. He contemplated dying with the same insightful honesty that illuminates his social critiques and journals of solitude, the photographic portraits and fictional characters, and the loyal, enduring connections with loved ones.

These same qualities are evident in Griffin's meditation on suffering, "The Terrain of Physical Pain,"[12] making clear that pain and suffering are as universal as racism and death. The redemptive quality of suffering cannot be measured quantitatively, as faith cannot be proved by tangible results.

Yet he experienced the truth of these effects in the solitude, believing that any sufferer, "if he has been deeply enough wounded, will remain reawakened to mercy and to that whole mysterious cycle of replenishment in which he has allowed himself to be used, to be an instrument." He accepted that his last "acts of faith and hope no longer lie in writing books, but in keeping contact with a few beloved friends, studying and praying as much as I can, and by growing plants with the incentive of living to see them blossom."

His meditations on dying are not about death but about being alive. He had "died" many times during his last three years, often suspended unaware that his lungs had ceased breathing, his heart had stopped beating, that pulse had gone silent. But a loved one had always been there in time to save him. Thus, dying had become commonplace. But living continued to be fascinating, especially keeping the spirit alive. At the end he was "refusing to count the days or weeks or months, refusing to think that soon I will die or that some medically inexplicable healing might occur." Instead he was "being obedient to the doctors and, insofar as I can discern it, to the Holy Spirit, hanging on to love and some kind of innocence, trying to have enough presence of mind in the bad hours to go on saying 'yes' and meaning it."

Griffin's intuition connected these seeming opposites at the level of Being. The body was not debased to purify the soul, and the mind refused to trivialize matters of the heart. He admired J.S. Bach equally as a family man and as an artist of the spirit. While he had been trained as a scientist, he believed in transubstantiation.

Even though Griffin was called a "Renaissance Man," this glosses the surface of his deeper spiritual orientation grounded in the ideals of obedience and humility. The Renaissance meant the invention of the ego, a focus on the secular, on historical time, and on progress—the opposite of his focus on spirituality, on eternity, on anonymity. His critique of white racism, segregation, and injustice links him to the nonviolence of Gandhi and Martin Luther King, which was based on Natural Law and the ancient ideals intrinsically attached to the sacredness of life.

Perhaps we can understand Griffin more accurately as a "Modern Medievalist," as one blessed with a contemporary alchemical imagination, creating novels shaped by sublime music, transforming film into magical images, and transfiguring the *I* into the *Other* in *Black Like Me.*

The Journal

Like *Man in the Mirror*, this biography continues a dialogue with a mentor, but expands the commentary on his life and work.[13] Most chapters hone in on crucial years or Griffin's significant books, while others are overviews of issues. The chapters are chronological, and although every year is not examined in precise detail, the text moves from birth to death. During the time frame of the *Journal*, (1950-1980), I lean on its spine. For aspects before 1950, I draw on personal essays and *Scattered Shadows*. In the years covered in that memoir, 1945-1958, I focus on aspects that are not in the book, but also quote from it. Of the many witnesses no one was more insightful than his widow (and my late wife of seventeen years, Elizabeth Griffin-Bonazzi, 1935-2000), who not only had a superb memory of events, but also worked diligently typing the manuscripts we prepared for posthumous publication.

One of the criticisms of *Man in the Mirror* was that the book quoted Griffin too extensively. This is a valid criticism, because he *was* often quoted in *Mirror* (and more often in this book). But I disagree that he was quoted too extensively, and there are reasons for my disagreement. Griffin was remarkably quotable, and his main themes are articulated in the lucid, truthful *Journal* entries. Passages are excerpted from personal letters and the voluminous journals, which will remain inaccessible unless one researches in the archival institutions that hold his papers.

Griffin's *Journal* is an open book, a text of identity through change. His entries are never those of an objective observer, but about the daily reality of going it alone through the isolation his radical experiments imposed. Like other literary journals from the last century (Kafka, Camus, and Anaïs

Portrait of Elizabeth Ann Griffin-Bonazzi (1935-2000) by JHG, in 1960, which was taken in Mexico where Griffin turned the *Sepia* articles into the best-selling book, *Black Like Me*.

Nin), he recorded the vision of the outsider. He thought that André Gide's journals were "too carefully written for effect," but discovered in Kafka's diaries a truthfulness that was "total reality and therefore total inconsistency." Yet Griffin was moved most by the notebooks of Thomas Merton, and he was the first to read them as the monk's official biographer.

> Such writing, needless to say, has no value to the writer if he has any idea that anyone will ever see it. It has value and authenticity only when done in the complete freedom of privacy, where one has no need to be consistent, where there is no concern for the proprieties that unconsciously begin to color the materials if one thinks that another will see them. These are mediations on paper, reactions, descriptions; and because there is no need to make them eloquent, sometimes they contain the greatest eloquence.

In these remarks about Merton, Griffin characterizes his own *Journal*, which is as unique as the man. His actual experiences were more fantastic than fiction. To the degree he wrote this reality into fiction, the journal form was his natural genre from the beginning, when he began *The Devil Rides Outside* in 1949.

His *Journal* also reveals the private man behind the public image, the spiritual epiphanies and breakthrough insights, along with a ledger of the most commonplace events. Experiential time is contextualized by historical time. We know what year and month it is and usually which date. Many entries begin in early morning, leave off, and are returned to later that night, often identifying the passage as "Later" in the text. Griffin discusses why he kept a journal.

> I always advise the keeping of a private daily journal in which the writer describes, with total honesty (and with no thought of another's ever seeing it), his feelings, problems, emotions, reactions, random thoughts, temptations, and all of the private dramas and dreams of his day; and also all of those striking things he sees and hears that soon escape memory unless set down. This is an important discipline for many reasons.
>
> It is writing, gaining facility and technique. And if it is honestly kept, it will have the tremendous advantage of giving the writer a true knowledge of himself, the motives for his actions, the wide range of his

> spiritual fluctuation. This can be horrifying, sometimes overwhelmingly so, for it is humbling to see oneself without illusions, but it is the old Socratic way to wisdom and compassion.
>
> What has this to do with writing? It has much to do with it, because it allows the writer to create directly and without wending his way through all of the jungles of delusions and self-aggrandizement. The act of creation is far more profound in its sources than most of us consciously realize. It comes up mysteriously from the very depths of a being, and that sound box which is the spirit must be tempered and balanced as near as possible to the truth in order to produce the truest work.
>
> Honesty and a type of selfless self-awareness are remarkable antidotes to the poisons of pride and egotism, and one of the best ways to achieve them is keeping a journal in which he submerges himself to the truth, in which he quickly learns the difference between "what is" and "what appears to be."
>
> The profoundest truth constitutes the greatest originality.[14]

Black Like Me, later chapters of *Scattered Shadows: A Memoir of Blindness and Vision*, and *The Hermitage Journals* are truthful books drawn from Griffin's *Journal.* He revised these autobiographical works for publication, but his core realities stand firm. He kept the *Journal* "because it puts on paper what would enter into the realm of forgetfulness, and I am thrifty enough to know that I can come back to these, and in these thousands of pages, find something that I could reproduce later—find some thought, some expression or reaction that lives and breathes."

The *Journal* was Griffin's sourcebook for transforming experience into insight, but he never overestimated its literary value.

> Anticipating writing these notes, I wondered what I write them for. Most of them are utterly insignificant. Who will ever read them? Surely it is only for myself that I write them, to get things down, to think at the typewriter—to capture the insignificance of details in history, for I find that I do not write of the great events, but of the little ones, which somehow touch our daily lives. Will some student a thousand years from now, or a hundred, find these pages somewhere and read them and wonder about this time and place, and find it all primitive, as I have found in reading the memorabilia of past civilizations—and yet perhaps universal in that only the conditions are primitive by some

> future standards? Will there be a future or will these pages disappear with us in some nuclear holocaust? Who knows?[15]

Yet his journaling was never about the ego.

> Nothing is a greater waste of time than admonitions to 'Know Thyself'—one must know, but objectively; to be able to stand off from self and observe, in order to learn, but not to judge. The only way is self-abandonment, to get rid of self. Otherwise, an artist can never succeed to make of himself anything but a mask. The only value of self-knowledge is to escape *the delusion of self* in which all of our culture wraps us—that fastidious delusion which even our intimate experience fails to show us is a lie.

PART I

Our conflict is not between body and soul, but between our potential longing for the decency of happiness (including all the pleasures of body and soul) and for the indecency of certain pleasures made poignant to us through our conviction that they are vitiating. It is between the decency that keeps instincts in the realm of life, within the orbit of the ordo universali; and the indecencies that turn us away from the universal order and signify the ultimate passion for death. Our longing is between the will to live and the will to suicide.

Humanity is tortured by guilt because we are constantly tempted toward base and evil acts, never realizing that though such acts may be base and evil, the temptation to commit them is not. We have so personalized, rationalized, and cheapened religion that it now appears to be less an answer to spiritual hunger than to spiritual lust. Many misguided souls seeking to attain to the supernatural life think they have succeeded when in reality all they have done is to divorce themselves from what is natural in life.

This is why we have neurotics and bigots instead of saints.

—JOHN HOWARD GRIFFIN

Acts of Immersion

Classical music was John Howard Griffin's deepest artistic passion, imprinting on him an indelible spirituality throughout his brief life.

"Certainly nothing, no other art, no other form of communication is capable of possessing my heart and literally transforming me into the core of harmony as completely and magically as music," he writes in the *Journal.*

Born in 1920 at Baptist Hospital in Dallas, Griffin grew up listening to classical music. "Every morning I had awakened to hear my mother practicing the piano—sonatas of Mozart and Schubert, Bach preludes and fugues. We lived in a world of great music and books, kindness and religious fervor."

Lena Mae Young, born in Dallas in 1901, was a classically trained pianist who taught at the Fort Worth Conservatory for thirty years. She was the first teacher to give private lessons to African American children in the Dallas-Fort Worth area. She realized early on that her second child had perfect pitch and taught Howard to read music and to practice at the piano. Closely bonded, they shared an intense dedication and joyful love of classical music. While he never considered himself an accomplished keyboard artist, he remained an ardent student musicologist.

His father, John Walter Griffin (known as "Jack"), was born in Dallas in 1895. As a young Irish tenor, he hosted a local radio show. Most of his adult life he worked as a salesman in the wholesale grocery business. Jack was twenty-two when he married Lena, who was only sixteen at the time. "My father is a man I will never understand," Griffin admits. "He was brought up in that fundamentalist Baptist religion which said that anything remotely pleasurable was sin—an incredibly racist atmosphere.

But he *never* implanted any of these ideas in his children. My dad was a kind of miracle, a matter of pure grace. He was a wholly decent, uncorrupted human being," despite genetic roots in the arch-segregationist Georgia Griffins.

Howard made excellent marks in school and served as an altar boy at St. John's Episcopal Church in Fort Worth (his mother was Episcopalian). His early religious views were partially formed under the spiritual guidance of a close family friend, the Reverend Sherwood Clayton. "Memory of all the discomfort, the sleepiness, the awful 'secret' that I was unworthy to serve with Father Clayton at the altar, that behind it I was distracted by worldly concerns. However the memory itself is simply a long series of moments of quiet, of gentleness, of goodness."

His mother characterized him as "the different child in our family; a wonderful little boy with the most beautiful disposition." The family included older brother Edgar and younger twin sisters, Jacquelyn and Kathlyn. They listened to vinyl records and radio broadcasts featuring the great orchestras and virtuosi of the 1920s and 1930s. The first recording Griffin bought was a performance of the Beethoven *Violin Concerto*, featuring Jascha Heifetz with the New York Philharmonic under Arturo Toscanini. His first favorite composer was Schubert. Later it was Chopin, then Mozart, and then the list grew and grew. He did not restrict his taste among the classical geniuses, but never cared for lesser composers or other musical genres.

Griffin tended to be a loner, and when reaching tenth grade at Paschal High in Fort Worth, he felt limited by the curriculum of the public school system. "I was bored out of my mind. I had what they used to call a photographic memory. I memorized a whole school course in one week." He was unable to study Latin and Greek because they were not offered. He was "utterly impassioned by the sciences," but found no guidance, planning "to study medicine eventually." He supplemented his education with the *Harvard Classics*, "containing works I have cherished throughout the years ever since my grandfather, Samuel Clements Young, left them to me at his death, after having lent them a volume at a time when I visited."

After reading a newspaper article about concert pianist Moriz Rosenthal, Griffin became devoted to learning, allowing later developments come as they would in the way of a career or vocation. Reading the piece "opened up a far more fascinating horizon," discovering that "Rosenthal, like Schweitzer, earned degrees in medicine and philosophy, in addition to being an eminent musician."

A few months later, Griffin spotted a magazine advertisement for a boys' school in France and wrote a letter to the Lycée Descartes in Tours.[16] Since his parents were of modest means and had other children to educate, the teenager offered to work as a janitor for tuition. His letter was written as a secret dare. He had not expected a reply and forgot about it. When a letter arrived six months later from the headmaster of the lycée, inviting him to attend at no charge, he was stunned. If his parents could afford passage, the headmaster offered a scholarship, but which did not include room and board. His parents scraped together the cost of passage and promised a little monthly stipend. They allowed him to go at the urging of Reverend Clayton. Griffin recalls, "They were worried that France was both Catholic and utterly immoral, and they didn't know which was worse!" But they were supportive of the teenager's new path, even as it invariably strayed from the conventionally average. "It was painful for them, though they never said a word. I missed the revolt against my parents, and this made me closer to them than most children."

In 1936—a few months before he turned sixteen—Griffin sailed for France in search of a "classical education." This first Atlantic voyage to the Old World where "you could advance as fast as you could learn" began the intellectual adventure he had longed for. He arrived a few weeks before classes and survived on his first stipend, sleeping in the fifteenth-century Cathedral of Tours. From sheer necessity (and with the aid of a tattered dictionary), he acquired enough conversational French to get by until the new school term began. Eventually, he became proficient in French, and teachers guided him to fluency and a convincing accent. Those astounding years opened a wider world, and that initiation was immediate and lasting.

The French encounter struck an essential chord presaging a new direction that meant spending time in solitude. "I am tremendously preoccupied with the problems of loners, men who struggle to go it alone. To go with the crowd makes a man seek the average instead of what is truly his own normalcy, his own truth. Men do this and end up being all alike—one mediocrity is like another. And then they realize it too late."

Following the examples of teachers he admired, Griffin developed his dedication to learning. Art articulated his emerging ideals and visceral resistance to conformity. "All the pressures of society tend to conformity, to the crowd, to the monolith that eventually tries to destroy the one who is different, the one who has tried to be true to himself, his vision. The merely average hates true normalcy, as though it were hating the reminder of a dream long lost."

Nothing was lost at the Lycée Descartes. Griffin found the quality of teaching and depth of scholarship he dreamed of, receiving the discipline he needed, since the regimen of that time was "almost monastic in its strictness." Students were not allowed off the grounds and rarely read newspapers or heard the radio. The lycée reinforced a sense of obedience to learning instilled by his parents.

> For recreation we read books and studied paintings, and our discussions centered in an awakening awareness of sex and art. The Latin and Greek classics, Moliére, Racine—these were our background, and our most heated enthusiasms brought forth the names of Braque, Vlaminck, Chagall, Matisse, and Derain in painting, of Rimbaud, Apollinaire, Claudel, and Reverdy in literature.

Griffin read philosophy and studied the sciences, finishing in two years with excellent grades. Continuing in music, he developed a "fascination with Beethoven from reading Aldous Huxley's *Point, Counterpoint*, in which my predisposition for the Beethoven's late String Quartets was established, quickly followed by Beethoven's late piano sonatas, and an extreme response to chamber music that led to Mozart's string quartets and Schubert's *C major String Quintet*." Two French classmates who became loyal friends exposed him to new music. Jacques Duthoo introduced modern French works and art songs. Jean Hussar "opened doors to the music of Bach, as well as Debussy's opera *Pelleas et Melisande*."

During Griffin's first year at the lycée, a teacher suggested he keep a journal, and "I wrote faithfully in the journals, everything I read, felt and did." But when France was about to fall, he buried them.

> Years later when I returned, I retrieved the journals which had been buried on the Duthoo's family farm and began to reread them. It was a sickening experience. Pages filled with literary and musical analyses, with scarcely a word about the supreme reality of the war which preoccupied

> us. It was pure escape from that reality rather than any attempt to handle it. I was heartsick to find myself so false that I burned those pages.

Visits to the Duthoos were "filled with books and music and walks or horseback rides in the beautiful forests around the chateau."

> In those days I was on my Wagner binge, and the Duthoos were determined I become convinced that Debussy and Ravel were just as great or greater, so Jacques introduced me not only to Debussy and Ravel, but also to such composers as Roussel, Dukas, Fauré, and Honneger. It was there that I came to love the recordings of Roland Hayes, and played them so much I almost wore them out. It was also in those marvelous rooms that I came to know intimately the Schnabel recordings of the Beethoven concertos and sonatas, and the Schubert sonatas; the Ravel and Debussy piano works played by Cortot or Gieseking.
>
> From the library each night I took books to my room and read as long as I could hold my eyes open—the complete works of Balzac, Rabelais, Flaubert, Proust, Gide, Anatole France and many more, including the René Bazin biography of Charles de Foucauld, which so fascinated me—and dozens whose names have not lived.[17]

In 1938, just after entering medical school in Tours at age 18, Griffin rented a third-story garret in a pension, a cubicle with an old bed, a writing table, and a coal stove that attracted boarding house students for warmth and conversations. From there he made a rail trip to Paris for a performance by soprano Kirsten Flagstad in Wagner's opera *Tristan and Isolde*. Counting his saved francs, he figured to afford a third-class railway pass and the cheapest opera ticket, which would mean no meal or bed for the night. He decided to take the risk.

> I had never done anything like this. I was far from adventurous then; I was a studious scientist. The whole idea horrified me. But I knew that if I didn't go, I might regret it all my life. I decided to go, and that decision had far-reaching effects. The experience I had that night made me what is known as "adventure-prone," and probably was directly responsible for my becoming a writer.

Griffin traveled to Paris, attended a "magnificent performance," and faced a cold, rainy night, with pockets empty except for a railway pass. Hungry and shivering, he began walking in search of shelter. About to give up, he saw a chestnut vendor closing down his stand. They struck up a conversation and he was given a bag of chestnuts and directed by the vendor to the *Cour de Rohan* (a thirteenth-century sector across the river from *Notre Dame*) where the poor found refuge. He was told that the doors were not locked and the first two he tried opened. But the air was so "fetid" that he went to a third, which was no different. Exhausted, he stretched out on the grimy stone floor, and became "acutely aware" of cold discomfort and "totally absorbed" in his misery. Then a curious change began to reshape his awareness.

> But slowly, another feeling aroused me from my self-preoccupation. It occurred to me that all of this was interesting. I began to detach myself from my discomfort, and as I did so, I realized that this was an experience worth having—or rather, one that would someday be worth having *had*. I asked myself how many men had ever slept under the stairway of a 13th century house? To sleep in a comfortable bed was fine, but if you looked at it in a certain way, this was fine, too. I would forget the many nights spent in comfort and safety, but I knew that I would never forget this night.
>
> Therefore, it was worth experiencing, worth giving myself up to. All things took on new values. The floor became instead of something hard and tormenting, stones that had been laid there centuries before with pride by some craftsman. It became a thing which had known the weight of saints and sinners long dead. It became itself, giving up its secrets to me.
>
> Why? Because instead of *immersing it in myself, I was immersing myself in it.* All I had done was change my attitude. I was still miserable, but it had become unimportant. I had ceased to be a person judging everything on the basis of pleasure or comfort. I had gone out of myself to the value of things in themselves; and I have never since been able to step back consistently into mere self-interest.

During that unexpected epiphany in Paris, Griffin had become immersed in *experiencing experience* rather than internalizing it. Instead of contorting the intrinsic value of reality to fit preconceptions or fantasies, he embraced it with a focused detachment beyond "mere self-interest."

In art this is the humility of a work not falsified by prideful self-expression. Instead of reducing an ideal to ego, Griffin attempted to dissolve ego in the service of an ideal. He believed the perfect example of this ideal in the spiritual realm to be the anonymous monks who had composed the unsigned masterpieces of Gregorian Chant. After the Paris episode he approached experience with a more open attitude. His adult *Journal* is a long immersion in truthful writing. Most entries were not reshaped into published works, but many recall vivid memories of France, before and during the war. One recollection after the trip suggests that his move toward immersion in otherness had not reverted to self-interest.

In the *Journal* entry for January 14, 1954, written 17 years later, he describes being "filled with energy and interest," while

> walking for long hours through the narrow cobblestone streets of the cluttered "old quarter" that dates back to the 12th and 13th centuries with little change—an unbelievably interesting section, smelling always of garlic and wine and vegetables and coffee and the reek of people living in greatest poverty. In the cold days, when the air was heavy with mist and fog, I would spend hours walking, looking up at the balconies that seemed almost to touch from houses facing one another across the tiny streets that curved and wound like back alleys.
>
> My heart would be filled with loneliness lightened by fascination, for it seemed as though I were walking through a world of the Middle Ages; and to contemporary eyes, accustomed to modern homes, every brick, every low door entrance, every worn stoop, every long passage leading into inside courtyards was a miracle of the past brought into the present. All was small—as though in miniature—and it seemed that the people who inhabited this quarter and these dwellings had simply lived on, without change, from the time of the original buildings.

This scene amplifies the Paris awakening that led to his transformational insight about *total immersion* and *selfless self-awareness*, remembering that "It was on one such trip into this section that I chanced across one of the most extraordinary (because so unexpected) experiences of my life—one I shall never forget."

> It had become my custom to open doors occasionally, for many led into somber, unlighted vestibules or passageways back into courtyards. Turning down a side street, I saw a great double door with ancient iron hinges on either side. I lifted the latch and looked in. All was darkness, except that light from the open door illuminated a patch on

the stone floor. The faint odor of dust and incense, not warm, but dry, floated to me, and leaving the door open, I ventured inside. As my eyes became accustomed to the darkness, I saw the faintest pinpoint of light glistening beyond the black hole of the inner door, and I walked slowly toward it. All was silence and it seemed that my shoes creaked with deafening loudness. As I stood in the inner doorframe, I realized that I was at the entrance of some hidden chapel, for the small light was that of a candle, and it was joined by other votive candles.

Beneath the flickering red of the sanctuary lamp, I distinguished a small altar which seemed to be ghostly blue in hue, and was perhaps marble. It was covered with white linens, and I was vaguely surprised that the linens seemed to stay white and not become pink or red from the reflection of the sanctuary lamp that hung, suspended on a fragile gold chain, above them. There seemed to be a number of potted plants and I had the impression that they were artificial—palm fronds made of green paper. The small room had no windows, so that the impression was like that of being in a rectangular cave far from the world. But a door led to the other side, into a dimly lit hall that showed a scrubbed and waxed floor, and beyond that, some winding stairs leaning upward. The only two entrances were the way I had come, and the door opposite, which led into some sort of cloister, for occasionally a nun, clad in white robes, would appear and walk over, genuflecting before the tiny altar, and touch another on the shoulder, and this second nun would rise and leave by the same door.

Other than myself, there were constantly two nuns, facing the altar on their knees, praying silently. The room was about ten feet wide and twenty feet deep, with twelve pews facing the small altar space. There was such an air of reverence, and I was surprised to discover this hidden corner in the midst of such a district, wherein thousands of poor souls lived with no more privacy than a bee in a hive—to find it so isolated and private, and so unutterably silent, that I could not leave it. And, as I stayed on, nuns came and relieved those kneeling, without speaking. This scene would have been warm, except for a door leading into the polished hall, which was lighted by an unseen window beyond the view of the chapel, for it all was filled with the soft light of votive candles, while the light from outside was coldly gray and pervasive in its sad reminder that it came from outside, from the world of misery. I left

> finally, with great reluctance, and felt the peculiar constraint not to talk of this to anyone— to keep it as a secret, a place where I might be away from the world.

That hidden cloister seemed strange, but not forbidding. He was drawn into the silent chapel but unsure why. He learned from a priest that it was the Chapel of the Sisters of Perpetual Adoration. The nuns worshipped day and night in their role of guarding the altar and praying for those who forgot to pray. Alternating two at a time, the tabernacle was never unattended.

Griffin returned a week later "but could not find it, and was strangely affected, for it seemed to me that it had all been so haunting as to have not actually existed. I returned to my room mystified and disappointed." But when he returned to the quarter six weeks later he found the chapel.

> The village was dark when I made my way out into the snow-covered streets, and the air was rare with the freeze. It was almost one in the morning. Without difficulty I went almost directly to the little alleyway and found myself standing in front of the door. Night was fathomless in its darkness, and there were no stars to be seen through the murk of low-hanging clouds, but a peculiar luminosity seemed to float down and reflect from the snow, so that all things could be seen as if they had no shadows, as though they were painted on the face of the night with grays, in two dimension, but without depth, and certainly without any clarity of detail. I was almost frozen, and my feet were wet in my shoes as I stood trembling outside of the door in that incomparable stillness.
>
> I wondered if it would be possible to find anyone inside, or if perhaps something had happened and the nuns did not keep perpetual watch after all, so inconceivable did it seem that anyone else could be awake that deathly night. I opened the door and it swung back on its hinges with a frightful scream. I stood in the doorway a long time, and the scene was almost unchanged—the same candles, the same statues and the same ancient odors of sweetness. I knelt in one of the back pews and allowed the peace to infuse me, becoming a receptive organism without thought, as remote from the world as if it did not exist.
>
> I did not worship, for I was not really capable of it, but I experienced in deep measure the worship that must have accumulated for centuries into the very marrow of each stone. It was such an overwhelming aura that all else was shut out. The very air was filled with

> the incense of prayers that went up from this hidden place. I knelt there in the cold, feeling only warmth, acutely aware of this reaction of peace, of the complete lack of necessity to think, or to be anything except a soul kneeling there, absorbing the evocations of silence and radiance; all made more precious and unreal by the fact that I was there alone—that no one in the world knew of my whereabouts except the two nuns who perhaps, even though taking no notice, were aware. The three of us—two dedicated women and one clay hunk of a man suspended for a time. Then I did not think any more, but drifted with the night and with the feelings of ease and well-being and peace that stopped time and ambition. Those few hours have never left me, although now it is perhaps only a feeling of ill-defined nostalgia; but it lingers, and will always be one of the most precious things that ever happened to my tattered life.

Griffin was unable to "worship," because he had drifted into agnosticism. He had felt "unworthy" for as long as he could remember. Ethics learned early were clarified by his "classic education" and the humanism of French friends.

There was the equally powerful consequence of World War II—Griffin's involvement with the French underground resistance (*Defense Passive*), attempting to smuggle Jews out of France to safety in England. Jean Hussar had introduced him to the underground. Griffin recalls their conversations in the *Journal.* "The talks would invariably contain an element of seriousness, for Jean was discreet beyond his years, and profoundly preoccupied with all that was spiritual in the most noble concept of that extraordinarily beautiful and passionate soul of his. What a priest he would have made, although at the time he was Jewish and had not decided to be converted—something he never did before dying young."

Before the loss of Jean Hussar, who died fighting with the Free French Army against the Nazis, Griffin had met Jean's older brother. "Today, for the first time in my life, I am sure I met God in the form of one of His saints—Jean's brother, André, who has been with the Trappists but was released to do what he could for his country now that France is at war. He came to my room where the two brothers were to have their reunion. He came here as a living legend, known before his Trappist experience for his heroic work among the poor in Paris." André took the name Marie-Bruno as a monk with the Dominicans. While Griffin did not have the courage to take out his camera and "make the photographs I longed to make," he "could not escape the impression that I was viewing him through the camera viewfinder, studying the light on his tonsured head, the steam from the tea that boiled on the hearth and rose up past the red poppies on the wallpaper to haze his face."

Griffin audited literature classes at the University of Poitiers and attended the École de Médecine de Tours in 1938, taking the Hippocratic oath seriously. "I recall an experience in my early days at medical school in France, in the anatomy lab, when we were to begin dissecting cadavers; the talk given by our professor to this effect—that these blackened, formaldehyde forms were once living beings, breathing, loving feeling beings created by God, and that we must handle even this dark leather with the respect this knowledge engendered."

In 1939 Griffin worked as a research assistant at *Asile d'alienés* (Asylum of Tours), where Dr. Pierre Fromenty experimented with progressive psychiatric techniques, including Gregorian Chant as a therapeutic tool to help "incurable" patients. In his first radio interview with Studs Terkel in 1960, he explained.

> I became interested in Gregorian Chant in an odd way. Our research consisted of attempting to do something for the type of person who long ago had been condemned to what we called 'upstairs'—that is, condemned there without further treatment. In those days, if a patient wasn't diagnosed within 30 days he was put upstairs. Over a period of years, without being reexamined in the light of new therapy, they began to lose their sense of language. We applied Dr. James Jean's theory of the physics of sound on the nervous system, studying patients at various intervals in an attempt to bring them back to speech again. Seven hours a day we exposed them to sound. The old modal systems had the most profound effect, so we used Gregorian Chant.

During the same period Griffin studied with Father Pierre Froger, a musicologist and organist at the Cathedral of Tours, with whom he coauthored a musicological monograph.[18] Along with his medical studies, it was the sort of scholarly writing he expected to do. With the outbreak of war in Europe, both advanced areas of study ended. Tours was bombed heavily, and Dr. Fromenty was conscripted into the French army, desperately in need of medical personnel.

"However, being an American citizen, I was placed in charge of the asylum" of 120 patients, along with eight members of an order of nursing nuns to care for them. "At night I would be called out to dress the wounds of our soldiers who were being shipped back to hospitals—at a time when the public was being told fighting had not even begun. Often, by three or four in the morning, runners would come for us, and we would stagger to the railroad to dress the wounds of soldiers returned from the front—almost every night under the black-out lights of the railroad station we would work for an hour or two bathing, bandaging, feeding the shattered bodies of the Senegalese troops being used for cannon fodder by the French."

The medics crawled into the cattle cars where the wounded soldiers lay on straw, providing them with dry bread and red wine, the only available sustenance. Despite the religious struggle he was experiencing, Griffin witnessed something beyond the obvious. It came as a revelation.

> I witnessed the Christ in each of those mangled and stinking bodies; one saw them for an hour and never again, and one had to open one's heart to a tremendous abandonment of love for them or else die of disgust and terror—there was no half way about it, no nice balance or sanity or fastidiousness.
>
> There in the torn bellies was the total wisdom of theology—the wisdom of charity in the old sense of *caritas*; empathy, love of the thing, holiness in the universality of pain felt and pain allayed and the gratitude or hate (it made no difference) that shone from these eyes of strangers as we probed them for shrapnel and hurt them to help them and handled their bodies as one does a baby's.

It was the "universality of pain" Griffin perceived in direct connection with the "wisdom of charity" that mattered to the young medic—rather than the "niceties of choice, the inanities of meaningless little cut-and-dried arguments, the intellectualizing of all these things." He was overwhelmed by the brutal cruelty and selfless charity that were continuous counterpoints in his memory of war.

He worked with Jean Hussar and other young Frenchmen in the *Defense Passive*, smuggling Jewish refugees out of Tours. The refugees were handed over to other teams and transported to the Atlantic port of St. Nazaire. Their most significant rescue attempt of Supreme Court Justice Hermann

Thorn and his wife was not successful. Unable to get safe-conduct papers for the parents, they did save their two children (those under fifteen did not require papers at that time), disguising them as patients in strait-jackets and transporting them out of Tours in the Red Cross ambulance. They saved more than a dozen Jewish children, but their ruse was uncovered when the politician Charles E. Bedaux alerted the Nazis. Three days later Bedaux was arrested as a Gestapo informer by the Free French Army. But Judge Thorn and his wife had already been shipped to a Nazi concentration camp.[19]

In a 1961 letter to novelist Lillian Smith, Griffin wrote: "This is what haunted the rest of my life." In his last radio interview with Studs Terkel in 1978, he expanded on that reality. "I will be haunted to my death by those scenes. Suddenly, I experienced a *double reality*. The first: Parents said, 'It's all over for us. Take our children.' You sat there and realized these parents were giving their children away to strangers. The second: I could go downstairs into the streets and find perfectly decent men who went right on rationalizing racism."

Soon after the Bedaux betrayal, Griffin received a telegram from his superiors in the *Defense Passive*, ordering him to leave France immediately. If captured by the Nazis he would have been tortured and killed. He fled along the same underground route and evacuated to England, passing through Ireland to America.

Back at his parents' home in Fort Worth, Griffin could concentrate on little else except news about the war ravaging Europe. He enlisted in 1941 and went through basic training, earning a technician's badge as a radio operator. Shipped to Guadalcanal with the Thirteenth Army Air Force in 1942, he filled duffel bags with books by Pascal, Molière, Racine, and Dom Mocquereau's classic study of Gregorian Chant.

He continued studies in sound therapy and taught music to combat fatigue cases. "I have always felt that music is truly healing in direct ratio to its greatness as art and communication; and that it is an injustice to subject people in deep and terrible trouble to anything less than the greatest music." He broadcast a program of classical music to front line troops. "I took the job on the *proviso* that I had full control over the selection of the music. I broadcast for two hours each Sunday night, resisting all suggestions from the officers, threatening to quit when they tried to coerce me into music-hall stuff. I played the very greatest music and got no complaints."

After a year in Guadalcanal, Griffin volunteered as a language specialist in 1944, spending that year in a native village on one of the Solomon Islands. He prepared a glossary of the oral Floridian dialect. His superiors considered the assignment important for understanding the native inhabitants, and for gaining their confidence. Since the islanders had been mistreated by the Japanese for generations, they became crucial allies. Griffin immersed himself in the village traditions, befriending Grand Chief John Vutha, who had unified the tribes and brought peace to the islands a few years earlier. Chief Vutha became a hero for keeping his silence about the Allied positions after being tortured by the Japanese. He was awarded the highest military honors from the US and British governments.[20]

In 1945 Griffin was reassigned to the landing base on Morotai as a radio dispatcher. After drawing straws to determine who would remain on patrol during the anticipated invasion, he drew the short straw. He was to keep watch in the radar tent and destroy technical data before it could be confiscated. There was nothing to do but listen to the radio, when he heard the opening of Beethoven's *Opus 132 String Quartet,* "one of the sublimest of human utterances."

> The slow movement absorbed all my attention. Though I knew every note, I listened spellbound once again, as it restored in all its simplicity and grandeur the fresh vision of compassion, gratitude and great tenderness—that vision against which men harden themselves in war. Defensive crusts softened and gradually dissolved within me, leaving me defenseless. In its slow unfoldment, its strange Lydian harmonies, its shafts of light leading the soul into worlds where all was order, it entered the brain and heart and nervous system and totally altered them from what they had been. It created response to the profoundest mysteries, leading to spheres beyond joy and sorrow where the soul is struck with wonder and longing before a fulfillment too immense to be contained.
>
> The war, the black alert, man murdering man—all of these things that had before been commonplace realities—suddenly were incredible, monstrous. With the trauma of callousness dissolved, astonishment overwhelmed. The music had transfigured vision. Above the khaki line of my outstretched arm, objects on the table appeared in sharpest clarity—a package of cigarettes, the red and blue thermos, the books,

> the loaded carbine. The gun fascinated my gaze. It lay like a lump of obscenity in clashing dissonance to the music's evocations.
>
> I wondered if a man, tempered to his fullest humanity by this mysterious order of sounds, could actually pick up that gun and kill another man. I wondered if one of the "enemy" appeared in the doorway, and paused long enough to listen to this music, could either he or I commit the tremendous act of killing?
>
> In this musical dialogue with God, Beethoven restored too clearly the universal order of things. Hearing this, feeling it, how could a man cause another's heart to stop, erase his future…? The music entered its sublimest phase, a part now of my being, more me than myself. With the upsearching viola theme, a phrase from Pascal filtered through memory: "Why do you kill me? What? Do you not live on the other side of the water?" The phrase turned the music coppery.[21]

As the wind flapped the tent roof, Griffin turned in his chair to see "lightning flare silently over the jungle," and the phone rang. It was a call from command, saying there was heavy rain at the base and they did *not* expect a Japanese air attack. He heard the rain as the "Beethoven continued into the final movement." He turned off the lights, sitting on a cot with the carbine across his lap. He felt deep regret when the music ended. "Beethoven had withdrawn, leaving me alone after he had dissolved all the callousness—including that callousness to fear that sometimes passes for bravery—and left me strangely defenseless against the night."

Griffin sensed "a foreboding of violence, a certainty of death." An involuntary vision of Beethoven, dressed as a parish priest, appeared as if "to prepare a condemned man's soul to meet death." He could not erase "the idea that Beethoven's quartet had been the last sacrament." Turning off the lights to see more clearly in the darkness, he observed that the rain had slackened, as sirens and horns blared, signaling an air-raid alert. He trotted down a slope toward a trench as the pattern bombing began at the other end of the airstrip. "A shell shrieked downward and I threw myself to the ground. Covering my head with my hands, I heard my voice boom back from the wet coral against my cheek—*Mater misericordiae.* While I cringed against the falling bombs, I felt astonishment that these words had burst into my consciousness."

His body was discovered the next morning and pulled from a trench. He did not regain consciousness at the base hospital until days later, when he was diagnosed with a severe concussion. The doctors did not realize that the young soldier had lost most of his eyesight, which he kept secret. After four years of military service, including thirty-nine months overseas, he was desperate to return home. His secrecy worked until the final examination, having "perfected the role in all its details, with obsessive patience and cunning—the role of the fully-recovered man." The doctors believed that he was still in a traumatic state, preferring to keep him under observation. He broke down, begged to be released, assuring them he would visit an eye specialist. They did not believe him, but he was released. Griffin's separation papers were dated December 15, 1945, and he was shipped out to San Francisco.

He had earned the rank of sergeant and several medals and commendations, but never claimed the medals or filed for service benefits. He rejected war and declared himself a pacifist. He lived most of 1945 at his parents' home in Fort Worth. Local specialists confirmed his vision to be 20/200, and deteriorating rapidly. He would be blind within a year. He was fitted with a pair of thick lenses that were tinted to protect his sensitive eyes, and he bought a powerful magnifying glass for reading. Any hope for a medical career was gone, so he concentrated on music. While in the South Pacific, he studied musical scores, played keyboard instruments, and developed new compositions. None of his scores survived the war.

Griffin wrote a letter to his old friend, French pianist and composer Robert Casadesus,[22] then director of the music conservatory at Fontainebleau. Within a few weeks a letter informed that all was being prepared for his return to France, although Casadesus was unaware of Griffin's failing eyesight. Soon after he received official acceptance from Claude Levi-Strauss, Minister of Culture.

In the summer of 1946, hoping to become a composer, the twenty-six-year-old American sailed again toward his adopted homeland. At Fontainebleau he studied theory with Jean Batalla and composition with Nadia Boulanger. Griffin told no one of his failing eyesight. "There, in the magnificent surroundings of the Palace of Fontainebleau, nourished by music, the act of seeing became its own drama—private, intimate and personal. And it became very nearly sublime. I led two lives—one as a conservatory student; the other as a man looking avidly on things with the peculiar light of knowing he sees them for the last time."[23]

Yet imperceptibly this secret reached the awareness of others, and one afternoon it became obvious that friends knew. While at a rehearsal with the eminent musicians baritone Pierre Bernac and pianist Gaby Casadesus, he was asked to turn the pages at the piano. Seeing the first page end in a descending scale that appeared as a streak among blurred notes, he accomplished the first turn but failed to make the second. The music stopped, he apologized, complaining of poor light in the concert room, and it was passed off gently by the musicians. While he listened from the first row, Bernac approached to sing Gounod's *Berceuse*, intoning the text about a mother who tells her child to close his eyes. In this moment of tender recognition, Griffin realized his secret was known, although it remained unmentioned.

Later he asked himself why he had not told them. "But the answer was clear. I feared myself. I was not able to cope with the temptation to play the tragic figure. My silence was the only guarantee against falling into that trap." Embarrassed, he returned to his room, turning attention to a Mozart score. "The jubilant mystery of Mozart—that second innocence—preoccupied me. I sought to analyze from the black notes on white paper, to catch this supreme secret, for it contained the answer to the way I wanted to go—not musically but psychologically or spiritually."

Griffin's understanding of "second innocence" was not clarified until 1953, when he recognizes in the *Journal* that it was "not a condition of the intellect, but of the affections. It is a liquid condition, transient, which can be lost and destroyed and then regained. The innocent mentality often is achieved through struggle after all innocence has been lost through experience." But in 1946 he could perceive it only in the artists he admired. "I looked at Casadesus's hands, those hands that were not ashamed to practice the simplest passage for hours. I looked into the faces of Bernac and Gaby and Nadia and saw faces long ago clarified and unmasked by work and sacrifice and devotion. I thought of the years of preparation in lonely rooms before they had revealed to the world the finished product of art's past mastery."

The incarnation of "second innocence" Griffin saw in the artists was an antidote to the ravages of facing evil, war, and death. They had experienced harsh realities in France, too, yet remained connected to the sublime secrets of music. He writes of fading visual reality. "Faced with nothing, very little becomes everything. The sight of a pin, a hair, a leaf, a glass of water—these things filled me with trembling excitement. The plants in the courtyard, the cobblestones, the lamp posts, the faces of strangers—I no longer took them up in me. I went out to them, focused on them, immersed myself in them—they retained their values, their own identities and essences. I became them rather than making them me, and found them more beautiful than I ever dreamed they could be. They taught, they nourished when one gave oneself to them."

This was the same *essential insight* Griffin had during his trip to the opera in Paris as a student. He had achieved the viewpoint necessary for immersion in something beyond ego—perhaps his first mature act of immersion, which would become his mode of behavior throughout life.

Casadesus's advice was to find a beautiful wife. "At your age you should spend all your time making love."

Bernac pointed out, "You find what you're looking for alone—never in a crowd. We can give you a hint, show you how to work hard and not to despise loneliness, but nothing much more. Each of us had to do it alone."

Griffin realized he had "studied music so much that it destroyed creativity in that area," and "ended up learning every damned rule in the book. I knew everything you could *not* do, and that silenced me as a composer. I could write a technically correct work, but was too constricted by the rules to breathe any life into it."

A few weeks later, Griffin received a letter from Friar Marie-Bruno, inviting him to Paris to visit the Dominican monastery. This was the first of many retreats he would make to monasteries, counting these times among his happiest. Marie-Bruno writes, "Your stay here will be a good transition between Fontainebleau and the studies you will make at the Abbey of Solesmes." The monk knew about Griffin's failing eyesight, ending with a note of concern. "My poor friend, why are you so determined to be brave? Bravery of this sort is nothing but a role you play. You must work hard toward finding a way that will not require you to play roles."[24]

Griffin's "roles" of "going native" in the Solomons, of acting as a "fully-recovered soldier" in the military hospital on Guadalcanal, and becoming a "silent hero" facing blindness alone at Fontainebleau were all manifestations of youthful theatricality. His denials were play-acting, no matter how humble the rags or festive the costumes, and Marie-Bruno could see through such masks.

The Great Silence

The Dominican Convent of St. Jacques in Paris, an ancient novitiate built in 1256 and destroyed during the French Revolution, holds a unique place in Catholic history. This rebuilt novitiate deeply impressed Griffin, who noted a fascinating backstory to the place in his *Journal* years later.

> I had stayed at the Couvent St. Jacques as a guest and attended the classes in logic for the Dominican novices. Some years later I encountered an obscure reference to St. Thomas Aquinas' first visit to Paris. It told of his staying at the Couvent St. Jacques during the time he lectured and debated at the Sorbonne. St. Bonaventure happened to be in Paris at the time and also stayed there. The two saints met for the first time and became attached to one another. Each evening they took their recreation walks in the little weed-filled courtyard, on a circular path worn deep. Here they discussed and compared notes. The other Dominicans followed to hear the two great men's conversation.

When a Dominican asked Aquinas about the difference between his rational approach and Bonaventure's mystical approach to God, they anticipated a debate on the best approach. They got no such debate. Aquinas explained that by his method any basic reality, for example the taste or smell of an apple, could be made into a logical edifice to demonstrate the existence of God. Bonaventure, having mystical perception of God, could experience it in the taste or smell of an apple. For Aquinas the apple was the starting point, while for Bonaventure it was the end.[25]

When Griffin was greeted by Friar Marie-Bruno at the abbey door, he felt "the instant certainty that here was a man who had burned with all the pain and all the love that men can know, and from whom nothing needed to be hidden." It had been nearly seven years since they had visited in Tours. "Even then, André's reputation for sanctity had made me ill at ease until the moment when we had faced each other and his kindness had melted my discomfort." Griffin witnessed a profound change in the monk, which he relates in a pivotal chapter of *Scattered Shadows*.

> It was as though a great simplification had clarified his features and expression, stripping him of all self-consciousness. His eyes spoke his awe, his astonishment with some mystery I could not fathom. I saw the heavily patched robe as the picture of voluntary poverty, realizing that the friar had entered a world where all standards were altered from those I knew. All the things that were important in the world—position, ambition, success, esteem, accomplishment—meant nothing within these rooms. If I were a derelict in rags, he would view me with the same expression. I found this frustrating. I was poorest precisely in the qualities he would value most.

For Griffin the mystery was fathomless. Within the cloister, separated by thick stone walls from the streets of Paris, there existed a conundrum of cells where solitary monks were united in prayer, and open to the Great Silence. Marie-Bruno was his first true spiritual mentor. In awe of the monk's simple holiness, he feared that spirituality was beyond his attainment. It was no accident that when facing death during the air raid, he had envisioned Beethoven as a priest preparing to give the last rites. Finding the quartet on a radio was accidental, but equating Beethoven with a "master of souls" was not. Now faced with a living master of souls, he would be forced to recognize spiritual reality beyond intellect.

Examining a text nailed to a wall with a magnifying glass, Griffin realized it was meant for novices. He read of the difficulty of liberating oneself from ego—"*because man's nature has a thousand artifices with which to delude him.*" These social artifices gave one "*the delusion that he loves God . . . and has reached the sublimest spheres of spirituality, when in reality there remains the infatuation of self.*" He felt "estranged" because "it was too new," even while he "sensed the drama of men's souls struggling to make themselves perfectly conformable to the workings of God within them. This seemed an occupation out of our time, out of our concepts of balance and proportion. It repelled, but it stabbed painfully inward for recognition."

Contrasting the harmony of the cloister and the dissonance of the Paris streets unsettled him. When leaving the cloister, he encountered young monks whose "eyes were all alike—painfully alive, painfully clear, painfully reflecting some mysterious joy." The pain was his, yet he did not perceive this projection. He saw no "smoldering traces of fanaticism" in their faces. Walking in the nearby quarter, he was filled with "an almost desperate desire to get away, to go to the brighter sectors of Paris, even though I knew there was no escape."

Griffin recalls that "often as a student working with Dr. Pierre Fromenty at the asylum how we struggled to get patients to accept and face the consequences of their actions, to draw strength by plunging directly into the core of difficulties. I knew it was the only way, and I told myself I must return to the empty cell and swallow the medicine prescribed by wisdom." Next came immersion in their monastic rhythms, attending the Divine Offices and taking meals with the monks.[26] He had confronted "the undercurrent of tremendous adventure that lies invisible beneath the tranquil surface of the religious life." He was not instructed and not asked to do labor, except to clean the cell. He absorbed the liturgical atmosphere, and kept up practice at the piano, playing Mozart and Bach to the appreciation of the entire community. It was through music that the seeds of his spirituality had been planted. Although "I had been brought up in a virtuous home and had been given careful religious training," he believed "that religion was nothing more than religiosity."

The horrors of the Nazi occupation and the brutal war in the Pacific had eroded Griffin's early religious training, and he drifted into the swift currents of agnosticism. His conversations with Friar Marie-Bruno set the stage for openings that led to his eventual conversion to Catholicism. What had been rhetorical arguments against the existence of God were challenged by the realization that his preconceptions of the monastic formation were "utterly false." He imagined "that men seeking union with God more or less languished in a state of mystical trauma, soaring above the baser aspects of their own daily living." He had been wrong. The monks were intimate "with the things of the earth—cold, fasting, labor," and "were filled with the rich polyphony of philosophy and theology rather than with some pastel and lyrical emotionalism." All was harmonized by humble obedience, which had not "threatened the superficial liberty and objectivity" that he prized.

Griffin had seen society protect its religion from scrutiny, but heard the opposite view in the cloister. The monks were taught *not* to fear authentic truths, reasonable doubts, or any criticism of their faith. The difference between society and monastic harmony was their belief in the meaning of prayer. "They sought no compromise between their aspirations and what the world calls their 'lower appetites,' but did not despise these appetites." The meaning of worship for the monks "was not a matter of truncating their humanity, but of perfecting it."

Friar Marie-Bruno visited him on the last evening of the retreat. When the light had faded, Griffin switched on the lamp, turning to see it highlight the monk's tonsured head. "He looked like some ancient engraving of a monk come to life, speaking, smiling." In that moment, the young agnostic was able to speak of his own confusion. "I hated it when I first came here, and now I hate to leave. What you have makes sense, inside these walls. It seems tremendously important to me here and now, but once I leave, I know I can't hold it. I wish I could believe, make the *fiat* and mean it with all my heart." The monk remained a silent engraving. "I am wrong not to accept what is," feeling he had failed his friend, "just because my mind insists on demanding proofs and knowledge that will never be given."

Marie-Bruno responded. "It is true that some knowledge must precede love, since you cannot love a thing that you do not know. But only enough knowledge to let you know the thing. Because a great deal of knowledge comes from the experience of loving." The monk mentioned the pastor in André Gide's 1916 novel *La symphonie pastoral* (*The Pastoral Symphony*), who attempts to evoke the essence of the color green to a blind girl, equating the difficulty of understanding green without sight and the difficulty of understanding God's truth without faith.

Griffin would understand both parts of that equation when totally blind. But he was *not* ready for a love that demanded transcendence. When a long silence became unbearable, he tried to express his attraction to the monastic reality, while admitting his fears. "I know my belly too well," he lamented.

The monk exposed Griffin's wounded pride with an immediate retort.

> You don't seriously think your belly is different from any other man's do you? Dear God, I believe you do. My poor friend, the religious life, more than any other, demands the destruction of such delusions.

> No man has ever progressed far in it without feeling this same terrible unworthiness—without seeing clearer than ever before the depths of vileness into which his nature has too often led him . . . and could so easily lead him again. You speak as though the Great Yes need only be said once and then everything is somehow arranged. God's grace comes, yes, but so too the full power of temptations to resist it. The Yes has to be repeated again and again through life. And it never gets much easier to do. Look at you, you are the picture of discontent. That, at least, is good.

Griffin wondered how discontent could be good. "But there is another discontent in all this—a sort of *divine discontent* which has not so much to do with you as with what life appears to offer you," explained the monk. "This divine discontent can grow. It may become so painful it will drive you to love. That is what is good about it. You have a will, you know, some choice in the matter. You can *choose* to love."

The young agnostic felt "a vague disappointment" that the Marie-Bruno might be trying to convert him. The monk's last words: "I hope God spares you, that He does not ever show you His ineffable brutality. He drives some men where they never want to go."

Before going to Solesmes, Griffin took time to visit with the Duthoo family in Tours. Suffering headaches and blurring vision, he bumped into furniture and "raged with embarrassment" at his clumsiness. He wished "to go somewhere where I could make the transition into blindness in solitude." It was shrewd of Marie-Bruno to predict that his retreat with the Dominicans would be a useful transition to the stricter regimen at Solesmes, where Griffin would begin to strip away his masks.

The next day in Tours, Griffin found sanctuary in the Cathedral Saint-Gatien. He considered entering the confessional, but resisted. Then a remark by André Gide came to mind. "Referring to a group of nuns, Gide had observed how they cherished the pearl of their faith, never realizing it was a false pearl. True, I shared his belief, but how could we know? Did we, ourselves, possess the true one? If so, why were we so tormented?" Suddenly he was struck by the harsh realization that he "played the classic role after all," and was "blistered by self-contempt," embarrassed "to catch myself in a falsity of which I was not even aware." Returning to the Duthoo's home that evening, he retreated to his room, lit a dark cigarillo and turned on the radio. He heard Bach's second *Bran-*

denburg Concerto, "overwhelmed by the vigor and sanity" of the music and "a jubilance that brought tears."

When the Bach ended, he listened to rain filling the silence. "So I would be blind. By all rights I should have been dead, buried somewhere in the Pacific. So, this was a new life, given freely." Hearing the family downstairs, he joined them for wine and supper. He feasted, drank enough wine to lighten his mood, joking with the children. Returning upstairs, he felt contempt for his sadness, deciding "it was a time of change, influenced by the Bach, the rain, the cathedral."

If a career in medicine had been obviated by Griffin's blindness and the ambition to be a composer was beyond his talent, then the "years to come had been given me to live an experience which I was free to color any way I chose." Perhaps a life without sight could be as transforming as one with sight. "Who was to say different? Society? The bulk of humanity?" He viewed most others as "living their first lives, cautiously aware that someday they would die. They had everything to lose. They could not take the risks. But I had been through death. . . . I was living a second life, freed of these cautious awarenesses. I had nothing to lose. I could take all the risks." It was not yet the great *yes* to God, but it was a crucial choice and again it concerned music. Bach had brought back sanity.

Then Griffin remembered a promise to deliver a package of clothing from the American painter Abraham Rattner to the French poet Pierre Reverdy, who lived in the village near The Abbey of Solesmes.[27] "It was a name to excite and intimidate anyone who had been a schoolboy in France, for it was one of the great names of French literature." The letter from Rattner had described Reverdy as "the purest of French poets. Not a self-pusher. One of the pioneer cubist group along with Max Jacob, Apollinaire, Braque, and Picasso. Fiery temperament. Discourses beautifully. Tender, considerate, gentle, warm—also violent."

The next morning, Jacques Duthoo drove Griffin and Father Pierre Froger to the Abbey of Solesmes on the Sarthe River. Father Froger was their guide, since his brother was a monk there. Stepping through the gates on that cold, clear morning, he entered "a world of the Middle Ages" for the first time, and the "change was sudden, physical, tangible." In the settling quietness, he stared up at the edifice. "The birds had gone for the winter. The rush of the wide Sarthe River, invisible below the monastery walls, added depth to the silence."

After Duthoo had departed, Griffin took Father Froger's invitation to walk the grounds. Past the gardens and fruit orchards, he noticed a monk tending hog pens, explaining that the monastery was self-sufficient and a complete community that included gardens, livestock, a shoe shop, a laundry, and a bakery.

"Up there, where you see that row of large windows, you'll find one of the world's great libraries," the priest explained. "They have either originals or photocopies of every known Gregorian manuscript in existence. I don't suppose you could find such a gathering of scholars anywhere else in the world. Certainly not living under these conditions of poverty, chastity, and obedience. They are true monks. When they enter here they take also a vow of stability. That means they can never ask to be transferred, never go to another monastery. They know they will live out their lives here behind these walls, die here, and be buried here."

Griffin could only say "How beautiful," to which Froger responded, "Yes, beautiful, but wait until you know it better. Life here is hard and primitive. They are never warm in winter. You will see how simple the food is . . . and the silence. It's the silence that gets me—after three days here I always feel like shouting."

They were led up two flights of stone steps by Father Froger's brother to the cell Griffin would occupy. There was a hard straw mattress on a plank bed, a straight-back chair, a writing table, and a washstand. The one window opened onto a courtyard. He was instructed that the "Great Silence" began with *Compline* that evening, and there would be no conversation, except in an emergency, until *Matins* the next morning. He was asked to utilize the chamber pot, and not to leave the cell during the night. They went to the chapel in time to witness 120 monks enter two by two from the sanctuary, bow before the altar, filling the pews to either side. As the organ music ended, he first heard the chanting of the monks of Solesmes. This description in *Scattered Shadows* echoes a fictional passage in *The Devil Rides Outside*.

> The *Introit* began with a soft upswing of monks' voices. Many voices in perfect unison breathed life into melody, spreading in an ocean of sound without sharpness, allowing the chant to float in long undulating lines as a feather might float on the waves of a sea.
>
> This was my reason for being here. This moment culminated years of study when I had sat in tents in the Pacific or in lonely rooms

> around the world, poring over this music. Now, imagined sounds became real. I listened to tender, awe-stricken chants of adoration and petition, buried myself in the timeless splendor of the Mass. Nerves detached and settled into peace. I knew that I was living one of the high points of my life.

He became part of a monastic community through music, with the chants as the language of exchange, a liturgical vernacular he knew with a measure of intimacy as a budding musicologist. He had learned from the monk-musicologists, and this chanting edified his ear. He was determined to be immersed in the solitude that a monastic cell could nourish, although realizing that the cell would not insure solitude any more than a crowded street might negate it. He did not seek mere physical isolation or an escape into diversions, and he did *not* play the role of a pseudo-monk. Intellectually he knew such delusions destroyed solitude, no matter where one chose to retreat. His obedience to study was a conscious act of shaping a silent identity beyond the noise of ego. It was a becoming and, during this confusing period of rapidly diminishing sight, he felt the need to become a musicologist.

The next day he went in search of Pierre Reverdy's house. Standing by a high stone wall, he rang the bell, waiting nervously. Madame Reverdy spoke out from behind the wall, informing that the poet was in Paris. When he convinced her that he had a package from Rattner, she opened the gate. Inside the small house, he discerned two paintings by Braque, a cubist canvas by Fernand Léger, and a portrait of Reverdy by Picasso. She said that her husband was visiting these very friends in Paris, where he did all his business and socializing.

Reverdy was at that moment in a Paris hospital, and she said that Rattner was the cause, explaining the painter had sent a new overcoat that had precipitated an altercation. Griffin placed the package on a table, astonished that he seemed to be delivering an unwelcome gift. He asked about the incident. She explained that while wearing the overcoat in Paris, Reverdy had been accosted by a communist who called him a capitalist. "He hit the communist in the jaw, so hard it broke a bone in Pierre's arm." Reverdy refused to do anything about the injury, suffered terrible pain, but did not trust doctors. Picasso intervened, took him to a hospital, where an operation was performed. Madame Reverdy assured Griffin that her husband would want to thank him for the delivery. He returned to the monastery.

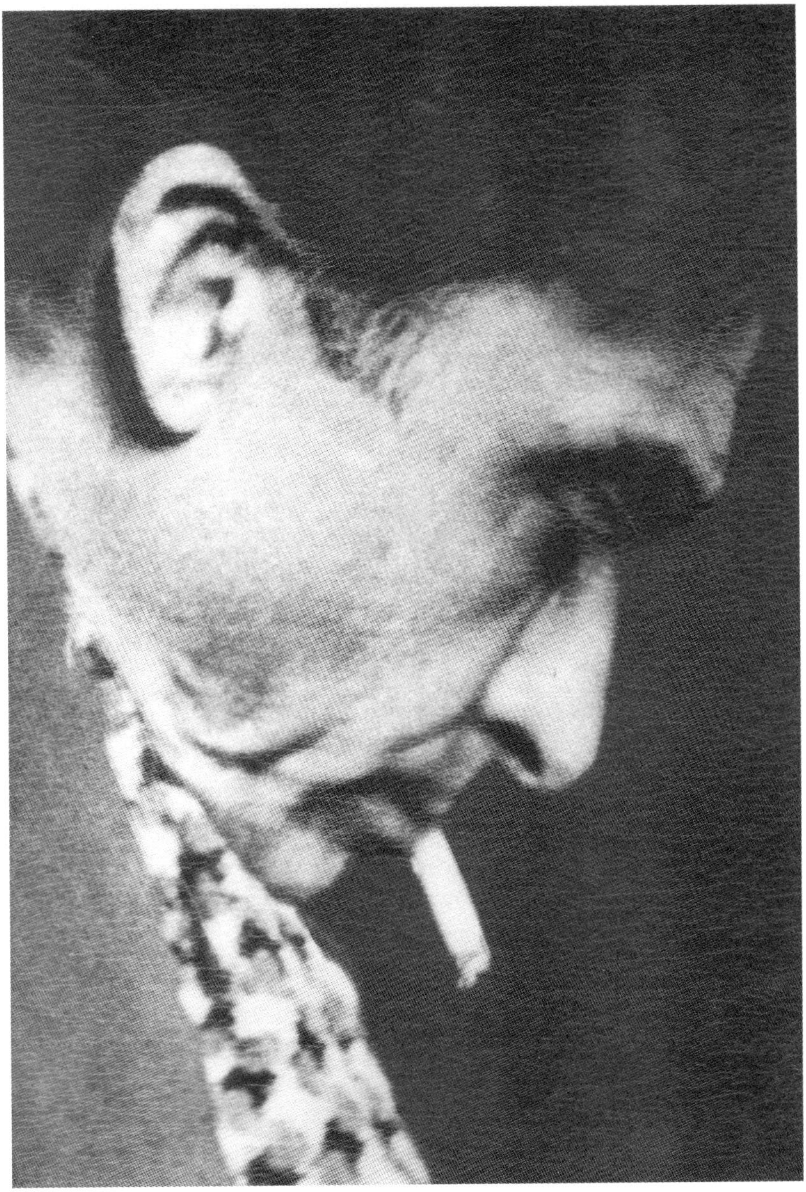

Portrait of French poet Pierre Reverdy by JHG, taken in 1946 at the poet's home in the village surrounding the Abbey of Solesmes, where Griffin studied Gregorian Chant, just before his blindness became total.

At the gatehouse an elderly monk holding a silver urn and a linen towel greeted him. A young monk stood by with a silver basin. The elderly monk introduced himself as the Father Abbot, explaining it was his duty, by the rule of St. Benedict, to wash the feet of guests. But since it was cold, he would wash the hands instead. Warm water was poured, and "the Abbot dried my hands as though handling precious jewels, with a care and reverence that embarrassed me."

The next day Madame Reverdy awaited him at the gatehouse to ask a favor. She handed him fifty francs and a folded piece of paper, requesting he call a few friends in Paris to let them know about her husband's health. As she turned to leave, he unfolded the paper. "Is this Georges Braque? Do you want me to call the painter?"

"Yes. What's the matter?" she asked.

"Nothing. It's just that I'm not asked every day to telephone a famous man like Braque."

She smiled. "He's a very nice man. You have excellent French, so you won't have any trouble. Will you come tell me what he says?"

He made the calls, but instead of speaking with the painter, it was Madame Braque who answered, saying that Reverdy was progressing well and had a telephone in the hospital room. The next day Madame Reverdy asked him to call the poet daily and to report back. It was a pleasure to sit with Henriette Reverdy, exchanging stories near a warm fire in winter, especially since the monastery was literally freezing.

> The days entered into a deep rhythm, not of clocks but of tolling bells, reverberating throughout the valley, telling us to attend the offices, when to eat, when to retire. But the jubilance of the chants, the awesome silence, the medieval tone of the monastery, grew so profound it obliterated the discomforts of the freezing cold, the dreary food, the lack of warm water or inside toilets, and even the rudeness of living without personal amenities or communication with women.
>
> In the chapel's wintry light, I followed the chanted offices with my reading glass and missal, renewing my Latin. Often I was the only visitor in the vast room, particularly at the early morning and the night offices. Imperceptibly, the liturgy entered our being, possessing the imagination, coloring all thoughts. I began to perceive how it could transform a life.

> This is how and what had happened to the monks here and in Paris. The liturgy had become the foundation stone for their lives. They were products of the liturgical formation; it shown in their gestures, their faces, their speech, producing a strange effect each time I met and spoke with one of them. I was aware of each monk as an individual human being of flesh, appetites, and a name; at the same time I was aware of him as a living liturgy. Though individuality was liberated rather than smothered, and even though our relationships were impersonal, we knew all the nuances of one another's being insofar as we perceived the nuances of the liturgy. If the element of mystery, the Divine Mystery, surrounded us, the secrecy between us had vanished, for our lives were transparent to all in the monastery.
>
> I felt out of place because the liturgy had not formed me, because my reactions were formed by and attuned to the world outside. It would take time before I could walk silently and know that presence did not shout. I waited without anxiety for the liturgy to do its work, in its own time. Within those walls, concepts of time disappeared beneath the natural rhythms of life. These rhythms captured the heartbeat and the respiration. One floated with them, effortlessly, unthinkingly, but aware that to rush forward in time or to feel impatience would be to defile the natural order of things.

When Reverdy returned home from Paris, they engaged in discourses on art, poetry, and solitude. The poet wanted to know why Griffin would "roam the world studying." The young scholar admitted he did not know, saying, "What else is there to do? I have no particular talent. Until I discover one, I thought I should spend my time studying." Reverdy replied, "I know what you mean, but in my heart I don't really understand it. I've had to write from the very beginning. If I hadn't, I'd have gone mad long ago. My writing is what saved my sanity."

Henriette called them to lunch. The poet protested, relenting when reminded that Griffin had been brought down by a fever at the monastery. Reverdy insisted that he try his personal remedy. "Reverdy poured coffee, cognac and aspirins down me. The conversation became brilliant for a time and then turned fuzzy. By early evening, I could do little more than reel back to my freezing cell at the monastery."

A few days later he had a letter from Reverdy, who had been ill also, apologizing for the "cure" that had always been effective.

Griffin reconsidered what Friar Marie-Bruno had said, along with a statement by French theologian Léon Bloy that "Sanctity is man's true normalcy."[28] This made perfect sense if one *believed*, but Griffin could only question himself.

> Could a man of such mediocre qualities, glued to the earth, with no religious instinct left intact, set about systematically to will a complete alteration in himself? Could a man deliberately and lovelessly set about to make himself the slave of God for whom he had not the slightest feeling? Could a man turn his back on the intoxications of the ego in order to open himself to other and greater intoxications? Could a man selflessly seek to become selfless?
>
> We who vaunted ourselves on being free were in reality slaves to countless masters, to social pressures, to opinions, values, and standards rooted in the cement and bricks of our age; to ambition and suspicion. Freely chosen slavery to God was scarcely a step down. It might even, through some mystery, become the ultimate liberation.

Despite the monastic rhythms permeating the young agnostic's spirit, he had been too calculating. "Could anyone really assault love with quite such sledge-hammer obtuseness? But how did one accomplish it? How had *they* done it? Could a man transfer techniques already learned?" He recalled an intriguing passage by philosopher Jacques Maritain in *Art and Scholasticism*: "The labor through which the zither player acquires nimbleness of finger does not increase his art as such nor does it engender any special art; it simply removes the physical impediment to the exercise of art."[29] He understood the metaphor, postulating that if "the chief impediment to the gift of self in love was self, then self was the thing to de-emphasize."

These ruminations chilled him. Knowing he lacked courage to make a leap of faith, could he choose merely to learn? Was it absurd for an "eternal" student to study the Eternal? He knew that Marie-Bruno was right. He did have a choice, focusing on sunlight illuminating snow-covered trees. "It rarefied the atmosphere within my cell, gave a hitherto unnoticed detail and dimension to the walls, the furniture and to my senses. This must always be, I told myself. If this ever vanishes into the other, then it will all be delusion. The body must not become my enemy."

Due to the severe winter, he was unable to recover sufficient strength after the fevers to withstand the monastic rigors. He was introduced to a couple whose villa remained vacant every winter. In January of 1947, arrangements were made to rent a furnished salon in their villa for six dollars per month. There was a large wood burning stove, running water, a sofa-bed combination, a chest of drawers, a bed stand, and a radio that aired classical concerts. To his delight the water closet had a supply of *papier hygienique* instead of the cut-up newspapers used by the monks. He could enjoy "the greatest luxury of all—to bathe" in a tub of hot water.

Solitude in the villa entered its own rhythm of study by day, reading and listening to music at night. He carried a portable library from the abbey, and became absorbed by theological texts. "On the one hand, my failing sight; on the other, the slow dilation of enthusiasm for philosophical and theological studies. Gradually, perceptions began to form in this area of thought so totally new to me. In the coldness, the darkness of gray days, the patristic writings struck me like dazzling sunlight." Silence expanded to the village in winter. There were no automobiles, the little railroad station was out of earshot, and the Sarthe River was frozen. Only the "crunch of footsteps in the frozen snow, the occasional crowing of roosters or baying of hounds, the peal of monastery bells—these alone gave dimension to the silence."

Griffin began to trace dwindling light perception by focusing on the colored wave bands of the radio, until they reflected a confusing haze of color. By placing white paper on a black tabletop, he managed to write, directing the pen in straight lines that were a blur. Headaches struck at night and a doctor prescribed sedatives and tinted glasses. When the magnifying glass failed to raise words to legibility, the monks read his mail aloud. "But even these developments were submerged beneath the great joy that sprang from growing familiarity with the monastic life and from the health that radiated out like the peal of its bells."

Yet he felt flashes of panic, knowing that he must leave to begin the necessary training for adjusting to blindness. He was grateful that sight had been lost in a solitary context. The monks held a refreshingly sane view of blindness, believing it to be as natural and inevitable as the arrival of spring.

Spring did arrive with milder weather and a chance to revisit Reverdy, who had no idea about his failing sight. He was met with a reproach "for having deserted them." Griffin explained that he did not want to disturb the poet's work, but Reverdy scoffed at the excuse. "It takes me a year to think of enough to write in five minutes. Besides, I do nearly all my writing at night. Come anytime."

During the next visit, Reverdy led him through the countryside on a clear afternoon, which offered the opportunity to take photographs of the poet with a cheap box camera. A few weeks later, when his left eye began to suppurate, he visited a doctor in Sablé, who cleaned the drainage, covering the left eye with a patch. While in town he picked up the processed film. There were two excellent sepia prints in the batch, which he attributed to the law of accident. Ironically these two prints became his first successful portraits, and Reverdy used both thereafter for book jackets. These images leaped beyond the poor snapshots he had made during the student days in Tours or while in the military. But he dreaded showing them to the poet.

As Griffin entered the Reverdy home, he spoke rapidly about the photographs. "To hell with the photos," replied the poet. "What has happened to your eye?" He told the truth and, as he feared, "it changed our relationship drastically." Reverdy went into a depression, taking it far worse than Griffin.

> Reverdy's reaction to my blindness brought home again the truth of my situation—that those whom I loved would suffer far more than I, that I carried with me the responsibility not only of accepting what came, but also of comforting them. The best way to comfort them, I realized, was to nullify the sad stereotype of blindness, to work for skills that would make them forget my condition.

Griffin realized the task was far beyond him. He would need help, knowing that he "must act in perfect, voluntary obedience to a greater force, do out of obedience what I could not do from my own imperfect initiative."

During the last week at the monastery, he entered the empty chapel, forcing himself to say: "If you exist, take what I am. I hold back nothing. Show me what you want me to do. I'll obey no matter how repulsive it is to me personally. I give you myself totally and without any reservations." His hope of making the great *Yes*, had left him "no joy, no relief, nothing but a sense of terrible finality in the knowledge that henceforth my life was not my own."

By May of 1947 the waiting was over. Griffin was unable to see the light on the face of the radio. It was time to contact his parents. He walked to the abbey, but had difficulty locating the gatehouse. The gatekeeper called out and took him by the sleeve. He felt the "temptations to dramatize, to seek the consolations of sympathy and the platitudes of condolence." He told the gatekeeper, "The sight is gone. The doctor says there is nothing to be done." He waited for the outpouring of sympathy. "Oh, come now, you're not going to waste time on that, are you?" The remark erased self-pity. He dictated the letter, thanking the monk for his honesty.

At the villa he continued to work on the skills needed to function in the sighted world. If he lost his way he retreated to the wall to begin again. His "nerves jangled with each unexpected noise," cursing with impotent rage, yet thankful to exercise "this initiation alone." As the radio's color bands once charted diminishing sight, its sounds now helped to locate a table or a door. He moved on to more difficult passages, like combing his hair and shaving. By sound and feel he was able to accomplish more than he imagined. "Alone and without any witness to my mistakes, the mistakes no longer irritated me, no longer impeded me from attempting to perform the action again." Griffin refused to take meals in the refectory, fearful of cursing at his mistakes, and the monks understood his reticence.

One of the oldest Benedictine priests sent for him.

> "You are too nervous, my son," he said in a high thin voice. "You must develop heroic patience. God has his own good reason for allowing such things to happen. You must go on faith, even though you don't understand."
>
> I listened to this old man's good-goderies with disappointment. Yes, here in the heart of a great abbey, a man could say such things. But what did he know about blindness? What did he know about living out in the world where a man had to fend for himself? I thanked him and rose to terminate the interview. My extended hand remained outstretched in the air, untouched. I sat back down.
>
> "You don't see either, do you, Father?" I asked.
>
> "Well no," he said with an explosion of wheezing laughter. "You are very quick. How did you discover so fast?"

> We fell into lengthy conversation. "Practice. Practice patiently," he said. "Learn to reach for a glass properly. Do it five hundred times and you'll never again knock one over. Get yourself a lightweight fork—then you can tell by the weight if you bring it to your mouth empty or if it has food on it. You're a musician. You have already learned that a passage of music you cannot play the first time comes easily into your hands after practicing it twenty or a hundred times. I still learn this way. I still am amazed all the time how quickly things come, and I've been without my sight for many years now—maybe twenty."
>
> I listened to this aged, almost gleeful voice and felt hope. "Your main task will be to persevere. Remember always the word *persevere.* Your main temptations will be against perseverance. But they won't be obvious. They come as temptations to lose patience, to murmur against the frustrations, to act superb."
>
> I noted that he unconsciously used the archaic language of St. Benedict.
>
> "It will take time. You will have to learn these attitudes but don't make the initial mistake that could cause you to give up before you have learned your techniques."
>
> When I prepared to leave, he snapped his fingers sharply so I could reach out to the sound and shake his hand. The gesture filled me with admiration and hope. It was a way of doing things, and I was happy to learn it. He grasped my hand in both of his.
>
> "Watch your pride, eh?"
>
> "I've got enough of it to watch," I said.

During the last days of waiting for his parents to cable money for passage, Griffin diligently practiced the scales of sightlessness, utilizing the radio to position himself in the room. He revisited the blind monk, recounting the experiments. The old monk cackled with amusement at the accounts, encouraging him with more techniques. Yet there was still an obstacle he could not overcome. "All the furniture seems to have shrunk exactly to the height of my shins." They both laughed uproariously. "Well, you need a stick. I've got two or three good ones. I'll give you one. You just keep it a little in front of you, easy, so you don't bang the furniture. The most important thing is not to let it out of your hands. If you misplace it you will spend all your time feeling around for it. Mine stays in my hand all day, and I put it beside my bed at night. Ah, poor lad, I should have thought of the stick earlier."

Photo of JHG was taken in 1952 by an unidentified photographer. This photo of the blind author appeared on the dust jacket of Griffin's first novel, *The Devil Rides Outside* (Smiths, 1952).

Without light perception Griffin's nervousness vanished. Evenings alone in the villa "were filled with the activity of experimental learning, now made much easier with the cane." He attended the services during Holy Week, receiving a telegram from his parents the day after Easter. Arrangements were made for emergency passage on a Lykes cargo passenger ship docked in Rouen and destined for New Orleans. He took the train to the dock, "listening to the clacking wheels carrying me away from the valley, the abbey, the place of my deepest happiness."

After a brief layover in noisy Rouen, where Griffin was helped by an elderly couple (the Burgesses), he boarded a ship bound for New Orleans. On board he met a doctor, who knocked at his cabin door on the first day at sea, opened it when asked to enter, declaring, "I am Dr. Rafael Carrazo from Guatemala. I understand you have a misfortune. I am the greatest doctor in my country, so if I can be of service to you on the voyage, have no hesitancy in calling me."

Since there were only a dozen passengers on board, they engaged in ongoing discussions. The doctor "revealed himself as a man of great erudition, both in classical studies and science, and yet he gave the impression of being an absolute thug." One distinction the doctor made, regarding consonant and dissonant scenes for the blind, made sense, since a psychological distinction was clarified by a musical metaphor. The doctor said: "Each of us must find some way to balance out the psychologically dissonant situations with consonant situations that allow tensions to resolve, or else our nervous systems collapse eventually. Now, without your sight, you still must live in a sighted world. You face many dissonant situations that people with sight are spared. Some of these will change into consonant situations, as you learn to solve your problems and handle yourself better."

Nearing New Orleans, Griffin's peace aboard ship became anxiety. "I knew the full meaning of the 'dissonant situation.' My dread was clear. I dreaded for my parents to see me like this." When the ship docked, he was put ashore first. Dr. Carrazo had applied clean bandages, packed his luggage, and led him to the launch.

Griffin's mother and Reverend Clayton were there to meet him. Embracing his mother, he wondered, "What was the expression on her face? Here, I knew, was the profoundest hell of blindness. One look would have told me. I strained to break through and see." The next day Reverend Clayton drove them to the airport. They boarded a flight to Fort Worth, where his father met them. They discussed a plan to purchase acreage near Mansfield, Texas. His parents wanted to live in the country, thinking it would be a good environment for their son's adjustment. It turned out to be a wise decision.

He studied Braille with Edith Bell at the Fort Worth Lighthouse for the Blind, some twenty miles north of Mansfield. By early 1948, he stopped going, yet continued practicing Braille at home. He never found it to be easy. While his parents worked in the city on weekdays, he practiced at the piano, studied theology and philosophy, and listened to texts his mother had read into a wire recorder.

His parents suggested that he try raising livestock on the forty-acre place, since half of it was open pasture. After consideration, Griffin decided "to raise livestock in order to become independent and to earn income." They bought chickens and hogs, and he began "doing hard physical work and experimenting endlessly, hoping to solve all the problems of feeding, judging, and breeding stock that would allow me to work without any sighted help." Within the year, regional specialists in animal husbandry became interested in his experiments.

For two years he raised penned Poland China hogs, learning to judge by feel, which was a useful method, since aspects that escaped the eye would not escape the hands. Working with the American Foundation for the Blind and experts from Texas A&M and Oklahoma A&M universities, he bred champion hogs that won ribbons, proving the blind could succeed as farmers.

During these years Griffin was involved in an entirely different activity closer to his heart—giving public lectures on classical music in Fort Worth and Dallas.[30] He began each series with a startling admission. "I have been accused many times of intolerance—of musical intolerance. Fortunately the arts demand intolerance, and I hope to clutter the place up with the germs of this disease, so that all of you may leave here with a slight case of artistic intolerance. There is too much wonderfully good music in the world to be tolerant of the less good." But what about humility, the prime lesson he learned at Solesmes? What about the ragtime tunes his mother enjoyed playing, or the jazz and blues that he refused to embrace?

> The criteria of musical judgment and of musical taste are the most intangible possible—so intangible as to defy analysis. That is one of the reasons why some of us spend a lifetime of research and enchantment. Perhaps we do not accomplish a great deal in clarifying what is essentially good or bad, but we inevitably become such an integral part of the science of music as to be able to give hints in the right direction. The genius of Mozart cannot be defined. We can analyze every element of his technique of composition but there is that element of genius, which we can neither assume nor explicate.

> This is a small part of the science of music, which leads us to certain conclusions. I have studied music for many years, going into uncharted paths, alone. This has been my great passion. I cannot presume to give you answers that do not exist, but I can presume to take you over some of the terrain and let you see for yourselves, let you build individual criteria based on knowledge and experience of your own. For music is a mystical thing. All of us have seen the snake worshippers, the religious fanatics, the desolating healers. This is the inevitable result of presuming authority without preparation, without knowledge. The most destructive person in our world is the unenlightened mystic. The most constructive saints in the history of religions were the great practical mystics. When we discuss any *thing* in which there are the commingled elements of the known and the unknown, we find that the known must be mastered, before the unknown can have any positive value.
>
> Great music is the result of such a perfection of the practical, coupled with the cultural environment, to produce the works that we hope to take unto ourselves. Can encyclopedic information be of any help? It can, but less than is generally conceded. This is the basis of my series here—an understanding of a civilization, the spiritual values, and the allied arts of any given period must be the basis for the assimilation of musical values.
>
> There is much that is debatable in such a thesis. We can say, as we do say, that art is created for humanity. All we have to do is sit back and wallow in all that beauty. That is a very facile way to see it, because it is not so. The great artists did not create for mankind, but for what they hoped humanity could evolve into—and they helped us evolve.

The Dallas series on Gregorian Chant allowed for a more detailed presentation, including technical aspects for the musicologists who attended. His last three lectures discussed modalities, rhythm, and pedagogy. But the opening lecture challenged the audience to embrace the aesthetic and spiritual aspects of the chants. "Until now, we have attempted to teach elements of Gregorian Chant by transplanting into the American choir the research and techniques learned in Europe. But we have failed in this, not rendering the true qualities of these great works. Our accent has been on technique, and we have produced a monster."

Griffin knew the monks to be spiritually enlightened, humble, and deeply aware of silence—the very aspects lacking in a noisy, egocentric, secular society. With the Benedictines "the chant becomes a great art form through the spiritual background of each man who sings them."

> From the seventh through the eleventh centuries we enter into a realm known as "The Golden Age of Chant"—we enter into a period of synthetic genius which has not existed since. How else can we account for the fact that thousands of chants were written, by many different monks, in many different places, of consistent quality? The great chants, written in the depths of cloisters by monks whose names did not appear on manuscripts, written exclusively for the glory of God, are works in which man became for a moment attuned to divinity.
>
> All these chants have similar characteristics. It is impossible to tell which chant was written by which monk. Never since has this feat of uniform greatness by so many men, unknown to one another, produced a work of art of such exceptional perfection.
>
> We find here the only expression of art in which the human trademark is completely subjugated to the ideal.
>
> It has been said that Gregorian Chant evolved from silence, and that silence remains one of its dimensions. This is true, and it is one of the reasons why we rarely hear it well sung outside the monasteries, for we cannot hear a whisper when our ears are *not* attuned to silence. Music replaces silence with form, rhythm and color. These sounds must create a reaction that causes mind and heart to improve on silence—otherwise silence should be preferred.

When discussing later musical periods, Griffin made different observations. "We have the very heights of music by greater masters—Bach, Handel, Mozart, Beethoven, Schubert, but never in the greatest of these works do we find music which loses the composer—always it can be identified." In the era of Tchaikovsky and Wagner, "we became accustomed to measuring greatness by climaxes of loudness," forgetting "how much more dramatic a whisper can be, as the music became brutalized by eternal storms of crescendo brasses and woodwinds."

Griffin had learned this lesson. "I had this forcibly brought to mind when I took a *toccata* written for Nadia Boulanger's criticism. She explained that the work was not effective because it began, continued, and ended in a climax, with no counterbalancing passages to relieve the tension. Since Mozart conceived works wholly in advance, they never contained these faults, for the passages of repose balanced those passages of tension." He enjoyed lecturing, but it was "too pleasant." Like the farm experiment it "reconnected me to people in important ways, supported by a very personal spiritual development that I kept secret." But he knew that "I would never be whole, never realize my full vocation until I took the next step."

He went on tour with pianist Robert Casadesus in January of 1949 and was introduced to Miss Sadie Hawkins in New Orleans, a renowned teacher of the blind. Sightless since childhood, she offered to teach subtle adaptations, including the use of a light cane to replace the heavy one, teaching him "to listen for the echoes struck by its metal ferrule," he writes in *Scattered Shadows*.

> Between lessons in advanced Braille and music Braille, Miss Sadie had me walk the streets of the French Quarter alone. She taught me how to judge traffic by the sound, until I had learned to tell by my cane's echo how far I was from a wall or a curb or when I passed an open area. Studying with Miss Sadie was like learning music from a master. I had thought I was fairly accomplished in the skills that nullify the handicap of blindness. Working with her, I quickly realized that I had made only the crudest beginnings. She opened a new world to me. Perhaps most importantly, she taught me to get rid of the "blind look." The sightless rarely look toward the person speaking to them. Like most, I tended to keep my head rigid and hold it too high, as if I was staring at the skies. The blind do this unconsciously. "Aim your face directly at the person's voice," she instructed. "Animate your face. Show expressions. Move your head frequently. Remember that to them you are not only Howard Griffin, you are a symbol of all blind people in the world. They will judge others by you."

Returning to Texas, he attended a Dallas lecture by New York theater critic John Mason Brown, conversing with him at the reception. Brown suggested that he write of his monastic experiences. "You have told me some great stories, you talk like a writer, all you need to do is get started." His "training in obedience to those I considered masters, which dated back to my early student years at the French lycée" served him well. "If a man of this caliber said I should write, then I would make every effort." He wondered if he had "stumbled upon" his real vocation, and if he possessed any talent as a writer.

He was about to find out the answers to those questions.

Experience Into Fiction

> The printed page is the tomb of human spoken utterance. The body of the speaker is elsewhere.
>
> —JOHN HOWARD GRIFFIN

During the early years of blindness, Griffin continued to live with his parents on their farm at the northeast edge of Mansfield. His father remodeled the feed room of the barn into a writing studio. The seven-by-ten-foot space—"roughly three long steps each way"—was similar to cells he inhabited in French monasteries.

Griffin recalls working on *The Devil Rides Outside:*

> In the beginning the prose was stilted. Then the characters, who at first seemed dead, began coming to life and acting with a vitality of their own. I wondered if this might be my true vocation, so casually stumbled upon. All of my past studies seemed to have been a preparation for those days and nights when I poured out pages of a first novel. My past training in giving up to something beyond myself tempered life now. I immersed my being in the atmosphere, in the movements and in the characters. The process became more hypnotically real than anything else. Soon the work took over so completely that I moved a cot into the feed room and lived there night and day.
>
> At the edge of the woods and amidst the farm animals, I led a solitary existence, living much like an animal myself. I forgot to feed the animals until the dog or one of the geese came into the studio to remind me. I forgot to shave, to eat. Basic comforts became unimportant. I felt warm

> in an unheated room, sitting with an old quilt around my legs. The only thing that loomed important at all was the book.

Even after false starts, Griffin never lacked emotional intensity, determination, or immersion in his new quest. One false start was a discarded twelve-page typescript. In "Metamorphosis," a British physician named Dr. Mansfield visits his brother-in-law, a stoic monk dying in a French monastery. The narrative advances in the doctor's voice and through alternating scenes in the cloister. There are similarities between this unpublished text, the first novel, and the author's autobiography. He had been a medical student, and his protagonist is as skeptical of monasticism as the narrator of *The Devil Rides Outside*. Dr. Mansfield and the novel's narrator confront the dying of a monk with disgust. The doctor's brother-in-law, Friar Serene, embraces death without rancor, as does the character Brother Placide in the novel (of whom the narrator says: "He is nothing, but already he is in heaven").

As in the novel, Dr. Mansfield comes under the influence of the chants that slowly change his attitude. The setting of *The Devil Rides Outside* in an unnamed Benedictine monastery and in the provincial village surrounding it are based on Griffin's experiences at the Abbey of Solesmes in France. The 596-page novel, written as a journal in the immediacy of the present tense, found its title in an old French proverb: "The devil rides outside monastery walls."

Several of the novel's characters can be traced to people Griffin knew in France, but he rightly called the novel a work of fiction. "It is obvious that the broader one's experience is," he writes in "The Men From the Boys," "the more sensations and sentiments and sights and sounds and reactions will be stored in the imagination to be drawn upon in creative work. It is not that we make factual use of experience—not at all—but rather that we make use of the insights that come to us through experience." Turning experience into fiction became transformational. Even though drawing on actual people and events, the novelist's past experience was changed by the aesthetic distancing in the act of writing.

> The true writer, like the true painter, is an observer of all things, and quite especially of himself; but of himself in detachment, as though a portion of himself stood away and appraised the rest of him, without self-love or partiality. If he experiences death close at hand, or the

> tragic break-up of his own marriage, he has the strange consolation, even while hating the experience, of knowing that all of these things, the seemingly tragic along with the seemingly pleasant, will teach and develop him, and that somehow that teaching and development will come out abstracted and refined as an enrichment of creative work.

The first draft of *The Devil Rides Outside*, composed at an ecstatic pitch during seven weeks in 1949, was executed by a very arduous method. Every night the blind author spoke lines in French into a wire-recorder, transcribing his English translation on the typewriter each following day.

By this method it seems nearly impossible for Griffin to have created a first draft of a massive novel in only seven weeks, since he was a beginning writer and a fledgling typist. He had taken a typing lesson at The Lighthouse for the Blind and practiced on his mother's standard typewriter over one weekend. After completing the novel, he started the *Journal*, "one that would be brutally honest" (unlike the student journal kept in France). In 1951, while working on stories, he notes in the *Journal*, "in the writing itself I discovered a process of understanding."

Since Griffin was unsure about writing, he turned to classical music. "When I began to write fiction, I had good knowledge of music, but very little knowledge of literary forms or techniques. Although I had read extensively in French literature, I knew little of English or American literature. When I began using words, I decided to avoid falling into the same trap I had experienced as an aspiring composer. I took musical forms and constructed my fiction on them."

He applied Beethoven's late string quartet, *Opus 131* (seven movements without pause) to *The Devil Rides Outside*, allowing "themes to develop from musical fragments, bringing characters on stage when Beethoven's themes enter the score. I have learned much from the moderns, but vastly more from Bach and Mozart," he pointed out, "and, most of all, from Gregorian Chant. However, Mozart and Beethoven of the last quartets and sonatas have dictated most of my work."

In a 1948 Fort Worth lecture Griffin speaks about Beethoven's *Opus 131 String Quartet*, a year before beginning the novel.

> In Beethoven's last works for small forms, he became attuned to a divine musical conception that burned out any Romanticism, which purified his music of "isms"—and made his genius contemporary.

> These last quartets were once considered too difficult, too abstract for even dissonance-tuned ears. I chose this work for several reasons—first, because it has the seeds of the type of composition which we consider as modern; second, because I have the score almost from memory; and third, because it is written with that economy of musical means, which characterizes the best in our contemporary composers.

The unnamed narrator is an American musicologist fluent in French. He leaves his sweetheart Lucette in Paris, in order to study Gregorian Chant with musicologist Father G'seau at a Benedictine abbey. Griffin's impressions of the Abbey of Solesmes and the narrator's experiences at the fictional monastery are similar in several respects. Both have their agnosticism shaken by the chants and the humble behavior of the monks. Griffin's account in *Scattered Shadows* is respectful awe, but the novel's narrator initially complains about the primitive austerity. He begins to open up to the clarifying insights of Father Clément, a character based on Marie-Bruno (also the model for the Trappist monk Friar Marie-Orneux). These dialogues grew from actual conversations with Friar Marie-Bruno in Paris. The themes of the dialogues are the same, but the transpositions are never verbatim.

The same transformation applies to the doctor Griffin met aboard ship returning home from France in 1946. Dr. Rafael Carrazo is the model for Dr. Rafael Castelar in the novel. Both doctors were Guatemalans who studied medicine in France and fathered ten children. Both are relentlessly intelligent and gruffly officious. Making his annual retreat at the monastery, the character of Dr. Castelar discusses blindness with the novel's narrator, who is *not* blind.

> Man is afraid of solitude and of darkness, both natural to him. We pity the blind, not because they can't see, but because their blindness makes them live in darkness and as solitaries. And yet we often find that the blind man develops a happiness which astonishes us, because he's been forced to revert to a single unit of himself, to live in a manner more natural to his basic character.

In *Scattered Shadows* the real Dr. Carrazo does not make this same observation, but his self-assured tone matches that of the character in observations that the actual doctor made about blindness during the 1946 Atlantic crossing.

> With no one around to pity them or make them feel self-conscious, they quickly shift from the shock of their condition to an interest in solving new problems. They begin to feel about for things. The danger comes when other people are around. . . .
>
> Listen, it's almost impossible to resist the temptation to use your misfortune to your own advantage. It's such a shitty trap for you to fall into. A man like you must never want people's pity, or their admiration. I hope you're above that kind of cheap self-indulgence.

Griffin accepted the doctor's harsh observations as truth.

> Isolated by the ocean, no one reminded me that I was supposed to be one of the world's unfortunates. So, I forgot it and spent time learning. The doctor followed my progress with full understanding and with the excitement of curiosity, verifying what I managed correctly and correcting me when I made an error in judgment or dedication.

There are no blind characters in the novel, but Griffin wrote two stories about blindness. A brief vignette about a blind man in the city ("Dark Noon") was based on a visit to Fort Worth. That same year he wrote "The Cage," a twenty-one-page story narrated by a blind teenager exploring his longing to escape the "cage" of blindness. It was revised as a twenty-three-page short story ("The Peas") in 1954. None of these stories were published or even submitted. He rejected the "cage" as an image projected by the sighted, who tended to judge blindness as a monolithic condition, perceiving the blind as tragic victims to be pitied. Quoting Epictetus's dictum, "What disturbs men's minds is not events but their judgments on events," and Griffin believed the problem was not the *condition*, but merely the judgment of blindness by the sighted. "Sickness is a hindrance to the body," writes Epictetus, "but not to the will, unless the will consent." Griffin did not consent, struggling with despair as he prayed for guidance.

After drafting the novel in 1949, which required revisions when there was local interest in publishing it, he experimented with characterization and dialogue.[31]

> As in *The Devil Rides Outside*—my only purpose was to say exactly what I wanted, no matter what the form. Sometimes this leads to extreme incoherence, such as scenes of drunkenness or coma. Write again

in that style, which is the most successful for me. This purposely-polished style, complete in itself, expression polished to a high gloss, does not really satisfy me in the slightest.

But now, I write of no themes as fascinating as the one I treated in *The Devil Rides Outside*. I study too much, learn too much about writing—it castrates, stultifies. The greatest danger for me is listening to different ideas on writing. All of them seem to make sense and none of them do. The only way for me is to write in a vacuum, choosing words, phrases, and constructions that seem the most natural; best I not be influenced into a hybrid cold style which I could at best only imitate, not assimilate. To write with honesty, simplicity, vividness—the best I can, with no knowledge of trends or schools, is my only hope for producing a fruitful output. Otherwise, it would all go into theories, and that would kill all compulsion to write for the sake of the story and reader and replace it with desire only to express myself according to set standards—all of which is ridiculous in the end.

Griffin converted to Roman Catholicism. He was baptized on July 13, 1951, often saying that *The Devil Rides Outside* "wrote me into the Church." He clarifies this point about conversion in *Scattered Shadows*.

I could not imbue him [the anonymous narrator of the first novel] with the wisdom to understand what I did not—the significance and the far-reaching effects that such an experience might have upon his spiritual evolution. In fact, since I was then agnostic, the novel was a lengthy argument *against* any spiritual evolution and a critique of organized religion. As to the spirituality of the narrator, he reflected only my most recalcitrant self, and he was not transformed any more than I had been at the time.

I had made a commitment at Solesmes, although it was anything but joyful in spirit. After the novel was drafted, I began making progress, yet my spirit was still as dry as dust. Without this powerful dimension of sightlessness, I would have remained as recalcitrant as ever, just like the narrator at the end of the novel. To have written about a spiritual conversion would have been not only false but out of character for the narrator, because I had yet to make that conversion real in my own life.

On April 16, 1951, Griffin composed "The Whole World in His Hands," which was published in *New Voices 2: American Writing Today* in 1955.

> At last, I've written the story I'm truly proud of. It all began last night when I listened to Marian Anderson, singing "He Got the Whole World in His Hands." The profound absorption of her great artistry into the core of the music haunted me. I recorded it and could not forget it.
>
> Suddenly, I had a feeling, an authentic feeling for the Negro, for the goodness, the tragedy of the Negro. It went straight to my heart, when I wrote the sentence: "Lissie wondered how far she could drive herself before the unbearable weariness closed her eyes." From there on the story evolved of itself, using the preacher's talk for much of the dialogue and using the spiritual. At the end, in the last pages, I was so touched, I felt like weeping. And yet the story is not emotional—it is not sad—it is practically static emotionally, but the restraint makes it more poignant. It is sparsely written, naked and true—somehow it seems to be exactly what I've been hoping to write.

Griffin empathized with the tragic plight of African Americans, but his tone is still paternalistic. He would not begin to know the reality until *Black Like Me*.

On May 2, Griffin wrestled with an unnamed story.

> How unbelievably trite is the piece I've been working on—for the reason that the characterization is not good—the amiable elements are carefully left out, the cynicism is hard and often cruel, whereas it must be made from the substance of affection to become believable and alive. Oddly, these things are in my novel—the love, the consistent balance of good and evil in all the characters—instinctively I skirted away from faults that with knowledge I now commit. Looking back, the least bad things that I have made acceptable, have been those in which the characters lived and whom I wrote of with consistent affection.
>
> I realize that now because living in the monastic atmosphere, being much more conscious of God in all of the monks, I loved them because I loved Him, and they lived because of that. I must find it in God again, for the sake of my work. This once more proves what I have always contended—that a profound adoration, on the highest philosophical and

> spiritual level, creates a sort of synthetic genius, which is often impossible otherwise. I must be like an unknown and anonymous filter, without sacrificing truth as I see it.

In the 1951 *Journal*, he mentioned being asked to write a biography of the French pianist Robert Casadesus, his old friend and musical mentor. He never wrote the biography, but refers often to Casadesus in *Scattered Shadows*.[32]

During 1952 Griffin struggled with aspects of writing fiction, continuing his internal monologue about craft in the *Journal*.

> The effort of creating characters, making them live—the tremendous effort of going inside of them and finding motivation—the effort of keeping a line of continuity in action and symbolism, developing tensions. No one can know the killing quality of that.
>
> The point is the struggle for money to feed a wife and children; the point is conflict between the religion of art and split dedications and the word "responsibility" in our century. But all of it ties together—all of it is necessary, all of it should nourish, because the most disastrous splitting of dedications are ingredients necessary to experience, to the building of spiritual resources. It is not so much the exhaustion of the brain, but the hunger and impatience for something quite simple and basic—the hunger and impatience for an end to loneliness, a contempt for the ivory tower of opinion.

Yet on June 16, he gives into melancholia. "Today I am 32 years old—I have lived too many lifetimes, under too much tension, and have driven too hard—now it seems I only wait for something." The next day he was self-critical.

> Today I begin again, and I believe that this time I will make it. I feel little and weak, but there is no longer this taste of bitterness, no longer the nausea in the heart. Everything seems clean, like ground prepared for a garden. I pray with all my force that this blackness may not come back, and in the depths, I feel confident it won't, that I have passed the crisis and been spared. My belly still trembles, but these are no longer the tremblings of despair, only the natural results of a great upheaval, for the heart is intact, as are the brain and the spirit. These things that block me are defeats that must be accepted.

I must stop the self-torture of struggling against blindness. It's understandable and appropriately pathetic that there are times when I'm overwhelmed by grief that I'll never see the faces of those I love. I must destroy the pathetic element. The struggle to overcome should be a healthful thing, without pathos. I must attempt constantly to reduce the fact to its minimum disadvantage. There are times when it is comforting to know that many things can plausibly be excused and explained away by others—but deep down, that is a fake comfort. I have not had the strength to resist. I've hated my blindness, and let it seem more tragic than it really is, and this has been a weakening thing.

In conjunction with this, and springing directly from it, another thing must be realized and accepted, and this is also difficult. I must realize that at least half of the words spoken, the acts and gestures of people, are spontaneous and involuntary, and have no meaning. This is a true aspect of blindness that is universal, and it is perhaps the most maddening and destructive single element of all. A word spoken gruffly, or a silence, or the sound of tiredness in a voice—these things can torture a blind person to distraction, whereas, if he could see the expression on the person's face, he would instantly understand and be relieved.

In my book I hammered home the first of these—that the blind man must be shown unequivocal affection and he must have that security above all else.[33] But the second point, which I did *not* make in the book, and which is equally important, is that the sightless man must be big enough to open enough to do his part—he must realize that sighted people have a different point of view, a different criterion for judging the gravity of things, and that each act, each word, each gesture is not, in itself, an ultimate expression, but rather a passing one. He must realize that those things to which he attaches so much importance are generally unimportant to the sighted, and that if he waits a while, he will be reassured, for the tone of voice will change, the silence will be broken, the tiredness will disappear, and he will know that, after all, he was not responsible, and that everything is basically all right. The sighted cannot always realize his point of view, and he must accept that also. The sighted too often think that this indicates a lack of trust, a lack of confidence, and it is in some way insulting to the quality of their affections.

> Sightlessness is an unnatural condition, it is a minority condition, and therefore it is largely up to the sightless to adjust themselves to the rest of the world, rather than expecting the contrary; and it is in these things that I have allowed myself to react without understanding, and it is basically these things that have defeated me, and that have pained all whom I touch. Another thing, which I come to realize, and which I must always realize from now on, is that blindness inevitably (and in some ways this is a compensation) renders its vessels away from externals and back to what seems a somewhat childlike state.

In the entry of July 15, 1952, Griffin hit upon an idea for a novel, *As of Now*, with the main character to be based on his dear friend, Clyde Parker Holland, but the novel never materialized. However, he combined the character with his own love of monasticism into two stories about an old monk called Friar Clud. The published one ("Sauce for the Gander") has an unusual backstory, as noted by Bradford Daniel, editor of *The John Howard Griffin Reader*.

> Griffin wrote it in a few hours one afternoon to lift up the spirits of a close friend, who was very ill, and mailed it to him without even keeping a carbon. Victor Weybright of the New American Library was present when the story arrived and immediately telephoned Griffin for permission to publish it. Griffin was horrified at the thought of the story being published, but Weybright assured him it was a nice little piece, and nothing to be ashamed of. It first appeared in *New World Writing* in 1953, and quickly sold to Sweden, Denmark, France, and England. It finally found its way into a textbook, *Communicative Reading* (Macmillan, 1956).

On July 22 Griffin heard from the Book of the Month Club. Slowly the first novel gathered attention in Texas and in national reviews, becoming a *Time* magazine recommended title for ten weeks, and a surprise bestseller. While the publisher was excited about it, Griffin felt mixed reactions.

> The jury is to meet this week and *The Devil* is one of the candidates, but the chance of its being selected is pretty remote now, although it will be recommended. Everyone agreed that the book was remarkably written, but from there on, the reactions were violently for and violently against. Due to lack of unanimity, it will most probably *not* be chosen as the *one* book. The primary objection is that it is religiously too controversial for the club's "mass audience."

> In a way it is an extremely encouraging letter, and good to have "violent reactions." I feel two things: More than anything I should have liked to help a lot of people financially, and this would have solved a lot of problems. For myself, that aspect of it means little, for my needs are extremely simple. Second, I am honestly relieved that it will *not* be chosen, particularly considering the fact that it will be by-passed for reasons of religious interpretation—a question therefore of policy rather than merit. It is better that I produce a violent reaction than that I produce a so-called "popular appeal" work. In my heart I can feel nothing but relief—I can go on now, and do more independent work without the brass ring of sensational success to sour the taste in my mouth and to infatuate me with my own importance. I think the work will produce a more solid and lasting satisfaction by making its way in less sensational channels.

Griffin understood that such success could be beneficial financially to his parents and to the publisher, yet he did not identify with their disappointment. Instead he was absorbing the news as a serious novelist, relieved that the novel had been given national consideration as a work of art.

> I think everyone is bitterly disappointed except me and it is remarkable that others can despair in such a case. They are afraid that this might cause a breaking point. And yet, in these past two or three weeks, something that I had lost has returned: the compulsion to work in that way that does not exhaust, that nourishes. It seems that my brain, my creative energies have been dormant for a very long time now, and that they have suddenly come back to life.
>
> I can't go back and absorb myself in the novel. That is what they can't understand. The thing that makes me live is what I am doing now and what I plan to do tomorrow. I did my damnedest on *The Devil Rides Outside*, but it has been out of my hands for such a long time. Yet I have gained a little time in which all of the paraphernalia of such success is to be spared me, and I don't have to be bothered with the ballyhoo, the hysterics, interviews, impressions, smiles, buttoned collars, and immaculate ties for a while yet.

During September of 1952, Griffin made a retreat to Mount Carmel, a small Discalced Carmelite monastery near Dallas, which kept a vow of silence and a rigid schedule. "This monastery is new, the conveniences are here—lights, water, heat—but comforts are not. It is bare, the beds are hard, the food is simple, and the kneelers are torturous." He was made a Third Order (or lay) Carmelite, which meant he must vow to pray daily and to fast when possible, in exchange for being remembered in their Masses. "Anyone wearing the scapular is the special child of Carmel," said the Abbot. "It is neither a charm nor a talisman, but simply the cloak of Our Lady."

Even though his knees were swollen from praying, he felt joyful about the retreat. Several times annually he made retreats there, writing and entering into theological discussions with the clergy. Many became close friends, and made reading tapes that facilitated his formal studies in theology and philosophy. Father J. Stanley Murphy also "sent an unceasing flow of tapes from books by Jacques Maritain and Etienne Gilson—the finest thinkers of our time."

On Christmas of 1952, Griffin proposed to Elizabeth Ann Holland, daughter of his close friends, Bess and Clyde Holland, presenting her with an engagement ring. He had been coaching Elizabeth, his mother's most gifted piano pupil, in preparation for her senior recital. Without realizing it, Griffin had fallen in love with the seventeen-year-old beauty. But since he was thirty-two and blind, he held out no hope. There is a chapter about this attachment ("She Played Chopin") in *Scattered Shadows*, including a conversation with her father, who did not approve at the time. Only later did both men discover that Elizabeth shared the same affectionate feelings.

In February of 1953, he began a second novel on a new electric typewriter. *Nuni* was informed by his year living among the aborigines of the Solomon islands. Since the natives' daily existence had not changed in centuries (buildings still rested on the ground, walls were made from split saplings with a roof of thatched palm leaves and driftwood shingles for flooring), he was able to texture a fiction.

When he had lived with the villagers, he was immersed in the reality of the tribe, eating the vegetables and fruits of a horticultural society, fishing, and hunting small game. He enjoyed the tobacco grown in small plots, smoked in pipes or rolled leaves, and chewed the ritual betel-nut, a mixture of areca palms, pepper vines, and lime (obtained by burning dried coral), which turned teeth and lips bright red and altered the mind

Photo of JHG with Grand Chief Vutha, who had unified and "cured" the headhunting tribes of the Solomons. He became a WW II hero to the Americans and British when he kept his silence concerning their positions, after being tortured and left for dead by the Japanese.

to a mild, hallucinogenic calm. Griffin had many conversations with the Grand Chief of the Solomons, John Vutha, who told him about the primitive era during which *Nuni* is set. In a 1955 essay ("A Hero's Silence"), Griffin relates a significant conversation with Chief Vutha.

> Vutha spoke quietly, his voice an emotionless rumble, as though he were telling it to the walls and to the night. He had tried to do right, he said. He had loved his people. When he had assumed rule over them, they were headhunters. They lived always in fear of being murdered by members of other tribes. At nightfall each family locked itself inside its hut and never opened the door for any reason until daylight. A man's greatness was measured by the number of smoked heads suspended

> from the raters of his hut, so it was raid and fight and terror all the time with tribe against tribe.
>
> During the reign of terror, captured women were made slaves and used by all the men in a village. If children were born of these unions, they were considered *zagáta* (no good), and tossed to their deaths.

This became the setting of *Nuni*, which means "world" in the native idiom, a jungle island "where there was no sense of time or goal." It was another allegorical novel about a narrator-as-outsider. Composed in the present tense (the Floridian dialect has no past tense), it reads like an undated journal in a place without calendars or clocks. *Nuni* was another novel of modernity encountering earlier civilizations—not the *Primitive Rule* of St. Benedict that guided the monks in *The Devil Rides Outside*, but the primeval law of the jungle. Griffin asks, "What would happen to the average American if he were stripped of all the paraphernalia and thrust among total primitives?" The American professor John Harper symbolizes modern man cast into an unspoiled environment after a plane crash, slowly being stripped away of all civilized trappings.

This second novel was based on music also, utilizing the antiphonal structure of Gregorian Chant. He developed a single theme with variations (not the sacred *Psalms* as in the first novel), but Harper's internal refrain of "driven along paths not of our own choosing," echoing through streams of consciousness. "I wanted to attempt a dissonant, contrapuntal work with but a single voice line (in contrast to the many voice lines of *The Devil Rides Outside*). I worked for a long time in this sense, wanting no flashback, no other accepted techniques of filling in," he says in a 1963 interview.[34] "But I did this at the outset, confident that the character would eventually possess me and something would develop. I spent three years of intense labor working on this book, which became a personal translation of a great struggle that I was seeking to handle in my own life."

Nuni was composed by the same severe method as the first novel.

> I had begun using two recording machines, transferring spoken text from the first, along with the edited changes, to the second. This sped up the process, in that I was spared tedious retypings by working out the problems orally. I used the first machine to edit all the bridge passages and, when that was complete and correct, I transferred it to

> a second in unbroken sequence. Then a third recording machine was added to the process. The third was used strictly for the tracing of background action, so it would be consistent and followed through, backing up thoughts and dialogue, and forming of itself, if taken out of context, a mute drama. This was when the actual fascination of *Nuni* entered the picture; this was the element of construction that must give strength and solidity to a novel without ever being made obvious to the reader, like putting on the undercoat of a painting.
>
> It was a brain-crushing job, however, the cataloguing of the specific sensual details of sounds, sights, smells, along with the progression of actions, which had to be made consistent with the general mood of the scene, or in contrast to it. Those first months of the year, too cold to go out anyway, had been days of intense and unrelenting work, when it seemed as though I had four hands and two typewriters, so rapidly and consistently did I work once the recording machine work had been done.

At first alone on the remote island in *Nuni*, Professor Harper comes into contact with a tribal culture that is steeped in superstition and brutality, and judges them to be primitives. Initially Griffin had viewed the natives the same way, exactly according to the conditioning of his Southern upbringing.

In his seminal essay ("The Intrinsic *Other*"),[35] Griffin writes, "I considered, with great affection, my subjects to be 'primitives,' 'unevolved people,' 'aboriginals.'" He did not question his belief that "theirs was an 'inferior' and mine a 'superior' culture." Yet after months on the island, "whenever I went from one village to the other through the jungles, I still had to have a five-year-old lad guide me. I could not find a trail. If I were lost, I would not have known how to survive, what to eat in the jungles. It became obvious that within the context of that culture, I was clearly the inferior—an adult who could not have survived without the guidance of a child. And from the point of view of the local inhabitants—a valid point of view—I was *Other*, inferior, and they were superior." This confirmed an intellectual point about the island context, but he did not yet know the experiential levels of *Black Like Me*.

Elizabeth Ann Holland and John Howard Griffin were married on June 2, 1953, honeymooning in Mexico City. They moved into a remodeled cinder-block structure on the fifty-acre Holland family farm west of Mansfield (where Elizabeth had grown up), a few miles from the author's studio on his parents' property.

Soon after settling into the wedding cottage, the couple's initial tranquility was shattered. On a routine visit to the doctor, Griffin fractured a shoulder. He was on crutches at the time, recovering from a foot ailment, and slipped on a freshly mopped floor, ramming his shoulder into a marble wall. In treating the injury, the doctor performed several additional tests, discovering that he had a type of diabetes difficult to control. Discovering the disease suddenly made sense of his previous pattern of emotional outbursts and diabetic comas, retarding the healing process of his feet (from plantar warts that were cut out at the core).

The medical problems contributed to financial stress, as the couple became dependent upon their parents for assistance, including Clyde Holland's hands-on help in driving Griffin from the cottage every morning to the barn studio. Throughout these difficulties, he recognized that Elizabeth had been a steadying influence. "She is a ceaseless and unfailing example of understanding, discretion, and devotion that is almost heroic in its quiet, good-natured way. She is a perfect counterpoint to my life, and I'm afraid I take advantage of it; but I could scarcely bear it any other way, and my gratitude to her is immense."

During 1953 the local dailies published features about Griffin's new novel. He revised *The Devil Rides Outside* for Collins of London, which was the edition he favored.[36] He checked the translation from Presses de la Cité with Ralph Walker, a friend and French teacher in Mansfield. The Dutch translation by Elsevier of Amsterdam was overseen by the Rosica Colin Agency in London.

He wrote on November 5 about a day "of steady, uninterrupted work," but felt that "the more I do, the more opens up that needs to be done."

> Trying to bring alive the scenes and characters—impatient for failing, for wanting to hurry, for feeling the block between me and the significance of details that remain static and sterile, for the violence that rings hollow in the character of the chief; for the strange falseness of passages written this morning. Good point to bring out—the permanency of the simple lust in connection with a senseless, feelingless "savage" and the temporal quality of passion in marriage—the former a primitive condition and emotion infinitely less tormenting and painful than the latter, a romantic concept of sexuality in civilized evolution of man. Here is perhaps the thing I have been looking for to solve the pages on Harper's reintegration from the sexual viewpoint. But it is not crystallized into anything convincing yet.

During the seventh year of blindness, Griffin endured another operation on the foot tumors. It was so unpleasant that he left the hospital early, returning home in a wheelchair on December 2. It was impossible to place feet on the ground, and he had to crawl into the bed, "making all the fidgeting movements required to get into position when there is no further use of the foot leverage. All of this interests mightily, but very little physical effort exhausts me." He pondered "the comparative quality of pleasures made rich in poverty" to the situation of Harper in *Nuni*, who "realizes that the pleasures of his life that have been acutely desirable through long denial (like sitting in an easy chair) can be transferred to those pleasures of his own existence, simply by considering them in their proper light."

Griffin did not point out that this comparison was parallel to his sleeping under the stairwell in Paris as a student, when he had realized that he would forget all the nights in a comfortable bed but not *that* night. It was a matter of immersion in the moment, since crawling into bed with great effort was memorable beyond all the nights of easing in without effort. His insights about *experiencing experience* became part of Harper's sensibility in *Nuni*, just as Griffin's early agnosticism and anti-Catholicism are part of his narrator's psyche in *The Devil Rides Outside*.

During the final weeks of 1953, he did not allow immobility to limit daily efforts. He worked on *Nuni*, contemplating it in the *Journal*.

> Tears destroy the need to write. I have felt this many times, when I would become so excited over the work that I would have to stop and cry, and the crying would then destroy the fire and speed of the work, and it would be dull and forced. Today, laying on the bed, thinking out the words of the book, I was overwhelmed by some tremendous desolation—some sudden clarity of death. It seemed that death was very close, and I thought of all those I love and have loved, and some great strangling weeping started inside of me, but I held back and rolled in the wheelchair over to the typewriter to start working, feeling that the emotion would write and that if I allow the great relief of weeping, I should lose the tension, the excitement.
>
> So, I wept on paper, without shedding a tear from my eyes, and although it took longer for that to bring the ease that comes from tears, it eventually accomplished the same thing. Perhaps all art is produced as this product of intense transferal—perhaps all great art is the unshed tear—the

> brushstroke that evolves from the same speck of tension and energy as the tear, and is put into form rather than into the evaporative liquid.

Later that night he followed this stunning strophe with a paragraph reminiscent of an observation in Sören Kierkegaard's *Either/Or*.

> In writing, you must see the details of life through the magnified lens of a telescope, but you must reduce them, fit them so that the picture is actually seen through the wrong end of the telescope. It does no good to describe the smell, sound, and color of a leaf in November, without connecting it with the tree and even with the forest of emotion that it must elicit. Always try to keep that in mind—see the leaf through the proper end of the telescope, but connect it with the scene as glanced through the wrong end of the scope.

Deciding to sleep alone in the studio, Griffin adds a final insight.

> There is, somewhere beneath this ape-skull of density a perception that lies unexplored, unused. The effort of penetrating it, of going deeper into the domain of the inter-connection between all things, all thoughts, all emotions and reactions, is killing. I feel myself screwing-up my head, twisting my brain to find that clarity that I know exists in all men, but I cannot get more than a glimpse of it. When there is that sudden flooding of perception, the work is good, when there is not, it is mediocre and therefore useless.
>
> I seek some way of attracting it, of hanging on to it, but there seems to be no formula other than sitting down and writing no matter what you feel, but writing always in that direction. Sometimes the excitement, the leading-lines of thought will open it up, and then you are gone. But it is never a sure thing. They say—"Art is selectivity"—but I think that the only selectivity is actually this—learning the reaction, the characteristics of those lines that are written during that moment, selecting them from the welter of cleverness, invention, accidental brilliance—and tossing the other away.

On December 17, 1953, Griffin noted that *Nuni* "goes superbly now, and there is great happiness. How I hope this will be a worthy book!—but I'm not thinking of that, not thinking of the people who are waiting for it, who have faith in me."

> Any attempt to justify their faith, to think of them, even, would put another tone, an effort to the writing that would change and alter it. Already, since I work from the point of view of writing only with the deep inner dedication to God, I have found the book moving along, taking on characteristics that I should most certainly change if it were I who were writing it—and my greatest confidence that this is the correct way to handle it is in this subtle change that has taken place in the script—greater freedom and abandon, descriptions of things that taste and backward modesty might prevent me from entering on, except cringingly, now pour from the typewriter with a gusto that is not [at] all characteristic of me.
>
> I am no writer when I try to write of my own accord, basing work on my own judgment and selectivity, it is nothing except occasional surface style, but when I forget myself, forget canons of criticism and taste, forget parents and friends and publishers, and write only for God, then the writing becomes something exciting.
>
> As I long ago learned to abandon all theological questionings to God, to abandon any desire to know the answers, so now I have begun to learn to abdicate my own knowledge, logic, and taste, and through prayer and meditation to make myself as blank as possible, which conforms to what St. Thomas Aquinas wrote: "Truth is the repose of the intellect." The strange, wonderful thing about it, is that these pages are more daring, more blood-bursting, more amusing and truthful and bold and outspoken than I would ever had had the courage to make them of my own volition.

That day he received a letter from critic Van Wyck Brooks, "somehow generous beyond expectation," and "he put his finger directly on the weakness of *The Devil*." Brooks wrote that the "only adverse criticism, a fairly serious one, is that I don't feel clearly enough the 'evolution' of the narrator."

> He comes around at the end, and very convincingly, but I saw little in the second half of the book that seemed to point to this conclusion. Otherwise, the novel is certainly extraordinary. There isn't a false note in it, or moment in which the vitality flags; it is honest; the tone is right, and your journal form gives it throughout a quite wonderful effect of immediacy. Especially remarkable is the effect of contrast between the monastery and the village. I feel that you have experienced

> and known, deeply, both, although I do not doubt that in a real French village the devil would not have *quite such unlimited power* . . .
> I do not at any point question your knowledge of monks, France, music or painting, to mention four matters that come into the picture. You are certainly a man of extraordinary talent. The novel made a great impression on me and I could not forget it.

He was greatly encouraged by Brooks's letter and also felt gratitude for the essay by Maxwell Geismar, the first literary critic to write about Griffin's novels in book form (in *American Moderns*): "*The Devil Rides Outside* is indeed, along with James Jones's *From Here to Eternity* and William Styron's *Lie Down in Darkness*, among the three best novels of the 1950s."[37]

Griffin told Thomas D. McDonnell in a *Ramparts* interview that with the second novel *Nuni*, "the great jubilus of Aquinas fully entered my life."

> It was the translation to a Pacific island culture, with a completely fictional character, the problems and solutions that were part of my own life—but a translation, nevertheless, with parallels all along the line. In addition, *Nuni* was written quite a long while after my loss of sight, at a time when my visual memory had atrophied terribly, when I no longer made visual images of anything. I felt the deliberate need to create a visual book that would, through the creative process rather than memory, not be handicapped by my own lack of sight. Unlike any other work I have written, it remains quite special in my life; too personal for me to have any competent judgment of it, or its function or place in the corpus of work.

Griffin's difficult challenge was to convince readers to see a world that he could not, and this accounts for the novel's intense senses of hearing, smelling, tasting, and touching, as well as its abstract, lush descriptions. The narrator's gradual forgetting of memories and language are metaphors for the author's loss of visual images. When editor Austin Olney at Houghton Mifflin said that the descriptions in *Nuni* reminded him of abstract paintings, Griffin responded in the *Journal*.

> I was secretly pleased because abstraction, if it is right, gets to essences; but secretly alarmed, too, because I had thought my concepts were described in a life-like visual manner. His remark brought the fact home. Like the narcotic who discovers he has become an addict, I

> hadn't realized I had *gone that far*, and thought this might occur sometime in the future when my memory of sight would have become more abstract, less tangible. Is there such a thing as compensation for lack of what we consider an essential in the creation of art? Beethoven wrote his sublimest sounds while deaf. Sight can limit as well as instruct, confuse, and turn concepts ordinary unless one uses it as the miracle it is.

The *Journal* of 1954 contains 255 single-spaced pages, the most of any year, and his attitude never changed. On January 16 he writes, "Why water down words? Why say things just to be saying them, and why not be frank with the idea that these pages will never be seen? That is what makes such a journal lose all value."

In March of 1954, Griffin felt healthy enough to travel, giving talks in Canada on classical music and monasticism for the Christian Culture Series. He lectured on censorship in Detroit, where Pocket Book's paperback of *The Devil Rides Outside* had been banned. He was interviewed after a speech in St. Louis on March 8, and a feature appeared in the newspaper's front page, "with a sickening headline, but the article was splendid, accurate and in good taste all the way through."

The Griffins vacationed for a week at the home of Mary and Alec Wyton in Belleville, Illinois, where he had spent military leaves during basic training. Reviewing record albums he had bought thirteen years before, he found Mozart and Scarlatti works by Robert Casadesus, recordings of Bach, Telemann, Couperin, and Brahms that the Wytons encouraged him to take back. He listened late at night, "and it seemed that I was that youngster again, who somehow sublimated through this music, as though the sounds were the absolution necessary to my very existence."

> I remember returning to France and finding my youthful journals there, and being disgusted with the youth I had been—a cow-eyed idealist wracked with the most hideous sentimentality and nobleness; and I was afraid of feeling the same thing in listening to these recordings. But no, it was a pleasure, and I could not help feeling real affection.

The couple returned to Mansfield on March 19, and on March 23, Elizabeth announced that she was pregnant. He was overjoyed. But on April 8, he lamented. "I have a wife, an expected baby, and the household expenses, and no money to pay for them," so he extended workdays at the studio into nights as well.

While his parents were gone for a few days, he wrote in the *Journal* on April 24. "There is a peculiar joy in this activity of solitude. It takes me for a moment into a world I should not like permanently, but one of which I often dream—a world in which there is no sight and therefore no lack of it—the strange release from the tension of being observed." Returning home, he spent two days with the Carmelites, writing about debating theology and feeling edified by the monks.

On March 30 he received a call from Pocket Books with a strategy for bringing their paperback edition of *The Devil Rides Outside* to trial in Detroit, where the League of Decency had banned it. In order to create a legal case, the book had to be offered for sale to a police officer, who would arrest the publishing representative. This plan was concocted with the aid of the district attorney's office. The goal was to lose the case in Detroit and the Michigan higher court, so that the United States Supreme Court could adjudicate the novel. Griffin was expected to be the principal witness for the defense. He testified in Detroit on July 9, 1954.

In a later article, he summarized the case in the *Dallas Morning News*.

> The censorship system in Detroit is based on a "containing" statute that says any book containing objectionable words or phrases can be banned from public sale, on the grounds that it will be harmful to children. The books are read by someone appointed by the police department, who simply copies down all such objectionable words and sends a typed list of them to the chief of police, who puts the book on his banned list without considering the book as a whole. Those who banned my book never bothered to read it. They went on a smut hunt for any passage "containing obscene, immoral, lewd or lascivious language."
>
> The ramifications of such a statute are staggering; logically everything from the *Bible* to Shakespeare could be banned on this basis. So the choice of *The Devil Rides Outside* for a test case was really only a peg on which to hang some clarification as to the constitutional legality of such a containing statute.
>
> Can any work of art be judged piecemeal? This is like calling a great statue ugly because you throw a veil over it and leave only the umbilicus exposed. In order to have any influence on humanity's understanding, art must exist whole. This statute denies the existence of that essential quality of wholeness, and allows a book to be judged obscene

> because of one or two words taken out of context. It is like judging a man's soul by a hand severed from his body in an anatomy lab.
>
> Must serious novelists, who wish to treat adult emotions and problems, aim their dramatic incidents through the filter of juvenile concepts and capacities? Can there be no such thing as essentially adult fiction? If such works as those censored, which are admittedly adult fare, are legally banned from sale, must the banning city not face the responsibility that in depriving the children of books not intended for them they are automatically depriving adults of books to which they have right of access?
>
> How I despise this puritanical trend that turns spiritual health into a type of hygienic destruction, which seeks only to kill in the hope that virtue will somehow be left intact in the vacuum; seeing as evil those things which God saw as good.

That summer Griffin began losing sensation in both legs. At first the doctors suspected it was due to the diabetic constriction of blood vessels. Back pain ensued and he had to wear a brace. Eventually the paralysis was correctly diagnosed as the result of spinal malaria, a virus he had contracted during the war. The malaria had an eight-year incubation cycle, and cases emerged among soldiers who had served in the Pacific. The virus was combated by minute doses of strychnine.

By keeping the *Journal* private, Griffin could understand the process critically, and by not vocalizing his doubts to others, he was free to risk writing it all. On July 29, when his mother broke into sobs over the deterioration of his health, he knew the rightness of that secret covenant. "Crises have played their full work on my life. I am like an old Steinway on which students have practiced *fortissimo* passages for years. I dread the *fortissimo* noises of emotion now, and long only for the Bach counterpoint, the Mozart melody line, the variations of Beethoven's last quartets."

On the night of August 9, he described his small solitary cell, the primitive place of solitude he knew intimately. "All the country sleeps and I am awake, sitting here in my underwear and back brace with the feel of warm cement floor beneath my feet and the clacking of this typewriter."

> All of the windows are open and the night air pours in to the accompaniment of crickets. To my back, the bed of timbers, with a thin

> pillow, covered with a cool cotton comforter. To my right, through a screen door, the birds, silent except for occasional stirrings and chirpings. I could turn on my fan, but I want the ruffling silence of natural sounds. I am aware of pain as a vague normalcy tonight, centering in my spinal cord, but not distracting me from the pleasure of the moment. Perhaps someone is reading one of my works, little knowing that I sleep in a barn, on a bed of boards, in a poorly furnished little room that has not even water; not knowing that I need a shave and a bath, not knowing that I idle away the moments by writing whatever pleases me in this *Journal.*

By August 28, his creative freedom was limited by paralysis in his legs and numbness in his hands. Deciding to keep this secret, he hit upon the idea of renewing piano practice as an activity to mask the difficulties.

> All was sloppy and uncontrolled, but I put the metronome on slowly enough to be able to concentrate on striking and releasing completely each note, doing those exercises that require the most muscles: the diminished chord, broken *arpeggios* in both hands simultaneously to stretch the muscles in my hands and forearms.
>
> Then the Czerny five note exercises with double mordents, the scales and regular *arpeggios*, the held chord with released notes and finally, very slowly so I could control them, the Bach *B-flat Prelude* and the Mozart *Fantasy in D minor*. None of the numbness has gone, but perhaps if I can keep doing these piano exercises each day—under the guise of wanting to get back into practice, I can retain usage that I now have.

Throughout the year Griffin kept up a correspondence with French composer Francis Poulenc, who had asked the Carmelites to pray for the completion of his opera, *Dialogue of the Carmelites*. While reminiscing about France in early September, he wrote of Pierre Reverdy in the *Journal.* He realized the value of putting down ideas in order to remember, causing him to remark, "how poorly I think when I am *not* writing down my thoughts. The activity of my hands has become an adjunct to my mental process." Since the piano practice aided dexterity, he returned to *Nuni.*

On October 11, Griffin praised Bach in the *Journal.*

> The crystalline music of Bach's *French Suite for Clavichord #4*, and the incomparable music makes the morning incomparable and full of

> the jubilation of the spirits and the heart and the affections. Affections most particularly for Bach. No wonder, after writing this, and then playing it for Mary Magdalena, they would produce another child! The joy of animal spirits made into a vehicle of the tenderest affection and vigor, combined with the sanity of the man, and the love of God, all of these together and centered in the family, in the loftiest concepts of soul and body, but without that ever sacrificing the gaiety and exuberance of genius. Only a man of the most profound sentiments could produce such light-hearted music.

He studied the *Summa Theologica* of Aquinas in November, which "constantly excites the heart with truths that cannot be digested properly by either brain or memory." While pondering the "boldness of sanctity," he slipped into "a diabetic vertigo, aware of all things in this eerie manner, almost as a bystander, but tomorrow I will not be able to recall any of it, so that is why I write it down now."

Later he thought "about a thing which rarely enters my mind anymore, much less my imagination, thinking of how it would be to see—to see my wife, to see our expected child, to see the walls of this place, the trees, the pastures, and the animals, and it seemed truly amazing and unbelievable that I have never seen any of that, although it is as familiar as the slow throb of my pulse. And it would seem strange—how strange—if I ever were allowed to see it, and probably all of it would seem completely different from the concepts I have of it."

A few days after the diabetic episodes, he felt the effects of the strychnine—"working like a whirlwind for a few hours"—then crashing. But solitary concerns disappeared from his notes made at the hospital, while Elizabeth endured sixty-four hours of labor in the delivery of her first child. The pages are an hourly account of waiting by the expectant father, both sets of parents, and by the nuns and nurses. Susan was born healthy on November 20, 1954.

By January 18, 1955, Griffin realized that "*Nuni* draws to its close and becomes tremendously absorbing, so that there is no thought that is not connected with it." By January 28, he worked "almost 24 hours and now I am tired, but tired in that strange incandescent way that desires no rest, so I take a few moments off to break up the work with this *Journal*."

Griffin continued working during the cold, rainy season and, on February 4, felt "immensely content, in that strange and luminous way when it is underlined by exterior peace and simultaneously by the rumblings of sensuality that invigorate it rather than enervate it." Often he typed "strange" when describing abandonment in writing, or the scales of sightlessness. "In the midst of intense concentration, a voice suddenly pierces the noise of my typing and dictating machine and tears me from the heart of my thoughts into the reality of knowing that it is time for lunch. And despite myself, I go in trembling, half torn with a fury that is not against anyone or anything, but only the result of being roused from this dream of the work. It is a terrible, and unsettling thing—the special problem of the blind."

> Solitude need not indicate inactivity but did need to indicate freedom from distractions. The artist should not be deprived of pleasure and live in asceticism. Rather, the artist must have the security and serenity of uninterrupted time devoted only to it, without fear of distractions. During these winter months, the bitter cold and frequent rains had prevented nearly everyone from distracting my concentration. I had been very close to *Nuni*—aware perhaps that I had been putting the problems of my own life into the lap of Professor Harper, desperate for the narrator to solve them. I had stripped him of everything that men generally consider necessary to function at the human level—family, friends, even clothing, and plunging him into a world he was ill-prepared to live. My prospect was similar, though I never mention it aloud. First my blindness, then this paralysis and loss of mobility, and the uncertainly of the prognosis. It must drive us to turning into vegetables of frustration or it must drive us to God or an equivalent thing above and beyond us.

Griffin has a brief intuition into sainthood on March 16.

> Today, for five minutes, I have known what it is to be a saint, and all else is unimportant. Not the writing, not the crackling fire, not the doctor's office. For these minutes I have known the greatest happiness I can know on this earth. Deep in my heart, despite its momentary vigor and robustness, despite the new blood coursing through my entire being, I know that some devil of smallness, some lust-splashed image will turn me out of this sunlight into that drab middle-plain, and that I shall diminish back to who I am."

A month later, he mailed the manuscript of *Nuni.*

> I have stayed awake almost every night for a long time doing the final draft. Parts had to be redone twenty or more times. Elizabeth has fed me and bedded me and been marvelous in letting me go through this final draft period as the energies came.
>
> Is *Nuni* any good? God only knows. I have worked at it three years, too long, and sent it away with fear and trembling. I think Harper found himself along the lines of humanity rather than those of civilization. Now it is gone. They are all gone, all of these characters who have been more real than many people I know.
>
> They walked out the door with stamps on them. Their existence disappears when words stiffen into print. I do not regret it. Now to come out of it. There is neither jubilance nor sadness, only a dullness and overwhelming fatigue.

By May 2, Griffin was regaining the ability to walk, and ventured alone into the woods—"the furtherest I have gone in over a year since I first became crippled." Reaching the creek, he shed clothes, dark glasses, and except for shoes and the scapular around his neck, went naked into the water.

> Health and sweetness seemed to flow out of the wilds, to envelope my nakedness with the softest balm of freedom. I was as free as God created man to be, unencumbered in the midst of nature, and there was a marvelous upsurge of jubilation in all of it, as I passed slowly from paths of sunlight into patches of dense shade, moving along the winding path. Walking, listening, smelling, feeling the atmosphere of the deep woods.

New Voices came on May 14, including "The Whole World in His Hands," and on June 1, he received *New World Writing*, featuring his story ("Sauce for the Gander"). He recognized a certain success, but in the *Journal* of June 6, he would not allow acceptance to delude the work, "created from a vast foundation of instinct that is never easy, never certain of itself, and that each time I send off a story or complete a novel, I am as thoroughly convinced of its unworthiness as I am hopeful that it may contain the germ of merit, of something new, of something fresh. There is no certainty, no jubilation except in the actual intimacy of the creation, none in the end product, which always inspires tremendous doubts and uncertainty."

Throughout the summer of 1955, he wrote less than a dozen pages in the *Journal*, working on a new novel set in Paris. In order to write about the monastery patterned after Couvent St. Jacques that fit into the plot, he studied the Dominicans and scrupled his own spirituality. He wrote five pages on September 16, a personal *agonia*, after not opening the *Journal* for three weeks.

> How strange are things that happen to the soul, and how completely must I give up trying to understand them. This has been, and still is, a prolonged period of aridity so great that I have, without realizing it, virtually abandoned the interior life, without in any way abandoning the struggle to maintain those exterior things—devotions to Our Lady's scapular and the rosary, attempting to stay in a state of grace, abandonment of my will to God, but all of that coldly, spoken words full of distractions, acts that were not virtuous but that were simply devoid of sin—a vast difference.
>
> What a dangerous moment in a man's life; and how well do I understand why people give up and become so calloused to religion that they simply have no more feeling for it, and cannot persevere. I turned on the tape recorder and listened to Garrigou-LaGrange's work, and suddenly lines and sentences were flying out of context, aimed directly at me. And I began to see my clumsiness. I had clung to this abandonment, but without love.

The classic study of St. Thomas Aquinas and St. John of the Cross by Father Reginald Garrigou-Lagrange was one of Griffin's bibles.[38] "Our failure to understand the holy inspirations of the interior Master," writes the theologian, "is probably due to the fact that we listen to ourselves, that we are not humble enough and desirous of the reign of God in our souls."

Griffin responded in the *Journal*: "The diagnostic hit me and all in feeling a revival of interest and the exterior knowledge that I must persevere to discover what I must do. This was a tremendous consolation and reinforcement, for I've made all these mistakes—listening without really being aware of it, more and more to myself and less and less to God. How dense is our ignorance, and how capable are we of drifting away from the truth. Now, He must take from me what He will, do with me what He will; and I must persevere—such a difficult thing because the obstacles are so subtle. You do not realize what is happening until you suddenly find yourself on the brink of giving up."

There was no giving up. The couple's second child, John, was born healthy on November 9, 1955, by a Caesarian section. Elizabeth admitted feeling guilty that the first child was a girl, which secretly she had wanted.

Darkness and Light

Clyde Parker Holland, Elizabeth's beloved father and Griffin's loyal friend, died on January 7, 1956.[39] Griffin never actually *saw* his friend, but often peered into the spirit of the man, who helped the couple in myriad ways—with sage advice, hilarious humor, loving tenderness, and financial support.

Advance copies of *Nuni* arrived on May 5, but Griffin left the package for Elizabeth to open. He turned to cleaning the studio, announcing that it had "become a sober and restful companion rather than a slovenly and irritating one."

By May 15, the publication date for *Nuni*, he had "a very touching letter showing profound appreciation" from family friend Sallie Gillespie. "Knowing that a few people will read what you actually slave to put into a work makes the slavery less lonely. Whether *Nuni* does anything or not, it is nevertheless a very important point in my life—the result of three years of labor and loving care—the end, I pray, of an epoch of sickness and pain. I feel immense quietness without words, withdrawing with the desire only to finish work on the new novel."

In the *Journal* entry for June 10, Griffin wrote that "Creative art consists first in putting everything in and then taking most of it out. The putting of everything in is an artistic necessity for only in that way can substance and pace be attained; but then those ingredients that can be supplied by the imagination must be deleted in order to allow the reader his share of the creative work."

The *Journal* of July 14 included a list of the events for the day: Bastille Day in France, the Feast of St. Bonaventure, and "the anniversary of my

First Communion." On that day older brother Edgar was visiting from Houston, reading a first draft of *Street of the Seven Angels*. It was rare to show anyone a work before publication, but he held Edgar's opinion in high regard.

> He has been sitting out there all day, and to my surprise, I have been unable to work at all, unable to think. I have been in here waiting in agony for some reaction; for he is a very astute critic and not easily impressed, and since he is the first person to see the manuscript in its completed form, I have sat here and wondered whether it would be found any good or would merely represent months of wasted work.

When Griffin left the studio for coffee in the house, his mother said, "Edgar is terribly impressed with the new novel; thinks it's far superior to *Nuni*." Griffin was "immensely relieved and we discussed it at some length, and I think he really likes it; in any case he offered some very valuable suggestions."

Drafted during 1955 and 1956, *Street of the Seven Angels* was crafted to balance every scene with an answering scene,[40] by alternating jubilant scenes with somber ones, maintaining a Mozartian balance of phrase and response. Griffin "played Mozart continually during the writing and rewriting of this novel, and anywhere the tone of the work did not coincide with the tone of the music, I changed the work."

Street of the Seven Angels makes light of musical references, including one extended joke, echoing the names the French composers once known as *Les Six* of Paris. By changing the first letter of each composer's last name, the six characters, who are obsessed by religious censorship, become a musical joke. The widows Ponneger and Duric are derived from Arthur Honneger and Georges Auric, Mesdames Hilhaud and Aurey are based on Darius Milhaud and Louis Durey, and the two spinsters Mailleferre and Toulenc are plays on Germain Tailleferre and Francis Poulenc. What Griffin intended as a send-up of his Parisian acquaintances, Milhaud and Poulenc, was written eighty years after the French composers made their only joint recording, honoring the elder composer Erik Satie.

Unlike the earlier novels, which are intensely realistic and deeply philosophical first-person narratives written in the present tense, *Street* is a satirical comedy written in the past tense from the omniscient viewpoint. Yet it contains substantial levels of consideration—a serio-comic discourse on censorship and a dialogue between common morality and uncommon spirituality.

He explained aspects of the novel in several letters to Maxwell Geismar.[41]

> The novel deals with the self-defeating hypothesis which do-gooder groups have—the compulsory return of the Kingdom of God on earth—and it deals with freedom of the will, in that any moral virtue which is compulsory therefore loses all value. It concerns the mentality of censorship—the book-banners, the guardians of public virtue, or 'the sanctimonious serpents,' as Gerald Vann called them. Underlying this, counterpointing it, though the themes never touch, is a subsidiary plot and a list of characters, an essentially somber one. *Street* is almost entirely written in scenes with very little introspection. It lays the foundation that comes right out with the idea that morality is an unamiable goal in itself, that it will calcify the soul of anyone who aims at the perfection of routine Christian morality.

In *Street of the Seven Angels* six women form The Society for the Preservation of Christian Morality Against Contemporary Indecency, "carrying on their work despite the efforts of their spiritual guide, the parish priest Father Trissotin, who scribbles religious tracts and advises them to tone it down a bit." The women "behave with absolute missionary zeal, and through their actions demonstrate the absurdity of the censoring 'watchdog' mentality, particularly when it is exercised with such moral obtuseness."

Counterpointing the comic scenes at Mailleferre's Religious Arts Shop (where the group congregates to plot strategy) are scenes in the Dominican novitiate that reveal the simple monastic life. "You have a contrast between the asceticism, the love of truth in the spirit of Aquinas that goes on in this completely enclosed Dominican house, and then you have this group muddling through all the obscenity and pornography they can find—to show the devastating effect they have for bad on this whole community, though they're under the horrible illusion they're cleaning it up." This implied contrast between enraged, opinionated censors and enlightened, humble monks illuminates a related but unstated theme—"that moral virtue is impossible without the virtues of prudence and intelligence which lead us to the right way of achieving a good end."

Griffin further explained to Geismar that "My concept of the faith is that no truth I can discover can possibly be in ultimate disharmony with the truth of the faith," in paraphrasing Aquinas. He reshaped texts to harmonize with musical forms but never realigned the content to match religious dogma. "I have a very profound belief that the virtue of art is ultimately the greatest of all virtues. If I had to pervert my characters or what they say in order to make them harmonize with some tenet of the faith, I would *never* do it. If a character is doing or saying something I'm *positive* he would say or do—even though it's enormously offensive to me—I still do it. A work of art that's as true as you can make it, with your focus entirely on *the work* and on nothing else—not on side issues or your faith, not on your audience or on yourself—then I believe this will ultimately produce health. This is the daring part of art to me."

Literary influences are not easily discernable in Griffin's earlier novels, but for *Street of the Seven Angels* he drew on the comedies of Molière. The novel suggests a cinematic sensibility in the arrangement of thirty-four scenes that continue without pause. The influence on religious subtexts resides in the passages of Scene Twenty-Six, including portions of Marcel de Corte's essay ("Incarnation and Pseudo-Incarnation"), methodically intoned by the Dominican reader in the sacristy.[42]

The leader of the *Société*, Mademoiselle Mailleferre, overhears it and, initially rejecting the discourse on the false dualism of mind and soul, she begins to reconsider. Then she hears the Dominican prior clarify the meaning to the novices, pointing out that the true goal of the saints was in loving God and not in judging humanity, and the key to sanctity was never to think evil of another, but to forgive the moralizers even though they tend to think evil of everyone else. Listening to the inherent wisdom stirs Mailleferre to a religious epiphany. The scene illuminates the core spiritual message while it exposes the logical fallacies of censorship.

The time frame of the earlier version of the novel was consecutive Tuesdays in the late 1940s, but when Griffin revised it in 1961, the comic hero Charles Durand establishes the new time frame, linking it with the 1960 death of Pierre Reverdy and the poet's last book, *La Liberté des mers* (illustrated by Georges Braque).[43] Along with these artists, theologians Jacques Maritain and Gerald Vann are among his friends mentioned in the novel. Other autobiographical references include the courtroom arguments that were loosely based on the censorship trial of *The Devil Rides Outside*. His fictional do-gooder's *Société* was modeled on The Legion for Decent Literature, the Catholic organization that was an aggressive force in banning his novel on the grounds that it was unfit for children and adolescents. While nothing in the novel would shock contemporary readers, it was daring for the 1950s.

After the Michigan Supreme Court refused to consider the Detroit case against *The Devil Rides Outside* on appeal, it was brought before the United States Supreme Court nearly three years later. "Like similar cases involving petty crimes, no absolute right of appeal existed and the Supreme Court of Michigan had to be petitioned for leave to appeal," writes Albert B. Gerber in *Sex, Pornography, and Justice*.[44] "The court denied the petition, setting the stage for a rule by the United States Supreme Court." The Detroit decision was overturned by the Supreme Court, adjudicating the novel *not* to be obscene in the landmark decision (*Butler v. Michigan*). It declared a section of the Michigan penal code, forbidding the sale of any publication containing obscene, immoral, lewd, or lascivious material tending to incite minors to violent or depraved or immoral acts, to be unconstitutional.

This decision was rendered on February 21, 1957, in a rare unanimous opinion. Justice Felix Frankfurter opined: "The state insists that, by thus quarantining the general reading public against books not too rugged for grown men and women in order to shield juvenile innocence it is exercising its power to promote the general welfare. Surely this is to burn the house to roast the pig." Justice Frankfurter pointed out that the law reduced "the adult population of Michigan to reading only what is fit for children [which] thereby curtails one of those liberties of the individual . . . that history has attested as the indispensable condition for the maintenance and progress of a free society."

The decision reversed the British ruling (*Regina v. Hicklin*) of 1868, which defined as obscene any work that *contained* words or phrases capable of subverting the young, the weak, and the susceptible." The prosecution cited only a few scenes from the novel and a list of objectionable words. Gerber writes that *The Devil Rides Outside* was "one of the least obscene or pornographic books that ever became part of a test case." The ruling established that no book was to be banned merely on the basis of selected words or passages taken out of context, and that all books had to be evaluated in their entirety. The decision also clarified that books could *not* be banned because such adult content might reach children. It forced all states to revamp existing *containing statutes* similar to Michigan's laws and changed the literary landscape. The American Book Publishers Council applauded Frankfurter's stern rebuke of the antiquated system, expressing debt to Pocket Books for fighting the case.

Griffin's cryptic response: "How sweet is justice." The controversy over what he acerbically called "my *Devil*" had drawn him into the debate. His real concerns were about the role of the artist and the right of literature to be read.

While some points are made indirectly in *Street of the Seven Angels*, the banning of literature is *not* the trial's central focus. Bookseller Chez Durand is accused of defacing a statue of *The Reclining Diana*, a public monument covered with graffiti for decades. He claims to have been erasing rather than making obscene marks when apprehended. "Durand thinks she is a big howl, and he can never decide if she is lying there on her marble pedestal spread-eagled waiting for her lover or her gynecologist."

Griffin connected Gregorian Chant with mysticism in *The Devil Rides Outside* and *Street of the Seven Angels.* Both novels feature scenes from a medieval cloister as a symbol of the eternal, juxtaposed with scenes from the world of time. The village in *The Devil Rides Outside* and Paris in *Street of the Seven Angels* represent the fallen state of temporal society. While there are humorous moments in *Nuni* and *The Devil Rides Outside*, the narrative tones remain serious. The satire in *Street* turns bawdy. Griffin was no stranger to censorship in the 1950s, and his involvement continued in subsequent debates during the 1960s, including challenges to *Black Like Me* that were dismissed by lower courts. His critical role remained passionate, and he controlled his outrage (if not always his outrageous humor), by approaching the subject with serious research, logical analysis, and ethical scrutiny.

During most of 1956, he became involved in the school desegregation battle that fermented in Mansfield after the 1954 Supreme Court decision. When efforts to enroll black children in the city's white school system were rejected, a lawsuit was filed by black citizens against the Mansfield Independent School District (MISD). The suit was tried in November of 1955 before the Federal District Court in Fort Worth, which ruled it "premature." But after an appeal before the Fifth Circuit Court, the lower ruling was reversed, and MISD was ordered to admit students without regard to race to Mansfield's only high school in August 1956.

Prior to enrollment days, there were cross burnings in the black section west of town on August 22 and 23. The president of the Mansfield chapter of the NAACP, a community resident for fifty years, received several threats warning him "to get out of town." On August 28 the effigy of a black man was strung up on Main Street in downtown Mansfield. One of the signs attached to the dummy read: "This Negro tried to go to a white School."

"During this time," related Griffin, researching the crisis, "no Negroes appeared on the scene and no word has been heard from them. They are keeping at home." About white citizens, he opines, "a small group of fanatics more or less control the town and have the backing of the majority of whites who do not approve of them, but approve of their championing a mutual cause."

When it was learned he was preparing an article, the White Citizens Council warned him "to stay out of it." Soon after Griffin was invited by Theodore Freedman to coauthor a field report to be produced by the Anti-Defamation League of B'nai B'rith.[45] "I agreed to research locally, since we did not think the people would cooperate with outsiders," letting it be known that the findings would be "objective" in the nationally published report.

On August 30, the MISD opened for registration at the high school. A crowd of four hundred gathered at the school, protesting the court order to desegregate, but only whites appeared that first day. According to Griffin's report, several white "interviewees indicated that the 'brutal element' began to take over the proceedings—the element that favored *anything* to keep the Negroes 'in their place,' to protect white children from 'mongrelization,' and to drive the NAACP out of town."

Members in the mob carried signs ("Nigger stay out, this is a white school" and "A dead nigger is the best nigger"), and an effigy of a black man appeared at the school. "The local constable went to the school and, seeing the size of the mob, placed a call to the county sheriff, requesting assistance. The sheriff arrived on the scene and advised the milling crowd that he was there to preserve law and order."

The following day more than five hundred gathered at the high school, including Dallas and Fort Worth media, for it was anticipated that three black students would attempt to register. "The members of the mob voiced open threats," writes Griffin, and "it was stated that the organizers of the protest had done a good job and taken over completely." White men carried handguns, making no effort to conceal them. Armed white vigilantes set up roadblocks at both ends of town, turning away all blacks and any whites suspected of favoring desegregation. None were arrested or confronted by local police. On September 1, the final day of registration, less than 250 whites appeared on the scene, but the black students remained home.

The school was closed over the Labor Day weekend. Governor Allan Shivers dispatched Texas Rangers to Mansfield with a document that granted the MISD full authority to transfer any student out of the district whose presence might incite a riot. On Monday, September 4, the three black students did not appear because their parents feared the mobs. They were transferred to a segregated school in Fort Worth. The crisis was over, but the problem remained unsolved.

The White Citizens Council declared victory. Governor Shivers had merely bypassed every court order to desegregate by having the students removed, because he determined that three unarmed black teenagers "represented a threat to the peace of Mansfield." The governor concluded his public statement, saying, "If this course is not satisfactory under the circumstances to the federal government, I respectfully suggest that the Supreme Court, which is responsible for the order, be given the task of enforcing it." Governor Shivers made his personal position clear: "I am opposed to the mixing of white and Negro children in our public schools. It won't work, and the thinking people of both races know it won't work."

Griffin recognized that the black citizens had been terrorized out of the right to equal education for their children and that the white majority had been manipulated by the White Citizens Council into pressuring the school board and law enforcement into neglecting legal responsibilities. The root cause of this aggressive activity was white racism—both the overt bigotry of the White Citizens Council and the covert prejudice of the white majority. The secondary cause was the lack of real communication and understanding. The desegregation crisis had given Griffin his first direct experience with the "race problem" in his own backyard. Even though physically blind, he perceived what the sighted failed to see.

> For the blind man, the whole issue of segregation on the basis of inferiority according to color or race is solved axiomatically. He can see

> only the heart and intelligence of a man, and nothing in these things indicates the slightest whether the man is white or black, but only whether he is good or bad, wise or foolish.
>
> This indicates the enormous superficiality of segregationist judgments that are based on mere physical sight rather than perception. Is not this gift of sight then being abused since it leads men to judge an object by the accident of its color rather than by its real substance—is a red table any more of a table than a green one?

Griffin had heard in those voices, both black and white, a certain truth without being "blinded" by the color of their skin. What he recognized was not only the difference between viewpoints, but also the tragic disparity between separate modes of experience. His direct encounters with white racism, and the local miscommunication about the field report, made a deep and lasting impression. "The world is crazy and disturbed tonight," he wrote on September 21, 1956.

> It is very late and the day has been spent digging into this crisis situation, interviewing people, trying to find the truth, the patterns that are formed in behavior when emotions take such complete sway that they dominate rationality. What characteristics turn these interviews into a source of depression—first the fearful caution of the people, and then as they begin to unwind, the profound sense of injustice that is laid bare in their souls and which they deny because they think everyone else is against this attitude, each feeling that he alone feels it and must not express it for fear of social or physical or economic retaliation.
>
> Yes, fear of becoming the same outcast that we force the Negro to become, fear is the common denominator here, and fear is most certainly one of social retaliation, fear of losing caste in the community, distrust now of one's neighbors, as shown in this inability of each to speak out what thoughts really lie in his heart. How much this group of bullies has taken on the quality of a dictatorship. Things come out in these involved interviews, and the most extraordinary thing is the immense power of these men and the degree in which they are resented by people who cannot see that although they may agree on segregation as an issue, they need not therefore agree on the methods these men are using not only against Negroes but against whites.

> I have learned from two separate sources today that they threatened each merchant in town with economic pressures if they did not show up at the school ground. They demanded not only passive acquiescence of the merchants, but active participation not according to their ideals, beliefs, consciences, but according to the demands of the racist leaders. Rarely, not since Nazi Germany and Communist Europe, have I seen such a science made of hate, seen people's minds so cluttered with confusion over an issue that would obviously crumble in the light of rational persuasion.

Griffin worked on the final summary of the Mansfield report on October 28, "insofar as the desegregation issue is concerned, and perhaps that took too much out of me, required too much thought and analysis, and so tonight there is depression." The MISD remained segregated until 1965 when, under the protection of the National Guard, black students desegregated the town's only high school.

Throughout the 112 pages of the 1956 *Journal*, Griffin writes about the lack of income, "tension-filled days as we struggle to know what to do against the pressures of being penniless again, and I try to cram in that much more work and wait for the mail, always hoping but with nothing turning up." By December 6, the situation had not improved. Two TV dramas he scripted were not saleable, and he understood "clearly their unsuitability to a mass commercial audience." His mother read the letter aloud, "and knowing how broke we are, I think it hit her harder, although I am feeling that desolation for seeming to be unable to make a living with the only thing I really know to do, the thing I want most to do."

> Both of my books have been nominated the best of their respective years, both have received critical success. I am acclaimed as one of the important writers of our day by serious and respected critics, and yet I cannot make a living, not even a humble one. I have prestige in the literary world, and no money in the Mansfield bank.
>
> Until now it has been a gentle poverty, but now it becomes the brutal, sharp, agonizing poverty, and we are too human to bear it well. I pray to God for a solution.

His prayers were answered on January 9, 1957, when Griffin regained eyesight unexpectedly. He writes of the rare experience in *Scattered Shadows*.

> As I was walking from the barn studio to my parents' house—redness swirled in front of my eyes. Then I thought I saw the back door, cut in portions, dancing at crazy angles. I stood dumbfounded. Elements continued to dance and there was pain in my eyes and head.
>
> Another thought struck me and almost twisted my brain. Was ever a man in a stranger position? My own wife and children, people who were my life, and yet if I saw them on the street I would not even know them! From the swirl of my own confusion, I thought of how my wife must feel. Should she run immediately to me? Should she take time to dress, fix herself up, so I could see her first in the best possible light? I felt my brain tossing it out, refusing to believe. Desperately I clung to consciousness, struggling not to collapse, struggling to hang on to the light and movement.

Griffin called Elizabeth first and she phoned the doctor. He wondered about his family. "Was I really seeing? Would their hopes be built up only to crash when this incredible storm passed?" Just then the doctor arrived. Griffin could see him only as "a splotch of blue in the corner." Keeping eyelids open was exhausting and his eyes ached from the effort to focus. "But there was no focus—only lights and colors in constant movement." The doctor asked if he was really seeing, and to tell him the color of his suit. "Blue, I think." The doctor was astonished and overjoyed. "I want you to be aware of everything. This is an experience few can ever have." Instead, he asked the doctor for a sedative. The doctor gave him an injection of Demerol, and he withdrew from awareness. "I wanted to sleep, to leave this terrifying shock."

Griffin's parents were the first to arrive. He was able to tell his mother that she wore a green dress, but he could not discern faces. He retreated into a stupor, until he heard the voices of his wife and children, and staggered up from the chair as his daughter ran toward him. "I concentrated beyond my strength and saw all the radiant wisdom of her face looking up at me. I saw her face and then it blurred." When Elizabeth hugged him he glimpsed only "raven hair." Then Johnny tugged at his pant legs. "I reached down, felt his short-cropped hair, but could not see him. That first clear view of my daughter had been like looking at the sun—blinding me to everything else. That image remained in front of my face during the next dim hours. The effort of seeing her, or perhaps the emotion, shattered me."

He was taken to a specialist, who prescribed a new medication to stimulate blood circulation. The doctor issued no prognosis. Since there had been no obvious cause for the return of vision, there was no assurance it would improve. Vision could continue to be fragmented and without focus—or disappear again.

The next day he was fitted with a pair of temporary glasses. The thick lenses forced him to focus, an act that was still painful, fragmented, and frightening. He felt safer with eyes closed, comfortable with darkness. The doctor told them he had to be hidden away, he needed extended rest and close attention, especially considering that phone calls and visitors to the cottage were creating a circus atmosphere. He was still in shock, and in no shape to handle any publicity or visits.

Griffin suggested a retreat to the Carmelite monastery, and the doctor thought it an excellent idea. In the cloister he would be able to rest and recover in seclusion. Over the next few weeks he remained at the monastery, except for visits to the doctor. A few days later he was fitted with a permanent pair of dark glasses that reduced the glare, and slowly he began to adjust to these changes.

He recalls in *Scattered Shadows* that his "recovery of sight was, if anything, more terrifying than the loss of it."

> At the outset, sight was more of a burden than a help. Nothing looked as I had remembered. I could not get around well. Instead of sounds to guide me, there was a visual confusion of objects and an extreme clumsiness. I knew I was acting in a dream, but I could not prevent it. The monks did not talk about it. They understood that to regain sight after so long was not accomplished quickly, that one must concentrate on other things. Just as I had the support of the Benedictines at the Abbey of Solesmes while becoming blind, I now had the support of the Carmelites while recovering at Mount Carmel.

He did not view his blindness as a fateful accident or sight recovery as a medical fluke, believing that it had been "God's Will" that had plunged him into a decade of darkness, then delivered him to mystical light. He did not pretend to understand these mysteries but simply prayed for guidance.

Vision continued to improve and, within a few months, Griffin recovered normal eyesight. He gazed upon the world as a series of magnificent paintings, perceiving the intensity in subtle levels of light. "To watch the daylight turn to the obscurity of beginning night, and to feel strange nostalgia for that, and to put off the moment of turning off the lights. And then to see all of this brightness, to see the scene change like a modulation in harmony. Is this what it is like to see? Is this the way other people see? If not, it is surely the way they were meant to see."

News of Griffin's sight recovery ran in *Time* and *Newsweek*, the Associated Press wire service, and in Texas newspapers. By March he was fulfilling requests to write about it. "Is This What It Means To See?" appeared in the Catholic magazine *Jubilee*, was reprinted in *Reader's Digest*, and anthologized in *The Spirit of Man*.[46] Then he embarked on a series of articles for the International News Service (INS) to be syndicated in daily newspapers that summer.

He gloried in seeing all that he had never seen and all that he had forgotten. He noted in the *Journal* on March 21 about the joy of reading directly on the page instead of listening to tape recordings. "Going through old letters dating from my adolescence in France; rereading them, seeing reflected there the passionate innocence, the wonderful, unconsciously seminal quality of those days." He reread letters from Jean Hussar, Friar Marie-Bruno, Robert Casadesus, and Abraham Rattner. "All friends who have gone their own ways, with whom I corresponded with only a brief note and a Christmas card!"

In the *Journal* of April 19, he wrote of reading the pre-Socratic philosophers in old editions owned by his maternal grandfather, Samuel Clemens Young, who had bequeathed them to his grandson.

> For the first time I actually see the pages and see there his markings. I see him with a strange new insight. This man ran a store and came home in the evenings to sit before the fire in his back bedroom (where he kept his books). He took off his high-lace shoes and warmed his white-socked feet before the fire and read a few moments. I remember that as a daily event from my childhood—everything from merchandizing methods to agricultural books to these Greek classics. I find his penciled markings around such phrases as "The beginning of philosophy is to know the condition of one's own mind."

Griffin walked in the woods, on April 27, marveling at flowers "more beautiful than I ever recalled seeing them" and feeling "happy only out of doors." The INS articles assured them of a year's income, "but now is the time when I must work, to insure our future." After the INS articles were appearing in syndication, he received many letters, "most of them good and heart-warming."

On May 29, Griffin wrote of being "bewildered most by two things—one exquisite, the other painful. The exquisite bewilderment is my home life, my wife and children. To see them and share sight with them is almost unbearably a source of joy. The other, disturbing factor, comes in the irresponsible and juvenile remarks I read in our national press and magazines. Before, I rarely had access to these in detail. Now, they form a pattern new and discomfiting."

Griffin began rereading the *Journal* on June 28. Nearly nine hundred single-spaced pages were typed during the years of blindness, accounting for one third of the manuscript. After regaining sight, he typed only fifty-four pages in 1957, spending more time with his young family and venturing out in the world.

> In going through and editing these journals, I notice how often I use the word *strange*; and it is right for me to, for all of life is strange. I live each moment as though I couldn't believe it, as though all of it were new. Each time I take a bath, shave, lie down to rest, it is new, seen and felt vividly. And the strangeness, too, of driving a car alone for the first time in so many years. In my younger days, before my blindness, I took such things for granted, drove everywhere and rather disliked it.
>
> Now I have had to drive a car on necessary errands. For two days I practiced, going only up the lane to the mail box; but today I had to go all the way into town. The car is easy to handle, and all of the old skills returned naturally. It was enthralling to be alone behind the wheel. When I'd picked up the groceries and mailed the letters at the post office, I drove on out the highway a mile or so and returned by a back country road, alternately speeding for the thrill of movement, and creeping in order to see all of the wildflowers, the barns, the fields of mown hay, the cotton patches and flower gardens of the various farms.
>
> How I should love to strike out and spend an entire afternoon in the car, going down side roads, going anywhere it took me, for nothing but the wonder of looking. These things, so commonplace to others, fill me with longing to experience them. And perhaps this sense of strangeness, of wonderment comes because most of my blind friends

> have never experienced even the commonest of these things. In a way, I do it for them, too. And certainly, I see it as few others in the world, from the perspective of absolute newness.

On the morning of August 5, Elizabeth suffered a fall and was rushed to the hospital. She was seven months pregnant, and the accident induced labor, resulting in the premature birth of a third child, Gregory Parker, on August 6. Elizabeth endured a long stay and was kept under close watch. The outcome was joyful, but soon there would be three small children in the crowded cottage.

From the *Journal* of August 17, we learn that Griffin proofread the galley for the *Street of the Seven Angels*, preparing a meal, while Elizabeth nursed Greg every three hours. It was like many other days he did not write about fully, but once looking up to notice that his wife "looked extraordinarily beautiful."

In early 1958, Griffin was informed about a writing project by Sam Bloom, head of an advertising agency in Dallas. He was commissioned by the First National Bank of Midland to write a history of the Staked Plains region of West Texas. The family moved to Midland, and he researched the history of the region for six months, beginning with the Comanches and moving on to the early white settlers, the great oil boom, and finally a portrait of modern Midland. He enjoyed the work immensely and was well paid for the project.

They returned to Mansfield in February of 1959, and Griffin turned to revising the historical book under a hard deadline. *Land of the High Sky*[47] was finished by the summer of 1959, and printed that autumn in an edition of ten thousand cloth copies as a gift to customers when the First National Bank of Midland opened in September of 1959. His first nonfiction book and least-known work was not distributed to the trade or read beyond its regional context. In the *Preface*, Griffin reveals his perspective, while discovering in the land itself the essential subject.

> I began to think of the viewpoint I must use to give the book some cohesion. No matter in what direction I turned, a phrase from Virgil recurred to me: 'Nature first gave us those customs.' The very nature of the land had so impressed me that I began to wonder what effect it might have had on the various cultures and civilizations that had known it, inhabited it.

> In this great deserted area, in the Carthusian silences, the circle of firelight dispels the forbidding aspects. However, the country, the plains stretch out beyond and you cannot forget they are there. It is easy to erase the present, for nothing here is contemporary, nothing is changed from what it has always been. One feels joined with eternity, somehow.
>
> Like the desert or the ocean, it throws many face to face with nature stripped of all distracting elements—no mountains, no trees, no beautiful views, though its very simplicity is more than beauty. It overwhelms. To stay here, a man must face himself and the realities of life and death. This was the essence of it. Often I returned to the land and always its evocation grew more powerful. I could understand the early-day rancher's love for it and the cowboy's, as I could understand another's hatred of it.

Griffin spent several summer nights on an immense ranch, left off at "an isolated spot near a water hole, where a stunted mesquite tree provided the only shade. The immense silence emphasized my isolation." He was not reminded of "Home on the Range," but heard the music of J.S. Bach instead.

J. Frank Dobie relayed a similar response in a letter to Griffin. "Many times I feel more closely akin to the land and its native wild life than to people. Very few understand or care to understand the Bach harmonies, the rhythms of the earth in its Wordsworthian diurnal round."

There are only a dozen pages in the *Journal* for 1958, by far the fewest of any year, and a mere sixty-three pages for 1959. However, during most of those two years, Griffin was working on *Land of the High Sky*. After recovering sight and overcoming paralysis, he spent more time with family. A less obvious reason for not writing in the *Journal* was that his spiritual struggles had been understood at the level of physical pain, although his internal discourse would continue throughout life, usually reaching temporary resolution in metaphysical study, music, and prayer.

After completing *Land of the High Sky*, he returned to developing the chapters for *Scattered Shadows*, which seemed to be the next book that Houghton Mifflin wanted to publish, due to the press coverage about sight-recovery.

On June 19 Griffin reflected upon a masterpiece in the *Journal*.

> Occasionally, in the realm of art, a work exceeds one's most elevated expectation and one sees greatness. I recall hearing the raves about

the pianist Glenn Gould, anticipating from him something almost impossible, and then I heard him and found he surpassed expectations. Yesterday, a similar thing happened. Robert Ellis has painted the dust jacket for *Scattered Shadows*. I have long loved his work, and I don't know exactly what I anticipated, but something very beautiful. I received notice his package had arrived and went into town to get it. The package was too well wrapped to open it in town, so I brought it home. All the way back I wondered what it would be like. My anticipation was high.

When I arrived here, I opened the package, almost dreading to look. When I did, I saw what is certainly a masterpiece. To come face to face with a masterpiece—especially a new one—is rather like meeting a saint. Both are overwhelming experiences.

I spent the afternoon and evening carrying it around, showing it to everyone—and all were similarly overwhelmed by the power, compassion and beauty of this work. For the first time I realized that painting of this type equals the art of music in its communicative power, its ability to imply and evolve almost limitless beauty.

No need to attempt to describe it—it must be seen. It is a mystery. It fits no category, and to say it is "modern" delimits it, since it is timeless, serene, powerful.

Griffin endured ten days of festivities in Midland to launch *Land of the High Sky*. Home on October 7, he wrote of "signing autographs constantly." His local flash of fame caused him to reflect on notoriety in the *Journal* of October 9.

I come back from a place where I was thrown strongly into the limelight, where there were all the seductions of attentions; where people felt it an honor to talk with me, have me sign my books, where I was considered a hero. What a sickening thing within me. I sat there and wondered how they could so delude themselves. I returned here feeling as though I should go to confessing and set things right.

Everywhere I go, I find this to be the center of the problem, a problem familiar from my own experience. How much time do we waste in seeking our so-called true selves! What a damned un-noble pursuit and yet a common one, the subjective approach that ought to vanish with some growth of spiritual maturity, but which clings

> because it leads us to think we achieve to heights when in reality we remain buried within ourselves.

A silent conversation among Griffin, Jacques Maritain, and Aquinas continued for several days in the *Journal*, culminating on October 12. "Then we return to our barn, our woods, our isolation—we take down the St. Thomas to read and within two minutes the great burst of sunlight floods us and makes all the other seem tawdry, unhealthful, incomplete. I realize once again, all the implications of what Maritain calls the *sanctity of the intellect*." Griffin received a letter from Maritain on October 20 about *Land of the High Sky*. "I forewarned him it did not merit his reading. However, at least the first half might merit his reading, since it shows something of a civilization he could be very familiar with."

On October 22, he typed that "If the truth scandalizes, then the fault is in the one scandalized." How true this became with *Black Like Me* and, considering the ethical issues it raised, we can now realize the spiritual force behind it.

> I think of our own ability to be shocked by the humanity of men who lead a higher spiritual life. Our image of the ideal in this realm would be so *angelicized* that he would certainly be repulsive to God. This is why men, all in admiring such, feel some uneasiness, some certitude of an ill (which they most often ascribe to their own fallen state rather than to something wrong with the person afflicted with angelism). To do such, one must keep his humanity, at least half of it, secret. This is not so much a matter of repression as of "playing a role." It is this "acting" that the public demands, and when the man who is involved in the spiritual life refuses to act, he invariably scandalizes the many all in refreshing the few.
>
> We see traces everywhere—a sort of hidden resentment man has against the clays of himself: the necessity for physical nourishment, for bodily functions—as though these were inescapable down drags to his humanity and stumbling blocks to his spirituality—a contempt in people with pious leanings for God's creation of man: the longing to deny these things, or to believe that others have "risen above them."

On the date of his first entry in *Black Like Me*, October 28, 1959, he typed this *Journal* entry that is *not* included in the book.

> It is night now, strange, warm, heavily overcast. I walked down to the barn from the house a moment ago, and the air was fragrant with the odors of autumn, plowed fields, moist and spring-like; and all the frogs have come to life and are croaking on the creek banks. No stars shine. The overcast is total. An immense sensuality pervades the atmosphere—a sensuality of nature reprieved temporarily from winter, a return to awareness, stretching lazily, wanting to procreate out of season.
>
> It catches you up with deep excitement. I stopped halfway to the barn. Above the rustle, I heard the night, the spring night in autumn and felt this awe, this pounding excitement, this giant, silent sensuality joining me with all of it. Mysterious moments that a man catches, quite by accident, on such a night. A strange attunement with it all—like some primordial seduction, taking him out of himself, out of his ways of living and doing things and draws him into the very center of something beyond himself.

Nature was not an abstraction, but holistic immersion. Her sensuality stimulated and reconnected Griffin with eternity. The "strange attunement with it all" resolved the seeming contradictions into a universal order. Human nature connected with Mother Nature and the supernatural in an unbroken continuum. This "attunement" seemed "strange" only because the eternal harmony, so often fractured by the daily dissonance, is rarely sensed. Yet once taken beyond oneself, awareness is not limited by physicality or linguistic constructs, and certainly not trapped in a "cage of blindness." He was conscious of the unconscious grasp of wholeness that tends to remain secret, intuiting the essence of reality rather than as a concept reached by the rules of logic or in the reflexive ruts of dualistic thinking. The "mysterious moments that a man catches" are not measured by time. They are intimate revelations into the eternal present, a glimpse of the real as transcendent. Even though he had lost *and* regained eyesight, Griffin never lost his spiritual vision.

In *Black Like Me* an Anglo writer disguised as a "Negro" travels through the segregated South for six weeks before returning to the white world of privilege. In *Scattered Shadows* an unknown soldier, injured by forces beyond his control, gradually goes blind, and a decade later unexpectedly recovers sight. He is the *same* man in both autobiographical works, perceived as a stereotype and reduced to the status of the *Other*, who discovers mature humanity in *Otherness*.

Griffin realized that blindness was perceived as a tragic handicap and as an intrinsically different condition, bearing no relation to the loss of sight, just as whites prejudged black people based merely on skin pigmentation, never considering their qualities as human individuals.

There is no question that blindness was one of the profound experiences that influenced his decision to embark upon the *Black Like Me* journey. "A man loses his sight then, but let it be understood that he loses nothing else," Griffin proclaims. "He does not lose his intelligence, his taste, his sensitivity, his ideals, his right to respect. It is a grave mistake to think that blindness places a person into a given category of behaviorist patterns or psychological reactions. One remains as much an individual as always. There is no doubt, however, that one is obliged to lead a different, more complex, and often a more vital life."

Scattered Shadows illuminates sightlessness as the sighted could *never see it*, and *Black Like Me* shines a light on the internality of black people as whites *never wanted to see it.*[48] Griffin could not reach the experiential depths known by African Americans, but he evokes honest empathy in both realities. His view of racism was considered *controversial* by those in power, because truthfulness always is.

While blind he embarked on a spiritual journey that mystics have called "the dark night of the soul"—a bold test of faith sinners must pass through toward the Divine, even though few reach such stratospheres. To immerse oneself in a larger reality meant *not* distorting it to fit one's preconceptions and prejudices.

In art this would be the genuine humility of creativity that does not falsify the work with prideful self-expression. Instead of reducing an ideal to ego, he attempted to dissolve ego in the service of an ideal. In the spiritual realm, the perfect example of this ideal for Griffin was the anonymity of the monks who had composed the masterpieces of Gregorian Chant in offering humble praise to the glory of God.

This attitude of immersing oneself in aspects greater than self was one of Griffin's primary themes, and its variations are played out through his memoir in relation to blindness and sight, joy and pain, music and silence, love of humanity and his unquestioned obedience to the Divine.

PART II

A man reacts to a situation *not* according to what he is, but according to how he was formed. In moments of crisis, a man rises to heroism or falls into defeat, according to his past conditioning.

—JOHN HOWARD GRIFFIN

Black Like Me

Today, more than fifty years later, *Black Like Me* is considered outdated by some, a mere tract of history about the segregation era. Yet Griffin had been right about the book's essential truth, which he emphasizes in "The Intrinsic *Other*"—"that the *Other* is oneself in all essentials." Since the 2003 Human Genome Project revealed what we now know to be a scientific fact—that while every human being has a unique DNA sequence that differs from everyone else on the planet, we differ from each other by just 0.1%, regardless of ethnic origin. All humans are 99.9% the same—thus *race* is not a biological reality but merely an ethnic prejudice.

Griffin decided to propose a daring project to the publisher of *Sepia*, based on an idea that had "haunted" him for years. On October 29, 1959, he went to Fort Worth to discuss it with George Levitan, owner of Good Publishing Company,[49] which produced several monthly magazines for a primarily black readership. At first Levitan thought it was "a crazy idea," attempting to talk him out of it. The writer argued that the "South's racial situation was a blot on the whole country, and especially reflected against us overseas." The publisher countered that he would "be making yourself a target of the most ignorant rabble in the country." After a long pause, Levitan sighed and said: "But you know, it is a great idea. I can see right now you're going through with it." They agreed that *Sepia* would pay expenses in exchange for articles.

Levitan suggested Griffin discuss it with Adelle Jackson before making final plans. He met with Mrs. Jackson, a black woman who had begun as a secretary and swiftly advanced to become editorial director of *Sepia*. She tried to dissuade Griffin, believing it would be too dangerous.

After further discussion he convinced her. He was invited to return the next day to meet with FBI representatives.

That evening he told Elizabeth about the project, expecting her to question his sanity. "I don't know why I didn't, but I was kind of fascinated by the idea myself," she said later. "After she recovered from her astonishment," Griffin writes in *Black Like Me*, "she unhesitatingly agreed." This meant that she must take care of the home in his absence. But she had already become a veteran of astonishing circumstances—giving birth to three children before she was old enough to vote, nursing her blind husband through diabetic comas and spinal malaria, and keeping the family together through stressful times. The experiment would hardly be a "normal" experience, but it was accepted by Elizabeth as another extraordinary yet normal event in their lives.

Griffin returned to Fort Worth the next day for a meeting with Adelle Jackson and FBI agents from the Dallas bureau. Even though the project was beyond their jurisdiction, the agents were given a detailed report. He asked them if they thought he would be treated as the same man, no matter what his skin color. "You're not serious," replied one agent. "They're not going to ask you questions. As soon as they see you, you'll be a Negro and that's all they'll ever want to know about you."

On October 31 Griffin ruminated about the idea in the *Journal*.

> This idea, which has so long preoccupied me, is now to be explored. But as the time draws near, many things reveal themselves. The intellectual, scientific fascination remains, but the emotional dread increases to a point of sickness. What will this do to my parents, my wife and children—not only the unpleasantness that we anticipate from racist neighbors, but in some deeper realm of our experience? We are, after all, white Southerners, living in a land where our lives have been formed by the tainted atmosphere of white superiority. Intellectually we know better and intellectually we have liberated ourselves from these basic concepts. We are on the side of justice. But can one ever root out these mysterious, spontaneous deeper reactions of the viscera? Are we still subverted by the clichés that form our concepts?

He pondered the question of identity, wondering who he would become once disguised as a Negro in the Deep South. Would his identity change by "becoming" the *Other*? While sightless he had known *otherness*. Would that "blind vision" of penetrating intuition be replaced by the domination of sight?

Then he asked a different question: "Why do I find this project so offensive now that I must face the reality of it?" He suspected the answer had "something to do with identity," and he speculated for several more pages in the *Journal.*

> Perhaps I feel that the physical change will drag along with it a transformation of identity, even interior identity. My family suspects this. It is precisely, I think, their fear that their husband, son and brother, even though theoretically he will change only pigment, will in truth be changed more fundamentally. The eye is more powerful than the intellect in such things.

The theme of identity is dramatized by Griffin's encounters with the mirror throughout the book. But in these passages from the *Journal* (not part of the book), he anticipated the role of the *stranger* on the eve of departure for New Orleans.

Reading his marked-up copy of Jacques Maritain's *Scholasticism and Politics*, he searched for certain passages. "In effect, I am acting his philosophy—based on the light of Thomas Aquinas—making it live in action, better than I could act on my own." He realized that Maritain's statement that "martyrs to the love of neighbor may first be necessary" had become prophetic for Catholics of Griffin's generation and students of Thomistic thought. But "that was the least of it," because the "real danger lies in a man accepting in conscience a task he is ill qualified to undertake." He knew nothing else mattered except the quest for justice. "Once again it is necessary to throw off (by an act of will) the great dung-burden of self-fears. But Maritain's statement now represents a contradiction within me . . . the justice that a man owes a marriage or the justice that he owes his neighbor?" Actually it was *his* fear and *not* the philosopher's statement that had raised the question. The "contradiction within" him was a personal doubt that had nothing to do with the concept of justice. Justice in Maritain's ethical view meant *absolute justice* for all. If there was not justice for all, there could be no justice for anyone.

Griffin's pursuit of justice meant a greater responsibility to both neighbor *and* family. It was not ethical lip service about martyrdom, which

Portrait of French philosopher Jacques Maritain taken at the home of the Griffins in Fort Worth, Texas, in 1966. Maritain was Griffin's "spiritual mentor," and this photo appeared worldwide as well as in Griffin's book *Jacques Maritain: Homage in Words and Pictures* (Magi, 1974).

meant nothing if not put into action. "In this instance I feel the conflict between this latter justice and the reality of a suspension of *amoris*; for I will not be loved as myself while I am gone. How can I actually be held in love when even my wife will think of me as a Negro stranger—thus what holds the man in existence will cease for the time that his existence as himself ceases." Once more he was projecting his anxieties, intensified by imminent departure. His family never confused the change of pigment with a fundamental change in identity, but were concerned only for his safety. There was no suspension of love in his absence. His fear of losing identity had nothing to do with the reality of his family and everything to do with his own fears. The metaphors were his, not theirs. The "Negro stranger" would not be in their thoughts, but only in his mirror.

Griffin felt the "undercurrent of excitement" but dwelled in safety. "I do not allow myself to think of the coming weeks. The full view of life is too much. I pull back and seek these more amiable diversions. But the diversions must be—as a sort of repose from the tension of facing what I am entering. Nothing is more difficult than to face this, than deciding to look squarely at profound convictions and to act upon them, even when doing so goes contrary to all desires."

Griffin gathered what he needed, and concluded the long personal entry (that is not in the book). "Yes, it must be done—deciding to abandon oneself deliberately and completely to that which is so beautiful, justice, and to that which is so terrible, the reprisals, the disesteem of men. We know it, perhaps we have even done it—made the act, said the yes." He returned home to be with family, and to enjoy the last diversions before departure.

On November 1, 1959, he boarded a jet from Dallas, arriving in New Orleans that night. He checked into a first-class hotel in the French Quarter and took a long walk. He recalled an earlier decade when, as a young war veteran, he learned how to adapt to blindness under the tutelage of Miss Sadie Jacobs.[50] With a flexible cane and other senses as guides, he had navigated the baroque passageways of the French Quarter that he never expected to see.

"Strange experience. When I was blind I came here and learned cane-walking. Now, the most intense excitement filled me as I saw the places I visited while blind. I walked miles, trying to locate everything by sight that I once knew by smell and sound." He wandered among sightseers "entranced by the narrow streets, the iron-grill balconies, the green plants and vines glimpsed in lighted flagstone courtyards. Every view was magical." He reached Broussard's, a favorite restaurant in the Quarter. As a connoisseur of French cuisine and an excellent chef, his love of all things French was rekindled when he visited. He had supper in the courtyard and viewed the scene "as though I were looking through a fine camera lens."

Suddenly, as if the cap had been placed over the lens, the view was no longer magical. He imagined the other side of town, which he would be forced to inhabit. He made a phone call to his friend Harold Levy. Relieved to hear Harold's voice, they spoke of earlier times, but the project was not mentioned. When he was invited to stay with the Levys, he accepted with relief.

Soon, under the direction of a local dermatologist, Griffin took medication orally and exposed his entire body to the ultraviolet rays of a sun lamp. For a week, up to fifteen hours each day, he stretched out on a couch under the glare of the lamp. His eyes were protected by cotton pads when facing the lamp, and he wore sunglasses when turned away.

The doctor prescribed Oxsoralen, a drug used to treat vitiligo, a cutaneous infection common among black people, which produces white splotches on the skin. Typically the medication was administered over a period of six to twelve weeks, but his experiment necessitated an accelerated pace that was accomplished by taking larger doses and enduring longer exposure under the lamp. Despite serious health hazards, the doctor agreed to the acceleration, monitoring the experiment with regular blood tests to chart any liver damage. None of the blood tests indicated liver damage, and except for lassitude and extreme nausea, Griffin felt no lasting ill effects. The legend about his dying from the drug is entirely fallacious. The acceleration did not succeed as hoped, but he acquired a dark undercoating of pigment that could be touched up effectively with applications of a dark stain.

In *A Time to Be Human* he looks back at his false preconceptions. "First I did not think I could possibly pass because, although I had the skin color, I did not have the kind of bone structure or facial conformation or color of eyes that we think of as 'Negroid.' Yet I did not have to be in the black community, as a black man, for more than an hour to see what I had never before noticed as a white man."

What Griffin failed to notice had been blurred by the racist mythology of his southern background. "I saw black people with every kind of bone structure, every type of facial conformation, and every density of pigment. . . . I saw black people with blue eyes, with green eyes, with gray eyes." He "never anticipated for one moment that I would pass as a Negro in the black community. The reasons I thought it would be impossible are explained by the fact that a deeply held prejudice will cause even the senses to accommodate to the image you want to see. I now wonder what we have been using for sight all these years, particularly those of us who live in the South, claiming to be in constant contact with blacks. I didn't have to be in the black community an hour before the truth struck me. At the age of thirty-nine I saw for the first time." Because Griffin was thinking white, he anticipated two problems where none existed. His selective inattention reinforced the stereotype that *all black people look alike*, blindfolding him to any differentiation in detail.

While the problems of passing to whites *and* blacks evaporated, a new problem arose, presenting an ethical dilemma. "I could not stay in the homes of black people under false pretenses, so I would try to tell my hosts the truth. I would say, 'Before I can accept your shelter and the food from your table, I have to tell you a truth about myself that may surprise you.' They would look at me expectantly and then I would announce, 'I am not really a black man. I am a white man.' The looks of pain and distress in the eyes of my hosts told me clearly what they were too courteous to say in words. Their looks said: 'Who is this black man who thinks he's white?'" This fact is not revealed in *Black Like Me*, because he assumed it would undercut the seriousness of the book. This aspect embarrassed him, and he did not confess the omission until his lecture tours, admitting that this naïve blunder was laughable.

Only Sterling Williams believed that Griffin was a white man in disguise, yet even he harbored doubts about the writer's true identity. Williams was the proprietor of a bustling shoeshine stand located on the edge of Jackson Square, where locals mingled with tourists at the French Market or relaxed on benches under the tree-lined walks of a nearby park. That stretch of sidewalk where he catered to a diverse clientele was the unacknowledged zone of tolerance between the segregated worlds. Looking in the direction away from the market, the eye took in a deteriorated row of abandoned buildings and clusters of derelicts.

Griffin visited the stand several times as a white man, engaging in friendly conversation with Williams, who took an interest in the unusual cut of the customer's shoes, but had little interest in what he said (that he was a writer from Texas, making a research trip through the South to study living conditions). But Griffin never disclosed the unique nature of the research project. He felt that Williams would be an excellent contact for entry into the black community, since the elderly man was "keenly intelligent, and a good talker."

Williams was a World War I veteran who had lost a leg from a battle wound. Griffin enjoyed his manner, which "showed none of the obsequiousness of the Southern Negro, but was polite and easy to know." Williams would become more than a contact in the project, and his shoeshine stand would prove to be more than a locus for data gathering. He would provide resourceful guidance, a place of vital interaction, and a valuable trust beyond expectations.

On the morning of November 7, Griffin made a final visit to the white doctor's office. The dermatologist established the daily dosage, informing him that it would darken the skin pigment over time. If he stopped taking the medicine the color would begin to fade. He noticed that the doctor "showed much doubt and perhaps regret that he had ever cooperated with me in this transformation." As Griffin left the office, "He shook my hand and said gravely, 'Now you go into oblivion.'"

Later that afternoon a cold front reached New Orleans, making the final sun lamp treatments bearable. He received a visit from Harold Levy, who was checking on him after an absence of several days. Alarmed by Griffin's appearance, Levy wondered what the writer planned. He said he would be leaving that night, but did not explain. Discreet as always, Levy soon departed, asking no more questions. Griffin began to feel anxiety mounting, so he moved to action.

Since he had straight brown hair, he mistakenly thought that he would *not* pass. He shaved his head until the pate felt smooth, washing away the soap and water. Next he applied coats of dark stain, wiping away the residue. He showered, dressed in casual clothes, and packed two duffel bags. One contained clothes and the other had toilet items, a second pair of shoes, spiral notebooks, and ballpoint pens. Then he turned off all the lights. He waited a few seconds while his eyes adjusted. Entering the bathroom, he stood in the darkness before the mirror. The moment had arrived to witness the disguise and he flipped on the light switch.

> In the flood of light against white tile, the face and shoulders of a stranger—a fierce, bald, very dark Negro—glared at me from the glass.
>
> The transformation was total and shocking. I had expected to see myself disguised, but this was something else. I was imprisoned in

> the flesh of an utter stranger, an unsympathetic one with whom I felt no kinship. All traces of the John Griffin I had been were wiped from existence. Even the senses underwent a change so profound it filled me with distress. I looked into the mirror and saw reflected nothing of the white John Griffin's past. No, the reflections led back to Africa, back to the shanty and the ghetto, back to the fruitless struggles against the mark of blackness. Suddenly, almost with no mental preparation, no advance hint, it became clear and permeated my whole being. My inclination was to fight against it. I had gone too far. I knew now that there is no such thing as a disguised white man, when the black won't rub off. The black man is wholly a Negro, regardless of what he once may have been. I was a newly created Negro who must go out that door and live in a world unfamiliar to me.
>
> The completeness of this transformation appalled me. It was unlike anything I had imagined. I became two men, the observing one and the one who panicked, who felt Negroid even into the depths of his entrails.
>
> I felt the beginnings of great loneliness, not because I was a Negro but because the man I had been, the self I knew, was hidden in the flesh of another. If I returned home to my wife and children they would not know me. They would open the door and stare blankly at me. My children would want to know who is this large, bald Negro. If I walked up to friends, I knew I would see no flicker of recognition in their eyes.
>
> I had tampered with the mystery of existence and I had lost the sense of my own being. This is what devastated me. The Griffin that was had become invisible.
>
> The worst of it was that I could feel no companionship with this new person.

This seminal passage reads like a "shock of recognition" scene in a modern literary novel, except that it was real. Yet there is a curious inversion because it is most notable for its *lack of recognition*. Within that illuminated exposure Griffin's psyche was overwhelmed by a series of simultaneous disruptions. His involuntary reaction to that sudden crisis was massive denial.

On the sensory plane Griffin conjured a visual distortion. What eyes saw mind refused to perceive. The dualistic subject-object relation was short-circuited by the unexpected "stranger" glaring back from the glass.

But who glared at whom? Was he that dark reflection in the mirror or was he the inner white consciousness that reflected upon it? This disembodied image stunned him into temporary dysfunction. Coherence disintegrated, continuity ceased, identity disappeared. The transformation obscured the appearance by which he could be recognized by those who knew him, severing him from all that had been familiar. Even his own name—recalled three times as if to declare individuality—echoed like a litany of disconnection and loss. Unconsciously, he had projected a primordial shadow figure on the mirror, causing him to recoil from the truth. The repressed prejudices he had managed for so long to deny or rationalize intellectually were exposed with brutal clarity in the "stranger's" glare. The stranger in the mirror was none other than the *Other*. Without warning, Griffin had encountered his own inculcated racism face to face.

Perplexed by this stark new reality, he was incapable of understanding what had happened. For the moment, he dismissed the experience as simply "the shock of first reaction," and that would have to suffice. It was time to leave, yet he hesitated. "How did one start? A thousand questions presented themselves. The strangeness of my situation struck me anew—I was a man born old at midnight into a new life. How does such a man act?" Just then the phone rang and he told the caller that his host was not at home. "Again the strangeness, the secret awareness that the person at the other end of the line did not know he talked to a Negro." After the clock struck midnight, he grabbed the duffel bags and stepped outside.

Seeing no one on the street, he walked to the corner and waited for the trolley. Soon he heard footsteps in the distance and a white man emerged from the shadows. Would the man speak or question him? He stared but said nothing. Two men, one white and one black, stood silently on a cold night at a street corner awaiting a trolley. It was as simple as that. He had passed the first test.

Feeling sweat under his clothing, he observed that the sensation felt no different as a black man. This childlike discovery gave off a flicker of illumination—all was new and, as expected, his discoveries would be naïve ones. Through a crude yet mysterious alchemy, a scientific experiment had been transformed in the seclusion of a secret laboratory. Since it was a "new life" into which even this "man born old" entered, the inevitable results would be fresh and fascinating, because the manchild became both the experimenter and the body of experimentation.

When the trolley arrived, Griffin let the white man board first. Even though the New Orleans transit system was no longer segregated, most public facilities remained divided along Jim Crow lines. He took a seat toward the back. Arousing no suspicion among the black people there, he began to feel confident. He asked one man where he might find a decent hotel. Informed that the Butler on Rampart Street was about as good as any, he got information about how to transfer to the correct bus. He exited the trolley at the Canal Street stop in the center of the city, passing the same places that had solicited his business on earlier evenings when he was white. This night he was not solicited. He returned to the drugstore he had patronized nearly every day since his arrival to purchase a pack of Picayunes. One of the clerks he had spoken with on earlier occasions did not engage in the usual idle chatter. She did not recognize him as the white man with whom she had been pleasant. Again Griffin was struck by the childlike reaction that everything looked and sounded and smelled the same, but now the soda fountain was legally off-limits.

Griffin caught a bus from Canal to South Rampart and found the Butler Hotel. He waited at a table in the restaurant while the clerk dealt with another customer. Then a large black man entered the restaurant, sat at the counter, and turned to him with a wide grin. The ensuing dialogue, which the writer's comic sense might have turned into farce under less stressful conditions, comes across as straight realism. The wit lies between the subtle deadpan lines. The local Negro grinned and said, "Man, you really got your top shaved didn't you?"

"Yeah, doesn't it look all right?"

"Man, it's slick. Makes you look real good." He said that the "gals" were really going for baldheaded men. "They say it's a sure sign of being high-sexed."

"I let him think I'd shaved my head for that reason. We talked easily. I asked him if this were the best hotel in the area. He said the Sunset Hotel down the street might be a little better." Griffin grabbed his bags and walked out the door.

"See you around, Slick."

In less than two hours, he had traveled a long psychic road from feeling that his white identity had been usurped by a black stranger to being a bald black man in the eyes of all he encountered. He walked a few blocks to the Sunset Hotel. It was located next to a loud bar in full swing.

The lobby was quiet, empty, drab. He woke the clerk, paid the rent in advance, and was led up to the second floor. The clerk informed him that no women were allowed in the rooms and that the toilet was down the hall. One look over the clerk's shoulder into the cramped cubicle almost made him back out, but he would not find a better room at two in the morning.

After the clerk departed, he locked the door, observing that the room was clean. He sat on the bed "to the loud twang of springs." The passage continues with a vivid description of precise visual details, the noises that intrude, and the very air he breathes. The objective elements of this squalid room match his mood. "A deep gloom spread through me, heightened by noise of talk, laughter and juke-box jazz from the bar downstairs," as subsequent sensations evoke this gloom. "My room was scarcely larger than a double bed. An open transom above the door into the hall provided the only ventilation." There were no windows and no mirror.

The room was cramped, the floor too flimsy to keep out the noises from below, the light "so feeble" that he could barely see. Even the air that circulated felt stale. The broken ceiling fan caught faint light, "casting distorted shadows of the four motionless blades against the wall." The shadowy distortions reflect a metaphorical mirror of his internal despair. Griffin becomes the room in all its aspects ("boxed in, suffocating"), unconsciously "mingled with that of other rooms," and specifically the room of the *Other* he has become. This scene at the Sunset Hotel choked him with "an almost desperate sadness." Worse were the aural intrusions creating a chaotic din, an ugly dissonance that jangled his nerves. He longed for sublime music, not "juke-box jazz," to harmonize the spirit, but not these sounds that "so degrade the spirit." Emotionally overwhelmed and physically exhausted, he felt mocked by "all this evoked" and the powerlessness of will that "could not shake" it off.

On November 8, he awakened as a "Negro" for the first time. It would be the most varied and eventful day in New Orleans, and the entry runs twenty pages. He began slowly, groggily, disjointedly, and in dire need of strong coffee. Before noon he dressed and entered the street, immediately aware of a different world.

"It was the ghetto. I had seen them before from the high altitude of one who could look down and pity. Now I belonged here and the view was different." He walked the streets in search of a café, taking in impressions at ground zero. "Here it was pennies and clutter and spittle on the curb. Here people walked fast to juggle the dimes, to make a deal, to find cheap liver or a tomato that was overripe. Here was the indefinable stink of despair. Here modesty was a luxury. People struggled for it." He carried his bags, knowing he would not return to the Sunset Hotel. Down to his last twenty dollars in cash (and two hundred in traveler's checks), he was wealthy enough to escape the ghetto. But such thoughts were overwhelmed by the harsh streets.

He withdrew from the panorama, focusing on a corner restaurant that attracted him with its spicy scent of Creole cooking. Entering the pleasant place, he sat at a table decked with a red-checked tablecloth. He ordered breakfast from a young black woman, who seemed to be waitress, cook, and cashier all in one. She served him breakfast for a half dollar—eggs, grits, and several cups of coffee (but no butter or napkin). A black man at the counter smiled and nodded greetings, asking if he was looking for work. Affirming that he was, Griffin inquired about a decent room in the area. The friendly local joined him. He suggested the YMCA on Dryades, informing him that a Catholic church was near the Y, when the newcomer asked. The local accepted a cup of coffee, characterized the area, and suggested possible places of employment. Griffin took mental notes and asked about the location of the nearest restroom. "Well, man, now just what do you want to do—piss or pray?"

They chuckled and the waitress chortled. The unnamed man was a wealth of information, pointing out the spots where black people could find the essentials, offering survival tips, and kind warnings. It was as if the street-wise local knew that Griffin needed to map out enemy territory fast. Finishing breakfast, he walked to the corner bus stop and caught the next carrier downtown.

He sat at the back of the bus with the black passengers. As it approached Canal Street, he noticed that more whites than blacks boarded. Soon the bus was nearly full, but white passengers who did not find an empty seat next to another white, stood rather than sit next to a black person. When he saw a white woman stand nearby, he began to rise and relinquish his seat. There was a wave of disapproval from the blacks that forced him to sit down. This movement caught the woman's attention and, as their eyes met, she scowled at him, "What're you looking at me like that for?" Flushed with embarrassment by the lurid implication, he mumbled an apology. This heightened her hostility and stirred deeper resentment among the black passengers. His innocent act had been twisted into reinforcing the stereotype that all black men lusted after white women. His apology confirmed rather than denied his social sin to the white gallery. The black passengers frowned at him, as if to say, "How can you be so dumb as to fall into that old trap?"

Burned by his blunder, he sat "sphinx-like, pretending unawareness." Soon the incident had lost its appeal, even though the woman kept on chattering in an attempt to hold the spotlight. Griffin was relieved to be out of that sudden glare, withdrawing into the shadows. His gaffe was the result of *thinking white*, and forgetting his disguised appearance. He had acted out of character for the context and the mistake was a harsh lesson. Griffin also learned "a strange thing—that in a jumble of unintelligible talk, the word 'nigger' leaps out with electric clarity."

Suddenly it was not a mere observation but a personal experience. Griffin was stung by the epithet because it was aimed at his skin and at all black people. He was ashamed of whites who uttered such slurs, but now he identified with black people and felt alienated from his own race. He was still relating to whites and blacks as groups, judging whites as not merely an ignorant group unaware of the effect of their cultural attitudes, but cast "into a category of brute ignorance."

Griffin departed the bus at Canal Street and walked to the shoeshine stand, wondering if Sterling Williams would recognize him as the white writer from Texas. When their eyes met he saw no sign of recognition. Climbing into the chair, he figured the bootblack would spot his unusual cut of shoes, as he had before. They chatted amiably until the job was finished.

"Is there something familiar about these shoes?" Griffin asked.

"Yeah—I been shining some for a white man—"

"A fellow named Griffin?"

"Yeah." Williams straightened up. "Do you know him?"

"I *am* him."

Williams was dumbfounded. Griffin reminded him of various subjects they had discussed in earlier visits. Williams shook with boisterous laughter, promising "perfect discretion and enthusiastically began coaching me; but in a guarded voice, glancing always about to make sure no one could overhear." The bootblack knew the local terrain and social interactions, and had mastered survival techniques in this segregated system. Griffin was raptly attentive to the black elder's wisdom, becoming an eager apprentice in Sterling's *Bootblack School of Survival and Social Discourse.*

That afternoon served as an object lesson for the model pupil. First, he was overdressed for the role. Second, he was taught the necessity of stocking food and water. Third, it was imperative to locate the nearest "separate facility" in order to relieve oneself. Then he was sent down the alley to said facility because Williams noticed light brown hair glinting in sunlight against the backs of the hands. He hurried down the alley to a wooden structure and shaved the hands by smearing them with shaving cream. The extra touch to the disguise met with his mentor's approval. The absurdity of the scene flashed in the bootblack's relaxed smile, grinning "the way one would after averting a terrible danger," and his "entire attitude of connivance was superbly exaggerated."

The apprenticeship scenes display serious caution and witty irreverence. The two men enjoyed the game and it was obvious who was playing the straight man. When there was a break in the flow of business, Griffin asked where he might find a drink of water. Williams gave him a tongue-in-cheek lecture on the subject. Then he "reached behind the shine stand and brought out a gallon lard can with wires looped through holes in each side to make a handle." He noticed a flake of ash floating on the surface, but did not hesitate to quench his thirst.

Griffin observed that some white customers, usually tourists, showed absolutely no reticence in asking Williams about arranging dates with black women. Courteous and friendly, they treated the bootblack as an equal. But when Williams made it clear that he was not in the business of satisfying such desires, the smiles disappeared and they moved along without another word. When Griffin mentions this, Williams wryly retorts, "Yeah, when they want to sin, they're very democratic."

Overwhelmed by the pungent aroma of roasted coffee and earthy odors of the market, Griffin recalled the old quarter in Tours, France. Aboard the bus, his attention shifted from a charming Old World tableau to a bustling cityscape that was typically American Modern.

Later he walked toward the ghetto. Since Dryades was his known destination, he tested responses of white men by asking directions. Each gave useful information and all were invariably courteous. Near Dryades, where blacks greatly outnumbered the whites, he spotted the impressive

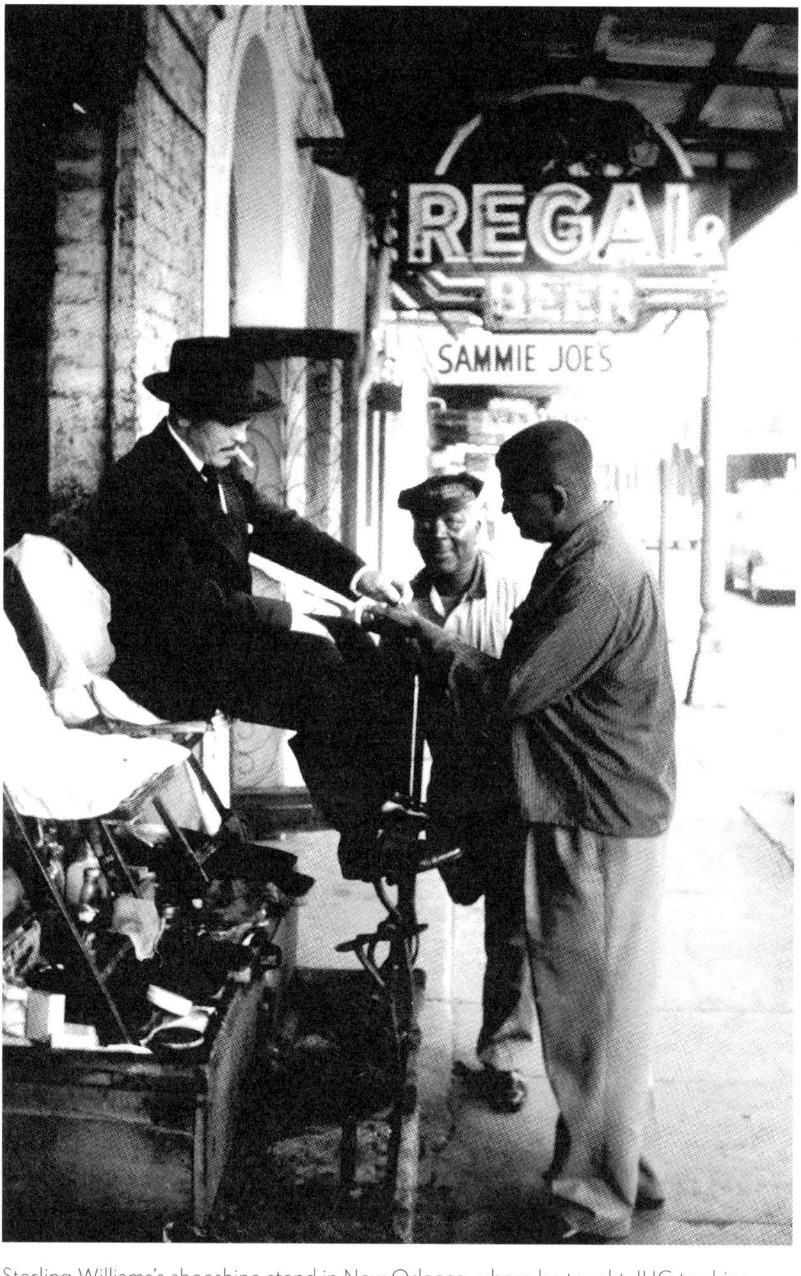

Sterling Williams's shoeshine stand in New Orleans, where he taught JHG to shine shoes. This photo taken by Don Rutledge in 1959 appeared in European and US magazines and in editions of *Black Like Me*, issued in cloth editions by Wings Press (from 2004 through 2017).

tower of an old cathedral. Inside the massive edifice of St. John the Baptist, he felt the silent grace and peered at the filtered illumination through stained-glass windows. A black woman was making the Stations of the Cross and other black people were kneeling in prayer. He sat in a pew with eyes closed and imagined his family at supper in their warm, well-lighted home. "They seemed so much a part of another life, so separated from me that I felt consumed with loneliness." These lonely distances suggested the idea of hiding until morning but, reluctantly, he decided to leave the sanctuary.

There were no vacancies at the YMCA, but the desk clerk phoned nearby boarding houses. There was a vacancy next door. He rented a room from Mrs. Davis, who led him to a freshly cleaned room, which had a window facing the street. The three-dollar-a-day rental afforded access to a bath and a kitchen down the hall. She brought a brighter lamp, so he could see well enough to write in his notebooks. She was such a kind lady that he lived there throughout his stay.

Griffin unpacked and returned to the YMCA coffee shop. It was the meeting place for the black elders of the community, and he was served a strong, chicory-flavored brew. He met an educated group of men who invited him into their discussion of "the problem" and forthcoming elections. He noted that his sense of "disorientation diminished for a time," and he felt comfortable telling them he was a writer doing research on conditions in the South. Their use of the phrase "the problem" showed they had *not* been lured into that semantic maze called "The Negro Problem"—a concept appropriated by white social scientists to fit their biased contours, and reiterated by journalists and politicians.

For these elders "the problem" was neither black nor white, but human. They were not concerned with what the white power structure *should* do, but what black individuals *could* do for their community. This peaceful yet active attitude was a refusal to accept the role of the victim. They asked him for impressions of the city. Explaining that he had arrived only recently, Griffin said he was surprised at the whites' courtesy and the atmosphere of reasonableness.

Reverend A. L. Davis, president of the Interdenominational Ministerial Alliance, explained. "Oh, we've made strides. But we've got to do a lot better. Then, too, New Orleans is more enlightened than anyplace else in the state—or in the South." Griffin wondered why he thought this. "Well, it's far more cosmopolitan for one thing. And it's got a strong Catholic population. A white man can show you courtesies without fearing some neighbor will call him a 'nigger-lover' like they do in other places."

"What do you see as our biggest problem?" asked Mr. Gayle.

"Lack of unity," Griffin responded.

"That's it," replied the elderly man who ran the café. "Until we as a race can learn to rise together, we'll never get anywhere. That's our trouble. We work against one another instead of together. Now you take dark Negroes like you, Mr. Griffin, and me. We're old Uncle Toms to our people, no matter how much education and morals we've got. No, you have to be almost a mulatto, have your hair conked and all slicked out and look like a Valentino. Then the Negro will look up to you. You've got class. Isn't that a pitiful hero-type?"

Griffin did not respond to the question, creating a pause in the owner's soliloquy. Into that brief silence, Reverend Davis declared that "the white man knows that," confirming the truth of the Valentino type as a deficient role model and divisive to unity. Griffin listened without making comment, sensing the awakening of racial pride and self-criticism in the personal tone of the elders who represented a transitional generation. Neither would they become black militants nor would they degenerate into Uncle Tomism. In their humane, non-violent, and responsible way they were enacting solutions at the local level where life is lived.

Griffin returned to the rooming house. As he made notes, Mrs. Davis lit the fire and brought in a pitcher of fresh drinking water. When he looked up to thank her for the kindness, he glimpsed an image in the wardrobe mirror that startled him. This second mirror reflection caused a brief dislocation, but had less impact than the first. There was only denial. He felt invisible, "observing a scene in which I had no part." He chose to perceive two anonymous black people engaged in a brief, inaudible dialogue, filmed by a remote camera. Unable to accept the *Other* as himself, he retreated to the inward safety of the white man behind the mask.

After Mrs. Davis departed, he withdrew into total exhaustion and sleep. But awakened by the ringing of a telephone down the hall, he struggled out of bed. He was hungry and went in search of a café on South Rampart Street.

When he had walked a few blocks from the YMCA, he noticed two white youths sprawled on a stoop across the street. The larger one, muscular and heavyset, whistled at him. He ignored the taunt, kept walking, and did not look back. Soon he spied the young white man angling across the street toward him. With the casualness of a late night stroll, the pursuer matched his steps without closing the distance. "Hey, Baldy," called the man in a soft, almost lascivious tone.

The chase was on and Griffin walked faster, not looking back, as the taunts echoed above the empty street. As if restrained by a long, cruel leash that connected him to his stalker, he could not extend the distance of separation. When he slowed the leash seemed to slacken. He knew the leash was imaginary, but its control was not. Picking up the pace, he felt his throat constrict in panic. He searched for options, realizing that fearful flight could not prevent the inevitable confrontation. Looking ahead to the next block, he spied an elderly white couple at the bus stop. When he approached they stiffened as he expressed his concern. The elderly white man asked who was chasing him. Griffin turned to point in the direction of the stalker, but the street was empty.

Griffin lingered at the corner, hoping a bus might arrive, but the tension became too uncomfortable. He moved down a well-lighted side street. Black people were there and he felt a brief moment of safety. But halfway up that side street he heard the voice again. The stalker shadowed his pace relentlessly, issuing threats and calling names along the way. Griffin imagined an absurd scene that might accompany his death, pondering the startled expression on the face of a white policeman, who would find the identification papers of a white man, perhaps assuming they were stolen.

When the white bully yelled at him to stop, Griffin let go of panic, and hit on a radically different tactic. Perhaps he could bluff his pursuer. He had been trained in judo in the military, and might be lucky enough to land the first punch. He darted into a dimly lit alley and issued a deep growl. "You follow me, boy, 'cause I'm just aching to feed a fistful of brass knucks right in that big mouth of yours."

Griffin waited, listening for footsteps. He heard himself whisper an involuntary prayer to the patron saint of lost causes, "Blessed St. Jude, send the bastard away." He was surprised by the spontaneous blasphemy and by its positive result. He peeked around the corner, but no one was in sight. He hurried to the church on Dryades and sat on its wide steps. As the bell tolled loudly over the rooftops, voices resonated in his mind. He heard a litany of insulting names spewed by the bully. Curiously he had not been called any racial slur, but Griffin did not analyze that. Instead he wondered if the doctor "could have known how truly he spoke, how total the feeling of oblivion was." When a patrol car cruised by the church and the white officers gave him a long stare, he moved on before they might circle back.

Griffin walked to a café, ate beans and rice, and returned to the rooming house. Exhausted by stress, constant walking, and mind-bending adjustments endured in the rush of the unexpected, his last thought was a despairing one. "The whites seemed far away, out there in their parts of the city. The distance between them and me was far more than the miles that physically separated us. It was an area of unknowing. I wondered if it could really be bridged." That distance seemed to stretch beyond all efforts, since that "area of unknowing" seemed like oblivion.

During the next four days Griffin searched for employment, wearing his best suit and tie, and the elegant shoes he learned to shine like a professional. He applied for jobs as typist, bookkeeper, and photographer. He was entirely qualified for any of these jobs. There were no hateful rejections, but the consistently courteous interviews were brief. Either they said there were no openings or, if he made specific reference to a recently advertised job, they said the position had just been filled.

At the end of daily job hunting, Griffin returned to the shoeshine stand. Usually he took one simple meal there, observing the same range of customers and invariable patterns of interaction. He gives few details of job hunting, but *A Time to Be Human* offers more. "The best jobs I got were menial—shining shoes, unloading trucks, or carrying bags in the bus station. The most I ever earned in one day was $3.95. Since I tried to live on my earnings and since my room usually cost $3.00, little was left for food and transportation. I was reduced to eating beans and rice, or beans and pig tails, or beans and neckbones, but always beans."

Every day Griffin studied the help-wanted ads and placed calls to prospective employers. He was truthful. He relates this scene in *A Time To Be Human*. "'This is John Griffin. I have just arrived in town and have seen your ad.' Then I would list the qualifications that made me feel I could do the job. I did not seek unrealistically ambitious employment." Phone contacts offered hope that interviews never fulfilled. "Twice I was hired on the telephone and told to come to work. But each time I appeared and it was seen that I was pigmented, I was immediately made to understand that I could not have those jobs. In every other case my qualifications were good enough for an employer to ask me to come in for an interview or fill out an application. There was no question that I qualified for those jobs so long as they thought that they were talking to a white man on the phone. The moment they saw I was black, even though I was the same man, I was turned away."

After two weeks Griffin's only job had been at the shoeshine stand. The few tips he collected were turned over to Williams in exchange for meals. He paid expenses from the traveler's checks. Most evenings were spent at the YMCA coffee shop, or making notes in his room at the boarding house.

On November 12, Griffin had breakfast at the YMCA coffee shop. He confided in the manager, recounting failures to gain employment. The elderly gentleman said that his results fit the overall pattern of "economic injustice," and that even educated Negroes could not get beyond the post office, the pulpit, or teaching in a run-down segregated school. "This is the cream. What about the others, Mr. Griffin? A man knows no matter how hard he works, he's never going to quite manage. Taxes and prices eat up more than he can earn. He can't see how he'll ever have a wife and children. The economic structure doesn't permit it unless he's prepared to live down in poverty and have his wife work too." Griffin agreed, saying "It's these things that cause the whites to say we're not worthy of first-class citizenship."

Other elders joined the conversation, sipping coffee and awaiting breakfast. They analyzed the racist myth of superior white intelligence, examined current economic realities, and outlined a necessary "conversion of morals" in the system. Their dialogue permits readers to hear voices that would *not* be part of the record. The survival masks worn in the presence of whites are removed in *Black Like Me*. Ironically, it was the effect of Griffin's own "mask" that created a unique space where real thoughts and feelings could be expressed. Without the disguise there would not have been real dialogue, because they would not have trusted any white man.

After another breakfast conversation, he walked to Chartres Street, pausing in front of Brennan's for the simple pleasure of studying the menu in the window. At first, he was lost in the unceasing continuity of his internal identity—the white Griffin, who enjoyed the intricacies of *haute* cuisine. In a reverie of "forgetting" himself, of losing conscious awareness of his disguise, he was actually remembering himself from his internal "white" perspective. Two weeks earlier, the same appetite, appreciation, and wallet had allowed entrance. Yet all was changed externally, and he was not permitted to step inside. Even his voyeuristic pleasure of reading an elegant menu struck the white onlookers as a grievous affront. When he saw their disapproving frowns, he was rudely reminded that he had crossed an invisible segregated line, and must get back in his "place" in order not to upset the tourists.

"The Negro learns this silent language fluently," he remarked, but without elaborating. In *The Church and the Black Man* (1969), Griffin discusses this concept as it related to his experience with racism ten years earlier in *Black Like Me*, when he was not yet fluent in the silent language.

> This problem of an imprisoning and blinding culture expresses itself in what Edward T. Hall calls 'the silent language'—a language by which men unknowingly express through attitudes, springing from learned behavior patterns, truths that contradict their actual words, and of which they may be wholly unconscious. This silent language is an intrinsic element in the duality of viewpoint that persists between black and white Americans. This duality is grounded in racist mythology so deeply inculcated that men tend to call it human nature, which it is not at all.

According to *The Silent Language*, which Griffin read before the journey, it is impossible to understand one's own culture until we encounter another.[51] Because we are immersed in culture, our attitudes and behavioral patterns reflect our "cultural unconscious," and we cannot see this consciously until we are made aware of it by a contrasting culture. *Black Like Me* made whites in America aware of the Negro's experience in a way that black writers of that era could not, simply because white ears would not listen to black voices. Yet white readers responded to the compelling drama of Griffin's book, identifying with his secret identity and eavesdropping on black conversations. Ironically his disguise mediated open communication between the races. *Black Like Me* does not solve the problem of miscommunication between the races, but does illuminate a critical blind spot.

Fear resides at the core of all hatred—fear of the unknown, and fear of those who we think are different. Whites who sincerely believed they were not prejudiced expressed their attitudes with unconscious disrespect and paternalism. But anyone who has felt the sting of prejudice learns to parry these irrational thrusts by understanding fluently the silent language of well-intentioned whites. Experience has taught black people to hear what one means rather than what one says. For those "whose lives have forced them to become masterful interpreters of such nuances, this is so degrading that it alienates immediately." While Griffin recognized this intellectually, he had not known it emotionally until he lived it. The incident at the window of Brennan's was a wake-up call that Jim Crow was watching.

Griffin made daily rounds in search of jobs, pursuing several opportunities to no avail. Everywhere he was greeted with false smiles of rejection. Weary from all the walking, he stopped in Jackson Square to rest on a bench. A middle-aged white man approached, ushered by a fragrance of pipe tobacco. The unexpected sensation seemed to reassure him that pipe-smokers were not racists. Then the man spoke with discreet courtesy, letting him know that Negroes were not allowed to sit in the park. He took the warning as a favor that would prevent being insulted by another white, yet failed to decipher the real intention behind the words. Later he was informed that Jackson Square was not segregated. The man simply did not want him there, but Griffin had misread the silent language. He left the park, "sick with exhaustion, wondering where a Negro could sit to rest," and walked to the bus stop. To travel anywhere by bus made more sense than walking on tired legs. He took the first bus without any thought about its destination. The bus took him to Dillard University where he rested, admiring the peaceful campus until dark.

On the return trip, he rang the bell as the bus turned a few blocks before Canal Street. The bus halted and, as he stepped toward the open door it was abruptly slammed shut. He politely asked the driver to let him off at the next corner. The driver ignored him, despite several pressings of the buzzer. The bus cruised past two stops, halting only when a few white passengers were ready to exit. Griffin followed them to the front and, when the last one stepped down, he quietly requested to depart. The driver was bored with the game and he was allowed to exit. This cruel exercise outraged him, even as he concluded that the driver's reaction had been against skin color and not against him. But it did not lessen the indignity.

Griffin's last day in New Orleans ended at night in Mississippi. This thirty-page entry for November 14 is the longest in the book, beginning with an assessment of the Crescent City. "After a week of wearying rejection, the newness had worn off. My first vague, favorable impression that it was not as bad as I had thought it would be came from the courtesies of whites. But this was superficial. All the courtesies in the world do not cover up one vital and massive discourtesy—that the Negro is treated not even as a second-class citizen, but as a tenth-class one."

The overt incidents of racism were obvious examples any white person would have seen. But the subtle behavior of whites toward blacks began to clarify Griffin's perspective. Every hour of "day-to-day living is a reminder of his inferior status," to which a black person "does not become calloused," and every "new reminder strikes at the raw spot, deepens the wound."

Some white reviewers argued that since Griffin was not yet desensitized to the abuse, he had overreacted. Yet this criticism reveals more about the reviewers' own rationalized racism than it reveals about *Black Like Me*. How could they know without being black? The real issue was the behavior of the white majority toward the black minority, and not the intensity of his reactions. Perhaps these indignities were more intense at first because unexpected, but cruelty registers in the human psyche, penetrating deeper than skin color.

On that last morning in New Orleans, Griffin headed for the shoeshine stand, observing that the community seemed particularly "glum and angry." When he saw Williams, he did not receive the customary friendly greeting. "You heard?" asks the bootblack, but Griffin did not understand the question.

He was told that a Mississippi jury had not indicted in the Mack Parker lynching case. Parker, a thirty-three-year-old truck driver, had been accused of raping a white woman. Awaiting trial in the Poplarville, Mississippi, jail after pleading innocent to the charge, he was dragged from his cell by a dozen white men in hoods. The jail had been left unguarded, and the mob entered Parker's cell with the key. He was dragged down two flights of stairs and kidnapped. Ten days later his body was found, and the coroner ruled it death from gunshot wounds. But prior

Sterling Williams and JHG share a meal at the shoeshine stand in New Orleans, 1959. This photo by Don Rutledge appeared in European and US magazines and in cloth editions of *Black Like Me*, from Wings Press.

to being riddled with bullets, Parker had been lynched. What crushed the black community was that the FBI had supplied a dossier of evidence naming the murderers, but the 378-page document (including confessions of guilt) had been ignored by the Pearl River County Grand Jury. The lynching of Mack Parker and the blatant racism of the grand jury's decision created a national uproar.

Sterling Williams read an editorial from the pages of the *Louisiana Weekly*, a scathing denouncement of white supremacy and mob rule. He read aloud in an angry voice. "They rant and rave about how the rest of the country's against the Southern white—hell, how could they not be? This is what we can expect from the white man's justice. What hope is there when a white jury won't even look at the evidence against a lynch mob?" He had never seen Williams so enraged. Certainly his reaction was anything but desensitized, proving that even a salty veteran who had endured racism for sixty years could not accept such an insult without protest.

Appalled by the grave injustice, Griffin decided to leave the relatively safe confines of New Orleans, and travel to Mississippi, but in order to leave, he needed to cash a traveler's check. Since it was past noon on a Saturday and banks were closed, he rode a bus to a store on Dryades, where he had been a steady customer. They denied his request to cash a twenty dollar traveler's check, and he had no better luck at other locations. He became angry at "the bad manners they displayed," giving the impression that the checks might have been stolen. Resigned to remaining in town until the banks opened on Monday, he walked back toward the Quarter.

Then he saw a shop he had not noticed before. It was a bookstore, and the small gold letters in the window read Catholic Book Store. He asked the lady if she would cash a traveler's check. She did so immediately. He was so grateful that he bought several books by Aquinas, Maritain, and others.

Entering the main lobby of the terminal, Griffin scanned the area for black faces and, seeing only whites, searched for a separate waiting room. No actual sign was in place, since the Greyhound system could not segregate under federal guidelines that controlled interstate commerce. He approached a white woman at the ticket counter, and her face contorted into a hideous expression. In a belligerent tone, she asked what he wanted. With careful politeness, he asked about the next bus to Hattiesburg. She glared "with such loathing," Griffin realized that he was encountering what black people called *the hate stare*. It was his first experience with this toxic example of the silent language. He would have been "amused," if not so startled.

Griffin begged her pardon, asking what he had done to offend her. She said nothing and continued to stare with contempt. The reason was obvious—his color offended her. He asked for a one-way ticket to Hattiesburg and laid a ten-dollar bill on the counter. She protested that she could not change such a large bill, turning away from the window. Bewildered by her venomous attack, he stood transfixed. When he did not leave, she repeated her protest in a shout. He expressed doubt that the bill exceeded the power of the bus system to make change, and asked to see the manager. Infuriated by his request, she grabbed the money and moved quickly from the open window. She reappeared and threw the ticket and loose change onto the floor of the terminal. He gazed at her with pity, and this caused her to blush involuntarily. He concluded the enraged woman "undoubtedly considered it a supreme insolence for a Negro to dare feel sorry for her." He picked up the ticket and coins. The final sentence of the scene has him wondering how she might feel knowing such rude behavior was witnessed by a white man. Intending to emphasize the irony, the unintentional effect of this last line reveals his habitual nature of thinking white.

With an hour to wait until departure, Griffin searched the nearly empty room for a seat. He encountered another hate stare from a white man seated nearby. "Nothing can describe the withering horror of this. You feel lost, sick at heart before such unmasked hatred, not so much because it threatens you as because it shows humans in such an inhuman light. You see a kind of insanity, something so obscene the very obscenity of it (rather than the threat) terrifies you."

Griffin's use of the second-person viewpoint here involves the reader directly in the experience of being hated without reason. His analysis exposes the pathology of white racism buried in the behavioral formation of a supremacist culture. Racism in Jim Crow's segregated society was "a kind of insanity" since it was irrational and reflexive. It was "obscene" because it debased a black person's individual qualities into a learned set of stereotypes that fit no individual. It was "inhuman" because it destroyed the humanity of those who hated, just as surely as they dehumanized their victims. This shock of "unmasked hatred" was "so new" to Griffin that he stared, thinking, "What in God's name are you doing to yourself?" By expressing to the reader what he did not say to the man, the question transcends injustice and appeals to a higher court of human conscience.

There were two reasons that Griffin distinguished between the threat and the terror of hate stares. What was not felt as a threat by a disguised white man would have been threatening to a black person, even in a legally desegregated public place. At that moment he was not identifying with his skin color, but with the hatred in those white faces for which he felt pity and shame. The hate stare was a brutal expression of the silent language that he had detected in his own glaring reflection in the mirror. The second reason Griffin felt terror instead of threat was his recognition that human beings were capable of such cruelty. The dramatic scene is relieved by the graceful intercession of a black porter who, with a touch of Griffin's arm, "in that mute and reassuring way of men who share a moment of crisis," directed him to the "separate but equal" waiting room around the corner. He found the *de facto* segregated space under the rubric of the *Colored Café* and took a seat.

When the bus was announced, the black people lined up behind the whites, conforming to discriminatory practices. Griffin boarded, taking a seat near the back. He overheard two black men express the bitter irony of the situation.

"Well, here we go into Mississippi—the most lied-about state in the union—that's what they claim."

"It's the truth, too. Only it's Mississippi that does all the lying."

Deep South Journey

The bus to Mississippi departed the New Orleans station, crossed the bridge over Lake Pontchartrain, and picked up passengers. Among those boarding was an elegantly dressed, light-skinned Negro, who later identified himself as Christophe. During the next few scenes he takes center stage with unpredictable antics and bombastic monologues that create tense encounters for Griffin and two black men. His exchanges with the black men hint at inevitable physical violence, but never go beyond loud name calling, caustic put-downs, and aggressive bluffing. The men find him to be an irritant, but not threatening. Yet Christophe has a nerve-wracking effect on Griffin, who hoped to avoid any conversation with "this strange man."

Christophe sported a mustache and a neatly trimmed Van Dyke beard. He passed through the white section of the bus with a "fawning, almost tender look" for the whites that turned into a sneer when he reached the back of the bus. He took an empty seat and began to hassle the two men who sat behind him, denouncing the ignorance of black people in a venomous tone. Out spilled polyglot fragments (in German, French, Spanish, and Japanese) to punctuate his superiority. One of the men reacted and a quarrel reached fever pitch, but after a lengthy, posturing exchange the voices subsided. Christophe moved to the vacant seat next to Griffin. He slouched and began to play an imaginary guitar, its mute music accompanied by a mournful singing of the blues. Attempting to ignore him, Griffin felt an elbow in his ribs.

"You don't dig the blues, do you, daddy?"

Griffin replied honestly, that he did not know the blues, and he hoped this would end the conversation. Perplexed by this reticence, Christophe cracked a smile, whispering, "I bet you dig this, daddy." He began chanting the Gregorian version of the Latin text *Tantum ergo sacramentum, Veneremur cemui* with such perfect diction that Griffin was dumbfounded. Christophe went on to recite the *Confiteor* in perfect Latin diction and, when he had finished, the back of the bus was silent. Griffin guessed that Christophe had been an altar boy, and the guess was confirmed. One of the black men from across the aisle warned Griffin not to believe anything he heard. Christophe's face "congealed instantly into hatred," and another exchange exploded the calm. Griffin feared there would be a fistfight but, as the confrontation reached its apex, Christophe turned and winked.

Christophe explained he was not "pure Negro," that his mother was French and his father was an American Indian. An instant later he contradicted himself, saying his mother was Portuguese. Then he began to speculate about Griffin's origins, claiming never to be wrong in such matters. He examined the author's face and, after a long pause, said "I have it now." Griffin feared he might be exposed as a white man impersonating a Negro, and tried to stop Christophe. But it was too late. "Your mother was part Florida Navaho, wasn't she?" Griffin felt like laughing at the absurdity of his mother "being anything so exotic as Florida Navaho."

Instead, Griffin said: "You're pretty sharp."

"Ha! I never miss." Then Christophe's tone changed. "I hate us, Father." Griffin insisted he was not a priest. "Ah, you can't fool Christophe. I know you're a priest even if you are dressed in civilian clothes. Look at these punks, Father. Dumb, ignorant bastards. They don't know the score. I'm getting out of this country."

Just as suddenly, Christophe's anger vanished and he whispered: "I'll tell you the truth, Father. I'm just out of the pen—four years. I'm on my way to see my wife. She's waiting with a new car for me in Slidell. And God . . . what a reunion we're going to have!" Again there was a sudden switch in tone. "Sometime, Father, when you say Mass, will you take the white host for Christophe?"

Griffin offered to remember him next time at Mass. That was "the peace my soul longs for," Christophe said, but returning to the church would be impossible. Griffin assured him it was possible, but Christophe's retort counters that suggestion. "Nah, I've got to shoot up a couple of guys."

These swift, erratic swings of emotion were too much, and Griffin's expression revealed his shock. As the bus slowed at the outskirts of Slidell, Christophe stood to straighten his tie. He stared contemptuously across the aisle and bowed ceremoniously. Everyone in the back of the bus felt relief to see him disappear.

With the departure from the Slidell Greyhound station, the mood of the bus ride shifted. The enclave of black people cohered into a survival community. They were now in the bowels of Mississippi, and the bus was commanded by a different driver, a bigoted autocrat devoid of any Crescent City gentility.

Bill Williams, a "stockily built young Negro," boarded the bus at Slidell. He introduced himself and sat next to Griffin. The conversation flowed smoothly between them and with other black passengers. Since all learned that Griffin was a newcomer to the area, it was not long before he received advice about how to survive in enemy territory. To add to strategies acquired, he learned new tactics from Bill Williams. He was warned never to look at a white woman, not even to look at a movie poster if it featured a white woman. If he encountered white boys who bothered him, he was advised to keep moving and never to answer their questions. Since he was well dressed he was told to stay clear of alleys where he might get mugged.

When it was nearly dark, the bus pulled into a nameless small town. The driver announced a brief stop and the whites filed off. Williams led the black contingent toward the front, but the driver blocked their exit. Williams deftly ducked under the driver's out-stretched arm and ambled off. The furious driver yelled, "Hey, boy, where you going? Hey, you, boy, I'm talking to you." Griffin stood on the bottom step, waiting, as the driver said, "Where do you think you're going?"

"I'd like to go to the restroom." Griffin smiled and moved to step down, but the driver tightened his grip on the door facings, blocking the exit.

"Does your ticket say for you to get off here?"

"No sir, but the others—"

"Then you get your ass back in your seat and don't you move til we get to Hattiesburg."

"You mean I can't go to the—"

"I mean get your ass back there like I told you."

"You announced a rest stop. The whites all got off."

The driver stood on his toes and put his face close to Griffin's, speaking slowly and threateningly, "Are you arguing with me?"

Griffin's protest collapsed. He sighed in defeat and the group behind him turned back. Some grumbled against these unfair actions and one woman said that Negroes were usually let off at that stop. For a few moments they sat dejectedly. Griffin was appalled at the cruelty of depriving this basic need.

Just then they heard the driver's loud voice addressing the return of Williams. "Didn't you hear me call you?" Williams innocently replied, "I heard you yelling 'Boy,' but that's not my name, so I didn't know you meant me." Everyone in the back smiled at this slyly comic yet serious gesture of courage. "In the immense tug-of-war," Griffin notes, "such an act of defiance turned him into a hero."

The bus plunged deeper into backcountry. The obvious communal caring among the black passengers was extended immediately to those who boarded at the small towns, joining them at the back of the bus. Griffin had seen nothing like that in New Orleans. This profound sense of inclusion connected at the level of spiritual unity with fellow human beings. He was alienated from fellow whites because they were out of touch with their humanity, just as Christophe had lost touch. That the logic of the segregated system was a fallacy, he was certain; that black people were individuals of subtle complexity, he knew now from experience.

As they neared Poplarville, the sight of the Mack Parker lynching, a wave of "agitation swept through the bus." Williams asked Griffin if he knew of the case and, even though it was a whispered question answered by a nod, several whites looked toward the back of the bus. The once "animated Negro faces turned stony." When they passed through town, Williams pointed out the locations where the tragedy had been played out—there was the jail where Parker was kidnapped, there was the courthouse where "Mississippi Justice" was sanctified.

Outside Poplarville the bus moved through the dark countryside on its way to Hattiesburg. They arrived about 8:30 p.m. and the black passengers scurried to restrooms. Williams gave Griffin the name of a contact in town and he took a cab to that address. The contact inside the black quarter referred him to another man a few blocks away. As he walked down Mobile Street, a car filled with young whites sped by. He was assaulted by obscenities and a tangerine that missed. He felt "the insane terror" of the black ghetto besieged by whites. Griffin entered the store of the second contact. This man related a few horror stories and sent him to a drugstore to await a third contact. These tense scenes suggest the intrigue of a spy novel, but the reality was no more fictitious than his involvement in the French underground. The third contact directed him to a secure room that, despite being "upstairs in a wooden shanty that had never known paint," was secure.

This sequence in the barren room of the Hattiesburg shanty marks the turning point in the narrative, a painful breakthrough to a fresh perspective foreshadowed by the evolving perceptions experienced earlier. "I switched on the light and looked into a cracked piece of mirror bradded with bent nails to the wall. The bald Negro stared back at me from its mottled sheen. I knew I was in hell. Hell could be no more lonely or hopeless, no more agonizingly estranged from the world of order and harmony." Detached from self-awareness, Griffin hears the voice of "someone else" uttering the unspeakable epithet, and sees tears in his reflected image. At the exhausted edge of breakdown, anger breaks through the gloom. "Then the onrush of revulsion, the momentary flash of blind hatred against the whites who were somehow responsible for all of this, the old bewilderment of wondering, 'Why do they do it? Why do they keep us like this? What are they gaining? What evil has taken them?'" Griffin's anger did not allow him to pity the whites. He despised them for their gross injustice. His "revulsion turned to grief that my own people could give the hate stare, could shrivel men's souls, could deprive humans of rights they unhesitatingly accord their livestock." With the cessation of this outburst, he turned away from the self-consciousness of the mirror toward anything outside himself.

The focus shifts as he surveys the room, noticing some discarded objects on the floor. "A burned-out light globe lay on the plank floor in the corner. Its unfrosted glass held the reflection of the overhead bulb, a speck of brightness. A half-dozen film negatives curled up around it like dead leaves. I picked them up and held them before the light with strange excitement, curious to see the image that some prior occupant of this room had photographed." Griffin discovered blank negatives and imagined a possible scenario to account for their existence. He posits a vignette for the prior occupant, but the "masterpieces of human ingenuity wasted" bring no warmth. They are the "dead leaves" of a blighted family tree. Negatives that might be transformed into positives remain as blank as the empty room and the burned-out light. In contemplating these objects he tried to fill a void with imagination, projecting himself into the life of the former occupant. Griffin tossed the batch of negatives to the corner with the discarded light bulb. Suddenly one of the negatives struck the bulb, "causing it to sing its strange filamental music of the spheres, fragile and high-pitched above the outside noises." This strange music signaled the possibility of a spiritual epiphany, but was drowned out by street noises, and this fragile harmony was shattered. He smelled the aroma of barbecue with the intensity of a man starving for more than food, yet he remained cautious about returning to the street.

He "attempted to write—anything to escape the death dance out there in the Mississippi night." Next he tried composing a letter to Elizabeth, but the distance he felt from true intimacy made this impossible. He stared at the notebook and, except for his intimate salutation, the page remained blank. "The visual barrier imposed itself. The observing self saw the Negro, surrounded by the sounds and smells of the ghetto, write 'Darling' to a white woman." He concludes that the "chains of my blackness would not allow me to go on," even as he "understood and could analyze what was happening." He knew the rational response to irrational taboo, but was imprisoned by emotion. Griffin perceived this "visual barrier" as a length of black chain, yet he was blind to the white lock that secured it.

Griffin descended into "the mainstream of hell" on Mobile Street to find a place to eat. A few blocks away he saw a dimly lit sandwich shop with a sign over its door: NO OBSENETY ALLOWED. He does not comment on the misspelling, but the tableau that follows illustrated the message. "A round-faced woman, her cheeks slicked yellow with sweat, handed me a barbecued beef sandwich. Standing so close, odors of her body rose up to me from her white uniform, a mingling of hickory-smoked flesh, gardenia talcum and sweat." The ghetto was the real obscenity. Griffin retreated and sat on the staircase to eat the sandwich, listening to the throng of shouts and the raucous music. He considered the reality of the ghetto in relation to an academic's assessment of segregation. "Despite their lowly status," claims the white scholar, "they are capable of living jubilantly." Griffin disagreed. "The laughter had to be gross or it would turn to sobs, and to sob would be to realize, and to realize would be to despair. So the noise poured forth like a jazzed-up fugue, louder and louder to cover the whisper in every man's soul, 'You are black. You are condemned.' This is what the white man mistook for 'jubilant living.'" This painfully accurate passage cuts to the immediate emotional reality that whites could never know.

It had been the longest and most despairing day of Griffin's journey, a day of horror followed by a night of stress that brought him to the breaking point. He decided on a plan of escape, a way to end the despair, if only temporarily. "Suddenly I knew I could not go back to that room with its mottled mirror, its dead light bulb, and its blank negatives." Griffin telephoned P. D. East, the only white man in Hattiesburg who might be able to help, and reached the journalist's wife.[52] She assured him that P. D. would be glad to make a rescue. Griffin waited in front of a brightly lit drug store, determined not to allow fear to chase him from the spot. As he waited like an illuminated target for the next night-cruising racists, he did not question his ethics or motives for seeking refuge from the ghetto.

East cruised past a watchful Griffin on Mobile Street, parking his station wagon down the block. The tall, lanky editor strode out of the shadows into the light. He shook the hand of the "Negro" and asked if he was ready. They returned to the car and set out for East's home. At first they spoke in "a strangely stilted manner," and Griffin wondered why. Then he realized that he had grown accustomed to expecting contempt from whites. He felt "embarrassed to ride in the front seat of a car with a white man," insisting East not help him if it meant danger or embarrassment for his family, but the editor kept driving in silence.

When they arrived, East's wife was in the shadows. "Well, hello, Uncle Tom," she said. "Once again the terrible truth struck me. Here in America, in this day, the simple act of whites receiving a Negro had to be a night thing and its aura of uneasiness had to be countered by gallows humor." Soon awkwardness dissipated, and he was struck by a sense of warmth, naturalness, and trust. He noticed that their modest home was a palace compared to his recent lodgings. He was safe yet anxiety remained, reminding of "the nagging, focusless terror we felt in Europe when Hitler began his marches."

Griffin summed up their feelings in a passage cut from the manuscript. "We felt that fear, and it outraged something in our consciousness, for it had its roots in the threats of unjust men. In reality, the Southerner, white or black, was no longer a free subject in a free land; he was a vassal of the pressure groups, the Klans and Councils, the racists. The race issue was merely a covering. The real issue, I knew then, was simply the conflict between just and unjust men."

Griffin stayed the next day, and the hours in their home were relaxing as he was able to let go of defenses, but the time was not restful. Before retiring the first night, East handed over the manuscript of *The Magnolia Jungle*, and Griffin became caught up in the journalist's autobiography, fascinated by the mixture of tragedy and wild satire. He did not stop until the manuscript was read.

At daybreak Griffin dozed off for less than an hour only to be awakened by his host. The entire day was spent discussing the manuscript, and later East regaled him with incredibly true tales. That night Griffin sifted through a massive file of materials. The contents formed what East called his annals of "assdom"—legal documents and hate letters. He found the evidence of "legalized injustice" to be more incredible than the hate mail, because the leaders of the white community wielded greater power than uneducated racists. What struck most deeply was the premeditated cynicism of the lawmakers. He was awake all night, making notes. They drove to New Orleans on the morning of November 16. The drive seemed like an instant compared to the eternal bus trip. They spent time at Dillard University, then East drove him to downtown New Orleans where the new friends bid farewell.

According to the published text of *Black Like Me*, Griffin purchased a one-way ticket back to Mississippi on a bus bound for Biloxi. But a three-day gap between November 16 and his arrival in Biloxi on November 19 is not covered in the book. He spent that time as the guest of Reverend Sherwood Clayton. The Episcopal priest was a gentle, cultured man who spoke French, loved classical music, and was a marvelous cook—just the ingredients needed at that time. During those restful days he called Elizabeth, saying little about the journey. He did not want to worry his family or parents, whom he asked Elizabeth to call, knowing they would be relieved to hear that he was staying with Father Clayton.

The November 19 entry begins with Griffin's arrival at the Biloxi bus terminal. Rather than languish in the station, he began walking. He slept in an abandoned shed and next morning had breakfast at a black-owned diner. Then he headed for the highway, hoping for a ride to Mobile. Walking on the shoulder bordering the lovely beachfront, he struck a leisurely pace in sunlight and checked historical markers along the route.

Many cars passed but none stopped. By midday he bought milk and a sandwich at a highway store. He carried the food over to the sidewalk along the low sea wall, and was soon engaged in a conversation with a local black man. He asked about the splendid beaches and was informed that the man-made beaches were intended for whites only, even though the project had been funded by a gasoline tax. The local man protested this segregated policy, saying that black taxpayers were considering political action to right the injustice.

By late afternoon he was exhausted by having walked more than a dozen miles. Then he spotted a place in the distance, a custard stand where he could sit at a table under shade trees. He noticed an "old unpainted privy" and returned to the window of the stand to ask about the nearest restroom. The man deliberated, directing him up the road about a mile to a black settlement. Griffin asked if there might not be something closer, "determined to see if he would offer me the use of the dilapidated out-house, which certainly no human could degrade any more than time and the elements had." When he asked about using the privy, the man replied, "Nope," in a voice softened by regret, but final in its refusal.

Griffin trudged several more miles without receiving a ride, but when the light of evening faded everything changed. He began to get rides, a dozen short lifts that took on the pattern of a nightmare. "All but two picked me up the way they would pick up a pornographic photograph or book, except that this was verbal pornography." The hitchhiking scenes are awkward, but described with elegant detachment. He viewed these episodes from a moral perspective, yet with flashes of humor that kept the discourse from turning sanctimonious. With the subtlety of an accomplished storyteller and the insight of a psychologist, he weaves a shadowy tapestry. The inherent mystery of night and the dark underside of forbidden fantasies are revealed, and the incidents are compressed into a clarifying critique of behavior.

Because Griffin appeared black, white men "assumed" that

> they need give no semblance of self-respect or respectability . . . . A man will reveal himself in the dark, which gives an illusion of anonymity, more than he will in bright light. Some were shamelessly open, some shamelessly subtle. All showed morbid curiosity about the sexual life of the Negro, and all had, at base, the same stereotyped image of the Negro

> as an inexhaustible sex-machine with over-sized genitals and a vast store of experiences, immensely varied. They appeared to think that the Negro has done all those 'special' things they themselves have never dared to do. They carried the conversation into the depths of depravity.

Griffin contrasted this behavioral pattern with other conversations in which "the atmosphere, no matter how coarse, has a verve and an essential joviality that casts out morbidity." But these scenes in *Black Like Me* are notable for their evident absence of respect and lack of decency. His responses were not prudish, since he found prudes insufferable. These men's attitudes were not just tainted by the lewd, but reeked of bestiality. He recoiled from the voyeurism debasing black people. If these encounters had not been so pathetic, they might have been comical. But they are incessantly humorless, and the only humor comes from Griffin, who could only hope "the next would spare me his pantings." When not spared, he attempted to dodge their obscene questions, which were "cynical in their lechery." When asked, "Did you ever get a white woman?" he responds with a question: "Do you think I'm crazy?"

"I didn't ask if you was crazy. I asked if you ever had one—or ever really wanted one." Then in a conniving tone, the driver says, "There's plenty white women would like to have a good buck Negro." When Griffin changes the subject, the driver calls him a liar. He was lying, but not for the reason the driver suspected. Soon after the driver became bored, pulled onto the shoulder, and summarily dismissed the hitchhiker, "as though he resented my uncooperative attitude, my refusal to give him this strange verbal sexual pleasure."

The next encounter, treated at greater length, forms the centerpiece of the hitchhiking sequence. This exchange was more of a joust than a mad chase. The young white man spoke with educated flair and posed no physical threat, but his challenge was more cunning. "His questions had the spurious elevation of a scholar seeking information, but the data sought was entirely sexual, presupposing that in the ghetto the Negro's life was one of marathon sex with many different partners, open to the view of all; in a word, that marital fidelity and sex as love's goal of union with the beloved object were exclusively the white man's property."

The conversation provides a forum for Griffin to argue against the inculcated prejudices of white society. The young antagonist is a "straw man" because his devious motives are laid bare, and his arguments rationalized the facts. The strategy of the discourse deconstructed the logical fallacies inherent in the white man's point of view, unmasking his real intentions. The antagonist's remarks created the illusion of seeking information to clarify intellectual curiosity when, in reality, he desired only the lurid details to satisfy his sexual fantasies.

Littered with the terminology of popular psychology, he pretended to be tolerant, admiring black attitudes toward sexuality. "Well, you people don't seem to have the inhibitions we have. We're all basically puritans." Translation: Black people are less inhibited because they have not been civilized. "I understand Negroes do a lot more things—different kinds of sex—than we do." Translation: Black people are more adventurous in sex because they are unbothered by promiscuity or perversion, and therefore breed like animals. "You people regard sex as a total experience—and that's how it should be. Anything that makes you feel good is morally all right for you." Translation: Black people experience sex as a totality, but are incapable of knowing the higher realms. He refers to blacks as "you people," implying that the difference is not a matter of diversity or extrinsic appearance, but the intrinsic difference of a lower species on the evolutionary scale.

"Oh, don't get me wrong," the man implores, "I admire your attitude, think it's basically healthier than ours. . . . Negroes don't have much neuroses, do they? I mean you people have a more realistic tradition about sex—you're not so sheltered from it as we are. . . . Isn't that the main difference?"

Griffin disagreed. "We've got the same puritanical background as you. We worry just as much about our children losing their virginity or being perverted. We've got the same miserable little worries and problems over our sexual effectiveness, the same guilts that you have." The white man was impressed by the hitchhiker's intelligence, but it was not what he wished to hear. His tone was "subtly conniving," asking about the details of black sexuality in pseudo-scientific language that failed to mask his intentions. It was clear to Griffin that "he was one of those young men who possess an impressive store of facts, but no truths."

He did not want to judge these night crawlers who insisted he "pay" for a ride by submitting himself "to the swamps of their fantasy lives." If that were not galling enough, the driver "ended up wanting me to expose myself to him, saying he had never seen a Negro naked." The hitchhiker kept silent, as the driver's shame intensified. "How could I let him see that I understood and that I still respected him, and that I formed no judgment against him for his momentary slip? For instead of seeing it as a manifestation of some poor human charity, he might view it as confirmation that Negroes are insensitive to sexual aberration."

Before Griffin could speak, the driver made his own defense. "I wasn't going to do anything to you. I'm not queer or anything."

"Of course not."

"It's just that I don't get a chance to talk to educated Negroes—people who can answer questions."

"You make it more complicated than it is. . . . If you want to know about the sexual morals of the Negro—his practices and ideals—it's no mystery. These are human matters, and the Negro is the same human as the white man. Just ask yourself how it is for a white man and you'll know all the answers."

"But there are differences. The social studies I've read . . . "

"They don't deal with any basic difference in human nature. . . . They only study the effects of environment on human nature. . . . These characteristics don't spring from whiteness or blackness, but from a man's conditioning."

But the young white man was oblivious to any wisdom that could not be distorted to his prejudice. He insisted that "we don't deprive you people" of such pleasures. They argued the point. Griffin made the case that in a segregated system black people were denied access to better schools and cultural institutions. The young man agreed that it was unfair; then argued that many whites lacked access also. Griffin made the obvious point that whites were at least given the choice of public access, but black people were denied access, even though they had to bear a proportionate tax burden to maintain the institutions that barred their entry.

The young man believed that "a man could do better." He did not want to know, and it was easier to deny injustice and rationalize segregation. Even as he attempted a rational approach, while the rabid segregationist used "noise, religion, bombast and diversionary considerations—such as states' rights and mongrelization—to cloud an issue that would be seen as absurd if stripped of these trappings," he still professed what Griffin posited as the "credo" of the segregationist. "His credo would seem to be:

If the truth makes you uncomfortable, don't change yourself but simply alter the truth to conform to your comfort."

The long ride through the Mississippi night was silenced by a rainstorm. Trying to turn the abandoned conversation in a positive direction, Griffin declared, "The situation is changing" because black people know for certain that "the only way out of this tragedy is through education, training. Thousands of them sacrifice everything to get an education, to prove once and for all that the Negro's capacity for learning, for accomplishment, is equal to that of any other man—that pigment has nothing to do with degrees of intelligence, talent or virtue. This isn't just wishful thinking. It's been proved conclusively in every field."

At the Mississippi-Alabama border, they approached a small, unnamed black settlement. The driver pulled off the highway and stopped, turning to the hitchhiker with an apology. Griffin waved it off and thanked him for the ride. He stepped out into the refreshingly cool mist, searching the unlighted settlement. There was no sign of life, no place to eat or sleep. Before this became a real concern, an old-model car pulled up. Griffin was "suddenly sick with dread at what this stranger would want," but there was nothing to do except open the door and smile.

The driver was another young white man, stout and "tough-looking" upon first impression. He asked where the hitchhiker was going and, when Griffin indicated Mobile, he was invited to get in. They drove east in the slackening mist and as each mile passed his stress diminished, listening to the driver talk in a "boisterous, loud and guileless" manner. "I could only conclude that he was color blind, since he appeared totally unaware that I was a Negro. He enjoyed company, nothing more. He told me he was a construction worker and tonight he was late getting home to his wife and infant son." They delighted in swapping stories about their children. Since the driver had not eaten, he suggested they stop for a meal. Griffin was hungry, but wondered aloud where there might be a place that would serve a Negro. The driver suggested bringing the meal to the car, and they could eat while they traveled. Stopping at a roadside café, the young man went inside. "I wondered how he had escaped the habit of guarded fencing that goes on constantly between whites and Negroes in the South whenever they meet. He was the first man of either color who did not confuse the popular image of the thing with the thing itself."

Griffin was relieved at the man's demeanor and fascinated that he had escaped every trace of racism. Through a series of questions, he discovered that the driver came from an ordinary background, was not highly educated, preferred popular music and TV westerns, and that his wife was religious and an avid reader. He could reach only one sensible conclusion—the man's "attitude came from an overwhelming love for his child, so profound it spilled over to all humanity." Griffin "knew that he was totally unaware of its ability to cure men; of the blessing it could be to someone like me after having been exhausted and scraped raw in my heart by others this rainy Alabama night." This driver, referred to as "my young friend," became a healing antidote to the racist poison. When they arrived in Mobile, he was dropped off downtown near the bus terminal, thanking his young friend for the ride.

Griffin noticed an elderly black man seated on a stoop across the street, and he went over to ask about lodging. As they conversed casually, he learned the elder was a preacher at a nearby mission. After asking if Griffin were a "nice man," he offered to share his own lodging. The preacher led him to his house, opened the door, and flipped on the light. The place was clean and simply furnished. The elder was living in two rooms at the front of his daughter's house. While he went to the other room to bathe in a large metal washtub, Griffin made notes. He surveyed the walls, noticing a calendar reproduction of *Christ in the Temple*, family photographs, and clothing on hooks. When the preacher returned, they carried the tub outside and emptied it. Returning inside, they prepared for sleep.

After a few minutes, the preacher asked if he wanted to sleep or talk. Griffin suggested they talk, "feeling the depression of the night and the poverty close in on the room." The preacher spoke of miracles and "banished the somberness." The preacher had two sons who went north to study law, never to return. He had remained to be with his daughters and grandchildren, but lamented the breakup of the larger family. They discussed white people and the preacher said, "They're God's children, just like us. Even if they don't act very godlike any more. God tells us straight—we've got to love them, no ifs, ands, and buts about it. Why, if we hated them, we'd be sunk down to their level."

From November 21 to 23, Griffin applied for jobs and researched conditions of black people in Mobile. The pattern of inconvenience was

Photo of JHG by Don Rutledge was the cover of first paperback, published by Signet in 1961 and by Gallimard (French paperback, in 1992). In subsequent editions both publishers used different covers, which were not photographs by Rutledge.

the same as elsewhere in the South, and only one scene of job hunting appears in the book. It was disheartening and revealed a new twist of cruelty. Griffin spoke to the foreman of an industrial plant who listened patiently to his skills and credentials. Looking him directly in the face, the foreman says, "No, you couldn't get anything like that here."

"This attitude cropped up often. Many otherwise decent men and women could find no other solution. They are willing to degrade themselves to their basest levels to prevent the traditional laborer from rising in status or, to put it bluntly, from 'winning,' even though what he wins has been rightfully his from the moment he was born into the human race." Again the phrase "you people" arises from the lips of the white manager, who supported the segregated system as if it were his duty and honor to be a member of a superior race. He felt no need to use epithets or to display anger; all that was necessary to uphold the sacredness of white supremacy was to close another door firmly without fanfare.

In Mobile Griffin made the rounds of advertised jobs and the nights were spent in the charitable company of the preacher. Griffin recalls his first visit to Mobile, the seaport from which he embarked on his first journey to France. He knew it then "as a privileged white," and Mobile had been impressive "as a beautiful Southern port town, gracious and calm. I had seen Negro dock workers stripped to the waist, their bodies glistening with sweat under their loads. The sight had chilled me, touched me with pity for men who so resembled beasts of burden. But I had dismissed it as belonging to the natural order of things. The Southern whites I knew were kind and wise. If they allowed this, then surely it must be right."

This visit was entirely different from the black point of view. The "gracious Southerner, the wise Southerner, the kind Southerner was nowhere" to be seen. He concluded that the "atmosphere of the place" changed drastically with one's perspective. "The Negro sees and reacts differently not because he is Negro, but because he is suppressed. Fear dims the sunlight."

On November 24, Griffin left for Montgomery, walking along the highway through swamp country on a cool clear morning. After several miles, he caught his first ride. When he opened the door to the pickup truck, he saw a shotgun propped up next to the driver. He backed away, but the driver laughed, assuring him it was for hunting deer. Griffin hesitated, but stepped in. He was told the man was an active civic leader in his fifties, married with grown children and grandchildren. He "began to hope that I had encountered a decent white."

The driver asked the hitchhiker benign questions until there was a turn in the conversation. What followed was his worst exposure to verbal pornography, more vile than earlier drivers, who left their lascivious fantasies in check until the night released them. But this driver spewed shamelessly in the glare of daylight. The civic leader said all the white men he knew "craved colored girls," and that he "had it in every one" of the black women he hired.

"Surely some refuse," Griffin suggested cautiously.

"Not if they want to eat or feed their kids. If they don't put out, they don't get the job." Griffin stared out the passenger window at the dense pine forest. The silent beauty of the countryside made a stark contrast to the ugly noises of the civic leader at the wheel. "You think that's pretty terrible, don't you?"

Finally, the hitchhiker said: "I guess I do."

"Why hell—everybody does it. Don't you know that? . . . We figure we're doing you people a favor to get some white blood in your kids." This "grotesque hypocrisy slapped" Griffin in the face.

In this passage deleted from the book, he wondered: "What moral and ethical difference was there between this sort of rape by coercion that threatened to starve a person and rape that threatened to shoot or knife a person?" There was no difference, except such weaponless coercion would not be reported, while the victim was trapped in her silent humiliation.

In a tragic climate of brutality there was no need to invent a Theater of Cruelty, since the reality was beyond fiction. The scene renders absurd the white man's view of black immorality, his horror of mongrelization, and the loss of so-called racial purity. "Mongrelization is already a widespread reality in the South—it has been exclusively the white man's contribution to the Southern Way of Life." It was no surprise this pattern went unreported in the press or was overlooked by the social scientists. If any victim had disclosed these crimes, she and her family would be targeted for violent reprisal. "Alabama nigger women are good about that," declared the civic leader, "they won't never go to the cops or tell on you."

Dissatisfied by the Griffin's lack of enthusiasm, the civic leader interrogated him. "He spoke in a tone that sickened me, casual, merciless. I looked at him. His decent blue eyes turned yellow. I knew that nothing could touch him to have mercy once he decided a Negro should be 'taught a lesson.' The immensity of it terrified me." The driver nodded toward a tunnel of pines that screened the swamps beyond. "You can kill a nigger and toss him into that swamp and no one'll ever know what happened to him," he declared.

In the original manuscript Griffin expressed rage in his private thoughts, but the following line was cut. "It took all of my control not to reveal myself, not to say the words that formed inside me: Why you sonofabitch, you're not talking to a scared Negro. I'm as white as you are." He remained silent, imagining the man in scenes with his grandchildren, standing to sing hymns in church, visiting with wife and friends on the front porch—everything he had been led to believe when he first decided to risk riding in the pickup truck. This was the mask of "the amiable, decent American," obscuring the rapist from detection. "It was the side he would show no one but his victims, or those who connived with him."

The truck pulled into a dirt road and stopped. "I'll tell you how it is here. We'll do business with you people. We'll sure as hell screw your women. Other than that, you're just completely off the record as far as we're concerned. And the quicker you people get it through your heads, the better off you'll be."

Off the record? Not so, because *Black Like Me* restores the record.

Griffin returned to the highway from the dirt road and sat on his duffel bags to wait for another ride. There was no traffic. He walked along the gravel shoulder, this time under the first stars, hoping to find a place to eat. After a few miles he saw a light flickering through the foliage. He hurried around the curve, seeing that it shone from a small store atop the hill. Reaching the crest, he waited across the highway. He saw an elderly white couple inside. He approached cautiously, not wanting to startle them. The woman came to the door, saying they were closed. He pleaded that he had not had a meal all day and he was on his way to Montgomery. He saw her hesitation, "her caution and repugnance struggling against instincts of common decency," and felt that she wanted to refuse. But she opened the door. He bought crackers and an orange soda and stepped outside. This was devoured quickly and he returned the bottle, buying another. Since sardine cans lacked keys and he was not offered a can opener, he bought a fried pie, a loaf of bread, and five candy bars.

Griffin returned to the highway, hearing a vehicle approaching. Although he "dreaded riding with another white man," he dreaded being out in the cold all night even more. He stepped into the view of the approaching car and waved. The old car came to a halt on the shoulder. To his relief, "the reflections from the dash light showed me the face of a young Negro man."

The driver offered not only a ride but also food and lodging. Griffin became the unexpected guest of a family with six young children. From the night of November 24 until the next morning, he encountered a black family imprisoned by a controlled system, living in a two-room wooden shanty with no indoor plumbing or beds for the children, who slept on feed sacks placed on the floor.

"As we drove several miles down a lane into the forest, he told me he was a sawmill worker and never made quite enough to get out from under his debts. Always, when he took his check to the store, he owed a little more than the check could cover. He said it was the same for everyone else; and indeed I have seen the pattern throughout my travels." Part of the white strategy, when black people were allowed to work at all, was to keep them in debt. The low wages and high prices at the "company" store, where black workers exchanged weekly checks for credit, worked flawlessly and maintained the closed system at a profit. Griffin asked why the mill workers did not organize and strike for higher wages. The man laughed at this suggestion. "But if they stuck together surely the whites would not kill them all."

"They could damn sure try. Anyway, how long could I feed my kids? There's only a couple of stores in twenty miles. They'd cut off credit and refuse to sell to us." In the harsh glare of reality, Griffin made no more suggestions.

Soon after they turned onto a rutted path that ended at the top of a knoll, and Griffin saw their shanty. The wife, silhouetted before the glow of a kerosene lamp, met them at the door. The children expressed delight to have a visitor. The wife prepared the meal and he was invited to join them.

Griffin describes the scene in terms as bare as the shanty, but in a tone that turns elegiac. "Supper was on the makeshift table. It consisted entirely of large yellow beans cooked in water. The mother prepared mashed beans and canned milk for the infant. I remembered the bread and offered it as my contribution to the meal. Neither parent apologized for the meagerness of the food." They ate from plastic dishes, adults at the table and children on the floor, with newspapers as a tablecloth. He congratulated them on their family and the wife said that they felt blessed. He watched as the cold facts of their existence transformed into the warmth of intimacy. He cut up the candy bars for dessert. "In the framework of nothing, slices of Milky Way become a great gift," as the children consumed the chocolate in animated celebration.

After supper, the two men walked outside. Under bright moonlight he stepped behind a pine at the edge of the woods, recalling a passage from Lillian Smith's novel *Strange Fruit,* about a "Negro boy stopping along a lonely path to urinate." He "felt more profoundly than ever before the totality of blackness and the immensity of its isolating effects." He contrasted Smith's novel with his reality. "The transition was complete from the white boy reading a book about Negroes in the safety of his white living room to an old Negro man in the Alabama swamps, his existence nullified by men but reaffirmed by nature."

Returning to the house they drew two buckets of water from the well, making a second trip to gather wood for the iron stove. When the water was heated, the mother sponge-bathed the children, while the men shaved. Then each child used the zinc bucket in the corner, since it was too cold for the outhouse. The adults spread tow sacks on the floor, feed sacks atop those, and gathered patchwork quilts as coverlets to complete the pallets. The youngsters asked about Griffin's children, then kissed their parents goodnight. They wanted to kiss their guest goodnight, too, so he sat in a straight-back chair, holding out his arms to the line of children. They put arms around his neck and touched their lips to his. Amid giggling, they said goodnight and slipped into their pallets. The parents retreated to an alcove bedroom, turning out the kerosene lamp. They climbed into a creaking bed while Griffin lay down, fully dressed, on a pallet in the kitchen area.

Griffin observed moonlight pouring through the cracks and listened to the children drifting off to sleep. "Odors of the night and autumn and the swamp entered to mingle with the odors of children, kerosene, cold beans, urine and the dead incense of pine ashes. The rots and the freshness combined into a strange fragrance—the smell of poverty." He thought of the parents' courage in "attempting to bring up a family decently, their gratitude that none of their children were blind or maimed, their willingness to share their food and shelter with a stranger."

Then Griffin went outside, sat on an overturned washtub, and wept silently, thinking of his children asleep between clean sheets in a warm house. He remembered the black children's kisses, as softly innocent as the goodnight kisses of his children, and visualized their eyes, "guileless, not yet aware that doors into wonderlands of security, opportunity, and hope were closed to them." His tears were not shed from self-pity, but were tears of grief for every child wounded by racism. "I saw it not as a white man and not as a Negro, but as a human parent. Their children resembled mine in all ways except the superficial one of skin color, as indeed they resembled all children of all humans. One can scarcely conceive the full horror of it unless one is a parent who takes a close look at his children and then asks himself how he would feel if a group of men should come to his door and tell him they had decided—for reasons of convenience to them—that his children's lives would henceforth be restricted, their world smaller, their educational opportunities less, their future mutilated."

If all parents knew such misery, they would "see it as the Negro parent sees it, for this is precisely what happens." What parent could knowingly impose this fate on any member of the human family? Yet it was happening a few steps away, where six innocent black children slept on a cold floor.

Returning to the shanty, Griffin stretched out on the floor to sleep. Later he was awakened by a recurring nightmare. "The nightmare worried me. I had begun this experiment in a spirit of scientific detachment. I wanted to keep my feelings out of it, to be objective in my observations. But it was becoming such a profound personal experience, it haunted even my dreams."

Griffin was awakened at dawn. In the lamp-lit shanty, the adults nodded and smiled, but said not a word. The six children slept, while the adults shared a breakfast of bread and coffee. Then the husband went outside to start the car. Griffin thanked the wife and reached for his wallet. The wife refused, but he pleaded with her to take it as a gift to the children. She relented and took the money.

At the intersection of the country path and the highway, Griffin stepped out of the car. His host waved farewell, and drove in the opposite direction toward the sawmill. Soon he got a lift from two young white boys, who left him at the bus station. He purchased a one-way ticket to Montgomery, not looking forward to another bus ride, but determined that there would be no more hitchhiking. In the segregated restroom he pulled out a hand mirror. "I had been a Negro more than three weeks and it no longer shocked me to see the stranger in the mirror. My hair had grown to a heavy fuzz, my face skin, with continued medication, exposure to sunlight and ground-in stain, was what Negroes call a 'pure brown'—a smooth dark color that made me look like millions of others."

Instead of avoiding the mirror, Griffin concentrated on the changing details of his disguise. He noticed that his face had "lost animation," and in repose "it had taken on the strained, disconsolate expression that is written on the countenance of so many Southern Negroes." His mind had also lost animation, "dozing empty for long periods," thinking of food and water, spending hours "just waiting, cushioning self against dread." He observed the internal despair that accompanied appearance, fixing his expression into a mask. Thought processes had lost their characteristic curiosity and liveliness, and his mind dozed as a sleeping object.

Desperate "for something merely pleasurable," beyond the squalid external reality and internal humiliation, he found some stolen bit of "joy in the mere fact that I could be alone for a while," safely locked away from "the hate stares, the contempt." The act of splashing his face with cold water seemed like a "luxury," as did the smell of Ivory soap, which "livened the atmosphere." He noticed that the stain had come off with the washing, and wondered when he would be able to pass for white again. He decided to stop taking the pills and removed shirt and undershirt. His body had "paled to a *café-au-lait* color," several shades lighter than face and hands. He wet a sponge and poured dye on it to touch up the corners of his mouth.

Refreshed and ready to resume the journey, Griffin boarded a bus for Selma in the afternoon. That evening he strolled around near the Selma bus terminal during a long layover. He sat on a park bench a few blocks away, waiting near a public phone booth, uncertain of local restrictions. When he saw a black man use the phone, he placed a long-distance collect call to his wife.

In a passage edited out of the book, he admitted feeling uncomfortable about "a Negro never speaking endearments to a white woman." His discomfort irritated him and he told Elizabeth, "Surely, we've enough sense to overcome this." She agreed. Speaking with the children was no problem, because a "Southern Negro can call children 'darling' without flinching." He spoke with them "as their husband and father, while reflected in the glass windows of the booth I saw another man they would not know. At this time, when I wanted most to lose the illusion, I was more than ever aware of it, aware that it was not the man she knew, but a stranger who spoke with the same voice and the same memory."

In this fifth reflection scene Griffin stands between the white world he hears confirming his identity and the black reality he sees reflected in the glass. He was suspended in an eerie limbo, an existential absurdity, perceiving the experience in the cross hairs of his double perspective. "The night was always a comfort. Most of the whites were in their homes. The threat was less. A Negro blended inconspicuously into the darkness." Griffin quotes the final lines of Langston Hughes's poem—"Dream Variations,"[53] the source text of the book's epigraph and title. "At such a time, the Negro can look at the starlit skies and find that he has, after all, a place in the universal order of things. The stars, the black skies affirm his humanity, his validity as a human being. He knows that his belly, his lungs, his tired legs, his appetites, his prayers and his mind are cherished in some profound involvement with nature and God. The night is his consolation. It does not despise him."

Griffin slept at the back of the bus during the trip from Selma to Montgomery, scene of the historic bus boycott. He arrived in the state capital near midnight, staying the following week. The hopelessness reflected elsewhere in the South was replaced by hope. "Nonviolent and prayerful resistance to discrimination is the keynote. Here, the Negro has committed himself to a definite stand. He will go to jail, suffer any humiliation, but he will not back down. He will take the insults and abuses stoically so that his children will not have to take them in the future." But he was uncertain about the white community. The attitude was "too fluid, too changeable," since their unity was based on old fears and cherished stereotypes. He prepared to test a new strategy of passing back into white society.

Secluded in a ghetto motel for the next two days to avoid exposure to sunlight, Griffin stopped taking the medication. On the third night, November 28, he scrubbed himself "almost raw until my brown skin had a pink rather than black undertone." He felt confident in passing back into the white world, but it would be nerve-wracking to leave the ghetto as a white man. In a reversal of his New Orleans transformation, he slipped out of the ghetto late that night to reenter the white world. He carried all belongings and headed toward the white side of town.

Along the way Griffin encountered a black teenager near the dividing line of the two worlds. The young man's caution in his presence seemed to validate his white identity. But not until he passed a white policeman in a well-lighted area was he convinced the reversal had been accomplished. Now he was accepted as a first-class citizen, but the psychic readjustment would not be easy. He crossed the street to a restaurant and sat at the counter between two whites. The waitress smiled and he felt as part of a trick of magic, but "felt no joy in it." The smiles and courtesies he had not known as a disguised Negro turned the "miracle sour."

The next dozen pages of *Black Like Me* cover Griffin's time in the tense capital. A series of parallel episodes brings his double perspective into sharp focus, revealing the tragic ironies and comic absurdities of the "two worlds," as he moves between them in literal and figurative senses. On waking up as a white man in a plush hotel, he writes that "Montgomery looked different that morning" of November 29, and the "face of humanity smiled—good smiles, full of warmth; irresistible smiles that confirmed my impression that these people were simply unaware of the situation with the Negroes who passed them on the street—that there was not even the communication of intelligent awareness between them."

Black reality was out of the awareness of white perception. When Griffin spoke with whites, he heard the same clichés, reeking of unconscious racism glossed over with paternalism. That same day he walked through a ghetto area. "I, the white man, got from the Negro the same shriveling treatment I, the Negro, had got from the white man." His presence meant nothing more to black people than a conditioned reflex to whiteness. In either place one was alien if a different color. "Was it worth trying to show the one race what went on behind the mask of the other?"

That week in the capital, moving between two worlds and changing masks from black to white and back again in transit, becomes the maddening climax of *Black Like Me*. "I kept a damp sponge, dyes, cleansing cream and Kleenex. It was hazardous, but it was the only way to traverse an area both as Negro and white. As I traveled, I would find an isolated spot, perhaps an alley at night or the brush beside a highway, and quickly apply the dye to face and hands and legs. . . . I would go through the area as a Negro and then, usually at night, remove the dyes with cleansing cream and tissues and pass through the same area as a white man." The effect of his "zigzagging" technique was unsettling, but he had become bolder, even somewhat reckless. The "zigzagging" made for more complex, compressed tests, but the results were the same. He pushed the limits of experience that only appearances needed to be changed in order to pass through either world undetected. It was almost too easy, yet beneath appearances its essence was difficult and sad. The double perspective of being a white man disguised as a "Negro" was redoubled by passing into the white world as an "ex-Negro." Everyone saw only "color" and judged by reflex. Griffin's point was made and he ended the experiment.

Griffin rode a bus to Atlanta on December 1. Departing, he went directly to the restroom in the terminal. "I had had enough. Suddenly I could stomach no more of this degradation—not of myself but all men who were black like me. . . . In the men's room, I entered one of the cubicles and locked the door. For a time I was safe, isolated; for a time, I owned the space around me, though it was scarcely more than that of a coffin." He was struck by the irony of Georgia, the land of his forefathers. "The town of Griffin was named for one of them. Too, I, a Negro, carried the name hated by all Negroes, for former Governor Griffin (no kin I would care to discover) devoted himself heroically to keeping Negroes 'in their place.'" Griffin "celebrated a triumphant return to the land from which his people had sprung by seeking sanctuary in a toilet cubicle at a bus station." He rubbed cleansing cream on hands and face to remove the stain. The hand mirror indicated that he could pass for white again. He left the cubicle and disappeared into the crowd.

On December 2, Griffin woke early at the YMCA, making a phone call to the *Sepia* office to inform them the experiment was concluded. They requested another assignment in Atlanta and he agreed, but only on the condition that he would not be disguised. He was directed to meet with a photographer assigned to the project at noon on December 4. Since this left him free for two days, he called the Trappist monastery in Conyers, asking permission to make a short retreat.

When Griffin arrived the monks were chanting *Vespers*. Greeted in the courtyard by a brown-robed monk, he was led to a cell on the second floor. "The contrast was almost too great to be borne. It was a shock, like walking from the dismal swamps into sudden brilliant sunlight. Here men know nothing of hatred. They sought to make themselves conform ever more perfectly to God's will, whereas outside I had seen mostly men who sought to make God's will conform to their prejudices. Here men sought their center in God, whereas outside they sought it in themselves. The difference was transforming." The distance between the hypocritical Christianity of the racists and the genuine sanctity of the monks was not merely spatial or temporal, but a spiritual transformation from fragmentation to wholeness.

That evening Griffin entered the chapel for the last prayers of the day. He knelt in the balcony to listen to white-robed monks chant *Compline*. The final chant was the *Salve Regina*, which was so tender "we felt the crusts of our lives fall away and we rested in the deep hush of eternity." After the monks had filed out, he remained in the darkened chapel, "not praying but simply resting in the warmth where all senses are ordered into harmony, where hatred cannot penetrate."

The guest master greeted Griffin at the door to his cell. He confided to the monk his recent experiment, asking if black people ever visited the monastery. Yes, but not many knew of it. How did the white guests react? The monk explained that white men on retreat "would hardly keep one eye on God and the other on the color of his neighbor's skin." After the conversation, the monk left to retrieve Jacques Maritain's *Scholasticism and Politics*, leafing through to find the page he wanted. "Maritain has some profound things to say about the religion of racists." Griffin was startled that the French philosopher perfectly characterized the racists of the South, but he realized that Maritain was "describing racists everywhere and from all times" and "that this is the trait of men who twist their minds to consider racial prejudice a virtue."

Griffin met Don Rutledge on December 4.[54] The young photographer from the Black Star agency had driven from Tennessee. He "liked him immediately," describing Rutledge as "a gentleman in every way." In *Black Like Me* he summarizes the activities in Atlanta, impressed with how far black and white citizens had evolved, "proving that 'the Problem' can be solved and showing us the way to do it."

Most of the research was done in the three-block area of black-owned institutions of finance and industry and a larger section where six black colleges were located. These social institutions formed a cohesive infrastructure, gathering these resources into one unified community. "In the matter of education, Atlanta has long been eminent," making specific reference to President Benjamin Mays of Morehouse and President Rufus

Clement of Atlanta University. In an interview with Dr. Mays, he recalls "the look of surprise and vast amusement on Mays' face when I confided to him my journey."

The Southern Christian Leadership Conference, under Martin Luther King Jr., was located in Atlanta, which had taken a different road that Montgomery aspired to reach. New Orleans, even though far ahead of rural Louisiana in 1959, was neither as organized as Atlanta nor as determined as Montgomery. Mississippi and most rural areas of the Deep South still resembled the dark ages of slavery.

One of his final dialogues in Atlanta was with the Reverend Samuel Williams. Griffin recalled what the professor of philosophy had told him, because it connected seamlessly with what he had read by Maritain and Dr. King.

"I spent years," he told me, "studying the phenomenon of love."

"And I spent years studying the phenomenon of justice," said Griffin.

"At base, we spend years studying the same thing," said the Reverend.

By December 9, Griffin returned to New Orleans, intending to retrace the terrain of his journey. He mentioned the plan to Rutledge, asking his advice about a first-rate photographer. Fascinated by the idea of making a documentary for the *Sepia* series, Rutledge took on the assignment.

The project presented problems, since a black man being photographed by a white man aroused suspicions. "Whites tended to wonder, 'What Negro celebrity is he?'" Black people were curious. "The Uncle Toms think that every Negro should bury his head in the sand," and "they distrust any Negro prominent enough to be photographed by a white photographer."

They invented clever strategies to overcome the obstacles. The result was a batch of sharp images and some humorous episodes. The general approach was to meet at the same place and time, pretending *not* to know each other. Rutledge acted like a tourist taking casual pictures, while Griffin found ways of slipping into the frame. One day they received some unexpected assistance at a fruit stand in the French Market. As one woman waited on Griffin, Rutledge talked to another vendor a distance away. The woman said to the photographer, "Why don't you hurry up and get a picture of that funny old nigger before he leaves?" Rutledge obliged.

Another episode occurred at a fish market where Rutledge asked the vendor to pose with a fish. The vendor went in search of the biggest fish.

Griffin followed the man behind the counter, as if the fish were intended for him. The vendor tried to maneuver him from the picture, saying that customers were not allowed behind the counter. Just then Rutledge spoke out. “That’s good right there, hold it,” and the vendor turned, wearing a smile, as Griffin smuggled himself into the frame.

At the shoeshine stand Sterling Williams was relieved to see Griffin safely back in New Orleans. Rutledge’s finest images are of Williams. The photographic work was concluded by December 14.

Griffin’s last entry in New Orleans ends the text of his journey. “I resumed for the final time my white identity. I felt strangely sad to leave the world of the Negro after having shared it so long—almost as though I were fleeing my share of his pain and heartache.”

Aftermath

> How difficult it is to put into practice the theories of the spiritual life that one never questions—the returning of love for hate, of tenderness for brutality. Most terrible of all has been this weird thing—I have become a hero-figure in a way that throws into my face the total unworthiness of it. The haters consider me a mortal enemy now, but the crowds consider me a great hero, and I cringe at both.
>
> I live on the ideas of St. Thomas Aquinas and Jacques Maritain, on Bach and the great musical masters. My brain is dulled by everything else, closed against the constant outrage of men who cheat against themselves in order to win over other men.
>
> —JOHN HOWARD GRIFFIN

On December 15, the "ex-Negro" departed New Orleans on a jet flight bound for Dallas. He was welcomed at the airport by Elizabeth and their three young children. His parents joined in the reunion that was marked by nervous jubilation and profound relief. They drove twenty miles south to Mansfield. "We came directly here to my parents' farm," wrote Griffin in the *Journal*. "We sat in the living room for a while as my father fixed coffee, smiling all over himself. My mother asked: 'Was it as horrible as I think it was?' I answered: 'Worse than you can possibly imagine.' A shadow crossed their faces but it was no time—and we knew it—to discuss the past weeks. It was time to visit with the children, who fought for places on my lap; time to talk of nothing, for the pleasure of hearing normalcy again."

Griffin had not been alone with his wife yet, and felt anxiety about their intimacy. He got up from the circle of children, saying he was going to wash up. As he walked to the bathroom, he heard the laughter of the children pouring out of the house into the front yard. Right behind their voices followed those of his parents. Then he heard Elizabeth's footsteps approaching the bathroom door.

> A sense of panic flew through me—a moment of fear. She opened the door, stepped in and closed it after her. We stared at one another, completely disarmed, defenseless. "Is it all right?" I asked, hearing my voice—hoarse, weak, full of strain. "Yes . . . oh yes," she said, and was in my arms and then kissing me in a way which left room for nothing but a flood of relief in me. I held her close and whispered against her hair, almost unable to believe that we could have this kind of good fortune in our relationship. "Are you sure?" "Yes," she repeated, breathing it out with an ecstatic sound. . . . I heard her weeping with relief. She quickly controlled herself, however, and said she'd better get back to the kids. "What would you like for supper?" she asked at the door. It was such a natural question there was genius in it.

This ends Griffin's *Journal* entry for the day and night of return, which was not published in the book. It marked a few weeks of intimate union, a private peace that would be erased by the upcoming public storm. The final pages of *Black Like Me*—from January 2 through August 17 of 1960—report the story of the public reaction. This was what he chose to publish, deciding that the complete *Journal* notes would have invaded his family's privacy. The unpublished pages fill in gaps, providing an inside view of a wounded healer attempting to heal his own wounds with a loving family and a close circle of friends. But to love those who hated him during the journey or to love the white neighbors who called him a traitor to his race, those adjustments would not come easily. Yet he felt a responsibility to love them in the manner of the *caritas*, and the spiritual direction he followed.

During the last two weeks of 1959, his work on the series went well. "The work flows," he said in the *Journal*. He thought of "how depressing it had been to sleep in the hovels I occupied as a Negro touring the South; and yet, here I was in one scarcely better (not even as comfortable as some of them) and was blissfully happy. In truth, I love this barn, and was happy to be stuck here through the storm. Today, it has continued—so dark I need lamplight. This afternoon snow begins to fall, with a forecast for snow tonight. I settle down to it, with the luxury of long hours stretching before me, hours isolated by snow and ice, long hours that will bring no interruptions." Later he turned out the light and sat near the fire to pray. The steady flame held his gaze while all else dissolved into the background.

After saying prayers, he turned on the lamp to resume the *Journal.* "Strange how when a man is alone, deeply involved with nature, everything—his prayers as well as his functions—all is taken up without separation, without contradistinction into the love of God. There is no dissonance, no conflict between body and soul. All of the elements of each fall into some basic harmony that is his love, his form of worship, his manner of glorifying God." He was speaking of what he was writing, the works he had written, and would write. "For in this framework, nothing can be contained—it overflows and must pour out in glorification, in a tremendous union with the Source of it all. Not bringing in the source to self, but throwing self outward toward it—until there is abandonment, until self is lost in this concatenation."

After days and nights alone in the studio, he returned to the family cottage to stay the night. At that time the children were growing swiftly. Susie was five, Johnny was four, and Greggy was two years, five months. After supper, he put on a favorite recording, Benedetto Marcello's *Concerti Grossi,* turned out the lights, and lit a candle. "We sat in the soft light and listened to this magnificent and tender music, and no one uttered a sound; but what a glowing joy lighted their faces as they would put fingers to their lips to call for silence and smile. When the music was over, we slowly came out of the deep calm delight into which it had plunged us."

Once the children had slipped into bed, the couple lay in darkness, listening to the Marcello and the sounds of children turning in sleep. Elizabeth whispered, "We mustn't ever lose this." They embraced and he watched her slip into a deep sleep. He remained awake until the music ended and the machine clattered off. "It was only then that I felt not the slightest doubt that no matter what happened, I would take it and be glad, for the one thing I had feared most damaging—my wife's love for me—had not been damaged at all."

What Griffin had not realized (and never knew), was that from Elizabeth's viewpoint her love had never been at risk. Her only concern had been for his safety. In terms of the "race question," her formation had not been poisoned by racist mythology. Elizabeth had been raised by her adoptive parents on the same farm she was raising her own children. On the Holland farm, where the family had lived in close proximity to black people, there had been no segregation. Everyone who lived and worked on the farm took meals together at the family table. In the Griffin household the "help" lived elsewhere and the maid or the handyman ate their meals at "the second table," according to the southern tradition. This meant that black people ate in the kitchen *after* the white family had eaten in the dining room.

Griffin's children never saw this tradition, growing up in a household that was not only liberated from racism, but with parents who were consciously antiracist. But in 1959 and 1960, the children had no idea their father had ever been disguised as a black man, but only that he took a long trip. The same high spirits of his return extended beyond Christmas into 1960.

The *Journal* recorded progress on the magazine series, as Griffin marveled "at the simplest and most prosaic things," remarking that "occasionally it worries me, for it is the child's reaction in the adult." It was the same reaction he had experienced during the initial hours of the experiment. As he watched their children, he was reminded of the six children sprawled across the cold floor in pallets in that shanty. The inequities were painful to contemplate, and it was an image he never forgot. Yet it was the humanity of those children that struck most deeply, for they were all "part of the universal order that none can go against," and for Griffin "there is constantly renewed harmony in it, a harmony of the most magical sort—old as time but always fresh, astonishing, and inciting us to love the way things are at this universal level of humanity beyond innocence or guilt."

The *Journal* entry for the first day of a new decade explored contrasts. It was one of those days he relished, "a dark, cold day, misty and hinting of sleet," which most would not enjoy. He made notes as he listened to Bach Cantatas that "jubilantly defy the mood of the day and change it." It was "a new day, a new year," and he felt "like spending the lonely day lost in work. But writing of my experiences as a Negro takes a turn back into the darkness. By comparison with the literature and the studies of the Dark Ages, the truth of the present appears a monstrous regression." He wondered if the new decade would be darker. "The whites in the South have simply receded from the human race. The man who is less than just is less than man."

Griffin was writing about a state of injustice that should not exist, but because it did exist, he was compelled to comment. "With pain and great excitement I write the pages I so detest, because I detest delving in corruption; and I have never seen more obscene corruption. And it is foolish. They wallow in their white misery, but will not do the things that will make them at peace. They will not let the Negro breathe, their deep prejudice does not want that, considers it unpatriotic, a sin against one's seed." And finally, "All of this bounces off the wall of Bach, like sickness bounces from the wall of health, or like viciousness from the wall of love. It cannot enter into the felicity of art's great order, because it is without order—it sneaks mole-like through the underground tunnels of the soul."

The *Aftermath* section in *Black Like Me* picks up on January 2, 1960 (after a gap dating to December 15, 1959), and then goes silent until February 26. On that second day of the new decade, Griffin visited the *Sepia* offices in Fort Worth. Publisher George Levitan tried to let him back out of publishing the series. "The only way I'll run it is if you insist," he said. "Then I think we must run it," replied Griffin, but "wishing with all my heart I could drop it."

Since the magazine was read by mostly black people in the South, he felt it was a way to let them know that the truth would be made public, and that there were some white people who cared enough to speak out against injustice. The initial installment of the series entitled "Journey into Shame" would hit the stands on April 17, although news of the story was known before in local newspapers and through national radio and television.[55] The *Sepia* series ran monthly and the final installment was published in the September 17 issue. His work consisted of a personal journal and an objective report on the relevant data accumulated. But attempts to make sense of the statistics about "race relations" did not progress.

Griffin realized the *real* story was in the experience and *not* in the data. In this context he was clarifying awareness of the prejudice that had conditioned his shocking reaction to the stranger in the mirror, the denial and rationalization, as well as the guilt attached to this complex set of emotions. He had begun to go beyond the intellectual concepts and ethical assumptions that had deluded him into believing he was free of racism. His self-criticism demanded more than clarity of thought; it also necessitated a purging of emotions and a purification of spirit.

On the night of January 13, 1960, Griffin attempts to outline an ideal of sanctity. "The man in love with God," begins a long entry, "is assailed by satanic impulses of a depth unknown to most men." He viewed these impulses as developing parallel "in clarity and sheen as his love of God grows, until a point is reached where the two forces threaten to tear him apart." Thus, one will be forced to make a choice. Either one succumbs to the pressure and finds a way to "balance the two forces in nice proportion, and cease all growth, or one takes a blind leap of faith."

Griffin believed the leap to be "the beginning of sanctity; that is, the beginning of a higher love, which no man can know in advance of actually experiencing it." This meant "a brute act" must be made—the act of abandoning oneself to God." Otherwise our "whole existence is haunted by an indefinable longing," which he believed was "the way of the routine practitioner of religion." The brute act was a conscious response to the higher order, total obedience to the Divine, a rejection of crowd conformity, and the erasure of self-interest.

Five nights later, on January 18, both the act of writing and the healing solitude helped guide Griffin through the processes of clarification and purification. He noted in the *Journal* that it was "down to twenty degrees outside," but the work flowed despite the bitter cold. "The silence is profound, but without the loudness it sometimes has. I work, and in the background listen to recordings made in a Benedictine convent—the nuns' chanting exquisitely evoking the strict life of the cloister, its peace, its timelessness." He was "filled with their tenderness. . . . They go all the way in it, and it is full of mystery—the mystery of the ancient rule; it touches depths that cannot be defined, but that are lost when the rule is lessened, when less is demanded of man's gift to God." Aware of his immersion in the "mystery of the ancient rule," he must demand more, not less, and he was aware of the contrasts. "The music fills my studio with its ageless serenity, and I find the contrast between the moment and the work (my trip as a Negro and the cruelty of man to man) almost unbearable. I play it deliberately to remind me to love what is still so close and personal."

Prior to the journey he had been concerned that his love "would not be great enough to embrace" the black people he encountered, but discovering that "familiarity brought its own love," and now "how easily I love them as brothers and sisters." But how would he find the humility to love the whites? "My bitterness to find my own people so distorted, so full of hate, has blackened me, and it is the devil temptation. I struggle against it. I pray for the ability to love them for they are sick and their meanness is a sickness that seems almost universally shared."

Griffin heeded the wisdom of many black people, especially the New Orleans elders and the preacher in Mobile, who exhibited the mercy and humility of loving one's "enemies" as fellow souls. "Without loving them, I feel I cannot write properly of them as humans, but will continue to write of them as mere operatives, and therefore in giving an accurate account, will not give a wise or completely true one."

This was Griffin's "great uneasiness," aware that too often he poured "out my deep distress with my white brothers—then erasing and trying not to call names." Lucidity continues in the *Journal* of January 19, and the "modality remains, the felicity lingers at midday the way it was at midnight—the chants add the patina of what is eternal, as do the views of barren trees and brown pastures, calm in the sunlight." He responded to this healing orientation as if it were a "prolonged prayer" in which "every act participates," including the clatter of typing. Yet the painful work was "immensely difficult," and he had to force himself back into it, "because it must be done, but it is a violence of sorts, like forcing a compass needle away from true North and all the magnetism of its nature draws it to that polarization."

Griffin's "true North" was in the direction of the eternal modality, but he could not avoid the South, forcing him to revisit that troubled territory in the dimension of time. By January 30 that time had arrived. The experiment was becoming known, and he received requests for radio and television interviews. "I realize the hatred it will bring me in the South and I look on the next months with the worst possible dread. I have the deep conviction that I am on the right side—the side of justice; but it will be a dirty bath, regardless, for the opposition refuses to reason, to debate, to seek truth. They brand and hate, that is all."

Throughout February the workload grew, and thus Griffin's pace quickened to meet its demands. The schedule for lectures and interviews was being set for April and those for March were being confirmed. His mother and Elizabeth fielded most calls, while he remained out of contact in the studio. Griffin lectured to a group of adjustment psychologists. "I advanced the thesis of cultures, suggesting we seek those isolates that contradistinguish the culture of a handicapped person from the surrounding culture. Then I correlated this model with that of black people in contradistinction to the dominant white culture."

While Griffin was blind, he was treated by the sighted as an object of pity. He felt this same "minority condition" was experienced by black people who were scorned by whites as inferior objects. In both situations, Griffin felt he had been judged as perceived, but never as an individual. He recognized these attitudes of superiority were based on cultural conditioning that placed limitations on the sightless and forced greater limitations on black people. Both realities illustrated that the prejudiced majority defined minority conditions, casting its victims into *otherness.* The intrinsic qualities were ignored in the comfortable embrace of racism based on extrinsic stereotypes.

On February 13, Griffin noted that "The depression has left me, despair from the after-effects of the experience, from the shock of seeing kind people's cruel capabilities —and the work has flowed now that the shock is over."

Black Like Me picks up the *Aftermath* on February 26, with the news that he has accepted an invitation to be interviewed on the Paul Coates television show in Hollywood. The book then skips ahead to March 14, when the first of two shows with Coates aired. Several internal events during the unpublished interim were recorded in the *Journal* and letters. Griffin received phone calls from Washington, one requesting he appear before Congress, another from the Department of Justice proposing lectures in April and May of 1960. These calls, along with the national programs already lined up, made him question his preparedness.

Griffin turned to his old friend Father J. Stanley Murphy. In an October 4 letter, he admitted concerns about going public. "My story is not sensational, it is an ethical study of an experience lived. I am in a petrifying position of having all possible communications media open to me and therefore of being capable of turning the entire history of our land at this point. Why it had to be someone so deficient, so unwise as me, I do not know." He felt anxiety because he had never been on national television, spoken before Congress, or lectured beyond the local level. Perhaps his "story" was not intended to be "sensational," but the media would make it so. His "first concern is to be a good Catholic, to speak Thomistically (as I do in my book)." He offers no explanation, as he knew the priest understood. "Pray for me, because it is possible that my appearances before the whole country can save lives and restore some respect for ethical values that have been tossed down the drain. This will be my plea, in any case, for it is something I feel profoundly, and it may communicate to the viewer. But I am sick that it had to be me and not some wise man."

What did it mean "to be a good Catholic" and "to speak Thomistically"? First, to be absolutely honest about the experience, including the revelation of his own racism; to clarify that our racist culture has taught us to judge and to condemn black people on the basis of skin color rather than on their qualities as human individuals. Second, to articulate in a rigorously logical manner that racism is irrational, while critiquing the illegal statutes of segregation and the extra-legal forms of discrimination that violated the basic human rights of black people and the ethics of Natural Law. And third, to plea for the resurrection of justice, peace, and Christian charity in concert with the elimination of injustice, violence, and hatred.

In relation to the presentations, he vowed to face criticism "without rebellion, without giving in to temptation to defend myself, to lash out." Griffin believed he was an instrument of communication, but not its meaning; and that what he had written, or what he would say, was only significant in the transforming quality of the message and *not* the messenger. He made no claims for his words or deeds, knowing he was merely the medium. What he had done, or might do, was "deficient," and what he wrote or said, or might write or say, was "unwise." He did not consider himself courageous. To Father Murphy: "They speak of me as a man of courage, but I sit here utterly devoid of courage, numb, waiting for the great axe of hatred to fall."

On March 12, Griffin wrote in the *Journal* that "the news has broken." He had just returned from taping interviews with Paul Coates. Both segments were about to be aired the following week. There were stories on the Associated Press wires, calls from *Time* and *Life* magazines and national television networks. At the center of the vortex, he was back in the solitary studio, "listening to Bach, waiting to be slaughtered, waiting to see how much they will misquote me, heartsick at what must come; though I expected it." He prays that the message would not be distorted. "I pray and offer up all the pain of it to God, and try to act easy around my parents, but I am in mortal fear—the hate merchants, the bigots, the racists have shown me I can expect no more mercy from them as a white man than I could as a Negro. I know I must pass through the Beatitudes—those dreaded ones of being despised, poor, degraded. I pray for charity large enough to encompass the whole thing." But the experience "makes me mute, bludgeons my brain." His "great sadness" was not what they might do to him, but that "our civilization could come to this."

Despite Griffin's belief that the greater evil is what happens to black people every day, he could not deny the fear that in the aftermath of public disclosures his family might be the targets of violent reprisals. "In such a state of dread, one must return to the basic teaching—that not my will but God's be done."

Griffin poured out his concerns in the *Journal.* "The challenge here is to act with sanctity while the public focuses on you; and the only way to act with sanctity is not to attempt it, but to fix all your attention on God. The great 'Yes' must be said again; my own strengths must be abandoned to a point where I even appear a fool in public. If I fail to love them that hate me, then no other victory can compensate for it. I will have lost my chance, fallen short." He did not fall short or appear foolish, but exposure would exact a price and place a burden on his loved ones.

Black Like Me resumes its narrative on March 14. The Coates interviews were aired amid heavy publicity in the Dallas-Fort Worth area newspapers. The first phone call after the telecast at the family cottage caused anxiety. Would it be an abusive call? No, it was from friends L. A. and Penn Jones. There was a discussion, and he realized the Joneses were tying up the line to block abusive calls. After their hour-long call was finished, another ring followed immediately. He picked up the receiver. It was his parents, saying the program had been fine. "How full of dread their voices were, but they sincerely approved of what I had said."

The next day Griffin flew to New York. There was a morning interview with *Time* magazine and an afternoon NBC-TV *Today* appearance with Dave Garroway.[56] He was particularly impressed with Garroway, who told him to be as honest as possible and not to worry about sponsors. "He kept me on camera 20 minutes and he asked pointed questions that did not evade the issue. Before the interview was over, we were both deeply moved. At the end, he asked me about discrimination in the North. I told him I was not competent to answer. I told him that the Southern racist invariably brought up the point that things aren't perfect in the North either—which is no doubt so—as though that fact justified the injustices in the South."

Between events he returned to the hotel room to phone his parents. Lena had received the first threatening call from a woman in Mansfield. The conversation began politely, but soon the woman became abusive and "succeeded in terrorizing my mother by telling her, 'If you could just hear what they're planning to do to him if he ever comes back.'"

He called Elizabeth, asking her to take the children to his parents' home, and to give Penn Jones a call. Jones watched over the family until Jack Griffin returned home. From then on his father kept a loaded shotgun by the front door.

Manhattan was frenetic, exhausting. When Griffin was not doing interviews, he had conferences with the *Sepia* publicist. He got little sleep, smoked incessantly, and checked with the family by phone. During the period of March 15-27, he made a television documentary with Harry Golden, stayed up one night doing a live radio interview with Long John, and did shows on NBC and CBS. The hotel room was populated with media and hangers-on. He was unsure how he was faring, feeling the Golden interview could have been stronger, although it improved as they progressed. The radio show with Long John featured phone calls from listeners but, because he was so exhausted, he was unsure of his responses.

Griffin recognized two glaring oversights in his report. First, he had no real knowledge of conditions in the North; and second, he had not been critical of the churches that practiced segregation in the South. He believed the Catholic bishops in the South would rectify the abuses once they were pointed out. He had been naïve about these expectations, and it was such a sensitive point that he vowed to walk off the set if Mike Wallace asked "one wrong question," or highlighted the issue in a way that might embarrass the Church.[57] He was assured that the newsman would be sympathetic. At the CBS-TV studio Wallace "fumbled uncomfortably

JHG 1961 television interview with Mike Wallace, which Griffin considered to be the strongest and most honest interview in which he participated.

for words," and Griffin "took a liking to him." Hinting that CBS had made a thorough investigation, he was "aghast," because Wallace knew "things I had tried to hide in order to protect the people involved." But Wallace was not specific.

"Look, John—hell, I know you've done nothing but answer questions . . . but will you pull yourself together and really work for me tonight?"

"I'd do that as a matter of conscience anyway."

"You want me to tell you something," Wallace said. "I'm scared to death of you—I mean a man who'd do what you've done—"

"Then you don't know me as well as I thought you did. The truth is I'm scared to death of you."

At that Wallace burst into laughter, insisting there was nothing to fear. That cleared the air, enlivened the mood, and they felt it would go well. The countdown began, red lights blinked on and they launched into a dialogue. "He poured intelligent questions into me and kept his face close, absorbing my attention, encouraging me. It was a super-charged moment. I answered, forgetting everything except him and his questions. Fatigue disappeared. Fascination took over. The excitement sustained us. I realized, when the time was up, that it had gone well. And when we went off the air, Wallace shouted, 'Top notch.' It was an extraordinary experience. Never have I been handled more superbly by an interviewer."

Most of the *Aftermath* entries are terse, while the unpublished passages from Griffin's *Journal* evoke the musings of a penitent. The exceptions to this pattern in the book are the New York scenes, which are vivid and immediate, because he kept a traveling notebook, making notes after each encounter.

Griffin returned on March 28, working three days with a film crew from *Radio-Television Francaise* of Paris, which was not his first appearance on French television. He was fluent in the language and culture of his adopted homeland, and was known to French readers as the best-selling author of *The Devil Rides Outside*.

The *Aftermath* text continues on April 1. News had circulated the globe, and telegrams, letters, and phone calls poured in. To Griffin's relief, most communications were positive, and there had been no further threatening calls from neighbors. He thought the local situation was oddly quiet.

The next morning he was awakened by a call from the *Fort Worth Star-Telegram*, cautiously asking how things were going. Griffin indicated that everything was fine. When the reporter said, "You don't sound too excited," the groggy author began to feel uneasy. Then the reporter revealed that Griffin had been hanged in effigy, and asked for comment. The newspaper had received an anonymous call about the effigy. When the reporter investigated it, the local constable confirmed that a dummy, half black and half white, with a yellow streak painted down its back, had been strung up at the intersection of Main and Broad Street. When asked what he was going to do, Griffin intended to ignore it. Later he drove to the dump to find that the effigy was hitched to a sign that read: $25.00 FINE FOR DUMPING DEAD ANIMALS. His only private response, according to Elizabeth, was "Not a very good likeness."

Nothing was heard from the town residents during that day. Griffin viewed the silence with disappointment, wondering if they condoned the lynching. His parents and Elizabeth's mother begged them to take the children out of town. The evening newspaper carried a six-column banner headline about the effigy, and the family received calls from friends offering sanctuary.

Decherd Turner suggested that Griffin work at the Bridwell Library on the campus of Southern Methodist University in Dallas. He accepted, agreeing to lecture to the SMU student body. The family stayed one week at the Turners' home in Dallas, and his parents stayed with friends outside Mansfield. On April 7, the *Star-Telegram* ran an accurate follow-up on the effigy hanging, also reporting that a cross had been burned on the lawn of the Negro church just down the lane from the Griffin cottage. The cross burning incensed him infinitely more than the effigy.

The family returned to Mansfield on April 11, deciding to hide no longer. A huge stack of mail awaited them, all from out of town, most of it favorable. Griffin's parents returned and received several phone calls threatening their son's life. "They have terrified my mother," he wrote to Father Murphy on April 12, "and the worst of it—to see those I love so forlorn before the cries for my blood."

There is another gap between April 12 and June 18, when Griffin embarked on a lecture tour for the Department of Defense, filing a report similar to those submitted to Congress and the Department of Justice.

The first installment of "Journey Into Shame" hit the newsstands nationally on April 17. Local calls increased and mail poured in. Elizabeth kept up with the influx. Griffin returned from the lecture circuit in early May, recording reactions in *The Petal Paper*. "In the South, teachers, school principals and other black people have described their indignities when they tried to register for voting; and others tell of threats, reprisals and the intimidating techniques brought against them," while at the same time in the nation's capital, "the Southern senators lied themselves bald, saying the Negroes in their states are not discriminated against."

On May 4 Griffin read that the Central Texas Division of the Citizens Councils for Segregation had met in Dallas, asking citizens to boycott businesses that served black people. "One wonders if these men are really of such retrograde minds that they believe this. Their attitude of white supremacy, suppression of the Negro, and deprivation of rights has given more 'aid and comfort to our communist enemies' than any single propaganda factor," he writes in the J*ournal*. "This is the Communist's most cherished line of attack—that in America a large group of citizens are not free to exercise their rights. They use this fact consistently to show the weakness of our system—and it is an immensely effective weapon against us, because it is true thanks to the racists. What can we conclude except that the racists' concern about our playing into the Communist's hands is utterly spurious and that the racists put the national interest far below personal and regional interests. Either they are invincibly ignorant, or they are the most un-American group we have."

Griffin returned to the lecture tour, speaking at colleges and universities, and giving radio and TV interviews. According to James C. Evans, who coordinated the tours, he was the most significant voice in race relations. Evans asked him "to go on trying to create a conscience and an understanding" in the white community. Griffin continued, even when there were diabetic flare-ups.

On May 20 he took the opportunity during a period of good health to catch up on correspondence. He thanked Decherd Turner for the chance to speak at SMU and to meet "people of that caliber." He writes to Father Murphy that "these are the busiest days I've ever known—lecture four and five days a week, make tapes, films." As usual, he opened up to Father Murphy. "I live close to the sacraments, but am not man enough to take all this. This work shows too much inhumanity, too much sadism, too much of man committing spiritual suicide." He felt blessed that he could "return home to the arms of my wife and children, completely devastated, wanting to flee the whole business." He had the support of friends, like the Joneses and the Turners. "Decherd remains a life-saver. What a wise man he is."

While experiencing hatred from local racists, Griffin was moved by the decency of white communities around the country where he lectured. "Forgive the complaining, I am simply unable to stand this look at hell, this mammoth sin against the spirit." That night he wrote to Sallie and Hannah Gillespie in Taos, beginning rather than ending with an implied apology. "It has been so long, but our life is one of extremes, always busy." He wrote of Mansfield where "we are despised and every dirty harassment they can think of is being brought to bear against us. The ignorance of these people who are ruining themselves and a great segment of our white children—the unmasked evil of their intentions and desires has turned my heart sick for them."

Meanwhile Griffin was making plans for a permanent escape. “Mother and Dad are selling out here and going with us to Mexico. It is the only solution—the only way to get sufficient peace to go back to my regular work.” They intended to move to a village near the city of Morelia in the State of Michoacán, where brother Edgar owned a house that needed overseeing. His lecture tour concluded in early June. By June 10, they had not departed due to the ongoing sale of his parents' property, including the old barn that had been Griffin's studio since 1947.

June 16 marked Griffin's fortieth birthday. “Delicious moment when I woke up yesterday, went and got coffee and then heard from the other room my children's singing of ‘Happy Birthday.’” But he decided there was too much work to take the day off and drove to the studio. When he returned that evening there were gifts, and Elizabeth had baked a chocolate cake. Since he had given himself a new Leica camera, he spent the evening taking photographs.

The *Aftermath* continues the narrative, after a nine-week hiatus, on June 19, which was Emancipation Day and Father's Day. Griffin counts six thousand letters from whites in the Deep South with only nine abusive ones, concluding that the “average Southern white” was frightened more by his white neighbors than by black people. There was a letter from Curtis Bok, Supreme Court Justice of Pennsylvania, enclosing a speech the judge made at the Radcliffe College Commencement of 1960. Griffin thought the speech “put it clearly,” in his “Angry Old Man” tone (quoted at length in the book). The coverage stops until August 14, eight weeks later.

But on the night of June 19, Griffin typed in the *Journal*. “The threat is there, just beneath the surface of existence, almost unconscious in my awareness, but always there—always there in the possibility that they could come to this studio, prowling through the woods, and see the light at my open windows. This strange awareness of my not belonging here haunts me, keeps my nerves on edge, keeps me heartsick.” He contemplated Emancipation Day, visualizing black people “dressed in their best, attending their churches for all day sessions, celebrating their freedom from slavery, all in feeling the inside thing, knowing that they are not free after all, that they are celebrating a myth.”

Griffin focused on the threats communicated in various indirect ways would be carried out. Isolated in the country, out of earshot of neighbors.

"Is tonight the night they have decided on? Is it tonight when they come to show the rest of the world what they do to men who dare question the mob's prejudices, who suggest we are no longer Americans so long as we force a segment of our citizens to remain on the junkpile? Is tonight the night the shotgun blasts through the window? Is tonight the night they have marked on the calendar to drag me out and castrate me as they have promised?" He felt like "a perfect target," illuminated in a bright barn window, but they did not appear that night.

He prepared to move his young family and elderly parents to avoid the racist threats. "We prepare to leave for Mexico, after 13 years here in this barn studio, and I try to sort my books—books gathered over the past 20 years of my life. Strange to go back over them, to dig them out and decide what to give, what to sell, what to keep." Examining books packed away since 1949, he made his choices. Griffin's entry floated to other worlds and times.

> Things forgotten, things not seen in years or, again, many that I got while I was blind and never saw until I went through storage boxes today. They range from magnificent volumes, like the *Paléographie Musicale* from Solesmes, to our little two franc school volumes of Molière and Hugo.[58] All represent periods of momentary enthusiasm that flared and then cooled to affection that remains to this day. Each was once held between my hands with that excitement nothing else can quite parallel.
>
> I find an old and worn copy of another French book, and it brings back the incidents long dead in my memory—the cluttered second-hand bookshop near the Cathedral of Tours. The purchase for little or nothing, the excitement then of hurrying to my room, up darkened steps, and finally sitting in a chair near the dormer windows and opening the world. . . . The experience of taking out and examining these beautiful things becomes almost unbearable—the evocations are fresh, stripped to their essences, and the essences were good, indeed terribly good for all of it was discovery, marvel, delight.

While the Gestapo had driven Griffin out of France in 1939, he was being forced from Mansfield by local racists. The family would leave before, while he stayed on to finish chores. Departure was bittersweet, and no more so than on this day, as he reminisced about other places he had been forced to abandon. That night he writes to Jacques Maritain, in response to a disturbing letter about his wife's illness. "Late at night—the fan fights the tremendously heavy heat and puts a hum into the Bach. I try to answer Jacques's letter, so full of pain."

> Above all, know that you are not alone, that everywhere in the world you are loved, not only because you are Jacques and Raïssa Maritain, the philosopher and poet, but because you are you. It's strange, simple, a peasant blushes in his clumsiness while trying to write a 'love letter' to the great poet-philosopher and the great philosopher-poet.
>
> How to say thank-you to two people who have been the greatest formative influence since your adolescence? How many others are spiritually your children in this sense? Many more than you imagine. How many others, ordinary types like myself, have taken fire thanks to you, and have worked in the "Thomist" liberation you have procured for them? I know authentic ones, who have taken this lamp, lighted by you, and have gone into the shadows to illuminate the obscure corners of the world.

Griffin wrote Father Murphy to let him know of Maritain's "very distressing" letter. The priest had known the Maritains since 1942, when Jacques was awarded the Christian Culture Award, the series Father Murphy had initiated in 1941. It was the last letter he would write from the barn studio.

> Jacques speaks of Raïssa's falling ill in Paris; better now but with a long and dolorous convalescence ahead of her. He has spoken repeatedly of the hell of his life since Vera's death [Raïssa's sister], without specifying. Lord, when you think of what this man has given the world; what some poor beggar like myself owes him in formation, and then to be impotent to do anything to make things easier for them.

On August 9, Griffin made his final *Journal* entry from the studio. The first half is a jubilant description of a sudden rainstorm "after weeks of drought, all the more wondrous because nothing led us to expect it." But after the mail arrived, nerves once again were frayed. "Dad brought the mail, with that long-suffering expression on his face, of pain and anguish; another no-return-address letter, another threat, another promise. I tore it open and read it. The writer tells me 'they' have definitely set the date for August 15. 'So fuck your wife good, you half-nigger bastard. After August 15 you won't have balls or peter. Your time is up. You are marked.'"

He stuffed the letter in a pocket and showed it to no one. But his father was able to read the postcard that also arrived. Scrawled in pencil was the simple message: "August 15 is the date." Griffin's mother walked into the room and responded to "the mournful, the terrible glance" of her husband's face. Even without having read it, she blurted out, "Well, let's go now. Let's pack up and drive away."

Six days later, on August 13, Lena and Jack Griffin left Mansfield and drove to Taos, spending a few days with Sally and Hannah Gillespie. From there they would travel on to Mexico to meet their son's family. Elizabeth and the children flew to Mexico City on August 15. They were met there by Robert Ellis and wife, Rosa, a native of Mexico. After more than three hours in customs, a kindly clerk intervened, allowing the Ellises (who were bilingual) to enter the glassed-encased area. Everything was settled quickly and the weary Texas family was waved through. Robert Ellis drove the forty-five miles to the home of Rosa's family in Toluca, where they met Erendira, the couple's two-year-old daughter, for the first time.

Griffin stayed on alone in Mansfield through August 15, to challenge the racists' deadline, but no violence occurred. He sold the last of his parents' furniture and traded his English Ford for a 1960 Corvair, figuring since Chevrolet had plants in Mexico, parts for it would be available. It was a mistaken assumption.

Early on the morning of August 18, Griffin loaded the car with everything he could squeeze in. Elizabeth had taken six large suitcases containing their clothes. He loaded photography equipment, a record player and boxes of albums, a recorder and tapes, and enough cookware, dishes, and utensils to begin a new life. It was their intention to relocate permanently in Santa María del Guido, a little village on a mountainside overlooking Morelia. The plan was to remodel an old hacienda owned by brother Edgar, and to send the children to a French lycée in Morelia. Meanwhile the car was packed to capacity, with only a tunnel between the rear-view mirror and the back windshield and, with a touch of unplanned humor, an ironing board thrust nearly halfway out the passenger window.

He described his departure after he had arrived in Mexico. "I began again to keep this *Journal* after a long silence. I, who wanted so much to leave the horrors of this past experience, to come to Mexico, left one morning with the car loaded. Instead of relief and joy, I experienced an immense, almost pathological sadness. I drove out of Mansfield where I have lived 13 years and no one said good-bye or good luck. Most were invisible, but those on the streets simply stared after me, convinced I have no doubt that they had driven the bastard away."

Griffin drove southwest across the Staked Plains region of Texas, which he had written about in *Land of the High Sky* a few years before. "A tremendous heaviness filled me and I could not shake it." He stayed in an El Paso motel, after a long, hot day and 450 miles. The next morning he drove to a border check, passed through customs, and crossed the bridge over the Rio Grande into Mexico. Late that night he drove around the sprawling metropolis of Mexico City, continuing west to Toluca.

He arrived at the home of Rosa's family at four in the morning on August 20. The house was dark and everyone was asleep. Robert Ellis responded quickly to the knock at the door. The two friends greeted each other as "*compadre*," in the traditional manner they had adopted in the early 1950s. Early the next morning both families set out in a car caravan across the mountains west toward Michoácan. After a grinding eight-hour day through two hundred miles of winding roads, they arrived in Morelia, taking rooms in a downtown hotel.

Within a few days they rented a furnished apartment in the mountain village above the valley surrounding Morelia. Santa María del Guido would be their home in Mexico, and once they were settled, the Ellises returned to Valle de Bravo.

From August through September, the Griffins lived in an apartment across the street from the Villa Montana Restaurant. Early in their stay, they became acquainted with the owner of the restaurant, Ramón Coté, and the delicious traditional cuisine he offered. They cooked in the apartment kitchen, shopped at the local market, learned the terrain of the little village, and began speaking Spanish.

Exile in Mexico

On the evening of October 2, 1960, as Griffin was playing a Mozart record, he heard a different Mozart piece through the thin wall separating the apartment from next door. He invited the neighbors over, astonished to discover that Luis Berbér, conductor of *Los Niños Cantores de Morelia* ("The Singing Boys of Mexico"), and his wife, Wilenne, a native of Fort Worth, were living next door.[59]

A few days later, the Griffins met Americans Barbara and Don Shoemaker, who owned a furniture shop in the village. Through the Shoemakers and Berbérs, the new family became known and trusted in the village. Meanwhile Griffin's parents had arrived from New Mexico, immediately renting the guesthouse at the Denton Estate, while the Griffin family moved into the main house.

"All of us are well," Griffin writes in the *Journal*; "we live in the Denton home, with high stone walls around a large grounds filled with flowers—a splendid and cheerful home to occupy while we wait for Edgar's house to be finished. I work in the guest room, separated from the main house by a patio. It is a typical native room with red brick floors, white adobe walls, a corner fireplace, windows looking out to the mountains. The room has a private bath which I have turned into a darkroom. I have lost myself in film work." He settled into a productive cycle of writing, photography, and research at the Denton house, realizing the frustrations of the Mansfield aftermath and the dislocation from moving had left him in a state of depression. "I knew I was reacting dangerously and sought to counter it, but the effects went too deep and it has taken me almost two months to regain sufficient voice to put anything down on paper."

Now that he felt secure in the new studio and darkroom, the emotional wounds had healed, and he gained a certain aesthetic distance from the experiment. His task became a matter of reshaping the story from the *Sepia* series into the book that would become *Black Like Me*. Before writing again, he had immersed himself in every aspect of photography, aiming for a higher level of technical control. "Thank God, there was this absorption in something new."

The Mexico period marks Griffin's breakthrough in photography, initiating a deeper understanding of the creative harmony achievable in combining photography with writing. He developed this fresh vision during the entire exile, from September 1960 to May 1961. He outlines his goal in the *Journal*.

> The desire to do my own photography, and in some way to combine it with my writing, would not leave me. I wanted to see if my eye could capture the particular modality that had haunted me in my loss of sight, and again in my recovery of sight: To catch humanity not in its drama so much as its truth, its intelligence.

When Griffin was blind he could peer into the heart of a person, hearing them in the naked tone of their unguarded voices. He could "see without partiality" a truth the sighted overlooked. In "Notes on Photography," a typescript composed at the Denton house, he searched for a way to clarify what might obscure his eye to what the lens revealed, to see what was really there, rather than being trapped in the unconscious phenomenon of "selective inattention." He believed that "the personal vision of the photographer can and does make the originality of his work."

> If his vision is purely visual, then he can only produce images. If his vision is philosophical, then the work will take on a density of concept that opens the door to originality even in the most banal shots.
>
> He must develop taste—so that what he selects (from all the possible elements to photograph in a subject) creates the illusion of reality rather than merely the greater clutter that is always involved in reality. He must go through great complexity, for every image, every communication is immensely complex, in order to arrive at simplicity—in order to make his vision speak his own language.

Griffin's approach to perceiving what is there, instead of substituting a stereotype or projecting subjectivity upon the subject, was evolving as "something more than the 'know your subject' conventionality."

> I looked upon my neighbors, the Tarascans, and sought those elements in their culture that were universal to all men, and then sought those elements that were special to their ancient and beautiful culture: qualities of tenderness and dignity toward children; extreme fidelity to friendship; generosity and simplicity. And in the framework of the universal, to capture something of these other individualizing elements.

He described the Tarascans as "aristocratic, beautiful, and aloof," discovering universality in their native rituals, a curiously rich mixture of indigenous and Catholic influences. He traveled to the island of Janitzio to photograph the Day of the Dead in November of 1960. Later he witnessed Holy Week in Tzintzuntzan. Besides these trips, he practiced with cameras, lenses, the Leitz enlarger, and chemicals. He walked the countryside to study light meter readings in relation to film-speed and exposures, making a dedicated effort to meet the Tarascans, so they would become comfortable with an uncased camera at his side. "The Tarascans, however, until one knows them, are extremely reluctant to be photographed."

The culture and landscape "offered endless wealth to the photographer in material." Yet the essential question remained: How to select the discreet image from the obvious possibilities? Griffin did "not shoot promiscuously," since overcoming his early inclination to shoot too much film. He searched out what was there, remained patient, and waited. Eventually those images and words were revisited by a different, evolving perspective. He approached photography as he had writing, going his own way, rarely influenced by other photographers. It was a matter of experimentation to pursue the mysterious, relating the artistic challenges of photography to what he had learned from writing.

In "Notes on Photography," he points out: "If I sought light, composition, expression—nevertheless I was aiming at something else, something the novelist must deal with—the expression of the basically inexpressible. In other words, a combination of elements that would produce the resonances in the viewer that I wanted him to have; works that would do something to the viewer rather than merely please the eye."[60]

His challenge involved aesthetics, ethics, and metaphysics, once dedicated practice had brought technical skills to a natural fluency.

> I realized that the photographer often errs when he photographs a thing that has great subjective importance, thinking it will strike the viewer with the same overtones. The point of challenge is to analyze this, and to set about deliberately, with technique and imagination, to create the artifact that would involve the viewer. This is also the novelist's constant challenge; it is the reason why the definition of art as "selectivity" is such a valid one.

Griffin meant selecting and reshaping reality into essential artifacts born of images or words—the opposite of "selective inattention" or lack of awareness or attempting to deform essences to maintain a prejudice. In the case of the photographer, "it must express what he wants to express, it must be deliberate and he must choose the means of making it so."

> The photographer must master the art of developing and printing, which are highly individual techniques that no one else can do for him, in order to bring out exactly his vision. He must feel, after the mastery of technique is out of the way, a continuously greater freedom to stretch his medium and his belief in its capabilities.

Griffin's vision of combining photography and writing came into sharp focus when he witnessed the Day of the Dead ritual in early November of 1960. On November 1, he recorded the experience in the *Journal.*

> I have returned this morning from the Island of Janitzio, a small, legend-rich Tarascan island that rises up out of Lake Patzcuaro. There, All Soul's Day is celebrated by a night-watch at the cemetery, in the belief that the dead return to visit their living—a mixture of pagan and Catholic ritual, dating from some aboriginal past and somehow intermingled with the Catholic faith. It is not a sad occasion, but a quiet one, a tender one to those who believe that their dead return to visit with them—and all more or less hold this belief.

This ritual challenged his technical skills as a photographer. The result was a folio of images arranged on matte boards (entitled *Return of the Spirit*), as well as an essay on the encounter ("The Watch of the Dead").[61] In the images from Janitzio and the essay about attending the ritual, we have a natural integration of senses in a silent hush of absorption. The images are simple, lucid, reverent. They resonate without shouting. The tone of the essay matches the awe of the visual experience, a brief narrative that does not call attention to its own voice.

Griffin had to obtain official clearance to photograph the ritual, and was informed that the request would only be considered if he met the strict prohibition on the use of flash equipment. He assured them he would photograph discreetly, without supplementary lighting. The islanders would have the final say, because they had grown weary of tourists with flash cameras, liquor, and poor manners. Arriving at the docks, he saw boatloads of visitors heading toward the island, doubting he would be allowed to go. But the orders against visitors had been rescinded. "Local police let us pass, one by one after making certain we did not carry flash equipment or liquor and with a polite admonition that we make ourselves no more obnoxious than necessary." He climbed the "steep cobblestone street toward the church halfway up the hill in the last dim light of dusk," pushing open the heavy doors of the church. Everything was set out to be blessed (long-burning candles, bouquets of flowers, baked bread) for the spirit of the beloved. "Shawled women and children and hatless men knelt, dark masses in the flickering light, absorbing the fresh odor of incense."

Griffin's portrait of women and children lit by candlelight at the "Day of the Dead" in Mexico, 1960. His essay and photos of the annual ritual were published in *Encounters with the Other* (Latitudes, 1997).

Griffin was advised to eat heartily before going to the site. After eating fish, he walked up the side of the mountain to the *panteón*—"a flat tabletop of perhaps two acres bounded on one side by the sheer rise of a cliff and on the other by a low wall over which we looked down on the lake below." He entered through "a high stone arch topped by a cross" that he photographed. There were no grave markers or burial mounds. Candles by the thousands and several wood fires illuminated the cliff. Parents awaiting the spirits of their children spread out toys and mangoes on colorful blankets. He moved quietly, being "another mere shadow in the candlelit night," and was not rebuffed. "The Tarascans, a people of the greatest natural dignity and beauty, asked only that we not openly intrude."

Suddenly there was a garish flash of a camera. A wave of murmuring protest followed as the man set off another flashbulb. The man was escorted away, and Griffin slipped the camera back in its case. He took no pictures for an hour, until the mood became less strained. By ten o'clock the night turned colder. He sat on the ground near an elderly woman, her austere face highlighted by the tall candles. "Do you want to photograph me?" she asked in Spanish. He noticed the magical flow on her face and clicked three frames.

By midnight most of the visitors were driven away by the increasing cold. Griffin's hands became so numb he was barely able to use the camera. Small children were wrapped in blankets and moved near the small fires. Most of them slept, but those who remained awake did not utter a complaint. At two that morning, "the quiet murmur of conversations hushed as a woman's sobbing shocked the atmosphere," but she went quickly silent. Just before dawn the priest arrived to celebrate Mass. After Mass the silent islanders disappeared from the *panteón*.

In a letter to Father Stanley Murphy (November 7, 1960), Griffin said that he had completed research on racism and the Catholic Church.

> It took a good deal of research, and the material is so vast I could not begin to cover it properly in 5000 words. At least it made me proud of the Church if ashamed of many of our fellow Catholics who, in their desire to possess both God *and* their prejudices, reek of the child in tantrum. Yet how nice it is to write from such a place. The great silence, the immense views on a sunlit day—the noises of my children in other rooms, my feeling of pride as I went back into the

> history of the Church and saw how uncompromisingly and courageously She has always pronounced herself in these matters of racism.
>
> Most of all, the sense of immense privilege that this might be the means of clarifying someone's doubts—of encouraging one poor soul to see through the fog of our imperfections as Catholics and blunderers to the true value of the Faith, and perhaps to go that way himself and find there what we know is there.
>
> How many have we defrauded with the Faith through our obtuseness?

A week later Griffin received an Aerogramme from Father Murphy, breaking the sad news that Raïssa Maritain had died on November 4. Immediately he wrote a letter to Jacques Maritain in France.

During the last week of November, Griffin worked nightly in the darkroom. By December he had made two hundred prints as a result of a marathon, including many 8x10 and 11x14 enlargements. Days were spent overseeing the remodeling of Edgar's house, which would become their Santa María Hacienda by December 23.[62] All was "glorious" until an accident on December 28 altered the mood and turned their attention to the youngest child.

> Gregory got kicked in the head by a horse when he tried to pet the animal's hind legs. They brought him in unconscious and so covered with blood he was unrecognizable. A skull fracture—"an insignificant fracture," according to the doctor as he put in ten stitches—was all the damage, thank God. But do you know that within one minute, every inhabitant of the village was standing at our front door, not making a sound. I was terrified about Gregory, fearing he was dead, but so moved by this demonstration of sympathy I could scarcely bear it. We got him to the hospital and every day while he was there, people anonymously left tortillas, tacos, fruits and cooked dishes at our door. We were fed by the village, never knowing who supplied these things.

Gregory was home on the last day of the year, and everyone was "greatly happy to have him back, though banged up a bit; and the whole house—the weather, the surroundings celebrate." Griffin sat in the courtyard and pronounced it "the most cheerful courtyard in all of Mexico." He played Mozart concerti on the phonograph, listening as the music filled "the air and beyond our walls, the church bells clang while behind us the nuns' hens cackle their delight."

On January 4, 1961, Griffin left their newfound paradise to fly to New York, doing two radio programs and a TV talk show. He returned on January 7, to resume his description in the *Journal*. "This morning, again in the patio being baked by a mild sun, surrounded by the music of Schumann and the twitterings of thousands of birds in the trees beyond the courtyard wall." At that point daughter Susan fetched a tangerine that was "vine-ripe and unbelievably sweet."

The danger for Gregory had passed, and the stitches were removed. He received special treatment from the village children. The children's chatter was carried on in English, Spanish, and Tarascan, and villagers welcomed their new neighbors. When Elizabeth went shopping in Morelia, she took neighbors along. "There are only two cars in the village, but they never impose for rides—they would not think of it except in an emergency. The days pass, too busily, and I no longer find the time to write in the *Journal*, and it is a shame, too, because the inclination is constant to put down the life we lead here."

By mid-February they had to renew their six-month visas. The next week they packed winter clothes and headed north.

Back in their cottage west of Mansfield, Griffin began to catch up on stateside business, as the family settled in for what was intended to be a brief hiatus. But during the first week of March, Elizabeth went to bed with the flu. She had not been enthusiastic about returning home, and her exhaustion reflected life in a racist atmosphere. Griffin was "filled with deep longing to go back to the mountains, to the peace of beauty of the Tarascan Sierras."

Griffin wrote of intense feelings in the *Journal* on March 11.

> Why? Because in that "underdeveloped" land there is kindness, courtesy. Why? Because here I am forever made to witness the lowness of men who hate; and because I am not man enough myself to look upon it with sustained pity. No, anger takes me—and the anger is deeper than myself, deeper than anything to do with me, deeper than self-defense. It is anger at the way things are; at the way men can look and *not see* what goes on. It is anger—or more exactly black melancholy—that lingers on in me, while the rest of the race shouts its confidence and joy over a better future.

His "black melancholy" was that of "a man who loves his country and is bitterly deceived by the silence of decency and the loudness of indecency." His only relief from it was to be with family or "to recreate the faces of humanity, the kind faces, the beautiful faces—my photos go entirely in that direction." Writing gave no solace. "My typewriter is silenced, because what I have to say now is neither loving nor beautiful—it is not art, but documentary; and I have not the courage to pour out great efforts for the documentation of men's stupidity."

On April 2, 1961, Griffin departed alone by car, arriving in Santa María on the night of April 4. His attention was refocused on attending the annual passion of Christ in Tzintzuntzan (*place of the hummingbirds*). As the ancient capitol of the Tarascan empire, one of the four cardinal points of Michoacán, it had been a metropolis of 100,000 people at its zenith. When Griffin reached it, he found a small, quiet village that was still a sacred city to the Tarascans.

Griffin arrived on Holy Thursday, April 6. He met the last monastic resident at the sixteenth-century Franciscan Monastery of Solitude, Padre Ernesto Tovar, who gave him background information. As the old priest spoke, Griffin photographed him. The role of Christ in the pageant was voluntary, and each year a young man offered to suffer the ordeal, including all of the physical agonies except the actual crucifixion. At that point, the young man representing Christ is taken for medical treatment, while a wooden *Cristo* with movable arms and legs gets nailed to the cross.

Griffin wandered through the second floor, his steps turning up low plumes of dust. In "Passion at Tzintzuntzan" he described the tranquil scene.[63]

> Odors of stone and age surrounded me. Ghosts of the past hovered over the ruin, telling me that this was once a center of Franciscan learning where friars copied manuscript books on mathematics, philosophy and theology; where they painted frescoes on the courtyard wall depicting the Sacraments. Drawn to these ghosts, I felt glaringly out of place and time as I opened my case of splendid cameras with their precision optics, set up tripod, and photographed the peeling frescoes.
>
> It was soon done, but I could not leave. I turned at the stairway and walked back down one of the corridors to the last cell on the end. I seated myself on a stone niche carved as a kind of chair against the

> wall and looked out the hole that had once been a window. Mountain peaks rose in the background. In the foreground below, children played beneath tall jacarandas that were covered with blue blossoms. I sensed some strangeness. Something was not natural in the sights and sounds. It came clear. The children made no sound. Nothing made any sound. Birds were hushed. Except for breeze-stirred leaves, silence brooded over the land. Christ was away, beyond sight and sound, on the Mount of Olives.

Below the window, guards in white "with faceless blood-red hoods" rode on horseback in search of Christ. The muffled hoof steps, "like the sounds of heartbeats, deepened silence rather than broke it." In the distance he heard an occasional sound, a musical motif to silence, "an oboe-like Tarascan shepherd horn sounded its plaintive call, flooding the sunlit countryside with melancholy."

This was not the "black melancholy" he felt in Texas, but it was tinged with terror. "The genius of the terror sprang from the silence, the strange shepherd call in the distance, the growing awareness that Christ, invisible to us, was being searched down." Griffin sat on the church terrace to reload the cameras, spotting the characters of Barabbas and Judas across the compound. Both wore "ghastly pink masks" as they chased the children into the terrace. Suddenly Griffin was surrounded by the children, while the two "villains" moved toward them. Barabbas rattled chains and asked for money. Griffin looked to the children for hint of what should be done. Barabbas pushed him to the ground, trying to force him to drink tequila. After a struggle, Griffin pushed him away, handing over to him a five peso note. Judas quickly snatched it, and both thieves skipped away. The children's reproaches made it clear that he had made a poor decision by contributing his part of the thirty pieces of silver. He wanted to exonerate himself, rushing after the thieves. He coaxed the thieves into putting the money into the church's alms box, correcting his error, and the children no longer feared the American with the camera equipment.

Despite knowing they were actors, he began to feel the hypnotic effect of the ritual. "We were so involved that I found it difficult to realize that this was essentially an *ad libitum* play. I felt split, part realizing this was the 20th century, part eerily involved in the event 2000 years ago," accounting for the different tones and varied pacing. Alternately, he was an observing camera eye and a participant in the ritual. Conscious planning was swiftly reduced to reflexive action. This Passion was no polite catharsis or Biblical morality play.

On Good Friday morning (April 7), Griffin was served a generous breakfast. He watched barefoot Tarascan girls walk past, wondering how it might have been when this village of five hundred had been the capital of the empire. He went to the compound where the crowd had gathered. Near the cell of the imprisoned Christ, he encountered two guards, who raised their spears as he lifted his camera. He explained that he had permission, but there was no response from beneath the red hoods. When he raised the camera again, a spear knocked the lens cap aside. Trying a third time, he was struck on the side of the head. Instinctively, he reached for a spear, jerking it so violently that the guard fell to the ground. He tossed the spear aside and photographed the other guard. The crowd voiced support. But he realized they lived their roles, and he felt sympathy for the fallen guard. "I was overwhelmed with my own sense of guilt at altering historical truth in this manner. Two thousand years ago no photographer had thus embarrassed Christ's guards. My action distorted the truth of the day, changed it from what it should have been."

Suddenly the crowd's attention was drawn to a loud voice, ordering the Christ to be brought forth. It was a centurion on horseback, approaching with four guards. The haggard Christ was dragged from the cell and shoved across the compound, where he was stripped and flogged. Without a word, he endured the relentless whipping until his bare back was covered in blood. Then the scene of Pilate washing his hands was reenacted, as Christ was clothed in purple. A heavy wooden cross was loaded onto the young Tarsascan's shoulders, and he was pushed toward Calvary. Griffin moved ahead of the procession to be in position to photograph Christ's approach, stepping into the dusty path and moving away as he shot film.

Barabbas, dancing gleefully ahead of the dragging cross, swung heavy chains against Griffin's legs, knocking him off-balance. "I concentrated away from the drubbing and photographed the Christ, his face hazed with pain in strange repose. I photographed the crowd of men and women, their eyes forlorn with tenderness and grief. Again, I burned with the embarrassment of my intrusion. Cameras did not belong in the Passion." The Christ fell forward in the red dust. Again Griffin hurried to help, but felt a spear jabbing his torso. "Intense silence surrounded all of this activity, accompanied by savage thuds as the guards beat Christ until he staggered to his feet." Griffin knelt in the path, while Barabbas' chains pounded his back. Then he lost balance, falling forward as the Christ approached. "His eyes were dazed. I froze, fearing he would stumble over me. I rolled on my back and reversed position, trying to scoot out of his way. As his foot touched mine, he stopped. His glassy eyes cleared. He looked down on me patiently, intelligently, and with an expression of such sorrowful love that I felt devastated. I reminded myself that this was not Christ, but a Tarascan youth playing the role. It did no good. The illusion was too powerful." He was transfixed for that instant in the presence of Christ. Stunned by the powerful illusion, he was face to face with the Christ's expression, radiating pure compassion. Swept up, he was a penitent drawn inexorably along the path of tragedy, while also the outsider intruding on the sacred procession with a camera.

The stark contrast between "Passion at Tzintzuntzan" and "The Watch of the Dead" cannot be exaggerated. At the "Watch" Griffin attempted to disappear into the darkness, careful not to intrude on the dignified rhythms of the ritual. During the "Passion" he blundered at crucial times. When encountering the Christ, he "realized that my instincts as a photographer were functioning, that I was working the camera, photographing first his face and then his blood-stained feet."

After that, Griffin continued photographing from a respectful distance, filming the "almost nonchalant cruelty" toward the stumbling Christ; a piglet crossed in front, and a moment later, a hen pecked the dried blood on the Tarascan's feet.

Christ's walk to Calvary continued until the Tarascan was carried through a curtained doorway of the church. He was replaced by the wooden *Cristo*, which was nailed to the cross. An elderly man went into the sanctuary to kneel at the foot of the cross, staring "at the figure, and with his arms outstretched in a gesture of abandon, began to intone a Tarascan chant, slow and flowing as an ocean wave." The crowd went to its knees, joining in the dirge, which "resounded through the countryside." Griffin left the church through a side door, walking across the empty compound. On the way to the village, he met a messenger, who announced that the young Tarascan Christ would live. Beyond the chanting, he heard the last mournful sounding of the shepherd's horn, signaling that the Passion was over.

During the next week Griffin immersed all energy in darkroom work. He was excited by the images emerging from twenty rolls of film. Sallie and Hannah Gillespie arrived for a visit on April 15. "How good it is to have them here, not only to see them again, but to dissipate the almost unbearable loneliness of the place since the family is not here. Without them I begin to be paralyzed by the consuming depression of not hearing their voices, seeing them, holding them."

The next night he took the Gillespies to hear *Los Niños Cantores* perform under the baton of Luis Berbér. "It undid us all," hearing them sing works by Palestrina, Pergolesi, Orff, and Stravinsky. "They sang spectacularly—flawless counterpoint, difficult dissonant counterpoint, with such a flair and precision and attack and tonal parity that it tied us up in knots and left us exhausted."

But what he heard later on the radio would become the ultimate dissonance to his brief paradisical life at the Santa María hacienda. There were various reports from Russian, Cuban, and American sources about the Bay of Pigs invasion—propaganda from the communists and denials from the United States. The effect would impact Americans living in Mexico. The next afternoon Luis Berbér brought bad news. An organized group of university students had invaded the Mexican-North American Cultural Institute in Morelia that morning. "They broke into the Institute, hauled everything into the street and set a great bonfire," reported Luis.

The *Journal* entry of April 18 read: "We pieced together the sequence of events. As planned, the students met ostensibly to protest US intervention in Cuba. Faculty from the University of St. Nicholas harangued the students into ferment against US citizens in Mexico. The Governor's secretary met with the communist student leaders. Director Eugene Kenny, his wife, and friends were in the Institute."

Demonstrators smashed through the doors and vandalized the Institute. The police did nothing, but everyone escaped unharmed. Griffin phoned Americans to brief them on the danger and to invite all to a strategy meeting inside the formidable walls of the Denton Estate. At five, Berbér returned from Morelia: "Get your parents quickly. The mob is coming to burn the hill." Griffin ran to the nearby seminary to use the only phone in the village, except for that of José Tocaven, editor of *La Voz de Michoacán*, the state's largest newspaper, which was propagandizing against Americans.

Griffin registered a protest with the editor.

"Why should I do anything to help you," Tocaven said, "when at this moment Americans are murdering our Cuban brothers in the streets of Havana?"

Griffin replied, "The Santa María Tarascans are our friends. They will kill any student who comes up this hill. Such deaths will be your responsibility, since you have agitated against us. Also, this will probably so enrage the Tarascans that they'll come here and kill you." That got Tocaven's attention.

A young priest telephoned the federal office in Morelia, asking for troops. The request went quickly through the chain of command. An officer called back to say the mob had swelled to several thousand. The young priest hung up, saying, "Troops are on their way, but we do not know if they will get here in time. You are in grave danger. Take the women and children at once to the Monastery on the mountain. If the mob gets this far, we'll see they get no further."

"How can you be sure?" Griffin asked the priest.

"We have three hundred seminarians," the priest said, smiling. "All are in superb physical condition. They will block the road."

Griffin went to his car, spotting some of the seminarians at the gate. They were in their best cassocks, smiling, looking eager for the clash. He returned to the hotel to gather the Americans to safety at the monastery. On the return trip, they encountered the young priest. He spoke to Griffin in French, not wanting to frighten the others. "The troops are at the bottom of the hill. The crowd will be intercepted." The mob was only five minutes away from a possible clash with the troops. The priest wanted to know if the Shoemakers were back from America.

"No, Father. But I warned the men to lock up and stay there all night."

"Good. It seems the crowd has instructions to burn them out."

"Why?" Griffin asked.

"They are important people in the village. Ruining them would put many out of work and make it easier for the communists to move in."

With his parents and the Gillespie sisters, Griffin led a caravan of Americans up the mountain to the monastery, where they were welcomed by the monks. Griffin commented in the *Journal* that the faces of the Americans "were calm in the dim light, but drawn with strain. Most were middle-aged, had never been subjected to this sort of crisis, and were bewildered to find themselves fugitives from a mob's anger." He returned to the village, where federal soldiers patrolled the streets and Tarascan villagers had organized. When he drove to check on the Shoemaker's shop, he saw Tarascan men on the roof. "The men are on watch," the foreman told him, "and the women have set up a shrine to Our Lady of Guadalupe, and will burn candles and pray all night." At the seminary, he learned the mob had been disbanded and all was quiet in Morelia. He returned with the news. The soldiers had returned to Morelia, but the village was being guarded by police patrol cars.

Back in the Santa María hacienda before midnight, Griffin began to make notes about the day's events. After midnight he drove in widening circles around the village. He saw no patrol cars, but the village was being protected by Tarascan men with rifles and machetes. He drove down to investigate in the pre-dawn hours. He "did not find a single patrol car or policeman. I drove through the silent streets that earlier had been feverish with the mob." Storefronts were boarded up, as young men were pasting a poster that read: DEATH TO THE YANKEE ASSASSINS OF CUBA.

On April 19 there was anti-American propaganda in *La Voz de Michoacán* and praise for the destruction of the Institute. Tarascans from the village dropped by to check on Griffin. "With superb delicacy, avoiding the subject, they managed to convey their apologies for the shameful incidents." They indicated that Tocaven had sold out for a price to the communists, and they considered him an enemy. Griffin went to see his parents. Official word came to hide cars and lock the gate. They heard another demonstration at the bottom of the hill. The Gillespie sisters urged his parents to return with them to Taos until the crisis was over. They refused to go without their son. He convinced them he would be able to work and to escape, if they were out of harm's way. Many Americans from the village departed.

Newscasts described the riots in Morelia and other riots in Mexico and Latin America. Sound trucks broadcast anti-Catholic slurs along with the anti-American propaganda. "This last move astonishes me, since most here are Catholics, and it would seem a perfect device to alienate them."

On April 21, members of the US Embassy in Mexico City began looking into the demonstrations. The governor had troops protecting the evening's meeting. Griffin met with the officials later. "I let them know that this great show of 'control' was new on the part of the local government." They said the governor rationalized the burning as "a spontaneous student manifestation that got out of hand." They asked for a full report from Griffin, which was delivered by government courier to the US Embassy in Mexico City. He rerouted other mailings through Celaya instead of Morelia, convinced that his mail was being intercepted.

On April 23 Griffin read Mexico City's *Excelsior*, the nation's finest newspaper. "They give an accurate, objective report. They tell it straight. They name the Russian agents who came here, and they name the student leader. No one in Morelia can now doubt that this was a plot of international communism—that it was treason committed against Mexico. Tocaven ran the photo of the burning Institute, gloatingly, as a symbol of the defeat of 'American Imperialism.' *Excelsior* ran the same photo, and in context with their article, it looked shameful."

During the morning of April 24 Griffin was proofing the galleys of *Black Like Me*, which had been shipped by courier from Houghton Mifflin in Boston. A week later, the galleys were corrected and shipped back by courier. There remained only a few clarifications to make and the book's *Preface* to compose.

Nonetheless Griffin was reluctant to leave Santa María. "We had a few peaceful and lovely months here," he noted in the *Journal* on May 2, 1961, "and now I must return to the hate, the taunts, the threats, the endless busy activity, the stupidity of men who have become expert in destroying reputations (since they cannot destroy arguments). I need to work, but I feel exhausted. I need to see my wife and children, but how I dread to return to that racist-ridden area."

He packed what his parents had left behind on May 4. The next day, when he checked the post office box in Morelia, it was empty once again. He had not heard from Elizabeth in nearly three weeks, and had no word from his parents in Taos. He inquired at the post office, but they knew nothing about the missing mail. He was convinced that his lines of communication had been severed. That afternoon, May 5, he called his wife in Mansfield. Elizabeth confirmed that no mail had arrived there either, even though he had written to her nearly every day. She urged him "to get the hell out of there."

Five days later, on May 10, there was still no mail in his postal box. "By cutting off my mail, they have cut off my tongue, forcing me to leave."

He had prepared for that eventuality. "I have never lived among a people for whom I have felt such admiration and love as I do the Tarascans."

The family never returned to their beloved "Santa María Hacienda." Griffin thought of the Tarascans asleep in the village, "with their trust in Nature and God and Humanity, their absolute fidelity and generosity."

Next morning Griffin packed everything that fit in the Corvair. Unfortunately he could not manage to get the darkroom equipment loaded, which he would regret. Knowing that a long, lonely trip lay ahead, he left the village after daybreak, heading north toward Texas.

PART III

In truth I practice and find my spiritual home in another time, one that is not held in very high esteem today, one against which there is even a revolution; and the strange thing is that I pray for the success of most elements of that revolution and support it—and yet all of my tissues draw away from it and back into the old houses of the soul—the *Precautions* of St. John of the Cross, the *Primitive Rule* of St. Benedict.

This would appear to be a contradiction, and I suppose it is. The contradiction of yearning to withdraw from public life into a life of silence, solitude and obscurity—this yearning that has torn at me so many years; and yet my life and work, precisely because it was long ago given without reservation to God, is in the world, in activity.

Somehow these contradictions are resolved within me, because there, at least, they are not contradictions.

—JOHN HOWARD GRIFFIN

Contradictions

Reporters hounded Griffin when he returned to Mansfield. One headline in the *Fort Worth Star-Telegram* blared: AUTHOR DRIVEN OUT OF MEXICO BY REDS? The article began: "John Howard Griffin, the blind Mansfield author who regained his sight, said today that he left Mexico because of 'pressure' from communists there who objected to the articles he wrote. The 40-year-old novelist appeared reluctant to talk about his reasons for leaving Mexico."

Griffin was reluctant because the turmoil there remained unresolved. When asked about his intention to stay in town, he responded, "You might say we're visiting here," without masking his sarcasm. His deepest hope had been to return to Mexico, but even with a complete resolution of the tense political climate in Morelia, he could not have returned, because he was flat broke. It was not the first time, and it would not be the last. The immediate financial difficulty was due to the two-year involvement with the *Black Like Me* experiment.

The *Sepia* series had been a trade-off for Griffin's expenses, and the balance was decidedly in the magazine's favor. His articles had, as Elizabeth pointed out, "quite frankly, put *Sepia* on the national map," stirring tremendous interest from subscribers, new readers, the media, and academia.

The contract with his publisher did not include an advance on *Black Like Me*, because his account with Houghton Mifflin showed a negative balance. The sales of *Nuni* had not covered the advance on that book. This pattern persisted throughout his writing career. The bulk of his income during the 1960s was made as a lecturer, not as a writer. Never did he earn enough from royalties to support his family, astronomical medical expenses, and the cost of photographic equipment and supplies.

Griffin had an uncanny instinct for what made a story or photograph or musical composition significant, universal, beautiful; yet often made poor financial decisions, trusting others to take care of that realm. He worked with those who shared his ideals, and always had the support of family and friends. No one was more supportive than his protective parents, who rarely complained about sacrifices. Others were helpful in countless ways: brother Edgar; his twin sisters and their husbands; Elizabeth's parents and her Aunt Bettie Adams, plus a long list of friends who formed a caring network. There were economic struggles in 1961, but several projects relating to *Black Like Me* were in process, including a paperback deal, translations, interest in rights for film, stage, radio, and television, promotions for lectures, and an advertising campaign for the book. Meanwhile he was finishing a final draft of *Street of the Seven Angels* and continuing work on *Scattered Shadows*.

The contract signed with Houghton Mifflin for *Black Like Me* provided new openings, but Griffin retained translation, British, and film rights. But there were two clauses in the contract that would cut deeply into future royalties. The first, less damaging clause involved Smiths, publisher of *The Devil Rides Outside*, who were due 2 percent of the cloth edition royalties, as compensation for releasing first-refusal rights on his next two books (*Nuni* and *Black Like Me*). In the case of *Nuni*, which sold less than nine thousand copies, the loss was minimal. The eventual take for Smiths on the cloth edition of *Black Like Me* came to about $1,400.00. The loss of income was significant at the time, but Griffin was relieved to have that chapter closed.

The second, more costly clause, would plague Griffin into the early 1970s. This highly irregular clause seemed simple and inconsequential at the time, but what was on paper did not reflect the expansiveness of the "gentlemen's agreement" that loomed behind it. The actual contract called for a fifty-fifty split of *Black Like Me* royalties between Griffin and George Levitan, publisher of *Sepia* magazine. Since everyone's impression was that the book would not become a popular title and certainly not a best-seller, he generously handed half the royalties to Levitan. He felt obligated to the *Sepia* publisher for financing the experiment, even though the expenses had been less than $2,000. He assumed that the fifty-fifty split would be limited to the Houghton Mifflin cloth edition, but Levitan expected to get the same split on the New American Library paperback, even though he had *not* negotiated either publishing deal.

What did George Levitan actually do for Griffin? He hired Benn Hall Associates of New York to organize a lecture tour and media appearances; he negotiated with King Features to run excerpts of the story in various media; he handled queries from motion picture studios that expressed interest; and the staff of Good Publishing Company disseminated media packets globally, including copies of the *Sepia* series, book galleys, and photographs by Don Rutledge sold around the world (even though the photographer was never paid a penny). The results of Levitan's efforts failed to produce a fraction of the value he realized from the split of royalties over the next decade. The movie deal was a poor 1964 production panned by the critics. Levitan got half of the small advance for the film, but neither received payment from the theater proceeds or television viewings.

During Griffin's initial lecture tour during 1961-1962, he shared fees based on a "gentlemen's agreement" with the unscrupulous Levitan, who had absolutely nothing to do with negotiating *that* agreement, either. Finally, the Redpath Bureau's managers convinced Griffin that he was under no legal obligation to split such income with Levitan. He took their advice, yet still felt pangs of guilt, even though he knew the publisher was a bona fide millionaire and that their "gentlemen's agreement" had been stretched beyond all fairness. Griffin was somewhat intimidated by Levitan, but too proud to admit that what he lost in the process put his family through unnecessary sacrifices. The aggregate financial shortfall was about $200,000, which was the difference between a minimal level of financial security for the family, and the reality of struggling to pay bills or even plunging into debt.

The public perception was that Griffin had become wealthy, especially from *Black Like Me*. A brief look at the financial history of his book will clarify the issue. In the case of the first edition, the official sales figure of the $3.50 cloth edition was 90,615 copies, a very respectable total for the time. His entire income from that edition was $13,793 over a four-year span. Levitan's take was the same. Griffin expressed concern in a letter to Paul Brooks of Houghton Mifflin. "Will you double check for me to make sure I'm not going to end up like Joe Louis paying taxes on Levitan's half some day? I never intend to get involved again with anyone. First Smiths, then Levitan—it's no way to live."

For overseas negotiations Griffin signed an excellent contract with the Rosica Colin Agency of London, to represent him in the United Kingdom and with countries interested in translations. Rosica Colin was a skillful negotiator who knew the British and European territories. Her correspondence with the author was always prompt, instructive, and friendly beyond business cordiality. By early 1962, Colin negotiated contracts for *Black Like Me* with Gallimard of Paris for a French translation, as well as German and Polish translations (all with advances). Unfortunately, she had no success with his two novels and little success with future books. But her representation, followed by Joanna Marston's with the Griffin Estate was impressive—sixteen European languages, a UK edition, photocopy rights, plus translated excerpts in newspapers, magazines, and anthologies.

Other basic problems beset Griffin. Not only had the Mexico exile exhausted his funds, but the family was also without a home. The cottage had been rented in their absence, under the assumption they would not return. The family crowded into the home of Elizabeth's mother, the rambling wood-frame structure where Elizabeth had spent her childhood. It was just large enough to accommodate three adults and three children. With the rental income to help with some expenses, and the groceries being charged on Mrs. Holland's tab at a local market, they survived.

This arrangement provided no space for a writing studio and, since he had not brought back the darkroom equipment, he was unable to develop prints, although he continued shooting film. He solved the studio problem by turning a little storage shed into a workable space. The shed was about sixty yards southwest of the Holland house, behind the big barn. The shed's front windows looked out on a thirty-acre pasture. With a loan from his parents, Griffin put in a floor, an air conditioner, and a wood-burning stove. He lined the walls with mounted prints of the Tarascan images and family portraits. It was reminiscent of the old barn studio on his parents' farm, where he had written his novels. He wrote a spate of letters to old friends, catching up on the backlog, while remodeling the shed into a writing studio.

The next week Griffin made a three-day trip to Los Angeles, giving two lectures, speaking on seven radio programs, and making three TV appearances. At one magnificent dinner party held in a palace, he met Gandhi's grandson, who "intimated, and certainly with some truth, that we of the West were more or less bound by the chains of an essentially unenlightened Catholicism."

Early June brought good news. The Ellises had moved from Mexico to Texas, building a home on the Gulf Coast near Galveston. The Shoemakers made a brief visit before returning to Mexico. Griffin loaded them with letters for his Santa María friends, because mail was still being intercepted. In early July a much-needed check for $1000 arrived from *Life* magazine, payment for his piece on the uprising in Morelia ("Terror in Mexico") in their Spanish language edition.

Near midnight on July 19 Griffin went to give *Street of the Seven Angels* one last look, then wrapped it up to mail the next day. "Strange to feel the book gone, all traces of it, out of your hands; good-byes said to the characters who seemed so close to your thoughts over the years. There is no sadness, really, only a pagan sort of release." He had grave doubts about any book he finished. "After all the work on this book, I doubt that it is worth anything but the waste basket." He turned to *Scattered Shadows*, developing the 1958 articles syndicated by the International News Service.

On July 23 Griffin began to feel the onslaught of a cold. He listened to piano lessons with Susan, "who learns with remarkable ease the finger exercises and the Bach preludes." Later attempts at Sunday entertainment turned dismal. "The radio offers nothing, the television is worse." He walked out to the studio and Gregory followed. Every time he tried to work, his four-year-old son kept talking. "He wants to go take a photo with his new camera. I told him there was not enough light, but then the sun popped out. He pointed it out to me and said, 'See, I was right and you was wrong.'" They grabbed their cameras and went on a spree.

That night Gregory wanted to stay with his father in the studio, because Johnny and Susan had gone to visit their grandparents. Gregory gathered his "necessities"—pajamas, fresh clothes, candy cigarettes, a baton, and a thermos of fresh water. Before going to sleep, he walked the floor saying scapular prayers, while Gregory followed in his footsteps, saying prayers with a great smile on his face. He told his father that the little camera (a German Retina Compur) would one day grow as large as his father's Leica. That did not matter, Griffin explained, because both cameras could make the same size pictures. "Yes, Daddy, I know that."

Over the next few days, he helped Houghton Mifflin with promotional work. Press kits and galleys were mailed to Roland Hayes, Roy Wilkins, Leontyne Price, Marian Anderson, Sidney Poitier, James Baldwin, and Ralph J. Bunche at the United Nations. Other copies were sent to Flannery O'Conner, Lillian Smith, and P.D. East. Griffin requested that the press releases *not* include his place of residence, saying that he was *not* living in Texas. He wanted to keep his enemies guessing, staying away from downtown Mansfield. As for lectures, he indicated that he was "not prepared to speak in any of the hard-core Southern states," since receiving "threats of assassination." He considered only Atlanta as a possible exception, saying, "if this seems utterly fantastic in Boston, it is only too real in the South."

Meanwhile Gregory was becoming a permanent fixture in the studio. On the morning of July 27, Griffin photographed the sleeping child, one of countless images of the children, even though they tended to be "so camera conscious, no matter how much they see me photograph," he noted in the *Journal*.

> Instead of being natural, they will find a thousand things for me to photograph. Susie and Johnny are as bad as Greggy. Johnny will go stand under a tree, leaning against the trunk with his arms casually crossed, with the sun backlighting his hair and say: "How about this?"
>
> "Would you like to photograph me sitting up here on the fence?" Susie will say, as though the idea were ravishing.
>
> I miss my darkroom equipment terribly. I keep making photos and feeling the frustration of not being able to develop and print them. I fritter the time, drawn to my major passion. I study a great deal—chemicals, emulsions, the lens combinations, and all the papers—all of the complex interrelationships that will allow for the finest end result: the print. Am now working with the microfilm-speed emulsions, very high resolution Adox Dokupan, and noting readjustments I will make.

During the next three weeks, Griffin worked full-time on *Scattered Shadows*, completing the final draft of the first six chapters. He did not write in the *Journal*, instead taking care of business in the daylight hours.

Two significant events occurred on August 20, 1961. Griffin received an advance copy of *Black Like Me*, pleased with the "extraordinarily tasteful job." It was "good to leaf through and note names that are dear to me, names I revere in a text where I can honor them, perhaps, or at least make their message go to people who might otherwise miss it." The *Journal* concluded, "Always a strange moment, to see one's work printed into this format, complete—a year of labor that weighs less than a pound; and yet few pounds of any substance have produced the explosion this has, the repercussions, the changes in our life and status."

The second event was an internal decision mentioned in the *Journal*. "I put my affairs in order, so that Decherd Turner becomes my literary executor."

> We begin the lugubrious business of seeking protection again, putting up blackout shades, so that if anyone comes up here at night they will not know if I am in—or at least cannot see to shoot me through the windows. This kind of "sitting duck" uncertainty, the fear of a racist crackpot getting through, or a communist doing this so it can be blamed on the racists—fills me with renewed tenderness for my family, especially the children—and yet it was for them that I did it, and no matter what happens to me, I can at least know that what I did was an effort to make the world better for them, to give them hope of growing up in a less prejudiced climate, and therefore a less perverting climate.

Griffin informed Paul Brooks of Houghton Mifflin that Turner would handle his unpublished works, consisting of eight volumes of journals and short stories, plus *Passacaglia*, a fourth novel, which was never completed. The *Journal* at that point ran to 1,105 pages single-spaced typed pages. He kept it in three-ring binders that were not divided by year, but simply filled to the brim. In a letter to Turner, he writes, "There is a great deal in the journals that is obviously not meant for public view. You will know what should be submitted and what should not . . . "

> I should not like for you to consult with my family about what elements of the journals should be published, since their care for my memory would not allow them to judge properly. I feel that you alone would know me well enough to be the judge of this, and that you would not hesitate to publish whatever was of value, regardless of how

> it made me appear. But I feel that you have the most complete knowledge of what my work tries to be, and would therefore be a better judge of what should be published than anyone else; which is why I should like all of this material to go through your editorial hands first. This letter will authorize you to take 10% in lieu of an agent's commission, which you will receive directly on all works you handle and that are published in any and all forms after my death.

The next morning, August 21, Griffin felt a sense of closure. His literary estate would be put in order, and Decherd Turner was the right literary person to oversee it. Since *Black Like Me* was about to be published and *Street of the Seven Angels* was out of his hands, Griffin was where he wanted to be, right in the middle of drafting later chapters of *Scattered Shadows.* His passion for photography, even though frustrated without a darkroom, had reached a high level of technical expertise and artistic vision. He studied the craft with enthusiasm, shooting film for later development and scrutiny. The new shed studio became a productive space, despite limitations.

"The poison starts," Griffin wrote. Before going to the studio, he got a phone call "from a good friend, distressed by the tales that are being spread about me by those who would discredit the work, would nullify *Black Like Me.*" He promised himself to ignore the flak. "I had prepared a good and enthusiastic day's work, but this sours it—the interruption, the determination to keep utterly silent and not waste time defending myself, because it can drag on forever, and I have other work to do, and this keeps it from getting done." The poisonous lies would not kill the truth of the book, but could devastate his resolve, if he allowed it. The lies came unbidden, but so did its antidote. "A moment ago, Gregory came sleepily out to the studio, not yet awake from his nap, carefully wiped his bare feet on the door stoop and staggered in." As the phone call had been an "interruption" to concentration, the innocent boy's unexpected arrival halted Griffin's frustration. "The thing that came clear is that I am not going to do this child's future any good except by working on my present book. The other is past. I have said everything I know to say—let them take it or leave it. I can spend months denying their lies, defending my work; and these months will be wasted, accomplishing nothing, not creating new works."

What "came clear" was not intellectual, but a deeper emotional cauldron stirred by personal attacks, by name-calling, and by lies aimed at his credibility. Griffin could not let it go, still caught in a net of contradictions. "Yet, though I understand all of this, was prepared for it, a great heaviness lies on my chest, the desire to weep—why?—because my feelings are hurt and it's that childish." He had been honest about his reactions, admitting to being hurt by the cruel attacks. Yet he was wise enough to focus on the essentials. "I have my manuscript, my typewriter, my paper, the silence of an August Sunday—nothing else really counts besides these" for the artist, who "must cast aside the stench, make use of the time to work and to love, avoid the temptation of defending one's good name, and yet, it is shattering. The instinct for self-preservation swells the glands, throws anger into the veins."

That evening he visited his parents, who lived a dozen miles away in the small town named Venus, unwisely telling them about the local gossip, as if they would be immune. Thus, he "was astonished at his mother's anger, and regretted telling her." He tried to make light of it, to act as if it was "too ridiculous and amusing," but they were not laughing. That night, listening to "the magnificent Bach Concerto for two violins," he reminisced about the music.

> Now it is the slow movement of the concerto; magnificently beautiful and filling me with tenderness. I recall many years ago, when I used to play the two piano version of this work with my mother—and the marvelous joys of that compared to the bitterness and pain that I saw in her today. How I regret that my work, which should lead to beauty, leads to all this terrible venom against us. The hell of it is that this is embittering her, for she sees it in a degraded light in a way that few people are given to see it closely.

The next three days Griffin stayed at the Carmelite monastery, keeping his promise to continue with *Scattered Shadows*, while avoiding calls and letters. Driving home from the monastery, he had "an extraordinary experience," which he writes about in a letter to Father Murphy (August 26, 1961).

> Extraordinary because I had been suffocated by the stories going on about town, a nightmarish account of the good ladies' lynch parties against pornography, when what should I see looming up from

> a gigantic drive-in theatre screen, there to my left, in full view, but a group of completely nude women, blown-up to the giant screen, in the most ravishing Technicolor, cavorting in green waters.
>
> "Well," I told myself. "This did it. I've cracked up, lost my mind." I slowed down, sure that it was an hallucination (otherwise, there would be a whole stream of wrecked cars on the highway) and glanced cautiously. Yes, there they were, naked, wet, breasts and backs and hips. Badly shaken, but happy, I drove home and telephoned Decherd to ask him if I should have myself committed.
>
> He gently reassured me that it was some nature-studies picture that was causing a great stir "in good circles"—and that I had indeed seen what I had seen.

This passage offers a taste of Griffin's comedic sense, in an intentionally silly combination of breast sighting and leg pulling, for a liberated friend who enjoyed harmless fun. Meanwhile Griffin avoided local involvement in a current clash between the self-appointed censors and defenders of free speech. He had "refused two such programs already, saying that I could not stand to debate 'police censorship' with grown men and women who accepted with indisputable fact that there was something intrinsically evil about sexual stimulation."

By mid-September Griffin had received calls from Hollywood studios interested in *Black Like Me*, including one discussing film rights to *The Devil Rides Outside*. He turned the contacts over to George Levitan, who was negotiating with other studios. Griffin received a letter from Houghton Mifflin, informing him of New American Library's offer to reprint *Black Like Me*. They wanted to publish the paperback exactly one year after the cloth edition. The advance figure of $6,600 was small, but it had been the only offer. He accepted it, realizing it would keep them from deeper debt, even if half went into Levitan's pocket.

Griffin wrote a brief entry in the *Journal*, on September 17, after three weeks of silence. "Autumn is here, with cool, clear delicious days. Hard to stay inside and work. Many diabetic upsets that leave me stupid and exhausted. They have never been so thoroughly ravaging before." On the September 21, he was with P. D. East, driving his friend to Denton (fifty miles north of Mansfield). The following day he accomplished little, suffering from "such exhaustion that I have to prompt myself a long time even to write these dead lines in this journal." His exhaustion deepened due to adverse reactions to a new brand of insulin (in pill form rather than injections).

The next evening he drove P. D. East to Turner's home in Dallas. When they sat down for supper, Griffin felt intense pain from a violent insulin reaction, "a real thunderbolt that kept me in a coma for 12 hours and had all the appearance of heart attack complications." After a battery of tests at the doctor's, he learned that it was an "insignificant flutter" of the heart, but the "devastating blood-sugar imbalance" had almost killed him. This was not the sense of closure he had contemplated, and there would be further adjustments to the new insulin.

On September 27, Griffin was "physically sick, as though I had eaten ground glass—it was the Orinase to which I can never apparently accustom my system." But he could not "escape the background preoccupation with death that always follows such an attack."

That same week Hurricane Carla struck the Gulf Coast with brutal force, and the Ellises' recently-constructed beach house was swept away. "Poor Bob and Rosa, they got out in front of the hurricane with nothing but the clothes on their backs. When they returned, they could find no trace of the house or lot." Ellis "lost all of his canvases—and the recent ones were truly magnificent—he has developed into an unquestionably great painter."

Elizabeth recalled their arrival in Mansfield after the storm. "They were still in shock and utterly exhausted. Rosa and I cried, and I could see that Bob was very shaken. He was always the most composed and relaxed person I'd ever known." After combing the beach, all they found were an iron skillet and a tiny piece of kitchen linoleum, which Bob "forlornly pulled out of his shirt pocket." The only fortunate relief was that their three-year-old daughter, Erendira, had been with relatives. Elizabeth considered the Ellises to be her dearest friends, loving them "as if they were the sister and brother I never had."

Ten days later Griffin was still suffering from the effects of the new insulin. "I feel I shall never really adjust to these substitutes," he told the *Journal* on October 7. "Almost midnight, and I lie here in a stupor." He tried to pray, but "the prayers skitter off into nothing." Attempts to write were "full of dullness and errors." He wanted to remain awake until the medication wore off, settling for classical music from the radio, but it was blaring the music of Offenbach.

> I write in this journal really to try to stir something, to come alive enough to do some work, to make myself think when my whole being drowses. This must be the way great age makes a man feel; the flesh dragging and hurting—the unwashed, uncomfortable animal. How odd and stupid Offenbach sounds on such a night. I listen to it with immense irritation, and wish the Offen were stricken from the name and I were hearing only Bach.

The Offenbach was followed by even lighter fare, which drove Griffin toward the house to make coffee. "Walking in the intense darkness of October midnight, fragments of thoughts flickered: The body's weakness reminds man of self when the only hope is to lose self. What happened to the God of tenderness?—the personal God so beloved by so many and once beloved by me, but isn't that a fatal error of thought?" Walking to the studio, questions turned into statements.

> God drove me to Him always with the most ineffable brutality. There has never been the sweetness in this relationship that I should have wanted to believe. How this would shock many, and rightfully. If I had been less stubborn, less recalcitrant, less smeared with the marrow of myself, God would not have had to badger and beat me into submission—into willing finally my submission because it was the only way. I came to God in utter defeat, and fell in love with God—coldly and passionately and tenderly—but now I fall away again and again, but with no loss of faith, only in my weakness, in stupidity, in numbness."

Griffin wondered: "How much of this is blood sugar and how much my own wantonness? God alone knows; I do not." He read the label on the medicine bottle. "It says on the bottle that this very thing is likely to happen, so why attach any spiritual connotations?" He drank the coffee before it turned cold. More questions came, as he typed and smoked cigarettes. "Why this strange pride that feels hurt? What self-love to be humiliated (or disappointed?) by such things. Or rather what vicious habit of fastidiousness—ah, the habit of the pious." He paused, turning off the radio. He lit another cigarette, watching the smoke rise. "If the effort were made, if the immense concentration could be summoned, the old warmth would return, the warmth of continual prayer, so I try it." During the pre-dawn silence, he walked the floor with a rosary, intoning the scapular prayers. He turned off lights, kneeling to pray silently. He prayed until he was no longer aware of praying, and anguish lifted. He returned to making notes with renewed energy and clarity.

> Much of religion—much of what we search for in religion and much of what we think we find in it—the peace and the delights are really the intervention of the ego, the escape into the ego we think sincerely we have cast out, overcome. We have escaped into the ego and keep building the ego, and then God sends us the agony, the deadness, the sensuality to clarify us and show us the immense duplicity of our whole religious stalemate.

In reaction to this paradoxical reality, Griffin did not create an illusory escape from suffering, because "the anguish is the thing to risk—it must be risked, and I see now, welcomed." Neither the "illimitable detachment of the angelic being" nor the sensate "plunge into the consoling pleasures" can be maintained. Both attempts to deny the reality that ego must die to be reborn into spirit. That mystery beyond language or silence, beyond logic or absurdity, Griffin believed must live in one's abandonment in prayer. To avoid the anguish of reality, "ego demands angelism," but "one does not overcome the beast within him by simply being affronted and refusing to admit its existence; and yet this is the immeasurable temptation."

The parallel delusion demands only diversions to escape the agony of inhabiting a spiritual dimension. Griffin believed that sanctity demanded reality, and that one "must begin again to make *the immense reconciliation of the contradictions* between the beast and the angel. It will go on with someone like me forever, starting over again with the pieces God has bashed into a mess." Faith was his solitary "virtue in a holocaust of error," the simple "willingness to persevere." If one had limitless faith, "the light never really goes out inside of self." He considered that light to be "that margin of safety." He tried the radio again. "Mozart enters with a work to ravish the mind and soul with compassion and magnanimity," and Griffin's "reconciliation of the contradictions" was brought back in balance once again.

The following week he purchased an inexpensive enlarger. He fussed over a photographic portrait of P. D. East intended for a book jacket. "How I miss my Leitz enlarger, with its greater brilliance and sharpness than the one I now use." He remained "haunted by the desire to do the book that will combine text with photographs. But I must put it aside and get back to work."

Griffin's writing schedule was derailed repeatedly by a surge of correspondence. He put work aside, attempting to fulfill public obligations and answer mail. He wrote the Gillespie sisters on October 21, to catch them up on the torrid pace, sending them the working manuscript of *Black Like Me* for safekeeping. "I have just finished making a neat package of the manuscript, which Houghton returned today at my request. This is the typescript on which the editors make their comments and write me notes and I answer, and then it goes to the typesetters. These notes are interesting and reveal much about the editors, and often show why a writer likes or loathes them." Griffin noted in the *Journal* that "mail on *Black Like Me* is so heavy I am hopelessly lost in attempting to answer it. Not one unfavorable letter—that's both astonishing and disappointing to a martyr like me!" Congratulatory notes followed.

A telegram from Maxwell Geismar: "Read your *Black Like Me* with utmost admiration and fascination." Eugene McNamara, a literary critic in Canada, wrote: "I received your book yesterday and read it last night. It is beautiful, true, terrible. It made me want to cry, yell, get up and do something. If it affects many of its readers the way it did me, then you will not only have created a living and moving work of art, you will have moved men towards justice and love." Griffin was moved by words from Father Murphy. "I cannot help but wonder how some of the local betrayers around Mansfield will feel when they witness themselves now reflected on a world stage. How easy it is for people in everyday life to connive with evil and temporize, with the flimsiest of excuses. It will be less easy for anyone who reads this book to keep doing it. The moment anyone for a second treats any person in any condition as less than *res sacra*, there is no limit to the ultimate effects of evil."

The Honorable Curtis Bok's letter reads: "I find it very moving and powerful and want to express my admiration for your having the imagination and courage to do such a thing. The great big factor that sticks in my mind is not the idiotic statement by white southerners that no one can understand the problem but themselves, but the realization that they themselves don't understand it."

Griffin replied to Justice Bok: "Thank you for your gracious letter, and thank you once again for having permitted me to quote from your

Radcliffe talk. It summarized marvelously what I was trying to convey. As you remark, the stunning truth here is that the whites, the racists, who accuse the world of not understanding them, do not understand their problem themselves. In effect, too many are convinced that they have no problem except the nuisance of the unflattering opinions of *outsiders*. As Gerald Vann says, 'the tragedy is not so much their unawareness of the problem, but their unawareness that they are unaware of it.'"

Griffin wrote two letters to Geismar on October 24, 1961, typical of their lighter side, poking fun at P. D. East's views on photography. Before mailing the letter, he received another brief note from Geismar, typed on stationery that was four inches square (dubbed "mini-max" notes). It was more of their badinage, as they attempted to outdo each other on the subject of bodily functions.

He wrote six letters on November 1, including his first to Lillian Smith, telling her that *Black Like Me* mentions her first novel (*Strange Fruit*).[64] The purpose was simply to say he was greatly impressed with *Killers of the Dream*, a new edition of her book about the Deep South. In a note to Geismar, he declared, "I'm filled with admiration for it and for Lillian Smith (I'm halfway in love with her)."

To Father Murphy, he wrote of his "admiration for this brilliant and courageous and charming work," telling the priest that P. D. East "shared with me, in confidence, a letter from Lillian that broke my heart. The poor woman is down to no money, and although she has immense capabilities, can see virtually none of her work except that about the South. It is very sad to see a person of this caliber—and one who has contributed so tremendously—in this neglect."

Griffin's central theme that day was *not* Lillian Smith but Jacques Maritain. He explained this most fully to Father Murphy in a long letter with this prefatory note: "In reading this, I see that you must guess at more than you read; it is not merely an expression of nostalgia for the past, but rather for the kind of spirituality one encountered *there*—full of wisdom, warmth, freedom, daring, and absoluteness—dedication without the heaviness one finds *here*, without the fears, really."

The *here* was America of the present day, including Texas that represented the South to him. The *there* was France, particularly the culture that had influenced him. In his letter to Father Murphy, who knew Maritain and understood the philosopher's difficult works, Griffin writes at length about his mentor.

> Another long and immensely moving letter from Jacques today. I had written him about the death of our mutual friend, the French poet Pierre Reverdy. To my profound joy, Maritain is going to give me the correspondence between Reverdy and Raïssa, which he says contains valuable comments on poetry. It is a very strange personal thing—quite aside from (how can I say it?) the sense of unworthiness I feel even to receive a word from Jacques, still this recent correspondence, and especially today's letter represents my last link with that part of my life that was most important to me—the "European" life (and specifically France) that formed me and now has left me, and indeed left the world—I mean that life where poets and philosophers were heroes. The great personal attachments I had during those years were with these people—with Reverdy whom I visited during the winter at Solesmes; with Robert Casadesus, who was once like a father to me; with the Dominican and Benedictine fathers—all of these personal and real; and again with those whom we never met but who were our main topics of schoolboy discussion and intellectual passion.

Griffin felt he was a living contradiction. He had been formed artistically by French modernism but lived in postmodern America. His spiritual roots were sunk in the light of the Middle Ages, yet he felt surrounded by the unenlightened Christianity of the contemporary age.

> The world has changed; none of this is left, really, as Reverdy himself once warned me. But somehow, Maritain alone among these friends and acquaintances is the bridge, for he knew them all, intimately. Each letter from him, each contact such as today's is therefore unique, for we shared something in the past, long before we were personally acquainted, that is gone in the present world—let's say changed, for the artistic ferment does not die.
>
> In other words, I was attached, as were my schoolmates in France, to the tail end of a great generation—Braque, Picasso, Gris, Rouault, Reverdy, Valery, Claudel, the Maritains, the Casadesus family—and it had a different quality, and Maritain alone remains the link. Each letter from him makes me realize that such a past existed, formed us for

> better or worse, nourished us in some profound affection, showed us something absolute and full of flair and verve in its absoluteness.

Griffin remembered precisely what Reverdy had warned him against in 1947. "Don't read me, don't love Braque or Gris like you do—we will be past before you are mature—you will be left alone. Attach yourself to the young ones. These others—Picasso, Mallarmé—these are for old men like me." At that time, he was on the threshold of total blindness, making a study of the younger generation of artists nearly impossible. "I never understood what he meant until he died, until Raïssa Maritain died, until the world changed and left me 'old hat' at the age of forty." There was more nostalgia than he admitted. But there was also "a great truth in the core of this," longing for the "fragrance of that world, that time, that atmosphere," feeling a "strange tenderness-filled elation—not to have the prized letters (which they are), but to have for a time that fragrance, to be 'at home' once again."

> There is something intangible in my feelings for Maritain, quite aside from the immense reverence for his work—it is a sort of empathy, perhaps false, but real to me—the feeling that if I feel estranged and bewildered in this culture where all nourishments, all values, all passions, and uses of pastimes are scaled to an utterly different standard from what formed me. Then I think how much more estranged, lonely, he is; and I feel it deeply, the solitary quality that moves with him. In the larger sense, the great consolation exists for both of us, the great love above love that makes everything secure; but in the human sense, in the sense of bread and dishes and tables and rooms at night, there is always the quiet and gentle loneliness for the homeland, for the many brothers and sisters who came from that same womb of time and who have disappeared from us. The difference is that though I have roots in that womb so deep I can only be bewildered by the transplanting of time, ideals, and values; he has infinitely deeper roots there, roots from which he cannot and should not extricate himself even in his loneliness; so that the resonances that pour out to him from his human existence must ring with intimate nostalgia that amounts to total loneliness—this despite his great mind which can face the now without my bewilderment, and which can bring out of this immense complexity that marvelous simplicity which is wisdom.

Griffin did not detail these remembrances to Geismar, who was a modernist, not a medievalist, a literary historian of the American novel; and neo-Freudianism was the central influence on his critical canon. Yet their different orientations sparked a lively dialogue. He recognized in Geismar independent brilliance and fraternal warmth. He wrote to "Dear Old Max" that "My other half, my other world, that of my past, my formation-homeland has been jolted back into existence these days with a heavy correspondence with Maritain before he leaves to enter the monastery at 80." Maritain joined the Little Brothers and Little Sisters of Jesus, the order founded by Father Charles de Foucauld, settling in the principal monastery at Toulouse.[65] Griffin did not mention Maritain's reasons to Geismar, or speak of his sense of unworthiness. "I have come to realize that except for you, every other critic convinces me that I have no talent whatsoever, which I always knew and was secretly tormented by. But now the great clarification has come to liberate me—I know I have no talent, and I don't care one damn bit."

If this sounded like coy gamesmanship, it was precisely Griffin's intention. This comment left Geismar with a no-win proposition. Either the critic had to disagree with the novelist's view and be out-humbled, or he had to agree, casting his essay on Griffin's novels into disrepute. Endgame, or so it seemed. But that was not enough. "Do you know how that unblocks an essentially ungifted creative person like me? There is a great truth here as I have finally discovered. Why fiddle around worrying because you can't write, and turning your energies into junk—oh, it's insidious—and I'm over it now, thank God." Griffin's satirical subtext nonetheless revealed his insecurity. He felt dread that the public discourse about *Black Like Me* was going to take over his life, and this concern would turn out to be justified.

The sixth letter that day was for Decherd Turner.[66]

> I sit here now at 1 a.m., surrounded by the debris of things that represent so much love and so much death that I can only stare mutely at them—and in the immense dazzlement of old things seen new again, they appear incredibly clear, sharp-edged, full of color and evocation. I see the cluttered desk as a painting.

Griffin disclosed details to Turner that were not in the other letters. Maritain asked for a print of Griffin's portrait of Reverdy, but the negatives had been left with Reverdy in 1947. "Then I began going through my old correspondence with Reverdy, and there found the *Figaro Litteraire*, an issue of 15 years ago, fragile now and faded, but with my portrait of Reverdy. I cut it out, put it between cardboards, and sent it to Maritain, and now try to think of some way to get the negatives without disturbing Madame Reverdy."

This letter went beyond others, developing insights from the day's meditative reminiscences. Even as the experience of hearing from Maritain had "cut the link with what made me, what I loved," he felt "perfectly content that it should and must be," for "in all of this a great gratitude comes into play on quite another plane—a gratitude that in the fog there are lights—men of courage, honesty, goodness, and it is my good fortune to know a few of them, to see their lights and simply be grateful that they exist. You are one of these."

On this night Griffin shared secrets that would no longer remain private, writing that "perhaps I am secretly so relieved that Maritain—who could have had anything, any position, any distinction, anywhere in the world, divests himself and chooses the bread and the table and the cell and the passions of a poor and obscure religious in Toulouse—went straight where he should have gone."

The old philosopher had returned to solitude and, Griffin believed, to his final resting place. "I know only that if we should meet, the immeasurable and somehow impersonal tenderness that has developed between us would reduce us to weeping." That would *not* turn out to be true, since Maritain lived until 1973, writing new books and making several unexpected journeys, including a return to Princeton University in 1962, when the two friends actually met (no tears were shed). "I don't know why," Griffin confessed to Turner, "but all of this has opened me up, unblocked something, and it is a great relief. It is all clear to me now. I don't have to be up-to-date; that is for the young—or for people like you who have the capacity to embrace newness, and this is as it should be. Now I understand and am no longer torn, no longer desperate in that intimate way. The clutter is gone and I feel free to work."

Griffin closed the letter in a manner similar to its opening, but instead of seeing the cluttered desk as a painting (that could change with a subtle rearrangement or a mood shift), he perceived a fresh opening. "The envelope addressed to me in Reverdy's hand still lies face-up here on the desk. Have you ever looked at the scrawled address on an envelope and seen in it, instantly, everything that a human life was—especially when it is an artist?"

It was "as though in a brief moment of addressing an envelope, Reverdy had let slip everything that he did, felt, was." Griffin's nostalgic epiphany concludes: "All of that is here tonight, crowding this tiny room, taking me back to that homeland from which the world took me—not back in memory, but in a far deeper sense where I belong—in time; and this is not retrogression, since eternity is neither backward nor forward. It is all now."

Censorship and Human Rights

> Groups desiring to censor not only textbooks but also some of our most reputable literary classics on the grounds they are fighting communism indicate that they would protect us from one form of totalitarianism by imposing on us another. Any attempt to preserve liberties by subverting freedoms soon reduces itself to an absurdity.
>
> As a member of the Texas Institute of Letters and a citizen of this state, I urge that these efforts to censor ideas, scholarship and literature be repudiated by the House Committee. I further urge that provisions be made to protect reputable scholars, writers, and the reading public from all such extralegal forms of censorship as coercion, agreement or the implicit blackmail of group pressures.
>
> —GRIFFIN'S STATEMENT BEFORE THE TEXAS HOUSE COMMITTEE INVESTIGATING TEXTBOOKS

Even though Griffin would soon be thrust into the temporal anxiety of public battle over censorship, the eternal present would dwell in his private solitude. Autumn weather arrived, tardy as usual in North Texas, finally matching the seasonal shift while wiping away summer.

On November 2, 1962, Griffin noted in the *Journal* that Gregory had run a pitchfork through his older brother's hand. "Greggy did it, quite by accident, thinking he was helping with the flowerbeds; and now Johnny is getting a tetanus shot. I listen for their return, fearing there might have been some bone or muscle damage to the hand." Elizabeth took their son to the doctor, a week before Johnny's sixth birthday. Gregory was sad and silent since the accident, "perhaps his first real introduction to a sense of guilt." Elizabeth reported it was a severe injury that would take a painful recovery, but there was no bone or muscle damage.

Then it was Griffin's turn to visit the doctor. "Tragedy of tragedies—he told me to stop smoking—there are noises in the lungs and constriction of the blood vessels." He was a chain smoker and, from the few references to smoking in the *Journal*, it was clearly an unconscious addiction that he would never overcome. "I got some Bantron, which is supposed to relieve the urge, but it is the mechanical gesture—reaching for the cigarette, smoking it unaware that is my greatest difficulty; and I do not anticipate the days to come with any relish."

The next day's *Journal* notes reveal his awareness of *not* smoking. Instead of working, he spent the morning in search of a wood-stove for the studio. He bought a small iron one and set it up on bricks, with the stovepipe curving out of a little opening in the east wall. That night it was below freezing, as he rhapsodized about the stove, "which takes only a handful of wood, and has a nice damper control, pops and roars or purrs, as I adjust it, and casts a marvelous warmth." That night he typed a letter to Madame Henriette Reverdy, asking that she send the negatives of his portraits of the late poet to Jacques Maritain.

Editor Margaret Hartley invited Griffin to review a new edition of Lillian Smith's *Killers of the Dream* for the winter issue of *Southwest Review*. He agreed, saying he "had been ill, dangerously ill—but in a way that is painless. My doctor has restricted all activity, forbidden all public appearances, which leaves me free to spend most of my time out here in the studio in quiet and solitary work." On November 6, he hastily typed reactions to *Killers of the Dream* in the *Journal*.

> Lillian Smith seeks to recreate the southern experience to help fellow southerners to understand the tremendous forces that have grown into the southern white and led him to "Kill the Dream" of our founding fathers, all in deluding himself that he is preserving something infinitely more precious—the South, segregation, southern womanhood.
>
> In order to show the tragic growth of all these forces, she writes a semi-autobiographical work, telling of her typical southern upbringing, the influences on childhood in a genteel family, the combined degra-

> dation of the South after the Civil War, and the assuagement they took in the only thing that could *not* be degraded—the white superiority of their skin (abetted by ruthless politicians and wealthy families). White supremacy became their firmest belief—the Negro became the "object" on which they could safely vent all of their hatreds and frustrations, even while they could form individual personal attachments.

Griffin's review opens, "Lillian Smith, as the whole world surely knows, is a Southern Lady. Twelve years ago, with prophetic vision she wrote *Killers of the Dream*, about the South and segregation." He read the revised version of the book as "a magnificent free-form essay, one of those rare works that literally pours out from a mind that has pondered deeply and come to many conclusions without ever losing the passion she felt for her subject." The book caused him to rediscover abandoned roots, and to "become a Southerner vicariously."

There are interesting corollaries between *Killers of the Dream* and *Black Like Me*. The tones are boldly critical and, by natural turns, deeply compassionate, yet revealing undertones of vulnerability. They share an aristocratic artistry and novelistic control, elevated beyond reportage. Both authors struggled with a sense of guilt, intending white readers to feel the same. They had similar upbringings. Griffin came from an educated background in Texas; Smith was "a member of a cultivated and respected Georgia family." Their differences were complementary: Griffin's concern with the "manhood" of segregated black men and Smith's demystification of the white "Southern Lady." Griffin's review examines the southern white's rationalization of segregation through the eyes of Smith's courageous stand for justice and equality. She spoke of her parents, "who so gravely taught me to split my body from my mind and both from my 'soul,' taught me also to split my conscience from my acts and Christianity from southern tradition."

His scathing remarks go beyond Smith's refinement, defending her position while extending his critique of white male sexuality.

> The southern girls learned other things—a puritanical crushed-violet concept of sex, kindness to the Negro, the superiority of whiteness. They learned that Christ appointed the southern white to care for the well-being of the southern Negro, and that segregation was the proper and Christian way to insure the happiness of both races. They learned

> that it was unkind to encourage the Negro beyond the barriers erected for his own good.
>
> Most important of all, they learned that a Southern White Woman is sacred—a sacred reality who must be protected from the lion that raged beneath the thin layer of domestication nurtured in the Black by the White.
>
> Open the door to the Negro's cage and the lion would bound out to rape the white sacredness, to despoil it and outrage heaven . . . and also create a servant problem.
>
> The southern white woman had her flowers, her kitchen, her illusion of sacredness. And there was a certain beauty in all of this if she swallowed her frustrations at being cheated by the husband who had chivalrously guarded her sacredness by lavishing his brute masculinity on Negro women and saving only the gentle leftovers for his wife.

Griffin realized that Smith was too genteel to write caustically, or to critique the perverse totalitarian caste system of the South that allowed white men to rape black women with relative impunity. Yet Smith knew "that the warped, distorted frame we put around every Negro child from birth is around every white child also. . . . What cruelly shapes and cripples the personality of one is cruelly shaping and crippling the personality of the other." She reached the same conclusion as Martin Luther King Jr., believing all humanity to be sacred. She asks the challenging question: "Are we—the nation that first embarked on the high adventure of making a world fit for human beings to live in—about to destroy ourselves because we have killed our dream?" Smith issues a warning: "Time has run out; we must right now adjust ourselves to the speed and quality of world events, world moods, world psychology or face probable extinction as a free nation."

Griffin closed the review with "Surely *Killers of the Dream*, from the pen of a remarkably cultivated and communicative intellect, is the master contribution to our understanding of the most gangrenous problem of our time."

In the *Journal* he lamented that Smith had been typecast, "somehow dragged down as an artist by the fact that she has demonstrated her gifts so superbly on this one subject that the world does not get to read her on any other. She has written many essays that have nothing to do with her

'Mother-of-the-whole-damned-South role.'" He perceived in her viewpoint the same spiritual essence and ethical conscience he found in the works of Dr. Martin Luther King.

When Dr. King was asked how he could advocate breaking some laws while obeying others, he said, "The answer is found in the fact that there are two types of laws. There are *just* and *unjust* laws. I would agree with St. Augustine that 'An unjust law is no law at all.'" He quotes Augustine and Thomas Aquinas, "the great Jewish philosopher" Martin Buber, and Protestant theologian Paul Tillich. His sources of wisdom were not only from the West, since he also studied Mohandas Gandhi, who revered Christ. King's open letter to fellow clergymen, *Letter from a Birmingham Jail*, offered several astute arguments, including this lucid clarification.[67]

> A just law is a man-made code that squares with the moral law or law of God. An unjust law is a code that is out of harmony with the moral law. To put it in the terms of St. Thomas Aquinas, *a just law is a human law that is rooted in eternal and Natural Law*. Any law that uplifts human personality is just. Any law that degrades human personality is unjust.
>
> All segregation statutes are unjust because segregation distorts the soul and damages the personality. It gives the segregator a false sense of superiority, and the segregated a false sense of inferiority. . . . Segregation is not only politically, economically and sociologically unsound, but it is morally wrong and sinful.
>
> Paul Tillich has said that sin is separation. Isn't segregation an existential expression of man's tragic separation, an expression of his awful estrangement, his terrible sinfulness? So I urge men to disobey segregation ordinances because they are morally wrong."

King went on to clarify: "An unjust law is a code that a majority inflicts on a minority that is not binding on itself. This is difference made legal. On the other hand an unjust law is a code that a majority compels a minority to follow that it is unwilling to follow itself. This sameness is made legal."

Dr. King placed these reflections into a context of Christian theology for fellow clergymen, revealing his nonviolent intent. "In no sense do I advocate evading or defying the law as a rabid segregationist would do.

This would lead to anarchy. One who breaks an unjust law must do it *openly, lovingly* . . . and with a willingness to accept the penalty." Breaking a law because conscience judges it unjust meant "expressing the highest respect for law." The determination to peacefully arouse public conscience about injustice, and the willingness to accept punishment by law, were rooted in Christ's crucifixion, which Gandhi called "a perfect act of Charity." For Gandhi, "an unjust law is a species of violence," but "the law of nonviolence says that violence should not be resisted by counterviolence but by nonviolence."[68]

Both leaders endured imprisonment and were assassinated for the "Christ Ideal." They accepted the mortal risk, placed their trust in a greater power, and expected to be killed. Griffin expected to be killed and was directed by Jacques Maritain's words, "a political ideal of brotherly love alone can direct the work of authentic social regeneration: and it follows that to prepare a new age of the world, martyrs to the love of neighbor may first be necessary."

In Griffin's article on the 1956 Montgomery bus boycott, he characterized King's challenge and strategy.

> Martin Luther King's first problem was to inspire his people not only to persevere in their battle for freedom but to limit themselves to a single weapon—the weapon of Love: to return love for hate; to embrace a truth strange to modern ears but which black people's lives had uniquely prepared them to understand—that unearned suffering is redemptive.
>
> He asked fifty thousand people to do that rare thing—to make themselves subservient to an ideal (the Christ Ideal) in the face of opponents who made ideals subservient to their prejudices. Dr. King's second problem was to place the Christ Ideal in firm opposition to segregationists who were persuaded that they themselves acted from the noblest Christian motives and who felt it wholly within the framework of Christianity to smear, terrorize, kill or do anything else to protect the traditional Southern Christian System from anyone who sought to alter it.

The "Christ Ideal" was a profound belief in justice that synthesized with Gandhi's creed of nonviolence. The evolution of Dr. King's strategy was "anchored in a realistic knowledge of man that countered false optimism."

He not only helped to achieve rights for black people, which should have been accorded them at birth, but his later protests were leveled against the economic injustice suffered by poor people (particularly people of color), and the militaristic culture responsible for the tragedy in Vietnam.

Gandhi's nonviolence and fraternal love awakened the conscience of the white colonizers, as King and Griffin raised the consciousness of white America. "Truth never damages a cause that is just," Gandhi said. While nonviolence succeeded against imperialist control, it did not unite Hindus and Muslims when their common enemy departed. Instead Pakistan was born of a divided India, and the two powers remain in conflict along a common nuclear border.

"Jesus lived and died in vain," Gandhi wrote, "if He did not teach us to regulate the whole of life by the eternal law of love." His criticism was aimed at the missionary merchandizing of progress for the privileged through the subjugation and exploitation of the poor. Henry David Thoreau's *Essay on Civil Disobedience* was an integral source work for both nonviolent leaders. Their peaceful resistance movements, committed to human rights, that eschewed any physical violence, but also the "internal violence of the spirit," according to Dr. King.

Griffin wrote that "Through physical attacks, jailings, framed-up assaults on his character, King continued to lead and inspire. . . . In the market place of harshest reality he proved his thesis: that the *Christ Ideal* is not only a valid way, but in the case of Montgomery, Alabama, was the *only* way to insure victory: that the highest idealism is the ultimate practicality."[69]

In a letter to Thomas Merton, dated August 30, 1963, Griffin said:

> I had a long visit with Martin Luther King in Atlanta last week—all of us in the world who are trying to stem the tide feel the same thing—our enormous inadequacy. We are gaining only through the fact that men are beginning to see that they must change—not through moral conviction—no right or wrong here—but out of fear and in self-interest; nothing permanent about it, for they still hang on to the maximum cheating that the historic moment will allow. In the meantime, what a bunch of rags and tatters the civil rights leaders become. We are all half-dead except Martin, who is numb with exhaustion and the awful compromises of men. So pray for saints and great men—not men with only the vigor of anger—to come and do well what we are doing badly.

The mundane practicalities of making a living turned Griffin toward researching a work commissioned by the University of Dallas, a deal struck by Sam Bloom, who had negotiated the *Land of the High Sky* book, and managed to procure a decent stipend for the project. The scholarly monograph displayed masterful objectivity, but Griffin's voice emerged near its end. "The distressing characteristics of this monolithic society have already become evident in America, to the grave concern of all thinking men and women. The mass media and uniformity of education standardize the mental concepts of the public and create a 'collective conscience' or a society of mass opinion—a guarantee of moral and mental mediocrity. In such a society the individual who differs from the mass is not tolerated."

This position was entirely consistent with Griffin's critical stands against all the "killers of the dream"—educational conformers of mediocrity, political demagogues of racism, smut-hunting censors, and self-righteous peddlers of pseudo-religious dogma. His historical text looked to the future, seeing the continued "contribution of religious institutions of higher learning" to be "crucially important."

Griffin viewed higher education as "a basic necessity for living in a world increasingly bewildered by the implications of modern science and technology. Automation is here," and what we might do with "increased leisure depends largely on their intellectual and spiritual formation. Idle crowds can become mobs if a demagogue knows his techniques," he warned, and the "titanic task of American education in the near future" would be "to solve the problems of mediocrity and to counter the temptations toward dehumanization."[70]

After the essay was accepted for publication, he wrote Decherd Turner to say he was "distressed about my piece on religious education," because those at the University of Dallas and "somebody at SMU thinks it's great—and you know that makes me doubt its validity." SMU had ordered fifteen hundred copies of the five thousand pressrun. "In any case, I'm sticking in a quote from Rabbi Levi Olan, just to make sure I've not involuntarily bugged the Christian bit too much—anyway, it's a hell of a good quote that I've always wanted to use."[71]

With completed work at local publishers, Griffin returned to *Scattered Shadows*, as well as to time with his sons. On November 20, both boys "decided to come down and spend the night while I work." Johnny's hand was healing fine, and he joined in. "Though Gregory has frequently spent the night, this is Johnny's first try, and it was amusing to see Gregory unconsciously assume the role of host." Griffin taught them the basics of judo he learned in the military. They reminisced about Mexico, stimulated by the Tarascan prints lining the walls. "The boys remember everything and want to return to that beautiful place. We began to speak Spanish, and they are astonishing—still quite fluent after about nine months away from it—and that is some time to retain a language they no longer use at all."

On Thanksgiving Griffin was struck by a "deadly day," initially because his legs "went completely numb and after supper I lay down and slept like a drugged man for an hour." He went to the studio, but had no energy for work. He listened to a radio broadcast of "the ravishing Mozart Prague Symphony," when suddenly enthusiasm soared and he wondered why. He speculated to himself: "Is it not perhaps that one is surrounded by such insanity in the press that depression remains almost constant; and finally Mozart or Bach or some superb lines in a book or a letter or a fragment of conversation sets things right again?"

Griffin's depression had been caused by the continual barrage of "insanity" from the world, despair over the "complicated medical picture," and anxiety about the future of the family. It was an old behavioral pattern, as was his manner of transcendence, because as soon as he became immersed in music or writing, he lost the negative symptoms. Yet some days even that did not work.

"This has been a day of blackest hell," he wrote on November 27 in the *Journal*. "In a moment of weakness, I admitted to Elizabeth that the doctor had told me to put things in order, and I told her what I had done—made Decherd literary executor. Anyway, now it is done, and we shall not talk of it again; but God, what a mess this business of making arrangements is, especially when there are children to protect." How peculiar that he considered it to have been "a moment of weakness." The old paternalistic pattern had been learned from his father, believing a husband kept things from his wife to protect her from certain brutal realities. Griffin's chauvinism persisted throughout the marriage, recalled Elizabeth. "My role was to be wife and mother and I never questioned that role during the first decade. When we were married, he was a man of the world, a famous author, and I was totally naïve, a teenage girl in love with romance, and the exciting world he opened."

The "complicated medical picture" that Dr. Ross Kyger had detected would be difficult to control. "The blood sugar is disastrously high, the legs are numb about half the time and have atrophied a full inch in the past month; most hideous of all, there is the danger that we cannot bring this into line soon, and the diabetes will bring damage to the sight again."

The next day, he received welcome news from Paul Brooks, editor-in-chief of Houghton Mifflin. *Black Like Me* was doing well by their estimate, as the first two printings had sold out. Brooks suggested publishing *Scattered Shadows* before *Street of the Seven Angels*, offering a contract with an advance. Griffin promised to send several chapters of the autobiography, putting in a plug for his novel. "I realize *Street* is an off-beat work and not a big one, but I think it is a valid one; and it is timely, in view of the great rampage of irresponsible censorship that grows on us."

Griffin was motivated by the much-needed advance.

> If you can get me the advance on *Scattered Shadows*, I want to get that done immediately, and will hold off on everything else. One other consideration that intervenes, and on which you should advise me right away. Redpath Lecture Bureau wants to do a whole tour next fall on *Black Like Me*. Does this sort of thing help book sales sufficiently to merit undertaking? If it does, I'm sure we both want it done; if not, then I should know.
>
> I appreciate very much your letter and your willingness to go along with me in helping to get the autobiography done. As you recall, you have seen some 350 pages of the manuscript. I believe this is a big and unusual work, though I confess it is immensely difficult to condense and distill properly.

That week he received reviews from the publisher: Favorable responses from small town papers (*Providence Visitor*, *St Petersburg Times*, *Sacramento Bee*) and large dailies in Atlanta, Detroit, Houston. He read reviews by Lon Tinkle and A.C. Green in Dallas papers. P. D. East reviewed it for *The Progressive* and Eugene McNamara wrote about the Canadian edition in several Ontario dailies. There were positive reviews in the Catholic press (*Christian Living*, *Community*) plus three responses in *Commonweal.* Bruce A. Cook's main review was insightful; Ann Freemantle recommended it for a Christmas list; and Thomas P. McDonnell spoke out forcefully in his monthly column, beginning with "This is a very brave book."

> It is still disconcerting to recall the critically pathetic and shabby treatment given by the Catholic press to this author's fine first novel, *The Devil Rides Outside,* surely one of the best books containing a Christian theme by a contemporary American writer. No one more than its author could hope that *Black Like Me* may one day become an anomalous footnote to the social record of our time. But this is more than a sociological experiment, or as some might argue, a psychic fulfillment: *Black Like Me* is an act of Christian commitment that few of us would willingly make. Perhaps, too, we may hope for some fresh appraisals of Griffin's work from both secular and Catholic forces.

Ann Fremantle said that "This the pilgrimage *par excellence* of our time, the story of an incarnation made by one man, in deep reverence for the Divine Humanity that is daily insulted, buffeted, scourged, beaten, and bled in every black man whites insult. Griffin's heroic charity and courage are a glory for the Church." Like McDonnell, Fremantle appreciated his first novel, which she later discussed in a chapter about the author in her *Pilgrimage to People.*[72]

Black Like Me was making waves across the Atlantic. The Rosica Colin Agency negotiated a contract with Gallimard of Paris for a French translation and with British publisher Collins—both in 1962. A condensation appeared in *Man's Magazine* and an excerpt in *Interracial Review. The Saturday Evening Post* requested a 4000-word article on the journey's aftermath, but after many rewrites it was not published (and a substantial fee evaporated). The *Journal* went blank for nearly a month, and Griffin abandoned photography during this frenzy of activity. He worked nights and early mornings, revising the INS series into chapters of *Scattered Shadows,* and insisting that the boys not stay over night in the studio.

The only other voice he allowed into his solitude came in the correspondence with Lillian Smith, which stimulated energy. The first real letter from her, dated December 3, 1962, was three typed pages. Smith read his *Southwest Review* piece, saying, "We might as well dispense right now with the formalities, as I see we are headed—at least I hope so—toward a long, enduring friendship."

Smith writes about *Killers of the Dream.* "It was a book written almost with my blood: afterward, I was desperately sad for a year. I couldn't throw it off: I saw more as I wrote than I had expected to see: it was a kind of year-long vision of what we really are." After it was first published,

Smith went on a book tour in the northeast. "I was so overwhelmed with sadness that the effete New Yorkers couldn't take it. They have left me strictly alone since!"

> To speak as I did to complacent exurbanites (often) about tragic matters was, to them, unforgivable. They had come to the books-and-authors luncheons to be amused. And here I was, like Kierkegaard, fearing and trembling. But if they had only known, it shook me more than it did them. After one talk to a large group of highly successful professional women in New York (I forget the name of their club), one said coolly: "Have you ever considered having psychoanalysis?" I answered sweetly, "Yes, I have often considered it; but psychoanalysts always tell me I don't need it." She floated away in one direction, I gently floated way in another. The Yanks shouldn't try to deal with a "sweet southern woman"—there is nobody more dangerous. Oh God—how absurd and how foolish we all are. But the northerners (some of them) don't want any of us to be disturbed by us; and also, as you may find out later, they don't want any of us to be opposed to segregation; you see, they receive a psychic blessing from feeling morally superior to "the South" and we, who don't fit the pattern, shake them up. We break the stereotype, we remind them, somehow, by doing so, that all is not well in the North. And they hate us. That is why they love the moderates so; as long as moderation prevails, the snail's pace can be continued; and this means the North will not have to look at its sins, either. And above all else, nobody wants to be disturbed.

Griffin responded immediately to Smith's long letter.

> Instead of diminishing the timidity I have always felt toward great writers, your letter only increases it. In the first place, I honestly never expected to hear from you; and when I woke up here in the country, on a cold and somber day and walked down to the mailbox and found this letter, well, it was a great and exciting thing just to see the envelope. And the generous tone of it—the things you tell me.
>
> You say that after writing *Killers of the Dream*, you were overwhelmed with sadness for a long time. It was the same with me—a sense of utter disbelief and then a sort of cosmic terror that we have stepped beyond the limits of absolvable sin. I have learned, like you,

> what it is to have the 'privilege' of being sneaked into the back doors of kindly, cowardly people. I did not want to send you *Black Like Me*, for I felt it would needlessly increase the pain of your own experience; and most of all I felt it unworthy of being read by you.

Smith wrote back the next week.

> Let me tell you how I feel about *Black Like Me*. I read it at one sitting, of course; how could anyone do otherwise! I stopped once to make a pot of coffee; I needed caffeine. I read on. I'd stop now and then and whisper, 'Dear God, how can You forgive us! You can't; we have sinned *in extremis*.' I knew this. But you pushed it straight into my heart. You know the difference in knowing about and knowing. And you chose to know: which meant you must experience it yourself. I shall never forget this personal confession of a special and valid experience. I still bleed from it.
>
> The sheer cruelty of the Negro's everyday life! How wanton and terrible is white-imposed necessity (placed upon blacks) to search for a toilet, for a glass of water. I felt this: we white southerners do not deserve to live. We are a soft, sweet, terrible people; a worse people, in many ways, than the Nazis: at least they knew what they were doing. (Yes, they pretend today that they don't; but they do, and they knew then. But we—we chant our hymns, we call everybody honey and sweetie, oh God . . . we smile, sprinkle sugar, every day we sprinkle sugar on pus-filled wounds.)
>
> Behind your story so terrible and true, one could feel, I could feel, a fine intelligence, a well informed mind as well as a well informed heart. And it made me want to know you. What you did was not only courageous, it was imaginative and intelligent. You chose to know: and then to write down what you knew. This is wonderful stuff.

Not so wonderful was her estimate of Ralph McGill of the *Atlanta Constitution*, one of the whites Griffin had lauded in *Black Like Me*. McGill "has not taken a clear stand against segregation," she wrote. Griffin replied she was right about McGill, but "In what appeared to be a desert, I am sure I over-rated each ray of hope, commended each attitude that differed even slightly from the low norm. I should have suspected, for when a tone of benevolent wisdom is applied to what is essentially a passionate matter it is a dead give-away; indicating not necessary balance, but rather a care to leave a few back doors open." Smith had seen McGill for what he was—a white moderate Atlanta blacks called "Rastus"—and not the progressive he characterized himself to be. Griffin saw Atlanta as a new model for race relations in the South, but his view had been based on one week in Atlanta when he was *not* disguised. The city's newspapers had praised *Black Like Me*. They had characterized his view of the city in this paraphrase. "Atlanta's hope, he says, comes from Negro unity, from the quality of Negro leaders in education and business, from the enlightened leadership of Mayor Harstfield and from Ralph McGill." This gave the impression that all four elements had equal effect on the success of race relations. This was misleading, since most of *Black Like Me* focuses on the unity of Atlanta's black community.

With his letter of December 7, Griffin sent a photographic portrait of P. D. East, "a very special human in my book, a man who can't be explained—at least not by me. Poor P. D. is in the torments of his new book and a new marriage." Griffin writes that as a PhD in psychology, "his wife is certain she understands all the nuances of his nature and problems; and he cannot bear this, is certain she does not understand anything about 'creative processes.'" Griffin had little faith in psychology, believing that understanding a writer's motives were impossible.

> My field was to have been psychiatry, where there is still some freedom in Europe, but which is so completely closed and shrunk here that it has no longer any interest. I mean it is frightened here, unwilling to explore, and extremely hostile to explorations that might take it out of the field of clinical evidence. Enormously depressing, for it has also become a "popular" science, in which many amateurs accept hypothesis as gospel, and thereafter form utterly fantastic value judgments within the restrictions of labels and definitions. I have done a good deal of work in the field of religious psychology, a "specialty" of the Carmelite Order with which I am affiliated [as a Third Order Carmelite]; and, since my return to America, I have been appalled at the neat pigeon-holing of religious vocations indulged in by psychiatrists who have no concept whatsoever of vocations to the mystical life.

Smith's reply turned to psychological matters. "I have known a few psychiatrists and psychoanalysts: Karl Menninger, Lawrence Kubie, Rollo

May." She preferred Rollo May, even though he was "not as keen in intellect," since "he uses his intuition more and is, therefore, more flexible." The others, she suspected, looked down on him, "and they look down on God." Menninger "has a tolerance for good and all forms of religion because, he says, 'many patients need religion.' This sends me into quaking terror: to think man will accept a back-door God." Kubie "vigilantly fights God off; he envisages a 'humanistic' world without God." When she wrote of God in *The Journey*, Kubie had "fired back at me hard: 'Why bring in God?' After we had dinner together and talked a while, he said: 'But you really think of God just as a symbol, don't you?' And I was too sick to answer."

Griffin replied by return mail. "*The Journey* is so magnificently complete and final and true that it outrages me. And to think that one falls for that, believes it, and is silenced by it. Part of my work has been a Thomistic analysis of the concepts of neurosis. Part of this study and translation of terms is to see to what extent the language invented by the scientists in the natural realm might be interchangeable with that of the great mystical teachers." Griffin confessed to having "great fears about *Scattered Shadows*, which is a long, discursive autobiography treating these problems of the mystical life in its coldest and most brutal or existential light." Then he asked, "Will you not be offended, if I tell you I sent out word to our discalced Carmelite convents and asked that you be made the object of a perpetual novena?"

Within days Smith replied, "humbly grateful for the novenas."

> My Grandfather was Catholic; reared in a Quebec monastery to be a priest. Left before his final vows; came South, met Grandmother, married her, fought on the southern side but was always opposed to slavery, to radical cruelty, to stupidity. Some of Grandfather is in me; and always I've had a feeling for the rituals and the prayers—not the Church, itself, as an Establishment (not liking any establishments) but for the profound way it has met the human need for reaching inward in prayer, the human need for mystery, for reverence, for awe; the human need to be forever humbled by majesty and grace and love—and the unimaginable. . . . I have doors in me and on the surface never closed to the Unknown—which I understand is the most important part of us mortals.

Inevitably their dialogue moved along personal lines and all "subjects" circled back to contemplation of the "Christ Ideal," familial tenderness, and cherished values. Griffin compared "the great excitement of this correspondence" to "finding a new piece of music that strikes one just right; the pure joy of it."

> However you have kept what I could not–a brilliant ability to analyze and synthesize. I once had this to a high degree, and it is almost completely gone now. Your passion has sharpened your intellectual powers with no sacrifice of spirit. It has turned you into an aristocrat (if I may use such a term) and it has done just the opposite to me, turned me into a peasant, a gross mentality. I feel the loss, but feel also that as I abuse everything, I should have eventually abused this gift of the intellect—I drifted from ice toward the flame; whereas you have superbly counterpointed the two, with no sacrifice of either.

This was hardly the utterance of "a gross mentality," but another variation of his sense of unworthiness. But without question, Lillian Smith and Griffin shared a deep perception of what it meant to be outsiders in the South.

During the 1960s, Griffin continued to be involved with censorship issues. "Current Trends in Censorship," a 1962 essay, begins:[73]

> The history of censorship is a history of abuses. Beginning as an attack on pornography, it traditionally grows into a passion to suppress whatever offends the censor's religious and political beliefs. Before long, the censorial fog surrounds art, ideas, and scholarship. These patterns, with some new developments, characterize recent censorship activities.

One new development was a curious twist on an old tactic, since the "ostensible" goal of censors, they claimed, was to protect America's youth. "Now, however, the extremist political groups have announced that obscenity is part of the communist conspiracy to destroy America's morals."

The smut that had turned 1950's youth into juvenile delinquents was now turning 1960's youth into communist sympathizers! The new law passed by the 1961 Texas State Legislature repeated verbatim the test for obscenity established by The Supreme Court. "Whether to the average person, applying contemporary community standards, the dominant theme of the material taken as a whole appeals to the prurient interest." This was not a definition but an imprecise legal conclusion. Who is an average person? Where do we find "contemporary community standards"? Will Mississippi adhere to the same standards as Manhattan? The "average" person and a "standard" community were legal fictions.

"Presumably," wrote Griffin in a charitable paragraph, "the US Supreme Court made the standard elastic in order to allow works of serious intent which contained passages of erotic realism some freedom from censorship harassment, while providing a trap for hard-core pornography." This assertion was based on the legal test he knew well—censorship based on "the dominant theme of the material taken as a whole," as opposed to censoring a work on the basis of "obscene" words or sexually-explicit passages taken out of context. This illegal practice of censorship continued in Texas, and the tactics expanded to include works *containing ideas* offensive to the groups doing the banning. These illegal means violated the First and Fourteenth Amendments of the Constitution, the current standard established by the Supreme Court, and other individual rights guaranteed to citizens. The long list of criminal violations includes freedom of speech and freedom of the press, the implied right of citizens to read material of their choice, the right to due process of law, constraint of trade, illegal arrest, search, and seizure, fines, defamation of character, and harassment.

"Censors, fearing they could not ban the books they wanted to ban through due process with this new law, simply intensified their efforts to get the books removed by illegal or extralegal means," Griffin wrote. When a work was forced off the shelves of a library "by the manipulation of public opinion" (read: coercion by various groups), the works, authors, publishers, and booksellers were left with "no legal means to defend or clear" themselves. "We have witnessed again and again the spectacle of people 'opposing' books, even in court, without having read them." Since it became evident after weeks of testimony, the "Texas House committee decided that it would accept no further statements unless the witness had actually read the books he condemned!" Not only were books banned for words, phrases, and citations of "subversive" ideas, but because their authors were "suspected of disloyalty."

The activity in Texas focused on three main issues: literary books in public school libraries removed from the shelves; a campaign by Texans for America blocking the adoption of *This Is Our Nation* by the state's educators; and the banning of Henry Miller's *Tropic of Cancer* in Texas bookstores (arresting the booksellers who did not comply with the illegal edict). Each issue involved different censorship groups and geographical areas, but all were linked by practices that fit the new pattern of banning books as part of the communist conspiracy.

Griffin addressed these issues after researching the data, corresponding with those involved, and examining the conflicts in terms of law, ethics, and logic. The removal of literary books from libraries was centered in Midland. In September of 1961, four residents demanded that ten books be removed from local high schools, based on a list of "obscene" words contained in the books.

James N. Allison, publisher of *The Midland Reporter-Telegram*, called the four "a breed apart," saying that even the local John Birch Society leaders considered them too extreme! Griffin mentioned the books but did not name the "citizens," except to quote testimony before the Textbook Investigating Committee. Explaining why the books were attacked, one witness claimed they had been "written and distributed as part of the communist conspiracy to lower the morals of youth."

The Associated Press quoted the witness, flashing the report around the globe. It was the beginning of the end for the group. The bombastic attack by the "Midland Four" was neutralized by city educators, who formed a reasonable policy for book selection aimed at the very goal the amateur censors had missed—a realistic and unbiased curriculum.

The second conflict involved attacks against textbooks by Texans for America (TFA), offering "vast lists of picayune objections to a number of history books, but their main target was *This Is Our Nation* by Paul F. Boller, Jr. and E. Jean Tilford." Griffin gave the issue wide coverage, since Dr. Boller, a history professor at SMU, supplied massive documentation to the TFA's charges.

J. Evetts Haley, a questionable historian speaking for TFA, accused Dr. Boller of having "the liberal's unusual obsession with Democracy," accusing him of affiliation with "a communist front organization" (never documenting the charges). Dr. Boller belonged to the Southern Conference Education Fund, educators working for peaceful compliance with the Supreme Court decision on desegregation. According to Haley, these values were signs of communist subversion.

Griffin responded to this false logic.

> The quality of their objections to the book is revealing. They say that the book is friendly to the United Nations. They object to material on American Indians, whose contribution to America 'is practically nil.' They say the authors seem to have an 'affinity to Roosevelt.' They object to the 'overemphasis' on slavery. They object to mentioning Crispus Attucks, a Negro who was killed during the Boston Massacre of 1770. The concluding objection concerns Sherwood Anderson, Ralph Bunch, Steven Vincent Benét, Aaron Copeland, Theodore Dreiser, Bernard DeVoto, Albert Einstein, William Faulkner, Ernest Hemingway, Sinclair Lewis, Eugene O'Neill, Willa Cather, Carl Sandburg, 'and many more!' It is sufficient to suspect everyone in America, with the possible exception of J. Edgar Hoover and Kate Smith, of criminal subversion.

The pattern of objections never questioned the facts, but merely mentioned points of emphasis. "They demand that textbooks be slanted to purely 'nationalistic history,' requiring the historian "to alter or 'edit' historical facts to conform to their prejudices." If the historian did not bend to the pressure, as these authors refused to do, "they will suffer character defamation and possible financial reprisal. It is a punitive form of censorship, which could cause years of work to be nullified." Haley's credo about the writing of history for students was out of balance. He opined that "The stressing of both sides of a controversy only confuses the young and encourages them to make snap judgments based on insufficient evidence. Until they are old enough to understand both sides of a question, they should be taught only the American side." Griffin disagreed with Haley's view, deeming it irrelevant.

> This begs the question, however, since most of their objections concern not controversial points, but historical facts. TFA demands the truth be truncated wherever it reveals an incidence of weakness or error in our national past.
>
> In effect, they require the historian to abandon the science of history and become an amateur therapist, or at least a propagandist to pump into the young a spurious and hard patriotism; and what is more, a patriotism that never wavers from the narrow harmonies of extreme conservatism.

Under the guise of protecting America's youth from communism, self-appointed censors were pressuring historians to obscure facts with propaganda. In the name of patriotism, they were promoting a reactionary age. "Censorship groups who engage in the suppression of art, literature, and scholarship on the grounds they are fighting communism," Griffin pointed out, "indicate that they would protect us from one form of totalitarianism by imposing on us another. They suggest that we preserve our liberties by subverting our freedoms." He recognized the *reducto ad absurdum* of false logic and the self-righteousness of those who claimed "loudly that they are maintaining a civilization based on what they call 'the Christian Ethic,'" attempting to accomplish their goal "by the unethical and un-Christian means of smear, intimidation," and the trespass of legal rights. Any means of protecting the ultra-conservative ideology and the parallel racist methods of suppression were sanctioned without question. "The patterns are old and crude, but effective," and "in view of the reasoning behind current censorship pressures, one can only deduce that impoverished minds and purified vocabularies will help America win the battle against communism."

Griffin wondered where America's youth fit into this picture. "Are high school students really subverted by so-called four-letter obscenities that they have heard all their lives? Are they really so fragile they cannot take nourishment from truths that make other men strong? Will they not feel cheated that truths were deliberately kept from them?" He had lectured on racism to such students, not finding them to be mentally incompetent, but rather "tough-minded and worthy of far more than the strained soup our censors would feed them."

In Griffin's essay ("Prude and the Lewd"), he answers these rhetorical questions. The responsibility of writers, publishers, and booksellers was *not* to protect children from adult literature, but to enlighten adults. The responsibility to protect children "lies squarely in the home, the school, the church," Griffin wrote. "By the time the corruptible youth reaches an age to understand what he is reading and to be sensitive enough to it to be corrupted, his background training and moral development will have been fairly well established; and if this has been properly done, art, no matter how realistic, will serve for him the same function it always has—the dissemination of truth and creation of perspective and compassion. Blaming truthful art for juvenile corruption is like blaming one's mother for original sin. Does not making literature the scapegoat indicate only one thing: defeat within the home? Literature is at the mercy of those who confuse temptation with the act."

To censor adult literature reduced it to the level of a child's library, depriving adults of the constitutional right to read under the false presumption of protecting children, for whom that literature will be extinct when they are prepared to read it. For writers this becomes a double victimization, because the rights of free expression and the ability to earn a livelihood are threatened. Invariably the situation that calls for banning the cheapest smut focuses on authentic literary works.

The main points Griffin makes in "Prude and the Lewd" are those in "Current Trends in Censorship," with the exception that communist subversion was injected into the 1960s (although the censorship battles of the 1950s were not free of McCarthyism).[74] Nothing changed the trend, not the Constitution, Supreme Court decisions, intellectual debate, or ethical scrutiny.

Who are the censors? Griffin asked.

> That censors appear innocent of any awareness of the supreme importance of art in the maintenance of a culture, particularly when the art offends some cherished prejudice, and are therefore willing and glad to sacrifice highly-regarded works "to the good cause."
>
> It has always been so, and there is little hope that the cycle will not again complete itself without going to an extreme that will make the demands for freedom of the press and pen the subject of bitterly-fought battles; for the public is always late in realizing that between the two evils, the prude does it ultimately greater harm than the lewd person. The prude and the bigot are what they are precisely because they lack qualities of prudence and understanding. Moral virtue, behind which they hide, is impossible without these intellectual virtues. Power, then, in the hands of people who are currently embracing censorship with neither prudence nor understanding, must inevitably result in abuse. Seemingly admirable motives obscure the true damage caused by such people. The difference between pornography and the legitimate and necessary treatment of evil in literature is one which appears to escape the censoring agents. Every great artist, whether he is conscious of it or not, in some way illuminates the mystery of evil. But the pornographer wallows in evil, illuminating nothing.

Griffin's analysis offered clear distinctions between prudishness and prudence. Without subtle understanding, the prude perceives no gradations between an artistic evocation of sexuality and pornographic manipulation of adult content. The prude tends to wallow in the swamp of pornography, without understanding the difference, and highlighting the agenda of smut-hunters.

Implicit in Griffin's view emerges an ethical hierarchy, placing the prude and the bigot at the bottom of the scale, trapped in a reflexive mode that results in abusive behavior. At the top are the enlightened yet prudent people who "do not confuse nudity with provocative stripped-down nakedness," or the responsible citizen who "never confuses Greek sculpture with cheesecake." In his ideal hierarchy, artist and citizen are capable of ethical balance and aesthetic appreciation. The reality of sex "is not synonymous with sin," but associated with love, beauty, health, and joy. Such a citizen "understands that innocence is not based on non-knowledge of evil, but on non-love of evil," and "unlike the smut-hunter, feels no need to glut himself on every four-letter word in order to deal with the problems of pornography in society."

Finally, Griffin turns to satire in "Notes on Smut-Hunters":[75]

> I have never met a smut-hunter who admitted that his constant exposure to the 'lewd, lascivious, obscene, salacious and pornographic' had for one moment menaced his body or soul. One of the best-known professional lecturers on this subject explained his infallible criteria for detecting pornography.
>
> He contended that you could be sure a work was pornographic if it contained any passages that gave you 'a kind of feverish feeling in the cheeks and a grinding feeling in the stomach.' Although his definition was felt to lack something in theological precision, he demonstrated by showing his collection of pornographic materials, presumably so that the distinguished theologians might gain empirical knowledge of the indicated physiological responses in themselves in order to judge the validity and universality of these criteria.
>
> When he died shortly thereafter in the midst of his arduous lecture tour, one of the theologians promptly diagnosed the death as stemming from occupational causes: 'undoubtedly too much grinding of the stomach.'

Reluctant Activist

> Take the teaching of logic out of a civilization and reason is reduced to the squalor of prejudice. All of the classic fallacies of logic then become a sort of weird virtue and man seeks by loudness, fear, and violence to win causes that could *not* be won by rational persuasion.
>
> —JOHN HOWARD GRIFFIN

The decade of the 1960s was Griffin's most prolific public period. He gave more than a thousand lectures, served as a bridge between minority communities and the white power structure in many American cities, and made secret trips to crisis areas at his own expense. Media exposure included programs for National Public Radio, documentaries for French National Television in Paris, and radio programs for the Canadian Broadcasting Company in Toronto. He lectured across America, in Canada and Europe, touring three weeks of each month.

Griffin's lectures retold the *Black Like Me* story, and he spoke directly to the audience without notes. One strategy was to focus on an audience member who appeared to be skeptical. If the doubter changed expressions toward acceptance, his message was communicated. Black people in attendance were encouraged to speak out during the discussion sessions. Yet after standing ovations, white members of his audiences refused to accept the comments of black members, even though they were saying essentially the same thing Griffin had presented from the podium. When he lectured with Dick Gregory, the same responses occurred, whites accepting his points, but not Gregory's when he made the same assertions.[76]

This pattern of white resistance to black people's remarks revealed the truth of his observation that blacks and whites responded from wholly different sets of cultural experience.

Griffin noticed the same pattern in his crisis intervention work in northern cities. When asked to mediate between the black and white communities in urban areas, he got the same responses from whites. "I came into those meetings as what was called an 'ex-black man.' It was a very peculiar role in which I was cast, a role that was enormously frustrating, because what I perceived had been a degeneration of very basic communications." This was a constant theme in all his books and articles. "I had the profound personal humiliation of sitting in the presence of the black man and the white man, realizing that any black man sitting at the table had to know infinitely more than I did, and express it better than I could—the kinds of things, sadly enough, that still tended to give offense to whites if a black man said them."

Griffin was plagued by the same questions asked by whites, believing they did not really want to know the truth, or they were thoroughly indoctrinated by unconscious racism. "The tragedy of this situation was that the white leaders who had brought me in (to bridge the gap between the races) nevertheless felt that they lived there and knew better and said I was being 'unduly pessimistic' . . . and then within weeks of my departure the very explosions I had warned about happened."

Crisis intervention work brought Griffin back to the South. He became part of an underground network that included high-profile leaders and activists, but he did not belong to any civil rights organization, saying little about this network, until revealing anecdotes in the new epilogue to *Black Like Me*.[77]

"In a sense we led absurd lives in those days of terrible tension," forming "a kind of loose confederation, without organization, exchanging information, helping one another." The most dangerous areas were in the South, since Ku Klux Klan members held positions in local governments, police forces, and county sheriff departments. "In one year we lost seven friends and colleagues," and "Dr. King and Dick Gregory became almost fatalistic in accepting the fact that they were dead men and that it was only a matter of time before that fact became a reality."

With characteristic humility, Griffin never referred to himself in these terms. "They and many others acted with a bravery and heroism almost incomprehensible to most men. They went into areas of extreme danger." He knew that such action was "possible occasionally, but it is almost impossible to keep it up," because "the human nervous system will not stand it."

Dr. King, Dick Gregory, and Griffin made a secret pact in Atlanta. Since violent death seemed inevitable, they agreed to ignore their fears, continuing the fight for justice. Gregory was assaulted and jailed several times. Griffin did not suffer the ultimate sacrifice that Dr. King, Medgar Evers, and many other human rights activists suffered. But he did experience a brutal beating at the hands of the Klan one night in 1964 on a deserted dirt road in rural Mississippi. Left for dead, he survived and recovered, but never spoke of the incident publicly. Griffin wrote of the beating only once in the *Journal*, on December 12, 1975.

> The deepest damage to the victims of torture is not the physical pain inflicted but the sudden devastating moment when one perceives that one is at the mercy of men or societies in which mercy simply does not exist. It was particularly in studies dealing with the after-effects on the victims of torture, that I began to see the universality.
>
> I remember my own torture: the beating, and it was not the physical pain that penetrated in any greatly destructive manner. What did penetrate was when I heard them say, "Get his kidneys," and they rolled me over and stomped the kidney area. That I have had to face in order not to be destroyed by it. I would not have been at all surprised if they had shot me or bludgeoned me to death. But they went one step deeper into depravity—they deliberately and even cunningly left me to live maimed and I am sure with the idea that I would die much more slowly, but surely. The lasting damage came not from anything physical at all—it came in that moment when horror swept over me at the words, "Get his kidneys."
>
> Not horror either (I am sure of this) for what they were doing to me, but horror that men who had "left their humanity at home" were doing this thing, horror to be in the presence of such human degradation.

Extensive travel in the Deep South presented problems and risks. Griffin was tailed by state troopers and county deputies in officially marked vehicles, along highways and by-trails through the South, often all the way to the state line where the lawmen disappeared. When followed, he avoided the homes of black friends, never picked up white hitchhikers, and adhered strictly to the traffic rules. When finding lodging, he made every effort to change rooms upon arrival, since other activists had been discovered and beaten. He knew not to be in the company of a woman, unless other friends were present, because false charges of rape had been made against activists. If he needed a telephone, he went to a public booth to avoid a tapped phone in a rented room. He spoke in a code to avoid detection. This stress was unhealthy, especially for one with his acute diabetic condition. He was reminded of the French underground and military combat training, where he learned to avoid danger. But it was nerve-wracking and exhausting.

When Griffin was able to return home for a week each month, it took a few days of rest to relieve the stress. When the phone rang, he was always jarred into asking, "What next?" Yet even with too little time and energy, he managed to produce a large volume of commentary on racism and censorship. Excerpts from *Black Like Me* were published internationally. He continued the intense pace, and his work was being recognized. He was given the first *Pacem in Terris* Peace and Freedom Award by the Catholic Interracial Council (with late President John F. Kennedy), and *Black Like Me* received the *Saturday Review* Anisfield-Wolf Award.

The movie version premiered in Manhattan in 1964, featuring Tony-winner James Whitmore in the lead role, with distinguished character actors Will Geer, Roscoe Lee Brown, and Richard Ward. But the production was as Judith Crist's review in the *New York Herald Tribune* opined. "A good-will gesture gone wrong—gone so far wrong in form and content, in fact, that its high purpose and noble intent are all but perverted. The seriousness and good intent of those involved in the film cannot be denied, but the incredible mixture of sex sociology they have come up with smacks with opportunism and ineptitude." The film was confusing where the book was clear; shrill where it was controlled; sentimental where it was empathetic. Griffin lamented Whitmore's characterization. "He plays it angry all the way through. I couldn't behave that way when I was doing it in real life. I'd have been killed."

Constant lecturing during the 1960s left little time for the *Journal*, and Griffin felt no joy in discussing racism and censorship. Although he was a reluctant activist, he was directed by his ethics and spiritual direction, discussing the dangers flooding over the country, waves of white fear at the core of prejudice against black people, and the pathetic ignorance of smut-hunters censoring literature.

Griffin typed sixty-three pages in the *Journal* in 1960, ninety-one pages in 1961, and one hundred ten pages in 1962. He made additional notes in the script during first visits in 1962 with two spiritual masters, Trappist monk Thomas Merton at the Abbey of Gethsemani in Kentucky and Jacques Maritain at Princeton. The notes would become the basis for books about them. Even as Griffin felt compelled to discuss racism and censorship with these thinkers (who had written on those subjects), he was delighted to have conversations about philosophy and theology. All three were steeped in European culture—from medieval monasticism and knowledge of Latin to the contemporary arts. All were converts to Roman Catholicism, with perfect fluency in French. Griffin was not asked the same reflexive questions by these thinkers he held in the highest regard, but influenced and enlightened by their wisdom. They did not believe the light of truth had been extinguished, but only that white America had lost sight of it.

Griffin saw society as churning out conformists, but few enlightened citizens. He believed that the church cultivated faithful practitioners, yet no saints. He viewed our culture as sinking to the level of mediocrity. The merely *average* was hailed as the norm. The secular system did not reflect sacred virtues. Utilitarian self-interest had replaced ethical scrutiny. "We have become *democratic* even in our response to values," he wrote in the *Journal*. "We give the same response to a mediocre value as to a high one. The result is not that the high value becomes mediocre, but that *we* do. This is why we have neurotics and bigots instead of saints."

The *Journal* for 1963 was only sixty-eight typed pages. On January 4, he was "back to reading the Desert Fathers, admiring the bluntness of these holy men. It is like fresh water after the sickening niceties and delusions that surround religion today. How comforting to read St. Jerome and the Fathers in the *Verba Seniorum*, like some music dimly remembered, and now once again distantly heard; as though one had lived these things in some past time; the return of a cherished memory long gathering dust." During this period he continued on *Scattered Shadows*, and remembrances were touched by humble, ancient voices, rather than by dramatizations of the ego.

> Nothing is a greater waste of time than admonitions to "Know Thyself"—one must know, but objectively; to be able to stand off from self and observe, in order to learn, but not to judge. The only way is self-abandonment, to get rid of self. Otherwise, an artist can never succeed to make of himself anything but a mask.
>
> The only value of self-knowledge is to escape the delusion of self in which all of our culture wraps us—that fastidious delusion which even our intimate experience fails to show us is a lie. I live the desert life today, thinking of St. Jerome.

For two weeks he was on the road, lecturing four times in Houston, seven times in Nebraska, and once in Michigan. On January 20, Griffin typed two paragraphs, preparing to leave again. He returned on January 24, writing on a cold night and loving the solitude in "this stone room with its brick floors—the world draws into here, with a radiance, filled by a great awareness of the Desert Fathers, their writings and mentality, their silences, matched certainly by the silence here tonight."

On February 5, he had a call from Zara Nelsova, informing him that Francis Poulenc had died in Paris. "Now he knows the answers to those questions that so tormented him, particularly in recent years. Strange man and amiable genius." Later that month he delivered lectures in Chicago, Cincinnati, and Louisville.

Since Louisville was less than an hour from the Abbey of Gethsemani, Griffin made a retreat during the first two days of March, handwriting notes about dialogues with Thomas Merton and making an "Official Portrait" of the monk.[78]

"Days of work and great guilts," begins the March 13 entry, "because I am working on the photography instead of the promised writing. And yet, such beautiful things come from the camera and the enlarger that I cannot resist them." He had worked the previous two nights printing film of cellist Zara Nelsova.[79] He felt "the tremendous gratification of seeing them come out well—among the best I have ever managed. They are exciting, because all of them were taken while she was wholly immersed in playing the Bach partitas; and her face is illumined with concentration—what the French call *allegresse*, as though the music were there in the expression, the lift of her face." But writing obligations gnawed at him, "and my days are spent in a constant *mea culpa* as the photography possesses me hopelessly."

JHG's Official Portrait of Thomas Merton, taken at the monk's hermitage in 1963. This photo was published in *A Hidden Wholeness: The Visual World of Thomas Merton* (Houghton Mifflin, 1970). The cloth edition included photos by Merton and JHG, along with Griffin's texts.

"And the photography continues to dominate everything," begins the brief *Journal* entry for March 19.

> Splendid pictures at Gethsemani—many first class ones, showing Merton in his various activities. The photos open up all sorts of speculations,

> especially when viewed in the context of his writings—particularly those about silence. And how these things mark the face of the one who lives them. Not with a spiritual quality, as we think of it, but with a toughness, a clarity of the eyes, a quickness to laugh—all of it a shell that is man and that hides beneath its surface a volcano of love.

More traveling followed in March and April. On May 5, before leaving to lecture at the University of Texas in Austin, he typed notes in the *Journal*, knowing he would "regret the lack of sleep and feel stupid tomorrow."

> This spring has been the busiest of my life—constant trips, lectures, and then every spare moment spent working with the photography, writing articles, studying. But tonight, a steady rain drums against the roof and in the great silence of midnight, I forget the whole sad mess of racism, man cheating man, and enjoy a moment like the old times—a moment of awareness, awake while the rest of the world slumbers.
>
> It is the delight of this cloister; the intimate, withdrawn sense of felicity—as though in this area of lamplight, you ceased to exist except to sense the presence of God and nature; all attention focuses on that, but yet a portion remains in self, enough to sense the rightness of it, to know that all is well for the moment in this body and this soul—that all is comfortable and functioning; and the rest goes out to the moment when every view and thought is magnified.
>
> But it is not grandiose, not the chorus of praise—no it is the smaller thing, the little space of lamplight—clear, sharp, precise—like a fine-etched plate. Everyone I know suffers. In Birmingham, a thousand Negroes, many of them children, are in jail for asking that they be allowed to be human.

Returning from Austin, he writes on May 8 that the lecture had gone well, but "the highpoint was a good session with J. Frank Dobie."[80] The most famous writer in Texas at that time had invited Penn Jones and Griffin out to his country place. They went "to a most disreputable-looking country tavern near Dr. Dobie's *Paisano*, and we had a marvelous conversation."

Then Griffin wrote an essay about another visit to segregated Louisiana with the outspoken black priest, Father August Thompson.[81] During the visit they recorded a startling dialogue for *Ramparts*. The interview stirred headlines: NEGRO PRIEST SAYS SEGREGATION MAKES SECOND-CLASS CITIZENS (*New York Times*), FEAR AND

FAITH IN THE DEEP SOUTH (*San Francisco Chronicle*) and NEGRO PRIEST SAYS SEGREGATED CHURCH EXISTS IN THE SOUTH (*The Catholic Messenger*).

It was one thing to speak against discrimination, but Father Thompson's revelations concerned his all-black congregation experiencing racism and separatism by the institutional hierarchy of the Catholic Church. The priest's white bishop attempted to suppress the interview, but Father Thompson would not be silenced. At one point in the interview, Griffin asked "about claims frequently made by whites that Negroes, never having known anything else in the South, become inured to all of these undignifying things." Father Thompson retorted: "How can any man ever become accustomed to getting cheated? When a body is never fully fed, it never stops being hungry. It is the same with a man's spirit—it hungers, hungers after dignity, freedom, and love; and it never stops hungering after these things until it is finally crushed. The Negro has never become accustomed, and he will never become accustomed to being treated as less than fully a human being." Then Griffin asked how black priests are treated in the South. "Well, let's just say that in some areas, we Negro priests might be called second-class Christs."

This stunned Griffin, who replied, "We know that we do have a profound scandal of second-class Catholics, but when it is the scandal of a 'second-class Christ' it becomes inconceivable. . . . This must burn you very, very deeply." The priest responded: "As a priest it does, because it degrades the priesthood. And that's why I try to do everything possible to right it. I'm not saying that Negro Catholics want any kind of special treatment. They feel they are getting special treatment right now, and that is the trouble. All they want is to be treated exactly the same as any other Catholic."

He discussed this with Thomas Merton, who had met Father Thompson at a Gethsemani retreat, encouraging the young priest *not* to hesitate writing with such honesty. Griffin responded as if it were a command to his vow of obedience, writing a scathing critique of the Church—"Racist Sins of Christians."[82] It caused widespread debate, and rationalizations of the Catholic hierarchy were met by a wave of support for black people from the laity and the clergy.

On June 2, 1963, the Griffins celebrated their tenth anniversary, "the first time that we have ever left the children on one of our anniversaries to go out alone together. It would have been perfect had we not been constantly preoccupied with the dying of Pope John XXIII." The next night he wrote in the *Journal.*

> Nothing really interests me in photography except human faces, because with each one I have that intense excitement—not of accomplishment, not of technical triumph—no, it is the excitement of photographing yet another aspect of the image of God; and these somehow work together to form a whole, a large and diffuse harmony, a silent visual music that is the sound of God—all of it bound up in a kind of universal image.
>
> Now I hear Beethoven's *Second Symphony.* Beethoven the Moor. Always I think that if this sublime genius lived in the South, he would be considered a *nigger* and would not be allowed to go into a café in Mississippi.

Pope John XXIII died in Rome on June 3. Griffin reread the pope's encyclical on June 5. "In the *Pacem in Terris*, speaking of the rights that accrue to man because he is human and has human needs according to the Natural Law, the pope mentioned among other things, food, shelter, clothing, rest and art. How splendid to put in both art and rest—two things seldom considered essential." Griffin received a letter from Father Murphy, "where he waited out those days of the Pope's death in Rome, which struck like the death of his own father."

Before retiring that night, Griffin heard a radio newsflash about the murder of Medgar Evers in Jackson, Mississippi.[83] The thirty-eight-year-old field secretary for the NAACP (since 1954) was shot in the back by Byron De La Beckwith of the White Citizens' Council. The assassination was carried out the day after President John F. Kennedy's speech in support of civil rights on national television.

On June 26, Griffin had an unexpected visit from Mrs. Annie Humphreys, an elderly black neighbor. She was searching for Elizabeth and her mother Bess, but they were in town to shop. He invited Mrs. Humphreys in for coffee. She marveled at his photographic portraits. "When I showed her the photo of Father Thompson, she tapped his face with her finger, explaining, "It looks so real, I wanted to see if he was alive." Finally the purpose of her visit became clear.

> With a great flow of joy on her face, she told me how the white people in Mansfield were changing in their treatment of colored persons, as she calls them. Now, the white ladies are calling her "Miss Annie" instead of just Annie. In the country, everyone here calls everyone Miss and the first name, but never have called Negroes Miss or Mister. Well, in a tremendous flow of words, she told me of her great adventure with dignity; how for the first time in her life, the storekeeper did not abandon her for a white customer.
>
> Never have I been more moved, more delighted, more keenly aware of the human thing that is happening here—this old lady experiencing for the first time in her life that for which she has hungered forever—respect and dignity—recognition as a person worthy of respect. It is a glory for her—there is no other word for it—a magnificent new glory. It is one of the most beautiful things I have ever witnessed—to see her unfold like this, lose that defensiveness. She wants to bring her husband to see the pictures. I told her to come by any time.
>
> Then I asked if she would let me photograph her in that sunbonnet, but she would not until she washed it and starched it, and "fix myself up." No one is going to photograph her without her looking her very best, in her full dignity.
>
> Delicious afternoon when I witnessed that deep joy of Miss Annie, who need never again be just Annie. I realize these are the crumbs she has been given, when she was born deserving the whole loaf; but she has been deprived of that loaf, and at least these crumbs of health have brought jubilance to her past life of humiliation.

Griffin was told of the passing of Clyde Kennard,[84] who died on June 6, 1963. Kennard was framed for a petty crime and sentenced to seven years of hard labor, because he was the first black person to register at a segregated college in Mississippi. He had been a paratrooper in Korea, an honors scholar at the University of Chicago, and a tax-paying citizen. Martin Luther King, Dick Gregory, and Griffin petitioned Governor Ross Barnett for Kennard's release from prison (where he was dying of cancer), raising funds for his surgery in Chicago.

He wrote about Kennard on June 9: "One feels the hollowness of finality, the full crushing weight of his death, especially for his mother and sister. The needlessness of it and the terrible cruelty he suffered for being black. We whites created and tolerated the climate that formed the brute minds who framed him, brutalized, and killed him. It is against this formation that I have fought—not for Negroes, but for all children, so that they can be spared this kind of perversion."

Griffin lost another friend, recording the news on July 16.

> Received word that Father Gerald Vann died. Strange this dear friend whose writings so influenced my conversion died on the anniversary of my First Communion. He had suffered the tremendous agonies of cancer. Thank God it took him quickly. But his going is like a light going out. The world is somber, and it is poorer without his wisdom and great good sense. No man, except Jacques Maritain, has taught me more.

The travel schedule continued unabated for Griffin during the final months of the year. After the final round in Detroit and Windsor, Ontario, he made the last *Journal* notes in a Manhattan hotel, on November 22, 1963, learning of the tragic assassination of President John F. Kennedy.

The brief *Journal* notes for 1964 (only 36 pages) begin February 15.

> The months rush and I almost never get to write any more. It is all lectures, travel, hotel rooms. But this morning it halts for an hour, and I listen to Robert Casadesus playing the Scarlatti sonatas. I sit here in my pajamas with a cup of black coffee, overwhelmed to hear this music again—a felicity intensified by the contrast to that knotted and crabbed world outside where men struggle to justify and perpetuate injustice.

Griffin was on the road again until March 19. "Home at last from the most strenuous lecture tour I've ever given." On the next trip he was accompanied by Elizabeth. They were together in New York, on to Montreal, back to Washington, DC, and finally New Orleans. Griffin wrote little about the trip, but from Elizabeth's interviews we learn that she saw the *Black Like Me* movie premiere in Manhattan, later meeting Sterling Williams in New Orleans. She thanked Sterling for his kindness, saying that Griffin "couldn't have made it without you." Sterling declared it a "highlight" to receive a first edition of *Black Like Me* with his photograph on the back cover. The couple dined at Antoine's that night, and the chef remembered Griffin accompanying Robert Casadesus on his piano tours. Elizabeth said that it was "a very romantic time, and I did not want that vacation to end."

On his forty-fourth birthday, June 16, 1964, Griffin was overjoyed to be home. Among the gifts he received were albums that included Casadesus playing Mozart piano concerti with George Szell and the Cleveland Orchestra. The next day Griffin made arrangements for a passport, since he was to live for a month at the University of Peace in Belgium. He lectured to international students at the invitation of Father Dominque Pire, architect of "Fraternal Dialogue" (recipient of the 1958 Nobel Peace Prize for his work with displaced persons after World War II). Griffin had dialogues with the leading thinkers from Africa and Asia, edifying his work on global patterns of racism. While there he learned of the murder of the civil rights workers in Mississippi (James Chaney, Michael Schwerner, and Andrew Goodman).

The *Journal* for 1965 includes 110 pages, beginning on January 1, when he was down with a kidney infection. He cleaned the cottage studio, giving "the illusion of order and propriety—a pleasant atmosphere in which to pass the hours of treatment for this infection." The next day he turned down television appearances in Portland and San Francisco, "because the schedule is now so full nothing else will fit." During the decade, he had earned sufficient income to pay all debts. The income came from a back-breaking lecture schedule, not from royalties.

> How I beg the hours to stand still, longing for this tranquility here in the midst of my family. When will I be able to return to my real work at the typewriter? I have hardly any free moments between now and the end of April. Then crowds, travel, snow, meals when they can be found (and almost never a good one), problems of chastity—how I appreciate the loneliness in *Death of a Salesman* now in such prolonged periods away from home.
>
> And just when I was working fairly well, the damned telephone rang. Would I mind flying at my own expense to south Texas to speak before 50 rednecks? I can count on getting perhaps one page of work done—getting into it, and the damned phone will ring. By the time I have got off the line, all of the train of thought is broken; and today I am too dead tired to make the effort of going back and picking it up.

From January 10-16, Griffin lectured in the Pacific Northwest, and since the next stop was Ohio, he retreated to Gethsemani (January 25-26). He had conversations with radical priests Illtud Evans and Daniel Walsh, who were visiting with Merton in his hermitage. Griffin returned home on January 30.

> Before going out again to almost a full month of lecturing, it is murderous to live under such a schedule and far more murderous to be away from the family that long. We cherish the moments together. Gregory stays at my side constantly, working on his photography when I am typing—now he sits by the large windows, cleaning his lenses, lost in concentration, as beautiful a study in the half-light as any Rembrandt drawing.
>
> Some George Wallace supporters, apparently Catholic, have issued hate material to try to stop my Milwaukee appearance. This has created a great stir, and I have had to spend time in rebutting, which is degrading, not because of what they say (that I am a pornographer), but because whenever anyone gets down to battle with them, it is exactly like wallowing in a hog trough. They call themselves Citizens for Moral Responsibility, and use the most irresponsible techniques—cleverly, though, to avoid libel; but nevertheless to achieve a goal of character-assassination, like dogs tearing and snarling after a man's good name.

With Griffin back on the road, the *Journal* goes blank throughout February and March. Returning to it on April 15, he noted that the "past months have been devoted entirely to lecturing and times in and out of the hospital. They did the first of four oral surgeries—a great mess, but it was well done and seems to be healing properly. It continues to ache." He was suffering from osteomyelitis (inflammation of the bone marrow), which was destroying the density of his jawbones. This condition plagued the remainder of his years, eventually forcing him to grow a beard during the 1970s. Two days after this surgery, the stitches were removed.

> Aside from the great ball of pain in my face, peace and contentment, with a settling of nerves into health. Tomorrow is Easter—tonight silence smelling of expectancy. It is a time for waiting, for doing little things without any sense of hurry—polishing the children's shoes—and what a joy for a father in that. I practice a little on the piano, some Bach and Rameau. And then rare sweet moments of silence, when a man can just be. I take nourishment from the silence, the stillness, even of all thought, from not needing to *do* anything.

On Easter, as he was photographing wildflowers, he heard the sounds of the Easter service at the black church near the Holland farm.

> The piano blared out, electrifying the heated air—notes of huge energy on the torpor—and hands clapped and voices raised. I walked up close near an open window. A few standing singers saw me near, grinned and nodded a greeting. A great worship of the Lord on a Sunday in the country. They do it better than we. When the church let out, men and women streamed through the doors to a few cars, but most will walk down the lane to their homes. Now we waved overtly. A happy Easter that is not sterilized.

Griffin went on tour from April 19 to May 3, returning home for further oral surgery. "Awareness of the awful pain I will carry for the next few days, but no longer any dread of it," he typed in the *Journal* on May 6.

> Talked today to Mrs. Leona Smith, Clyde Kennard's mother, who asked me *not* to send checks anymore, since the banks are too "mean" about cashing them. I am arranging to send them to another person—a white—who can cash them and deliver the money. What a great joy to hear that voice, so filled with strength and faith. "Now don't you worry. I'm making out just fine."

In the *Journal* of May 16, Griffin wrote pages reminiscent of meditations during the 1950s when he was blind, but rare for the turbulent 1960s.

> This has been a day of strange perceptions. Everyday living continues to fill me with astonishment. Awareness that out there, an infinity away, is sanctity—that it is the only worthwhile reality that makes all other things make sense; the nostalgia for it that lies at the core of my every act and hope, buried there beneath all the layers of seeming realities of behavior and motive. Men seek always to discover the "motive" for my work.
>
> It is so terribly simple. But I cannot dare explain it without giving them the impression that I am something I am not. One can only struggle to make the gift of self complete and *motiveless* and trust then that one's acts will be better than those one could summon on one's own; to follow in the faith that the resonances will work out, and they need not concern one, and accept the questioned motives, the character assassination, even the hatred of those one seeks to redeem in this silent act of endless charity.

Back on the road, Griffin's lectures were picketed in Milwaukee and Minneapolis by the Knights of Columbus (which he called "the Klan of Catholics"). He lectured in Columbus, Ohio, drawing more than two thousand people on a night the Ku Klux Klan had its organizational meeting. Returning home for more surgery, he wrote in the *Journal* on June 5. "I take all nourishment through a straw and cannot speak clearly. This is all for the best. I am tired of speaking, clearly or otherwise."

By June 7, Griffin was free of pain, hoping to avoid sedation. He watched the children chasing butterflies as he went to the studio. "I look up from the typewriter and the portraits I have made of friends—and all of those faces come out of their frames, take on warmth and dimension, and share silently in the moment."

Griffin was considering the "new priests" he met on his travels, men who would take the Church in a progressive direction toward healing its racism. At the same time he was uttering a prayer of the reluctant activist for release.

> I have acted under obedience, pure and simple. I have acted in a way that is contrary to my every inclination, and I have come almost to the end of my forces. Now, I continue to make the same *fiat*, the same offer, because one can will such things; but my every tissue and bone and longing is to move into a whole different realm, to let the action become incessant prayer; to let the renown become invisibility and obscurity; to be relieved of the awful burden of being known, so that I can dedicate time to deeper and more effective writing, so that finally, at middle age, I can become myself.
>
> Is my vocation—this thing I feel so tremendously—really there, or will I be called on to re-enter the public arenas? I hold back nothing, obviously, but I pray that these new priests and younger thinkers signify what it seems to signify. I feel I could disappear from sight, from all of these temporal problems that sometimes ramify into the eternal and nothing would be greatly changed. It is the profound sense of being pushed toward contemplation, to love in silence, invisible, unknown, without distraction—the need (and how profoundly I feel this) to withdraw now that better men than I can ever be, wiser ones, can come in and serve as the kind of symbol that it has been my fate to serve up until now.

> How frequently in these years have I bitten back the cry that surges up spontaneously as an appeal within me, the cry: "I want out of it. I want off the stages of the world, I want out of the blinding glare, and to be allowed to come home to God without falsity. This is the way of reality—all the rest is false; and now a whole new generation of magnificent people with the energies of enthusiasm and commitment are coming to the fore, and perhaps answering that prayer that I have never really allowed myself to utter.

The next day (June 16, his forty-fifth birthday), there was release, as the doctor postponed surgery a week to allow for healing. "I will spend the day reading Maritain's *Carnet de notes* (Notebooks) and working with photography—two things that make for great delight—a way of celebrating the occasion."

Griffin endured three hours of surgery on July 1, but was back to photography by July 3. He was assisting with Gregory's photos of animals to be submitted for an exhibit at the Brookfield Zoo in Chicago.

> I have never heard of a seven-year-old who worked so hard and in such a sustained manner at anything. Now, on the radio, to keep me company, Casadesus playing the Mozart Concerto (No. 22) with the Cleveland orchestra. My affections go back to the years when we traveled together on concert tours, when we had such glorious times and reveled in such music making. I feel somewhat restored with the exception of this pain.

He continued reading Maritain, but this time under sedation.

> The eye fixes avidly on every word and phrase, absorbs them completely, and sometimes, merely to savor them, goes over and over a paragraph—so the reading is interminably slow. Names swim to the surface to evoke a thousand nostalgias: Garrigou-Lagrange, Yves Simon, Olivier Lacombe, Berdyaev, Reverdy, Gilson, Peguy, Bloy, Rouault. And then the radio announces that 700 college white students are in jails throughout the country. As black people say that you cannot trust the white man, so they say you cannot trust their parents' generation. According to their lights, they are probably correct, considering the tawdry values against which they protest and which outrage them.

Griffin worked July 23 on prints, waiting for Bradford Daniel to arrive to work on the *Reader* that night. In the *Journal*, he described a trip to town.

> Went to Mansfield to pick up some supplies at dusk. Strange magical synthesis of the moment—intensely hot (100 degrees), dusty, a grey last light of day with the garish neon lights. I smelled the odor of a parched country town, felt the pressure of heat on my face and thought of God as the great formless blaze of charity—the thought, the image imposed itself with such hallucinatory insistence it fixed all of my faculties. God was there in the purest form in a country town on a summer's twilight; no lovely image, no recognizable image—but the world-fire of roaring charity. And then returning here, down the country lanes, past houses where people sat fanning themselves on the front porches by the last light of day. I thought of our picayune charity, our acts, and our acting.

For a month Griffin was on tour, returning August 16.

> I lectured in Oklahoma City, the Knights of Columbus Hall. We heard a lot of discontent from the Knights about it, but the Bishop held firm. Great tension. Already the Catholics who are also racists were circulating photographs, alleging to prove that the Sisters who marched in Selma were in reality whores from New York City hired to wear nuns' robes. This appears to have been the Birch element, which is very powerful there. I repudiated it, and I think no one could doubt anymore. I said the truth, that I knew those nuns in their convents, and that this kind of doctoring was typically vicious. I got a standing ovation. One of the ironies of this whole situation is that I find we get our best protection from the Anti-Defamation League rather than from any organization within the Church.

By September 1, Griffin scrutinized his work, as he always had.

> How can man trust himself, to put ideas on paper? They show all the crudity of man in his unguarded moments. I stop, spend a long time reading Augustine, trying to give over the formation of my thoughts to Christ's thoughts, so that at least nothing I finally say will be in contradiction to that eternal logic, seeking to undo what is most me so that what is most Christ will speak through my fingers and mind. The major differences make themselves felt—I learn again, for

> the thousandth time, to refuse to judge men but to content myself with seeking ultimate causes and effects and simply revealing them.
>
> I learn again that my antipathies are a luxury I cannot, in any wisdom, afford to let penetrate either my mind or my work. I learn again that the ME is not either interesting or important in comparison to what is interesting and important. Why cannot this knowledge become habitual? Why cannot these learned things stay as the firm basis of all knowledge, not at the intellectual level where they exist, but at the profounder levels of conviction so deeply rooted it is spontaneous? No, I find that I have to exercise myself in them before each writing, just as a pianist has to exercise his fingers and mind all of his life in order to keep things functioning at the high level demanded of his art.

Another tour of duty took Griffin away for a few weeks, returning home only to face more surgery. After surgery, lectures through October in New York and along the east coast, then on to the Midwest most of November. He was looking forward to a return to Belgium in December to the University of Peace in Huy.[85] "So with summer's ending," he lamented in the *Journal* of September 22, "it means the beginning of a whirlwind of activity that is essentially repulsive to me."

> I do not mind lecturing, but always on why men must have their rights to be men, why it makes sense to stop cheating against fellow citizens, this gets to be immensely depressing. I should cancel and remain here to get the writing done, but I cannot in good conscience do that. One mind might be clarified, one life might be saved by going."

There are no typed *Journal* entries until December 22, after Griffin returned home from two weeks at the University of Peace. He kept a handwritten diary and met several Nobel Laureates. It had been a restful time, and he returned refreshed. In the days preceding Christmas, he had "a thousand things to get done" and, to his surprise, they received a quilt from Clyde Kennard's elderly mother.

> With her failing eyesight, the stitches are large and garbled, but I have never seen anything that so eloquently spoke of love—the hours she must have spent sewing and quilting. The white man killed her son in the most unspeakable manner, and she makes a quilt for another white man.

That same day he received the galleys of Cornelia and Irving Sussman's study, *How To Read A Dirty Book*, "which deals with art, censorship and pornography in the most mature and cultivated handling I have ever seen on this touchy subject. I stayed up a good part of the night reading it, and relished every word of it."

Transitions and Trances

I feel the terrible need to go out—not in the lecture halls, but in those rooms that obsess me, those rooms where the mothers of martyrs, the widows of martyrs sit; those rooms where the parents wonder what in God's name they can do to save their children.

I have "the apostolate of misery" in my heart; and yet I know this is *not* my true vocation, else why would God have given me a wife and children who are in a sense rendered an injustice if I fulfill that apostolate? Why would God be placing this health impediment in my way if that were my apostolate? No, I know this from a very long time back—when I ached for the monastic life and found that God was right and I was wrong. God drives men along these paths, the *right* ones.

If I cannot physically go to those rooms, I have been now in so many of them, and have come to see what is in those rooms, and come to be broken with love for what is seen there. I know this is what God wants of me, because each of those rooms is clear in my creative being, every stick of furniture, the tone of voices, the looks on the faces.

But while I write of those who have wept and prayed in the past, who will sit with those who weep and pray in the future? But I do that as an act of the will, and I believe in it and I trust in it.

—JOHN HOWARD GRIFFIN

Since enduring several operations in 1966 to remove tumors from feet that would not heal because of diabetes, Griffin was restricted to home by his doctors, avoiding the hectic travel schedule.

It was a prolific year writing in the *Journal* (248 pages). Yet as early as the first day of January, it was another typical year for racism. He had several calls from Father Thompson about another bombing of the only area service station owned by a black man. "They terrorize us without the slightest hesitation. Perhaps if the nation were watching through proper press coverage, they might think twice before picking off their victims."

Griffin tried to get newspapers to the scene, calling AP and UPI, as well as the FBI and Justice Department. There were upcoming trials, one concerning police brutality against the CORE workers, the other about the black man who was bombed, and came out carrying a weapon. "It will be an interesting example of justice," the priest points out, "and the country should know about it. If there is no coverage, the black witnesses can end up getting killed or maimed for testifying at these trials. "Griffin noted in the *Journal* on January 4 that "This has gone on over a year now. The fruitless appeals, the constant reporting to authorities, with absolutely no result. Soon they will kill someone like Father Thompson, and the world will rage and cry out and everyone will say: 'We didn't realize it was this serious.' But we've had this happen too often."

Griffin lectured most of January, but contracted pneumonia in Minnesota, "where I nearly froze and had to be taken to the hospital immediately after my lecture." The next day his fever rose. "Wrote some today, although the day seemed interminable and actionless; rather afraid to work for fear that it might worsen this pneumonia. But to write some each day—it mounts up. That is the important thing." He received a gift of Nell Dorr's *The Bare Feet*, magnificent photographs of Mexico, from Penn Jones on February 3.[86] "I have never seen a work so stunning. Tremendous excitement pours out from the pages, a life that breathes and touches reality in a way I have never experienced through photography."

His health showed improvement by February 5, so he traveled to Canada a week later. On February 16, he wrote about recording sessions with the fabled folk singer Josh White at the Canadian Broadcasting Company in Toronto. Then he lectured in New England, returning on March 7.

Griffin was awarded The Christian Culture Award (of Canada), bestowed on an "outstanding exponent of Christian ideals."[87] The family traveled with him to Windsor, Ontario, where he received the award, lecturing on "Fraternal Dialogue" rather than about racism. A photograph of him with a pregnant Elizabeth (and the three children) appeared in the *Michigan Catholic* on April 7.

In the *Journal* of April 13, Griffin wrote of sending the family home and going on another speaking tour. He "got attacked by the Birchites in La Crosse, Wisconsin, who tried to serve me a summons contending that the reading of *Black Like Me* had damaged their children. The community reacted in my favor even as *The Wanderer* carried a smear that lost some of its effectiveness when it was revealed the writer was Governor Wallace's campaign manager. The court hearing is repeating the innuendos brought by the Milwaukee group of Wallace supporters."

During two lovely spring days, April 15-16, he felt intense diabetic pain—"my blood sugar is in the mountains—the test tape black." He resisted the pain by praying for Elizabeth in her seventh month of pregnancy. "She is beautiful and handles all of the discomforts with great good humor."

April 20, reading *The Eagle's Word* by the late Gerald Vann, he jotted quotes in the *Journal*, and evaluated his own vocation.[88]

> To say that I leave public life because of the attacks on me, rather than that I leave because my vocation directs me into greater solitude, meditation and writing—is like saying that I listen to the mosquito's word when I am listening to the Eagle's word, which tells me that I must wane so that God can wax in me.

On April 30, he received a note from Thomas Merton, who was in a Louisville hospital, along with his poem about being trapped there. Griffin identified, "and that is why I dread hospitals—radios blaring country music, TV a poor counterpoint, nurses entering without warning to jab your butt or demand an immediate urine specimen, usually minutes after you've just finished pissing."

Griffin was getting ready on May 10 for a return to the hospital. "Tonight I cleaned my electric shaver and decided to take it apart and oil it. It is now a complete wreck. I could not put it back together. It doesn't even look like the same razor, and of course makes no pretense of running." He was taken to therapy to learn how to use crutches. On May 20, he had difficulties with the wheelchair, but found relief in listening to daughter Susan practice at the piano.

On May 27, the children were happily on vacation from school, but Griffin was not relieved by the doctor's news. "The wound is healing slowly and precariously, but the flesh on the bottom of the foot, due to diabetic lack of circulation, is turning black and dying. I made an attempt to print last night—a real nightmare. I shall not try it again until I am able to use both feet and stand up." The following Saturday was "a day of wonder and shrieking pain, immense haziness—all of it as in a dream, possibly hallucinatory because of the effects of the medication." But that evening his mother visited, and with Elizabeth and Susan, played the piano.

> Mother played Scarlatti sonatas and a great number of the most brilliant and profound and exciting works of Bach. The walls of the studio still echo this tremendous music, like the odor of baking bread that lingers strong.
>
> I have never heard Mother or any pianist play these pieces so well—brilliant, technically flawless, and she selected the most jubilant and life-giving ones, not the introspective ones. What a wise lady she is. The music was better than all the medicines in the world. My tissues came alive with the joy of these great sounds.

During these days, Elizabeth and the children made trips from the house to the studio, cleaning thoroughly with a naturalness he found touching. On June 1 Griffin types these words about pain, yet with a twist of wit.

> I come to the typewriter the way another would put a stick between his teeth to bite on when the pains hit, or another would slug whiskey. I will read back in these entries one day and wonder how in heaven's name a man could do so much bitching. Dead tired but I cannot stay on the bed for the pain that drives me wild, pain that strikes like lightning up and down my operated foot and all through the tumors of the other foot. I keep running (what a laugh, I *wheel* in the wheelchair) to the desk, stick paper in the typewriter, sit here staring at it, feeling somehow that anything I write is better than sitting there feeling the pain.

Griffin learned that James Meredith was shot in Mississippi on June 7.[89] First reports indicated that Meredith was killed, but none of the pellets hit a vital spot. The sniper who tried to murder Meredith was arrested. That same day he had a visit from Adelle Jackson, the editor of *Sepia* magazine.

> We talked about the city fathers' sabotaging of the various programs for black people in Fort Worth. It is simply maddening to see the manner in which the so-called pillars of the white community are so blind, so stubborn, so stupid when it comes to understanding the effects of their cheating. It is a wonder we do not have Watts explosions everywhere and that any black person retains any sanity. The lived experience of black people today is a mountain of these "little things"—each a slap at the individual's humanity. Whites who are good citizens can go right on countenancing these abuses, this murder of souls, and even conniving to perpetuate them with perfect ease of conscience. We will go right on until we drive black people to guerilla warfare, and then never understand how they can be such "poor citizens" who have so little "love for their country."

On June 8 Amanda Claire Dominique was born healthy, without complications, and by June 17, both mother and child were home.

Griffin got unexpected relief from pain when Father George Curtsinger, one of the Carmelite priests he befriended during the mid-1950s, visited on June 23. He was put into a hypnotic trance by the priest, and afterward felt no pain for six hours. A second treatment occurred on June 27 when Father Curtsinger and Dr. Alan Reid visited. "Dr. Reid took a good deal of physiological data before, during, and after the trance. I went in once, profoundly, for 40 minutes. The last 20 minutes were marked by total anesthesia of the foot. In the trance, the leg felt wooden, and after the trance it felt extremely light and numb for a long time."

The next night he contemplated Bradford Daniel's bridge passages from *The Devil Rides Outside* for *The John Howard Griffin Reader.*

> I have ambivalent feelings about this kind of work. Mostly it irritates beyond measure to go back to a work that is a stranger—but there is fascination, for I can read it almost as the work of another. There are good passages and those that embarrass by their lack of concision, their immaturity and ineptitude (what a temptation to take the blue pencil to them!). This is a young work, one I would never write again. It pains me, too, to be obliged to go back to it and tamper with it by analyzing Brad's bridge passages.
>
> On the other hand, there is the certainty I will not write like that again because it is such a passionate outpouring, a work of such

> energy—and I do not feel that kind of energy any more. I remember running across a passage in *The Devil* where I stupidly remarked that we make children, revel in our roles as fathers, when all we have really done is produced an effect through our physical passions. What a truncated, mutilated statement, since our child is *not* just that but she comes from the great love that our bodies knew in union; she comes bearing all the resonances of eternities when couples have loved one another—tenderly, strongly, and sought the natural goal of that union with the beloved object.

Griffin felt better during the following week, taking no pain medication. On the night of July 4, he worked in the darkroom seven hours, developing prints of family members holding Amanda. The next day he had a letter from Merton's Abbot (Father James Fox), assuring him that visiting the Trappist monastery in a wheelchair would *not* be a problem. That night he read "an excellent article in *Saturday Evening Post* by John Oliver Killens, concerning why black people are justified in using violence in self-defense against violence.[90] He says that if the law will not serve to put out the first fire the white men start, then Negroes will have to be their own fireman. He wants no violence, white or black, but let them stop the white violence or blacks will be justified in defending themselves."

Father J. Stanley Murphy visited during the second week of July, specifically to baptize Amanda. Griffin remarks on July 12: "We have had an easy time, visiting quietly, having our marvelous celebrations of the Mass in the studio each day. No one is less of a strain than Father Stan with whom I feel as perfectly comfortable as if I were alone." Griffin spent most of the next day reading "a most impressive piece by poet John Beecher in *The New Republic*.[91] He writes marvelously on racism—simply, straightforwardly and honestly." On July 14 Griffin was pleased that *Life* magazine was publishing two of his photographs of Merton.

The next day he returned to the doctor's, writing that "he had to cut the foot again, so the remainder of the day has been a haze." On July 16, he had another session with Father Curtsinger and Dr. Reid. For the next session they agreed to try to relive the novel *Street of the Seven Angels*, "to see if my recall of the creative experience is as total as lived experience."

I have done this vividly with my own experiences, but never yet with a created work. Would I be able to relive the scenes as though I were observing them? We had no idea how this might work, but presumably if you have worked creatively with a set of characters and scenes, you know them almost as though you had actually experienced them. They set me up in a deep trance for time distortion—which means that you live in one minute what it would take you an hour to live ordinarily. Well, it was simply incredible. Most of all the smells of the Café Zeus, a bistro where the main characters come to drink wine. Dr. Reid explained that the sense of smell is the most primitive of all our senses and it comes to the fore powerfully and early in trance. Then I proceeded through all the scenes, leisurely, reliving every detail as if I were actually there—many of the things I never put in the book but which were in this living-experience and quite overpowering.

The extraordinary thing here was the fact that I relived all of this exactly as though I had once lived it, seeing many things I had never thought to put in the novel, seeing some scenes as irrelevant, and to be condensed or deleted. But seeing it all, when in truth I have only been "there" in my creative imagination.

Which is correct? Which should I trust? Some characters I consciously created as interesting were in the trance not so interesting and some not really interesting at all, so I have tailored them. In the time distortion, all of this occurred, and leisurely, in exactly four minutes—which means it would probably take four or five hours to read the book. I must have made a hundred little additions and deletions based on this extremely clear and logical trance session.

During the next week there were "days of weakness in which little or nothing has got accomplished, as though time were suspended in a haze."

I sit in the wheel chair and read magazines. Getting into work is almost like practicing the piano. I have to work up to it, as though doing mental scales and *arpeggios* to warm up, to build enthusiasm and excitement until that creates the energy to sustain itself. These are days of incomparable opportunity to work and yet so little writing done. Finally, I may as well admit it, photography has become such an obsessive interest it eclipses everything else. I am constantly thinking

> about it, solving photographic problems, and everything I see is seen in double—as it is and as it would look through the viewfinders.

The *Journal* goes blank until August 5, because they were searching for a house to rent. Driving the children to Fort Worth every day had become difficult, since Elizabeth was caring for the infant. Moving to 3816 West Biddison turned out to be a significant transition. It was near the public schools and to Texas Christian University (TCU), where Elizabeth eventually found work in the library and a few years later in the music department.

> We were finally lucky enough to find an ideal house in an ideal location—four bedrooms and a connected den house. I will use the very back room, which is perfect for an office, and miraculously, has a perfect light-tight space for a darkroom. In all of it, though we are thrilled with the house, there has been the strange, focusless anxiety, a vague depression at the thought of moving out and starting over again—particularly with me in a wheel chair. It is maddening not to be able to be more helpful, to feel so completely useless.

Griffin proofed *The Devil Rides Outside* and the bridge texts, as well as going through *Street of the Seven Angels*. "This is the first really intensive work I have been able to sustain since May, and it is exciting to see that I can do it. Peculiar to go back through books I have almost forgotten. I have never read *The Devil*, and it has been quite a long time since I had done any work on *Street*."

Brad Daniel transported the darkroom equipment to the Fort Worth home on August 10, setting up everything for future photographic work there.

> On the way back, Brad asked if I thought I would have any difficulty adjusting to the city after so many years in the country. I said I could be happy anywhere with my family and work undisturbed, and that is true. My studio in the new house is hardly larger than the bathroom in the country cottage, but I am delighted with it. I look around and feel not the slightest regret.

After more than a week without *Journal* notes, Griffin made his first entry on August 19, feeling "the increasing relaxation in our new home. I am trying to keep my presence here a secret in order to get as much work done at the typewriter. But it gets known. I have gently informed all that I intend to do nothing locally, pleading not only my illness, but also that I do not want to become active in a way that will be detrimental to the work."

Griffin was dealing with pain over the next several days and not writing. He read an interview in *Look* with Lillian Smith. "She is now in hospital, apparently with terminal cancer. A most moving account."

He had another hypnosis session on August 24.

> Father George was over earlier, and we had a remarkable session. I spoke to him of the great difficulty I always have with interruptions to my work, the inability to see long stretches of unbroken time before me in which to work in one's own natural rhythms—as I once could in France and again in Mexico. We worked on that in trance.
>
> His suggestions were so remarkable I almost came out of the trance in admiration for the profound knowledge he has of the creative processes, the incomparable understanding. It was as though I were listening to a concert of the most personal and authentic music. Afterward, when I talked of this, he said it had been a preoccupation for 30 years. In the trance he took me back to Mexico to help recapture the calm of the uninterrupted hours. It was a remarkably beautiful experience and its resonances have clung since.

What Griffin did *not* say was that Father Curtsinger, an accomplished pianist, would later turn his creativity toward photography.

During the next week, Griffin was greatly encouraged by Attorney General Nicholas Katzenbach's testimony before a Senate subcommittee: "The Department of Justice has looked carefully into the causes of the riots. We conclude that they were indeed fomented by agitators named disease, despair, joblessness, hopelessness, rat-infested housing and long-impacted cynicism."

Griffin noted in the *Journal* of August 31.

> The pain is unbearable as it can be without becoming truly paralyzing. The thing that I have noticed is that it takes something immensely powerful to divert attention, and the one thing that I go to is photography. I went through all of the thousands of negatives and put them in

> order. Then I took photographic books to bed and studied them avidly. It helped. I went back to the marvelous folios of Marion Palfi and Nell Dorr.
>
> There is a deep mystery in the work of these great artists—a mystery that demands study and contemplation. How do they do it? Where does this profound vision start, how do they make it come through the camera, development, printing? And the same with Atget—those beautiful, serene, luminous works. I think writing could do the same, but I cannot handle ideas when I am sedated and my fingers constantly strike the wrong keys.

By September 4, Griffin had "worked some, as much as these ungodly pains would allow." The children were to start attending nearby schools, so the commuting from Mansfield was over. When school began on September 6, he felt "oddly at loose ends, the way I feel after finishing a book. Little left to do on *The Reader*. I should plunge right into the next book."

On September 11, he was prescribed penicillin for the infected foot. "The doctor cut the foot—there are a number of abscesses—so I have been in bed since. The sedation put me out of commission completely. It is impossible to work and there is intimate frustration in being unable to focus."

Griffin received a telegram about the death of Lillian Smith on September 28. Even as he expected this, it was still a shock.

On October 2, another telegram informed that Maritain would arrive at the airport the next day. "I keep feeling I have left undone important things, but cannot think what they might be. I have the kinds of food he can take, have plenty of film, the cameras are clean, his room will be fixed this evening, the children have been threatened with mayhem if they do not behave and remain quiet while he is here, will make mayonnaise this afternoon."

All went well with the visit. Maritain was accompanied by Babeth Manuel, the daughter of old family friends. On October 4 Griffin made photographs as "Jacques prepared eggs a la Mere Poulard and we talked about Reverdy. Jacques read Reverdy's poems in French and I recorded it." On October 5, "knowing we would be crowded with visitors, we got up early to begin recording Jacques' reading of Raïssa's poems." That evening there were several visitors: Father George Curtsinger and his brother, novelist E.C. Curtsinger; Dr. Alan Reid, Father August Thompson; and Edward Keating (*Ramparts* publisher).

Photograph of Jacques Maritain & JHG by Gregory Parker Griffin, in Fort Worth, Texas. Griffin and Maritain were on their way to meet monk Thomas Merton at the Abbey of Gethsemani in Kentucky. Many photos of visiting the monk are in *A Hidden Wholeness.*

The next day Penn Jones drove them to the airport and they flew from Dallas to Louisville, where Father J. Stanley Murphy joined them.[92] Reaching the monastery, Abbot Fox invited Maritain, Father Murphy, Penn Jones, Babeth Manuel, and Griffin to dine with Thomas Merton. They discussed the problems of racism in America. "Merton feels as I do that we are headed for an open war unless trends change rapidly and unless we begin to see the causes of these explosions." They were served a lavish meal, including steaks, and Griffin "was secretly relishing this for Merton, since Trappists never take meat, not even fish. I wondered how long it had been since he had tasted meat and when, if ever, he would taste it again." The monk consumed the meal with gusto. The Abbot excused himself, giving Merton rare permission to stay up late with the visitors.

Early on Friday, the monks took Griffin in the wheelchair up the freight elevator. The congregation attended Mass. Then they went up the hill to Merton's hermitage, where they were met by professors Dan Walsh and Jack Ford (from Bellarmine college in Louisville, home to the Thomas Merton Studies Center).

They discussed the problems of the extreme right wing pressures on the Church, the John Birch Society's appeal to certain Catholic mentalities, and the problems this caused liberal priests. Then Merton played records by Bob Dylan.

> He put on "Highway 61" and this extraordinary music poured out. He explained that he had permission for the phonograph and recordings as research. Still, it was almost eerie to hear such music in a Trappist hermitage. Merton almost glowed. He helped repeat the fierce words to Jacques, so we could get the nuances. Meanwhile I was constantly photographing. Here was something at least for Jacques and me that was completely new. When it was over, Merton read some of his new experimental poetry in which there is much of the vitality and whiplash of the Bob Dylan, though there the resemblance ends. Merton's new work was the most impressive poetry I have known since Reverdy.

During lunch, Penn Jones discussed his work on the *Warren Commission Report* in the book, *Forgive My Grief*, giving everyone a copy. In the early afternoon, they met again with Merton, traveling in cars to the woods near a pond.

> They spread blankets and sat among the trees, Jacques supporting his back against one and me in the wheel chair. Then Penn and Jack Ford went to get some beer and cups. I loaded my Alpa for Merton so he could photograph. He was delighted with this great instrument. We photographed for a while and drinks were served—and then the talk really began. It was mostly about the Vietnam war and growing problems concerning the loss of individual privacy as computers become more prevalent. Merton foresees the days soon to come when every time one buys an airline ticket, this information will be sent to Washington, so that everyone will be known wherever they go and in all of their activities.

By late afternoon, they returned to the Abbey. That evening Maritain addressed the community, speaking of contemplation and contemporary Church problems. Griffin was in too much pain to attend. "I sat like a statue in my room, watching the day turn to night, exhausted, but at complete peace." They were awakened early on Saturday, the day of departure. "Merton celebrated a Mass in Latin for us at 6 a.m. When it was over, the sun was rising on a clear crisp morning of great beauty. A perfect experience in every way—especially the freedom of conversation and the brilliance that sparked from Maritain and Merton."

Back in Fort Worth, Griffin typed in the *Journal* on October 12. "Processed 144 more negatives and still have that many more to do. Did 218 yesterday. These are beautiful negatives. Am extremely eager to print them. The work is painstaking and slow, but the results are worth it." For three weeks he developed more than five hundred negatives, not writing in the *Journal* until November 2.

> Have not kept journal notes for some time, since being so preoccupied with photography and writing the interview with Jacques for *National Catholic Reporter*. A note from Jacques yesterday indicates he thinks the interview is all right. A great relief. His visit and new book have helped immeasurably in clarifying obscure points. I had not deciphered the proper balance for what I needed intuitively to say, but could not justify philosophically.

Griffin had good news from the doctor November 3. His foot was finally healing, and "the black area which I feared was more dead flesh turned out to be a hemorrhage under the skin, so will not need removing." But he read election results on November 9 as bad news, especially the Reagan win in California.

> They showed how profoundly racist and fascist this country really wants to be. With what a patriotic lust the people throw away freedoms in the illusion that they are preserving them. Their eyes are fixed with such horror on the communist menace that they walk hastily into the equal menace of the extreme right, which will purge and censor as the communists, except it will do it in the name of freedom and Christ.

Griffin received two unexpected gifts on November 12, a photographic print from Nell Dorr and a new photographic book by David Douglas Duncan. Then the *Journal* goes blank until December 2, a day after the doctor had him practice walking in shoes. "As a result, I am in a rigid state of pain, which prevented any work. Yet how strange this new house looks from the upright position. I have never seen it except at the wheel chair level. The view is entirely different, as though I were standing on a rooftop looking down. And my children, who for eight months have seen me only seated or in bed, are dumbfounded at how tall I am."

The December 7 *Journal* entry recorded a "frustrating" day.

> For the first time in a long time I had some energy and got into work just wonderfully when the damned phone started to ring and people dropped by. I sat there in that special way of seeing ideas and mental syntheses evaporate while people talked. Such writing is gone unless it is put into some salvageable form.
>
> And poor Elizabeth, she has run from morning to night. She has her hands full with this household, but everyone calls on her for everything. I am no damned help at all because I have to work all my energy into earning our livelihood, and I can do so little in this wheelchair. I do baby sit Amanda but that is not much.

The final *Journal* entry for 1966 was on December 16. "The soft rain-filtered light of midmorning falls across my desk—the most beautiful and merciful kind of light. This is what people usually call a gloomy morning, but I have always loved this light that turns shadows hazy and produces the finest gradations of grays and whites. It is a time to sit and simply observe. Silence goes with it."

The *Journal* for 1967 (162 pages) opens on January 3. He was relieved that the children were in school. The holidays with "too many visitors" had ended. The house seemed "strangely quiet," and he worked well. The last entry for several months, on January 19, revealed his typical contradictions.

> Cold brightness in this office as Mozart clarifies the atmosphere and gives glimpses of the sublime so seldom experienced in our world today, which gives overwhelming sights of hatred, cupidity, and confusion, surrounding us like glittering whirlwind fogs that preoccupy our attention to a point where these Mozartian glimpses come almost as a shock to the system. They shock us back to remembering that such things exist and for a moment they melt the avalanche that attacks. In listening to his music bounce from these walls, the whole nervous system relaxes, the great pull to contemplation resurges, the hands fall from the typewriter, the head falls forward as the inner self seeks harmony with the sounds, seeks to let the music, like the voice of God, come in and do its work.

> And this work is simply a flooding of pure love into the void, the terrible smoke-filled void of self that is cluttered with a thousand details of man's brutality and avarice, all accomplished in the name of some high motive like patriotism or religion.
>
> Then the paradisiacal moment vanishes. The Mozart is followed by shit. The head pulls back, the hands return to the typewriter and all that needs to be done in explaining why all men need rights, particularly the right to live, and how massive is the tragedy of one soul alienated, one body tortured. They excuse the killing and the torturing by saying that more people die here of car accidents and soldiers are taught that a good way to make the Vietcong talk is to throw one of them out of a helicopter. Humanity is filled with those who would defend such actions, who have been calloused away from all realization of what it means to destroy another's life. How the soul shrivels with horror at these actions, and I have seen a thousand such evidences in my life.

From February 11 to April 12, Griffin returned on tour, keeping the *Journal* in a composition book. He was wearing shoes and walking again. His first two lectures were at universities in Philadelphia. In Plattsburgh, New York, for two nights at the Witherill Hotel—"ancient place, comfortable, charming; high ceilings, steam radiators, old-fashioned fixtures, a huge bed and faded prints on walls." Even with the temperature at 30 degrees below zero, he did an interview with students on February 13, delivering a lecture that night. He photographed the room at first light with "the illusion of being in France in some small hotel."

Griffin's next stop was in New Hampshire on February 14, where it turned warmer. Then he returned to New York, speaking at St. Bonaventure, "that marvelous Franciscan college. Merton's *Alma Mater*. Largest lecture audience they ever had." It went well, except he received the usual hate material, which "vastly amused the Franciscans, because the *coup de gras* was a sheet saying: 'You Can Judge A Man by His Friends: Daniel Berrigan, Philip Berrigan, Thomas Merton, Jacques Maritain, and other Pacifists.' The crazy bastards thought friends like that would prove my low ideals! It is almost unbelievable."

On February 16 and 17, he visited with Nell Dorr. "Saw her new work. We both got the trembles. She is a great artist at the height of her powers. This is no longer photography as we know it, but a profound visual mysticism, illuminating the mystery. It is to photography what the last Beethoven quartets are to music."

Griffin's next lectures were in Vermont and New York, hounded continually by the right-wing groups. "I am tempted to stop speaking at such events, as my chief harassment comes from fellow Catholics. The bishops support publicly my stance, but never repudiate the racist elements. How sick I get of their muck of racist hatred." He lectured in Maine on February 22, and during a connecting flight along the shoreline, "the pilot identified fishing villages and light houses in the land of Winslow Homer." The tour continued in New England until he flew to Baltimore for additional lectures. Then in late February, Griffin gave talks in Michigan.

By March 6, he was on the west coast, speaking at universities in Washington state. Two lectures on March 8 in Sacramento included "the largest audiences they ever had. Immensely responsive and enormously moving are these young audiences." He had two off days in Bakersfield, hoping "to take a car into the desert and do some photography." On March 10, he scribbled, "This desert vastness emphasizes the spirit of Holy Week." He photographed in Death Valley and two "ghost" towns. Then he lectured at colleges around Berkeley and San Francisco, enjoying the Pacific and "the constant roar of surf and the mild salty air, which are a blessing."

The *Journal* is empty until May 1, when Griffin typed the first pages since January. He was due to return to Washington and California, but the doctor would not allow it. He worked in the darkroom instead. "Got magnificent photographs in Death Valley and the Mojave Desert this time."

On May 26 Griffin wrote that "After the long silences in these journals, it is not easy to get back into the heart of journal keeping. I find myself skirting the things I want to say, writing anyway, knowing that when I have worked my way back into the spirit of it, the things will come." The next day he proofed galleys while listening to the "marvelous new recording of Beethoven *Sonatas* for piano and cello with Jacqueline du Pre and Stephen Bishop."

On May 28, he wrote in the *Journal.*

> The hours in the darkroom are in a way parallel to (or a replacement for) the fantasy-life. Instead of falling into daydreams, I tend to

> make prints. It has a certain sensual gratification, too; in that I struggle with a kind of intense inner excitement in bringing out textures of flesh, of cloth, of stones and grass; and am also deeply involved in the richness of symbols, like the burros ambling past the monastery of solitude—elements of reality that complement one another in the long gradations of living.

By May 30, he had returned to the piano "in the slow process of getting hands back to the feel of the keyboard, doing mostly Bach, very slowly, and some of the simple scale exercises." The exercises were useful for coordination, as they had been when he faced paralysis a decade earlier. He did this secretly, since the baby grand needed tuning. It had been played by an incredible array of great pianists who visited over the years, but Griffin never played for company.

Throughout the month of June, he worked on photography, making these observations in the *Journal* of June 24.

> Soon I will make a firm resolve to photograph no more women. The truer I make the photos, the less they like them. Women do not like the reality of themselves, they cling to some strange illusion of what they should like to see on the emulsion. No wonder successful commercial portrait photographers do such poor photography. They obviously have to alter their prints in order to "satisfy" the client.
>
> Only three ladies can I recall who saw the truth of photographs that refused to flatter: Anne Fremantle, Nell Dorr, and Ella Lourié. All three are profoundly beautiful women, but none is pretty. Why women prefer prettiness to beauty is beyond me, but they obviously do, this is the heart of the matter, and the reason why I cannot see photographing them so long as they will want to "approve" the results. They do not want portraits—they want illusions—and to give them the illusions they want is to be aesthetically dishonest. It is to give something far less than what ought to be given—it is to cheapen the work. It is not the nature of photography and not the nature of art. It is artifice.
>
> I do not call it vanity. God knows women have no more vanity than men. Perhaps it is simply a human trait, more highly developed in women, the trait of wanting always to be masked. The photographer struggles always against the masks people wear—to penetrate the masks and get to the essences. To penetrate a woman's mask is simply to

> unmask her, and I suppose when she has been thoroughly inculcated to the absolute necessity of the mask, the reality strikes her as a shock.

While there is generational chauvinism in Griffin's remarks about photographing women, subsequent views in the *Journal* of July 11 are based on the pure observations of the new photographs by Father George Curtsinger.

> Father George came to work in the darkroom and brought some negatives. They were very beautiful indeed, and though he intended only a brief visit, we got so excited with them that we printed until eleven last night, and then I went on working with his negatives for three more hours. He has the extraordinary vision that sees harmony and order in the most common sights—looks into the "essences" of things. He has always had this ability, but never knew any way to preserve what he sees. Now he knows, and he is doing some of the most beautiful photography I have seen. They are beautifully composed, with a wonderful balance of tensions and resolutions—almost inevitable in his non-interference (but for selecting the angles and light) with natural composition. He does not intrude in them—he simply presents to the emulsion what he has seen: and what he has seen is what I love to see myself; what most would love to see. He sees far better than I do.

Returning from a piano recital by Lili Kraus, he wrote on July 16.[93]

> Suddenly, in the middle of July, a handful of us have the privilege of experiencing one of the rare and great musical events of our lives. Lili Kraus, one of the idols of my youth, is in town giving a master class. She played a concert for her students and their guests—not open to the public. Father George took Elizabeth, Susan, and me. I thought back over the years when I was set on fire by her playing of the Mozart and Beethoven sonatas and her marvelous Mozart *concerti*. Would the years have taken their toll, Would the beauty that I recognized all fresh in youth remain the same—I mean, would my own concepts be more sophisticated now, to a point where perhaps she was not the marvel I had thought?
>
> We got to Landreth auditorium at TCU early and took our seats in the first row. Her students had chairs around the piano in a semi-circle on the stage. She said she did not know what she would play. Perhaps the Beethoven *Opus 109*, which she had been analyzing for them. She

> then began talking about Haydn, and played a Haydn sonata beautifully. Then a set of Mozart variations and, breathtakingly, Mozart's *A-Minor Sonata*.
>
> Certainly it was the most beautiful and moving performance of the work I have ever heard. Scarcely changing her body position or facial expressions, the music poured from her magnificent hands and spirit. Then she performed the Bartók *Rondos* very excitingly, took a little intermission, and returned to play, again better than I had ever heard it, the Beethoven *Opus 109*. We were breathless toward the end. Then, though she had played enough to exhaust most pianists, she played the Schubert *Wanderer Fantasy* and the music set fire to the auditorium. Such heroic technique.

One convenience of living in Fort Worth was easy access to such recitals, while it also meant seemingly endless interruptions. Since friends did not take Griffin's hints, he worked in the darkroom. Returning to the *Journal*, he registered complaints, and "a sense of desperation at the frustrations of getting work done." After interruptions, he called the *Journal* "my own personal wailing wall. I guess it is better to bitch to it than to humans, who would just be miserable."

Griffin was planning a trip to Europe on July 21. He would be in Paris for one day, hoping to meet with critic Stanislas Fumet and painter Abraham Rattner. Then he would go on to Kolbsheim in the French countryside to meet with Maritain. "It is probably the last chance I would have to photograph Abe Rattner, something I have always wanted to do and never been able to do. I just hope he will be free in Paris when I am there." It did not happen, and as with pianist Robert Casadesus, he never photographed these two favorite artists, who had been significant influences on his approaches to art.

Griffin flew to Paris on July 28. He kept a hand-written account of the three weeks in France, later published in *Jacques Maritain: Homage in Words and Pictures*. He left France on August 12, returning to the *Journal* on August 20.

> Have been proofing—with much help from Father George—the pages of *The Reader* and also processing film I took in France. The work is piled high, trying to wade through, all the while keeping my ear cocked to developments in our civil strife, which seems to degenerate

> more and more. John Beecher wrote yesterday that he was leaving Alabama, saying that it was beyond redemption now. My studio is a great mess of mail, unopened packages of books and magazines. I must clear it out somehow.

During August Griffin worked on photographs from France. "A great deal of work done this week," he reported on September 2. "I try to say no to every request for appearances or for anything that will mess up the work schedule."

By October 1, for "the first time since I returned from France, I am having a few quiet hours to work." That day he received a letter from an unnamed man (called "H" in the *Journal*), who confessed to reading Griffin's private entries.

> I don't know when anything has burned me more. The idea of his daring to presume that he could read these things without asking—and if he had asked, I would have said no so sharply and rapidly he would have been taken by surprise. I will never allow him in my home again. The very knowledge that someone might ever read these pages immediately falsifies my whole tone in writing them. They are thoughts on paper, most of them worthless—but valuable to me in keeping the writing going, in attempting to express what happens, and above all as a reference for later—of the things I was doing and thinking in these years. I do not write these pages for the eyes of anyone.

Over the next two weeks Griffin was revising chapters of *Scattered Shadows*, but had to prepare for a lecture tour. "I go out on October 24 to a meeting of educators in Saginaw, Michigan. Dread going out, but I must."

News about the trial of the Ku Klux Klan members who murdered the three civil rights workers in Mississippi confirmed Griffin's need to keep lecturing on racism. In the entry for October 18, he discussed the trial.

> The papers here carry practically no details of the trial in Meridian of the 18 Klansmen accused of killing Schwerner, Goodman and Chaney; whereas if 18 Jews and Negroes had planned and carried out this frightful execution of three WASPS, the papers would have been full of the trial in all its gruesome details. It will pass relatively unnoticed, and this is a crime against society, not to show that white men can become utterly dehumanized. You do not need any special

> credentials to be a monster—it can happen here, has happened here, and will go on happening here. No cry to change the laws and make this kind of murder a federal offense; but if the reverse had occurred, the cry for a change in the laws would be heard throughout the land. No, the most they can get is a fine and ten years in prison and there is no outcry. The testimony is shriveling to the guts. Klansmen bragging about killing; during the act, one of them calling out dibs on one of the victims—save one for him to kill! The later expansiveness of the KKK leader, who remarked how pleased he was because this was the first time the execution of Jews and a Negro had been successfully carried out. How a so-called civilization can fail to be horrified by this incredible testimony is what dismays me.

While in Kansas two days later, he got news of the verdict. Seven klansmen were found guilty, eight not guilty, and the case of three others was declared a mistrial. "What an incredible decision, since it was established that all 18 were together. But frankly, because it was in Meridian, Mississippi, I had expected all of the murderers to be acquitted by the all-white jury."

He returned home from Kansas. His lecture had laid out background causes to the urban riots, and in the seminar he was joined by other speakers. Chester Lewis of the NAACP rebutted the claims of the white clergy members, saying, "I hate this piousness, this bootstrap bit," and destroyed their rationalizations. Rev. Kelsey Jones delivered the most skilled analysis I ever heard—hard, funny, terrible, and brilliant, showing why black people have given up on whites and have lost hope in the white man's religion, clarifying how every solution has been betrayed by the white majority until now the fire is here."

> Then a young black student beaten by police during the Wichita riot took the microphone. So filled with emotion he could speak only in short phrases, literally carried the audience into the heart of the issue—to the paddy wagon where, handcuffed, he was sprayed in the eyes and beaten by officers who kept telling him—"You're all right. You're not hurt, boy"—until they broke his wrist with nightsticks.
>
> His face was like an open wound. He spoke in an agonized voice. "A year ago I knew right from wrong. They treated me like a mad dog. Now, I'm sorry to say it, but if I walk into some supermarket and just

> one man looks at me in a certain way or calls me 'boy' or 'nigger'—then I'm going to fix him so he can't see the sky. A year ago the thought of hurting any man would make me shake all over. Does the white American love the Nazis? He acts like it. The Nazis killed six million Jews. Well—FOOL!—do you think we're going to go like that?" The younger black audience members responded: "Amen, Brother."
>
> He continued in a rage: "We're going to kill back. We're going to take ten whites for every black man they kill. They can't say we haven't tried every other way, everything *decent.* We demand justice and we get a committee. Self-determination? The white man even has a committee to see how much self-determination *he's* going to give *us.*" The room was silent. The young man went on. "They're talking about us being deprived, unqualified. Hell. I go to college. I was holding two jobs when they beat me. Now we're going to take ten, ten more and then ten more if we can for good measure." The white audience curled up and died.
>
> My only follow-up statement was to explain that what he was saying was as repulsive to Negroes as to whites, that no Negro wants to be driven to violence. But we have not acted in good faith on any of the other solutions. We have consistently maintained the impediments of racism that prevent men from becoming truly men in their ability to function and to determine for themselves what their destiny should be. We will reap inevitably the stench of soul that we have sown with persistent injustices and psychological destruction.

Griffin went back on the road to San Francisco and to cities in the Midwest. On November 22, he wrote that "Now, four years later, we are finding that our early suspicions and disbelief were right, that men like Penn Jones was not a 'kook' as alarmists called him, and that we know several men were involved in the assassination of President John F. Kennedy."

By November 28, he was working with son Gregory on the Merton photographs. "Gregory did a perfectly magnificent job." The next day Houghton Mifflin delivered a copy of *The John Howard Griffin Reader.*[94] "It is strange to hold this big volume—600 pages—strange and final, somehow, like one's 89th birthday—a vast number of hours tied up in a couple of pounds of paper and print. Now it is finished, and nothing further can be done to improve it."

On December 4, Griffin was reading Stanislas Fumet's new book, *Leon Bloy, Captive of the Absolute.*

> I let it flip open where it would and simply began to read notes from Bloy's diaries for 1916-17, in which he speaks so much of Jacques Maritain and his contemporaries. Pages that carried back to a time before my birth, but a time that seems far more familiar than my own time, a time that I feel deeply in some pre-memory.
>
> J. Frank Dobie once said that Lon Tinkle and I were the only two writers he knew who were not "ruined" by France; and yet, if this is true, and I hope it is, it is even more true that we were forever marked by France that is not a country but an experience, a background, a culture and I, at least, am moved particularly by the names that Bloy's long dead hand brings back in his writing tonight. He speaks of Jacques and means a young man. Speaking in my *Journal* of the same Jacques, I mean an elderly man.
>
> All this is connected with *Scattered Shadows*—on Reverdy and Maritain, and reading from Bloy's journals in which he speaks of the same men. Strange, all of it.

After finishing the book on December 28, Griffin reflected. "Some accused Bloy of always analyzing the 'problems' but not offering the solutions! This happens in my lectures. You have told us how bad it is, they say, but you do not tell us what to do to make it better. I always keep silence, while within me the solution tumbles out: What solution can I offer that was not perfectly offered 2000 years ago? It is because you do not accept that solution that I have to keep telling you, and you deny the damage that has resulted."

Griffin discovered the "only answer" is faith and loving, in the works of others and in his own experience, but no one seemed to be listening.

PART IV

Is it true to say that one goes into solitude to "get at the root of existence"? It would be better simply to say that in solitude one *is* at the root. He who is alone, and is conscious of what solitude means, finds himself simply in the ground of life. He is "in Love." He is in love with all, with everyone, with everything.

He lives, then, as a seed planted in the ground. As Christ said, the seed in the ground must die. To be as a seed in the ground of one's life is to dissolve in that ground in order to become fruitful.

Speaking as a Christian existentialist, I mean by *soul* not simply the Aristotelian essential form but the mature personal identity, the creative fruit of an authentic and lucid search, the *self* that is found after other partial and exterior selves have been discarded as masks.

The original and authentic *paradise* idea implied not simply a celestial store of theoretic ideas to which the Magistri and Doctores held the key, the inner self of the student who, in discovering the ground of his own personality as it opened out into the center of all created being, found in himself the light and wisdom of his Creator, a light and wisdom in which everything comprehensible could be comprehended and what was not comprehensible could nevertheless be grasped in the darkness of contemplation by a direct and existential contact.

Christianity is a religion of the Word. *The Word is Love*. But we sometimes forget that the Word emerges first of all from silence.

When there is no silence, then the One Word which God speaks is not truly heard as Love. Then only "words" are heard. Words are not love, for they are many and Love is One. Where there are many words, we lose consciousness of the fact that there is really only One Word. The One Word which God speaks is Himself. Speaking, He manifests Himself as infinite Love. His speaking and His hearing are One. So silent is His speech that, to our way of thinking, His speech is no-speech, His hearing is no-hearing. Yet in His silence, in the abyss of His one Love, all words are spoken and all words are heard. Only in this silence of infinite Love do they have coherence and meaning.

Only in silence and solitude, in the quiet of worship, the reverent peace of prayer, the adoration in which the entire ego-self silences and abases itself in the presence of the Invisible God to receive His one Word of Love; only in these "activities" which are "non-actions" does the spirit truly wake from the dream of a multifarious, confused, and agitated existence.

—THOMAS MERTON

Rediscovering Solitude

Griffin's 1968 *Journal* contains 249 pages, beginning January 1, although he was writing what he did *not* want to write. "I have been making notes for an article on the super patriots, who talk about law and constitution, who dream of returning to America's origins. But in truth their actions and ideals indicate they want to return to the hateful nightmare of suppression, racism, and bigotry that caused America to be formed as a revolt against the things they advocate."

Listening to Schubert's *Ninth Symphony* on January 10, Griffin wrote of the exact opposite impulse—his great respect for solitary artists and thinkers.

> They produce not just brilliance but works that are large, full, which take time, and represent many hours of *solitude*. Did Schubert write at night? I look at Fumet's works—the pages that sprang not out of facility but out of hours of uninterrupted time, hours of meditation—a man who remains invisible when working; and of Maritain, alone in his room—the *solitude* of these men, that alone permits them to go with sufficient depth, reflecting undisturbed. I feel that kinship only in these silent hours when the pestiferous world snoozes and I am alone here, enclosed in the small room, surrounded by the music, the books, the thoughts that allow creativity the space in which to come unstuck and begin to flow. I take in the thoughts of others who are my brothers.

Yet the "pestiferous world" never allowed uninterrupted solitude.

On January 16, "deeply concerned about the arrest of Dr. Benjamin Spock on the charge that he obstructed the draft, and had only spoken and demonstrated against it," he asks: "Have we come to this, that men are no longer free to express opposition? I believe that *fascism is here*, deeply entrenched and in far greater force than we realize. The press has whitewashed this entirely."

Publication of *The John Howard Griffin Reader* was on January 22. The massive compendium features a folio of photographic portraits, chapters from *Scattered Shadows*, portions from novels, stories, excerpts from *Black Like Me* and *Land of the High Sky*, plus articles on racism, censorship, music, and *Journal* entries.

If the constant interruptions had not destroyed Griffin's concentration, there were phone calls and unannounced visits after the publication of the new book. He thought of a temporary solution, staying in a house on the property of Penn Jones, a place Jones called Mexican Joe's, which was less than thirty miles south. Griffin's plan was to work alone from Thursday morning until Sunday afternoon, the first four days of February, since he was to depart for a lecture tour on that Monday. He brought the *Scattered Shadows* manuscript and a typewriter, but no cameras, avoiding temptation away from writing. The house had lights and a refrigerator, but heat came only from a wood stove, and water had to be drawn from a nearby well. The outhouse was further away, surrounded by trees near the edge of a stream. The place was somewhat primitive compared to the home office in Fort Worth, but extravagant compared to the barn studio he had for eighteen years. "I have been delighted to return to this simpler form of living, and wrote 58 pages during this time of solitude and silence," during his first of several stays in the country place.

> I note a far greater response of the senses to everything here, due to the primitive living conditions and the great silence. For example, at home one goes into the heated bathroom and washes or shaves and never pays attention to it. Here, water must be fetched and heated, preparations made, for all is physical and attention must be given to it.
>
> I think of the freedom I sensed in the life of Thomas Merton, up on his mountainside in the wilderness in an even smaller place. My life here is similar, except that I do not have the fierce cold to combat. No wonder his work retains such a close contact to reality. A part of the slime of our times comes from the disease of atrophied awareness, even the loss of that memory of it in our congested and nerve-frazzled lives, and the search through conveniences to minimize all reality totally.
>
> The irony: When man becomes totally comfortable, he will have

> achieved finally no more resemblance to man. He will be able to gratify all his needs and they will become automatic and no more a part of his conscious apparatus than breathing. Life will be reduced, along with its arts, to the idle dullness of a crossword puzzle that helps pass the time between birth and death, marked by vague periods when man feels he has missed something, until finally these things will simply cease to exist in consciousness. Computerized man, numbered, automated, passing along the assembly-belt of life and time, fixed, destined from beginning to end, everything programmed, even the electronically filled contents of his brain and the simulated products of his genius in poetry, music, painting.

Griffin left this country setting to tour cities in Iowa, Virginia, and Maryland. Returning February 11, he felt the trip was successful, but "they act as though they were hearing something new, because these should be self-evident observations." After a few days at home, he was back on the road to Michigan and Virginia.

He returned February 26, worked two days at the country retreat, leaving again. This extended trip included lectures in Canada, Illinois, Washington DC, Alabama, and Louisiana.

Back home on March 26, Griffin hired a replacement for Bradford Daniel. "A great help from Charles Rector, a black painter just released from the Public Health Service Hospital for addiction to drugs. Extraordinary man, 33, raised in the slums of Kansas City, a most gifted artist. He commands a superb English, but confessed that here in the office were the first classical music programs he had ever heard and that he had never been in a "nice house" before. He has answered all of the mail, rearranged the filing systems and got some order in this office. His face is so extraordinary I have photographed him."

The next day Griffin left for a week in California, attempting to illuminate the reasons behind the riots, which led to the assassination of Dr. King on April 4, 1968. He did not write about this shocking tragedy until April 9.

> This day has been spent witnessing the lengthy rites for Martin, a day of grief and horror. I thought I should write my memories of our contacts, but that will have to wait. My sons were tremendously impressed by the bravery of the King children at the funeral, and

> wondered if they would be that brave if the Klan assassinated me. Their fears all broke through. They would not let me out of their sight. They could not understand why I do not even carry a gun or a knife for protection against the men who consider themselves my enemies. I was overwhelmed by the cares they expressed, and bitter that my children should have to carry such worries. Charles Rector and I talked about it this evening. He was so moved that they should be so concerned and they asked him many questions. Then Charles said: "You know, I'm as guilty as that man who fired on Dr. King. I have so hated the whites, so preached my hatred that I was the same kind of man as he, only black, but consumed with the same kind of hatred."

Griffin did not write again in the *Journal* until May 1, noting that while on tour, he had presented the year's *Pacem in Terris* Award to Father James Groppi. Then he had a session with the publisher about *The Church and the Black Man*.

Finally, Griffin shared a day with Thomas Merton, writing one sentence in the *Journal*. "We photographed because the talk made us feel too somber—and it was a beautiful day, made for photography." Neither realized it would be their final visit. Griffin's essay on Merton in *Continuum* discussed that day.

> On my last visit, shortly before his departure for Asia, I went particularly to have a session with him concerning *The Church and the Black Man*. We talked about this for a few minutes, and fell into a depression about some of the things that were happening. Our conversation frittered off into talk about the Black Priests Caucus, and the poor response it had received. We got gloomier and gloomier.
>
> Tom was sitting in my room, slumped down in a chair, looking at his hands. A silence settled between us. We had accomplished nothing.
>
> "We're not going to solve this. It's beyond human solution now. It's in God's hands," he said. "Do you feel like going out and photographing?"
>
> The gloom was instantly replaced. We got into the rented car I had brought and drove up to the hermitage. He grabbed his camera and film and directed me toward an old whiskey plant nearby. We photographed everything—the peeling paint on window facings of abandoned buildings, plants, weeds, rusting railroad cars, a stack of woodchips. He would see something, wander away to photograph it

> from all angles. From a distance he would yell that he had found something interesting. I marveled at his vigor and enthusiasm. Every time he became absorbed, I would photograph him photographing. I did not know that he did the same with me. Once I turned with my camera at my eye to find him aiming at me with his camera. He lowered it briefly and I photographed him.

The Swiss Alpa was loaned "in perpetuity" to Merton, who called it the "Picasso camera" (the model used by David Douglas Duncan for *Picasso's Picassos*). In a letter to Griffin on March 29, Merton wrote of the camera.

> It is fabulous. What a joy of a thing to work with. I am sending the first rolls and hoping that they are ok, that I have not done something all wrong. The camera is the most eager and helpful of beings, all full of happy suggestions: "Try this! Do it that way!" Reminding me of things I have overlooked, and cooperating in the creation of new worlds. This is a Zen camera. As for the F.100 lens, I tell you I'm going to blow my mind with it! It is fantastic, at least in the viewfinder. I'll wait and see what the contacts look like.

From March 22-28, Griffin was at the country property, doing the actual writing of *The Church and the Black Man*. His portrait of Charles Rector became the cover art. He wrote ten pages in the *Journal* about what had changed. "In this kind of concentrated work, I find that I can not hold up as long as I used to. And in handling this kind of material, I tend to get too angry and I have to remind myself not to slash, to use the truth only to cure, not to wound; to present the materials without offering judgments; to allow the reader to do his own judging."

Griffin did not return to the *Journal* until June 7, reeling from the assassination of Robert F. Kennedy. "Nightmare days and nights. I have the deep feeling that the violence in this country—the riots particularly, detonated by whites, surely with an element of collusion from the police—are becoming our equivalent to Rome, to the great blood lusts that were served in the arenas—never assuaged because such lusts quickly become insatiable and demand more pain, suffering, blood."

The next day they watched the funeral on TV, he recorded Elizabeth's reaction: "It looks as though you have to be a racist, a Nazi, a fascist, or a Birchite to live to old age." Her cogent observation turned out to be true.

Griffin continued on *The Church and the Black Man* throughout June, baking bread every day, and writing briefly in the *Journal*, until July 4. On Independence Day he typed three pages, mostly about his family and parents, who were visiting. When he checked on his loved ones, they were all dozing after a mammoth lunch. He laughed to himself, and "when I returned here, I spontaneously bent forward and kissed the typewriter. The act astonished me, and only afterward do I realize what an affection I must have for this machine, which has become an extension of my fingers and responds faithfully to everything I pour into it—the junk, the hash, the good occasional line or paragraph."

He typed five pages on July 9, concerning the inequalities suffered by poor black people from *their* viewpoint, the same futile anguish he experienced during the journey of *Black Like Me*. It was not the tone he wanted to establish in the new book, but it was a way of venting emotions and cleansing the spirit.

Returning from a tour through the Midwest in mid-July, he met Grace Halsell on July 21, to discuss her plan of disguising herself as a black woman to travel through the South *and* the North.[95] In her first book, *Soul Sister*, Halsell did what he had done a decade earlier.

Griffin went to what he termed "the ghetto" in Fort Worth on July 25, making photographs for *The Church and the Black Man*.

> I started by photographing, from across the street, Our Lady of Sorrows Catholic Church (appropriately named) and got several shots with black people walking in front of it. Then a youngster came up and asked if I would take his picture. I agreed, delighted really, placed him in the foreground, with the church in the background and made some good photographs—his face glistening with sweat in sharp focus, the church slightly blurred in the background. It is such another world down there, so filled with pain and resentment that every act by a honkey is suspicious. The resentments are especially acute now with the Wallace convention to be held in Dallas in a few weeks. I drove past the shanties baking in the sun, past people sitting on porches, trying to find a breeze, past the clubs and eating places where young men sat in groups on door stoops. A feeling of explosive misery and resentment pervaded the area—and the heat turned it raw.

The next day he reported in the *Journal* that "the work went well and the great rolling inventiveness got going as it has not been going in so long. After I had written 30 to 35 pages of the book, I was pooped." He kept working well on the book, including in early August at the country retreat.

Back home, he commented on the August 7 television coverage of the Republican national convention. "The whole thing, right under the surface, is the mighty push of the racists who thinly disguise their racism behind states rights; Nixon's alleged promise to southerners that he would not ram anything down their throats, which means he would keep blacks out." The next night, he read "a very fine work, John Hersey's *The Algiers Motel Incident*, filled with the kind of insights one does not anticipate from a white man, no matter how gifted."

Returning home from lecturing on September 2, Griffin did darkroom work on the prints of Maritain. He made 11x17 prints "so that the massive gardens can be seen, but the near certainty that Jacques cannot live a great deal longer gives these images historic importance. There are very few photos of him and most are mine from recent years." By September 6, he had the necessary ingredients to make developers since commercial products were oxidizing and not giving artistic results. He observed the difference on September 9, while reprocessing the Maritain negatives. After "typing all day, I processed the beautiful negatives in my home-made developer."

They celebrated Elizabeth's thirty-third birthday on September 12, buying a frostless refrigerator to mark the occasion. He did "good work, without too many interruptions" on the new book from September 13 to September 27.

The couple went to the Book & Author luncheon in Dallas on September 28, which was preceded by a discussion for the educational television channel.

> William Barrett is a nice man, straightforward, and they talked about *Lilies of the Field*. Then we got into less pleasant things and Kozol, a brilliant, perceptive man was most impressive in talking about what led him to write *Death At An Early Age*. We hit it off immediately. Then to the hotel press conference and luncheon. A huge crowd. Kozol spoke first, magnificently; then Barrett—a pleasant talk on writing. I spoke about racism.

> One regal matron at the front table just glared, but I caught the eyes of black people and their nods prodded me to tell it straight. Afterward the people descended on us and I felt so sick of answering white people's questions, especially within the hearing range of black butlers and waiters. Kozol and I were acutely aware of this silent, impassive audience of black people, though the whites asking the questions were apparently no more aware of them than they were of the furniture. I wondered how they kept silent, how they kept from laughing out loud at some of the ignorant white questions.

Griffin was on tour in early October and, though "the lectures went extremely well," he returned home, "dead tired, but with the need to make love and be loved by my wife—to lie in her arms and love her and feel the life come back. How much I sense this need after mulching brain and physical energies lecturing."

He interrupted work on October 7 to hear Marian Anderson's farewell recital at Constitution Hall. "I had not remembered what a spellbinding artist she was, though my memory of her is as a supreme artist—still, after all the times I have heard her, it was wonderful to hear that glorious voice sing Schubert."

The next day he processed the Jonathan Kozol negatives, pleased with the result. "The negatives printed out beautifully and make moving portraits." He did not go back on tour, turning down lectures in mid-October due to symptoms that appeared to be mumps with a high fever. The doctor prohibited travel, discovering that it was not mumps but a reaction to his medications. The following day he felt better, mailing a portrait of Jacques Maritain as the cover for his last book, the Macmillan paperback of *The Peasant of Garonne*.

Checking the mail on October 23, Griffin was "thrown into a cold shock" to discover that the bank account was overdrawn, since checks for lectures had not arrived. "I felt that awful sinking, because I thought we had enough in the account and had to get bank loan to cover the overdraft. At best it will be close next month and I pray that I do not get sick again and have to cancel any more lectures. To owe money paralyzes me." When that was settled, he prepared for lectures in Michigan. His usual fee was $500. He had received $800 to $1000 for lectures at larger venues, but also lectured for $300 to $400 at community colleges and high schools.

Back from another brief tour, Griffin's problem of working in the office had not been only phone calls and visits, but time with the family. The day before he had spent most of the day with Amanda, who visited "every few minutes, with a great smile on her face and a book under her arm—irresistible. Finally I took her to the zoo to see all the animals she knows from her books. We had a glorious time."

In the *Journal* of October 31, he declared it "a good day's work, the best I have ever had on this book. From early morning until ten last night, with no interruptions, no distractions—happy to have got over so many difficult hurdles." The "return was all I had hoped—great warmth, love, fulfillment," he noted on November 2. Since it was All Souls Day, he made a list of the dearly departed. They voted November 5, taking the day off. Griffin listened to the Bach violin *Partitas*, sorting through prints he had made the night before. "I baked a brown bread and the loaf was so beautiful when I cut into it that I photographed it—a picture of health and sanity that matches this magnificent music. Then Amanda, wearing Greg's hat and peace medal, came in, radiant, and I photographed her. I attach these photos in the *Journal*, both of which are like the music and the morning—glorious."

Sunday, November 10, Griffin was alone, as the family was visiting Elizabeth's mother at the Mansfield farm. He reveled in the fireplace and Wanda Landowska's performance of the Bach *Partita in C-minor* for harpsichord.

Veterans' Day, November 11, was a holiday with no mail delivery, which he realized later with a sigh of relief. His preoccupation with the new book presented a serious challenge. "How difficult to conceive the right tone; to present the materials without judging the Church. The idea of the Church as Christ (now seldom heard) of assuming the 'habit' of Christ, doing and thinking only according to Christ until self fades and this becomes normal. But the man who did this would be in almost constant conflict with the Church, as would Christ himself."

He was on tour of the east coast throughout the rest of November and into early December. While in Manhattan on December 11, Griffin received news of Merton's accidental death by electrocution on the previous day in Bangkok. He wrote about the funeral for *Continuum*'s special issue on Merton.[96] "I returned to Gethsemani on the day of the funeral, December 17, and closed my photographic archive with some shots the next morning of the red clay mound of his grave beneath a large cypress tree in the monastic graveyard."

Griffin returned home on December 21 to a "vast amount of mail," deciding to respond to it incrementally while helping Elizabeth. On Christmas night, he wrote about a new French edition of Pierre Reverdy's poetry.

> Weird how it echoes my own feelings on so many matters. These lines read tonight, written many years ago by Reverdy, strike perfectly at my own reticence. He spoke of himself as "an obscure animal who sometimes writes." He spoke of his nervousness, his shame in speaking of God in his books: "In any case, I believe that I have already my just recompense for having dared write and publish, without modesty, what one should never know too well how to hide. It is God I love, and I find religion. Misfortune, misfortune, misfortune!" At the end, a key line: "I found, at the extreme point where my forces allowed me to go, a light marvelously alive, but that burns like fire."
>
> Here alone tonight, so tired that a kind of clarity comes, all my thirst is for silence and solitude and the obscurity that hides what is real to me from the world, because the moment it is spoken or revealed it takes on a falsity.
>
> At Gethsemani I was enormously aware of this very thing in Merton's life and the reticence with which he spoke of the great thing that was happening between him and God until he finally did not speak of it at all, and above all not write of it for publication; and as he said, "just let it take care of itself." Merton had few tears, but those he had were for those same people, and finally he refused to be dragged along with them by isolating himself more and more (just as Reverdy did). How these things speak to me and for me.
>
> Yet I have that other vocation, and have to believe that what is done despite us is better than what is done by us. But I don't handle it well. I do it. I act. But I grow into a deeper fatigue, and only the word *perseverance* sometimes keeps me staggering on, being, doing and acting in ways that have little to do with the things that happen in the core of my being. It is not my vocation to wear God visibly. It is my vocation to be silent in these areas and to trust that the ferment from within and that alone and invisibly and secretly will produce whatever natural resonance God wishes. It is not for me to be concerned with the results.

The violent legacy of the 1960s took a terrible toll on Griffin's psyche, and also his friends and colleagues, who had survived the senseless waste of human life. The roll call of the dead was long: Dr. Martin Luther King Jr., Malcolm X, Medgar Evers, Vernon Dahmer, Clyde Kennard, and civil rights workers both black and white; President John F. Kennedy and Senator Robert F. Kennedy; the horrific "body count" from Vietnam and the riots. Equally painful losses: Pope John XXIII, Gerald Vann, Raïssa Maritain, Pierre Reverdy, and Lillian Smith. But the unexpected death of Thomas Merton hit him hardest. Devastated by the sudden and unexpected loss, he was asking why Merton and not himself. For Griffin it was "only with the awareness that there were people like Merton who didn't have to be out in those alleys which gave me the strength to do it; otherwise I couldn't have done it."

The tone of the 1969 *Journal* marked the beginning of a profound grieving process. Death was a reality never far from consciousness for a sensitive soul in intimate touch with the rapid dissolution of its fragile body. In the passing of Merton, who was only five years older, Griffin felt the loss of a brother.

The *Journal* of 1969 runs to 143 pages (80 typed in Merton's hermitage at the Abbey of Gethsemani in Kentucky), but he begins in Fort Worth.

> New years day. The year will bring what it will. I do not speculate about it. Surrounded by large prints made yesterday of Merton with the Dalai Lama and with Brother Patrick Hart. Must send these out, but do not know how to address the Dalai Lama. His Holiness? From the look of him, he couldn't care less about such precisions, and from the way he and Tom hit it off immediately, I cannot imagine that it would matter to him.
>
> I stare at the photographs of Merton. A mingling of loss and solace in doing these things. A letter from Brother Pat moved me tremendously: "Christmas is over and in spite of the efforts of all to put joy into the feast, it has been the saddest of my life. The vacuum created by Tom's death is almost unbearable."

During the first week of January, Griffin lectured in Arkansas and Missouri. In the *Journal* of January 8, he reviewed materials in a file about Merton's death. "I have to force myself to turn to the typewriter. I wish I had a full month, instead of these stolen moments, to complete the darkroom work on the Merton archives. It is strange, after printing some of the photographs made on my last meeting with Tom, I realize that he never saw most of these."

Griffin worked on *The Church and the Black Man* on January 13, "but things move so fast these days that I fear it will be obsolete by publication, impossible now to foresee which way things will go."

He lectured in Michigan for two days, returning on January 26. Again the *Journal* registers his frustrations. "The book is driving me crazy. For all these years we have lamented the Church's sins of omission in regard to racial justice, the condoning by silence, the *special treatment* accorded black Catholics (the missionary treatment, the separate churches, the discrimination within the 'integrated' churches, the unconscious racism widely displayed to black people in attitudes expressed by bishops, priests, laymen). Now something is really in ferment—to make the Church view man as man, and not as black or white."

In excruciating detail, Griffin wrote of processing Merton's last roll of film that was sent to him by the Abbey of Gethsemani.

> I tried to open it, but my hands trembled so uncontrollably that Elizabeth had to finish the job. I was overwhelmed to see how immaculately Tom had cared for the equipment—the body and lenses were spotless. I glanced at the frame counter and saw that 18 shots had been taken of the roll then in the camera body.
>
> More carefully than I have ever done anything in my life, I removed that roll of film and held it in my hand, realizing that on 18 frames were undeveloped images of scenes Tom had been the last to see when he clicked the shutter and I would be the first to see when they assumed form and detail in the developer. What had registered in his brain and senses, what had interested him, existed latent in that undeveloped emulsion.
>
> I mixed all fresh chemicals and worked with care. Rarely have such tensions cluttered the small space of my darkroom. If these negatives were ruined or spotted or scratched, they could never be replaced. These scenes could never again be photographed with the special vision of Thomas Merton, never again composed and captured with the whole culture of Thomas Merton. I began to breathe again when finally I held the strip of dripping negatives to the light and saw good clean images.

> When they were dry, I put the strip into the enlarger, selected one of the last images at random, focused and exposed it on photographic paper.
>
> Moments later I held the enlarged photograph in my hands. I looked through Tom's eyes on a scene viewed from some high place, downward past an edge of a building and a foreground of shore across a broad body of water from which reflected sunlight glinted back into the viewer's eye—a kind of universal all-embracing view of men and boats and water seen from the perspective of height and distance.

In *Journal* notes that day, Griffin speculated about the camera. "I never dreamed when I gave the Alpa to Tom that I would ever get it back, because I never thought I could survive him. I told him never to worry about it, that the camera was hardy and made for tough use, but he assured us that he would guard it with his life. I feel it should be in some museum. But no, he would scoff at such an idea."

While in Iowa on February 1, he heard about the death of Dominique Pire. "First Tom and now Father Pire, only 59, the great Nobel laureate, colleague and devoted friend. Is God going to allow us to be stripped of all our great ones? I got up prepared to work all day here, but I cannot get this down, and all I feel like doing is praying for him and Tom and Martin and the Kennedys."

After a few days of lecturing in Illinois and Iowa, he returned February 5 to fifty-six pieces of mail, including a tape of the Merton funeral Mass. "Enormously moving to hear it again after the passages of weeks. I relived the whole thing."

For two weeks, he worked on the racism book with fewer interruptions, because Elizabeth was monitoring phone calls. He bought recordings of Mozart piano concerti, performed by Robert Casadesus, under the baton of George Szell with the Cleveland Orchestra, responding in the *Journal* on March 6. "These plunged me into memories when I traveled with Casadesus, days of complete happiness, because I loved him as a friend, but really hero-worshipped him as a musician."

The next week Griffin was back on lecture tour, including a well-paid talk to the Teachers of College English Convention. But he came home ill on March 15. After a week recovering, he took to the road during the last week in March and the first days of April. Home for Easter, he writes in the *Journal* on Good Friday, April 4. "Long, hot day, and it remains sweltering tonight. An overwhelming day, here alone without interruption, working well, but beyond the work tremendously aware of the day. Am very hungry, but hunger tells me that others feel this constantly. I hunger voluntarily to share their involuntary hunger."

Returning home on May 12, Griffin wrote of the highlight of a commission from the Merton Legacy Trust to begin the "Official Biography" of Thomas Merton, to be published by Houghton Mifflin. By May 14, he had settled contract terms. "And most generously, so that is now final."

Griffin visited the Abbey of Gethsemani on May 28. The next day he had "a magnificent visit" with Father Eudes Bamberger.[97] He found in Bamberger's essay for the *Continuum* collection ("In Memory of Thomas Merton") to be "a model for the manner in which the biography can be handled. More importantly, it sets a goal, a tone, that makes me realize what an immense amount of work I must do in order to achieve the understanding necessary to do the biography adequately—but I am relieved at the same time to know better now in what direction to go, what to watch out for, what to search for." Later Griffin was alone for the first time in Merton's hermitage, describing the cell in great detail.

The next day he went to Bellarmine College "where I will get a first view of the materials" at the Thomas Merton Studies Center in Louisville. That morning he "offered my intentions at Mass for the book: that I may be guided to do it truthfully and with justice to Tom's life."

Returning home he wrote in the *Journal* of June 1, examining negatives that Penn Jones brought back from a trip to Bangkok.

> Penn is not the only one suspicious about Tom's death. The visiting priests there felt it should be investigated more. I must check out everything, though it seems impossible that anything other than what appears to have happened could have happened. I made prints of these negatives, and that fan is a jarring sight. Was it truly God's instrument to terminate Tom's life or was there more to it than we want to believe? I pray that the death was truly accidental, and that I am not walking into a nightmare in this investigation.

June 2 was the Griffins' sixteenth wedding anniversary, but Elizabeth had a severe throat infection. He would become infected the next day. "Though she did not want to spread any germs, I insisted on kissing her and did so several times. Regrettable because I have to go to bed—and on our anniversary, when we should be celebrating and love-making. I am just knocked out completely."

Griffin did not write in the *Journal* until July 21. "Sickness, travel, and work have kept me from these pages, which I resume now." The family had vacationed in Taos, and he recorded documentaries for the Canadian Broadcasting Company—Griffin's interview with John Reeves and his interview with Archie Moore, the former light heavyweight boxing champion, whom he photographed. On July 31, Griffin complained about overworking and fatigue. "I told Elizabeth today that I work so hard on my backlog I cannot do anything on my front log, and that is about true. Each day I plan a great many things, each day a few of them get done."

Griffin returned to the Abbey of Gethsemani on August 5, and this date became the first entry in *The Hermitage Journals.* From August of 1969 until June of 1972, he worked in the hermitage about one week each month, totaling over two hundred days. "I try to approximate Merton's schedule in my own research. I keep a running journal of my own experiences in living and researching this material—in other words, a complete journal of the writing of this work."

He recorded impressions of being in Merton's space, aware of the natural rhythms and simple rituals of solitude at the hermitage.

> Since Merton perceived the connections in many diverse elements of his life, I simply do what he did—put down everything and wait for the connections to come in their own good time. The truest and deepest sense of wholeness comes when the solitude itself is truest and deepest, when you are emptied of all the junk of self and simply function as a part of nature and silence and odors and feelings, at your own natural rhythms of spirit and body, with nothing to distract you from a sense of union with what Merton called 'the Christ of silences.' Tom made the point again and again in his journals that he did not come into this solitude and silence of hermit life seeking but rather he came here because this is where he believed Christ wanted to find him.

He awakened in Merton's hermitage for the first time, early on the morning of August 6. Using a borrowed typewriter, he noted that "even this quiet typewriter motor sounds an ungodly racket in the silence that possesses the countryside." He was served breakfast by the monks he had

Griffin at Merton's desk in the monk's hermitage at Gethsemani. It was taken by Griffin with a self-timer, and appears in the posthumous cloth edition of *The Hermitage Journals* (Andrews and McMeal, 1981),

come to know while visiting with Merton: Father Tarcisius Conner and Brother Maurice Flood. Brother Patrick Hart joined them, bringing research materials. The three monks assisted him during his visits, celebrating Mass each morning in the tiny chapel of the cinder block hermitage. Since the building was too distant from the monastery for him to traverse on foot, the monks provided him with all he needed.

Griffin began with accounts of Merton's death, translating from the French of Dom Jean Leclercq.[98] He quoted the final lines of the article in *The Bangkok Post* about Merton's talk the night before.

> The last words of his talk had to have a resonance that he didn't suspect: "And now, since the conferences of this morning will be the object of this evening's discussion, I am going to disappear. *I will disappear*." The moment having come, according to his last words, he disappeared. But at the same time, and forever, he remains.

Intending to retire early, Griffin stayed up until the early morning of August 7, to finish reading Merton's last journals from Asia. He decided to "put off reading the correspondence, preferring to do other things first—but really because I have not yet adjusted myself to reading anyone else's mail." He had scoured materials on Merton's death and adjusted to the monk's rigid schedule.

On August 9, Griffin clarified new perceptions.

> I am really feeling my way, absorbing everything I can. From all this there comes that deeper experience of the silence and the solitude from which Tom drew so much of his preoccupation. The sense of loneliness is gone. In its place there is a growing reliance on the solitude and silence, and these things serve merely as the background for the intimate preoccupation of the Christ that Tom sought in the silence, of the Christ that surrounded as the silence surrounds: and out of that a tremendous enthusiasm and vitality that fills the hours, even the hours of contemplation, with a flow and rhythm that stimulates everything and reconciles superbly the realities of the body's needs with the needs of the spirit, the mind. This is one of the things that made Tom unshockable in the face of any reality.
>
> What I am learning here is that in his own discoveries, in his own lived experience, the greatest part remained unexpressed, the greatest and most valuable part was hidden, secret. I cannot become him, God knows; and such an idea would utterly repel Tom himself; but I can become enough of him to perceive that the hidden part was the essential and the revealed part was infinitely less important, given only in hints (which is one of the things that gave an illusion of ambivalence and contradiction to much of what he revealed).
>
> He was simply not interested, despite his vocation as a writer, in revealing. His most vital writing is private, what he did for himself, because he made constant notes to help clarify things for himself.

Griffin ended the long passage, observing, "I believe one of the marks of the authentic contemplative is a growing need to hide himself, to draw ever more deeply into secrecy, to efface himself, become invisible." Perhaps he was over-identifying with Merton's last comment about "disappearing" and projecting his desire to be invisible. Or perhaps the authentic solitude was working its silent spell.

Up at dawn on August 10, he was listening to a tape of Lili Kraus playing Beethoven's *Fourth Concerto*. "This music fits the morning and seems to spring directly from the trees and mountains." He cleaned the hermitage and was taken to the monastery, where he had separate visits with Father Flavian Burns, the new Abbot, and Dom James Fox, the former Abbot, who had become a hermit.

"Dom James took me to his hermitage, hidden away through miles of woods on a small peninsula high in the mountains—a place of magnificent vistas and total isolation." During the talk, "Dom James stressed two things—Merton's 'profound, *almost childlike faith* and his *ultimate humility*.' If he had ever left, it would only be to go more deeply into solitude and isolation in his search for contemplative union with God. That is certain." He believed "Merton felt that western monks were not yet profoundly enough skilled in contemplation and he was trying to learn—that was the real reason for the trip."

Griffin was reminded of the similarity of the poets he most admired—Reverdy and Merton. "Dom James said that writing was a compulsion for Tom, and that Tom had told him that if he could not write, he would break down mentally. I remember Reverdy telling me that 'If I had not written, I would have gone mad.'"

On August 11, Griffin researched Merton's 1968 letters written just before he went to the Far East. The next day he reflected on Merton's solitude.

> All the private archival papers indicate one overwhelming fact: Tom was driven almost from the beginning to total abandonment to God: absolute and perfect. And in his struggles, the chief difficulty lay always in seeking to find ways to become more solitary, more united—seeking to remove the imperfections, the intrusions, the sounds: he died really looking ardently for that place where there would be nothing but him and God in uninterrupted silence and solitude, far from the proximity of men, though united to mankind.
>
> It was thought that when he was allowed to live as a hermit here, the problem of solitude would be solved. His solitude was guarded and respected, certainly, but he lived constantly with the *potentiality* of its being unexpectedly interrupted. . . . This fact made for an imperfect interior repose. . . . He did not seek self-fulfillment, but self-abandonment; not to become something, but to become nothing.

Griffin departed on August 13. "Magnificent week. I look forward to my return next month but now I look forward with the deepest joy to getting home." He accomplished little, as he was "downed by a pancreatitis attack and spent most of the time catching up." Two weeks later, he confessed to being involved with a book about photography. "Much work to get done this week," he reports the next day. "I hope to God I can do it before leaving for Gethsemani next week."

His second stay at the hermitage lasted five days, September 15-19. He read the Merton journals on the first day and awakened early on the second, continuing the research. By September 17, he was adjusted to the early schedule. That afternoon Brother Hart took him to Louisville for lunch with Carolyn Hammer, widow of artist Victor Hammer, and author Wendell Berry. "She gave me a copy of the Merton-Hammer *Hagia Sophia*, a priceless gift."

On the afternoon of September 18, he heard from the President of Bellarmine College, Monsignor Alfred F. Horrigan, requesting that he speak at a function on November 9, to establish the Thomas Merton Studies Center at Bellarmine-Ursuline College in Louisville. Merton had donated his archives to the Bellarmine Library in 1963, the very papers Griffin was researching.

Early on the morning of September 19, Griffin observed that the "thirst for this solitude grows. The week here comes to an end too soon, but thank God for this week each month." Galleys of *The Church and the Black Man* arrived from Pflaum, but he did not correct them at the hermitage.

> No music could add anything to this kind of silence, and no music could ever equal it. Music is necessary elsewhere as a substitute for it. Here, I choose the better of the two—the silence that is filled with Christ. I know that I am living a tremendous privilege here—I am awe-stricken with gratitude: that is all, everything within me goes out and fuses with that Christ-filled silence; every action, everything I do. Whereas in places where there is never silence or solitude for any extended period, these actions distract one from thoughts of God, here they simply fuse into that tremendous awareness. Such an awareness does not destroy the solitude as any human presence might (though not all human presences do); no, it simply fills solitude which, without

> it, would be only void, only hollowness. . . . this solitude has no hollow, no void, no loneliness—only felicity.

From September 20 to October 10, he completed several projects between lectures and a trip to Canada. He corrected galleys for *The Church and the Black Man*, finalized "The Terrain of Physical Pain" essay, and nearly all of the photographic work on *A Hidden Wholeness*, the photographic book on Merton.

October 11 was the first of four days during Griffin's third visit. "As ravishing a morning as I can ever remember," and he celebrated "the most perfect solitude. I had solitude, but always with the awareness that it could be destroyed. One has to sink into it and it has to be total before the real work begins."

> I am aware that in addition to doing the very best work here that can be done on this book—the most concentrated and sustained—I am also privileged to live some of the highest moments of my interior life. This hermit-existence, which in no way nullifies or reduces my family existence, is deeply and profoundly tasted in all its rarity.

This was Griffin's rediscovery of solitude.

> I had known certain types of solitude, having been blind for a prolonged period, having lived on islands in the South Pacific, having studied with the Dominicans and Benedictines in France, but this was entirely different. Here one was alone without the slightest sense of loneliness, and the longer it lasted the more profound grew the felicity, the sense of freedom, the faith, the loving. . . . And yet I wondered how could one find such solitude in the world for a sufficiently long period to learn what it had to teach, and how many of us spend our entire lives without ever experiencing it, or even a hint of it. Solitude in this sense differs vastly from merely being alone or simply passing the hours. The Creator and all of creation are one's constant companions, day and night, in all one's occupations. Living in that solitude, I often thought of Cassian's 'We pray best when we are no longer aware we are praying.'

Early on October 12, Griffin made *crepes* for the three monks who usually prepared breakfast. He had a scheduled lecture that night, but dreaded leaving the cell. He listened to music after all, playing the *String Quintet in G-minor* by Mozart. "The slow and final movements of this quintet come the closest to expressing in sound the felicities of solitude and silence of any music I know."

Griffin's talk to an attentive group of nuns went well, but he retired too late to wake early on October 13. He felt tired, even numb, "but it will return, the energy and enthusiasm will come with the work and the day and the deeply curative silences." With sunlight, he played Bach that "blazes out full of humor and vigor, catches my lethargy and pumps life into me."

> I could not help an old puritanical feeling that there was something vaguely sinful in taking such pleasure. It is the happiest work I have ever done in my life, the most satisfying, the deepest adventure. *Black Like Me* was crushing and depressing as a lived experience. This is enthralling as lived experience, nourishing in the most robust and jubilant way; overwhelming in its graces, especially when guided by such a hermit as Merton, as I penetrate his interior and exterior existence through these journals of his; studied right here on the very ground where he lived, and lived also by me under his tutelage; or through him, because we are vastly different men, though similar in our love of the silence and solitude.

It was raining in the pre-dawn hours on October 14, Griffin's last day of the current visit. "Lord, when I think of my first visit here alone in the hermitage—the forlorn kind of terror at the immensity of the solitude when I carried in me still the spiritual and nerve-seeped smog of the cities, and wondered if I could bear this kind of solitude, I am astonished."

He left Gethsemani for three days of lectures in Canada. Then he went to Indianapolis for talks on October 18-19, returning to Fort Worth on October 20. Since he could not bring the Merton materials along, he concentrated only on final darkroom work for *A Hidden Wholeness*.

The fourth visit began on the night of November 5, and it would be different. He had created a problem without realizing it. Since this stay included a celebration at the Thomas Merton Studies Center, he had made arrangements for Elizabeth, Susan, and Amanda to attend. There were retreat houses for men and women, but because the guesthouses were empty, Griffin assumed the couple would be allowed to sleep together. According to Elizabeth, they were hoping to "desegregate the monastery." This unprecedented request sparked conversations—mostly humorous on the part of Griffin and the monks. The eventual outcome placed him in the women's guesthouse with his wife and two daughters. They enjoyed the event at the Merton Center, where he delivered a talk about researching in Merton's hermitage.

Griffin wondered why dreams were so vivid in the hermitage. "Tom had them, too—he talks of them a great deal in his diaries. Perhaps it is part of the purging that takes place here, the 'emptying,' as he called it."

> No need to hide it here: here one is called to face squarely the realities of oneself: of one's body, one's mind, one's conscious and unconscious life; not deliberately—it is just part of the solitary life, part of the natural transparency of self that is accomplished in silence and solitude when one does not try to direct or guide it, but simply goes along with it. These dreams of deep anguish are part of the filtering process that takes place within—removing the impediments to love, the inner murkiness.
>
> A man has to be converted over again each hour, so man has to be aware of his profound vulnerability each moment, because the world demands in each an illusion of strength that amounts to an illusion of invulnerability: thus the illusion of growth that is not authentic growth at all. Here, where man gives himself over to the times of nature, to the inner silences as well as the surrounding ones and the growth is more natural, not that unspeakable hothouse growth of the world. The reality he faces is the reality of his vulnerability, which is why he can hardly escape the awareness of God's mercy: here, in the solitude and silence, the world's image, the 'mystique' of what a hermit should be simply falls away. . . .

Back home for the Thanksgiving holidays, Griffin was writing brief paragraphs in the *Journal* on November 27, the first entry since September, noting "something keeps me from writing in this journal." The photographic work for *A Hidden Wholeness*, to be printed in a 9 x 11.5 format on glossy pages, was in the hands of the publisher. He worked against a deadline on brief texts for the picture book.

Griffin arrived at Gethsemani on the evening of December 4, for his fifth visit. The next morning he awakened late, but managed to accomplish research. "This work is intense, but without strain, and by late evening, I am completely and healthfully exhausted." However, he had a sleepless night, concerned about what to say to the community of monks he was to address on December 10. "What could I say that would be interesting, that they do not already know? That will not insult them with its idiocy?" These thoughts kept him awake, until he was reading Merton's journals from early 1966. "Tom lived extraordinarily halcyon and grace-filled days here as a hermit. Tremendous journal entries."

By seven on the morning of December 6, he was tired and bleary-eyed. He took a nap, expecting visitors at noon. He survived the visit, turning in early. By five the next morning Griffin was on schedule and, since it rained hard throughout the next day, he was left entirely alone for twenty-four hours. He read Merton's journals and copied out many passages, which appear often in the working manuscript but not in the published version of *The Hermitage Journals.*

The first anniversary of Merton's arrival in Bangkok was December 8. It was the last entry in the monk's journals and the date of his final letter to Griffin. Editor Jim Andrews was on retreat and invited up for Mass at the hermitage.[99] It was their only meeting, and they did an interview for *National Catholic Reporter.*

On the evening of December 9, Griffin wrote in *The Hermitage Journals* of his day in Lexington as the guest of John Jacob Niles, folk musician and composer.[100] He heard a private concert of Niles's cycle of Merton poems, "performed with incredible beauty" by soprano Jacqueline Roberts and pianist Janelle Pope. "They are art songs of high quality, particularly high melodic quality. They come from deep within, giving an impression of great naturalness and spontaneity."

Griffin spoke to the community on December 10, marking the first anniversary of Merton's death. The event left him exhausted the next day, yet "at the same time the need to remain conscious of these precious hours of silence in this magnificent and curative solitude." He worked through the next day "on that difficult section about Merton's calligraphy, trying not to use the word Zen, which carries such a tone of false meanings to most Western minds, even those who think they practice it." Griffin completed it after several rewrites, but more texts were due for *A Hidden Wholeness,* and he did not meet the publisher's deadlines.

Not looking forward to 1970, Griffin dreaded the upcoming lecture tour. The visits to Gethsemani had been productive, but the stress of meeting deadlines, falling ill, and going back on tour left him depleted. He took the Christmas holiday season off to recover, not writing in the *Journal* during the remainder of the year—not even to mention that *The Church and the Black Man* had been published in November of 1969. He would learn of the poor fate of the book in 1970. The backlash by conservative elements of the Catholic Church rejected his conclusions, along with the views of black and white clergy and the secular critics who are included in the book.

Lightning Strikes

> I'm a firm believer in Black Power, as I believe anyone who wants the good of the total community must be. It is a tragedy that non-violence didn't work. The black man was trying to cure his white brother with it, but the white man wouldn't be cured. Non-violent resistance has done more than we realize, though. I think history will show that it accomplished an enormous thing in men's souls. It didn't fail, it just didn't complete the job. Black Power is a progression from it. It's the black man's assertion of his humanity, and it requires us to confront one another as equals.
>
> —GRIFFIN'S STATEMENT FOR THE REDPATH AGENCY LECTURE SERIES

Griffin continued lecturing and writing about racism during the 1970s, but at a diminished pace. In the new decade, America had moved toward the repressive "law and order" stance of the Nixon administration. This mood had already been evident from the white backlash after the 1967 urban riots. The discourse changed, and the evolving struggle would be carried on by Black Power advocates and not by white liberals. Griffin was relieved to retreat into the background, because of his great respect for the Black Liberation Movement, encouraging other white activists to do the same. But even if the political landscape had not altered irrevocably, failing health would have moved him toward the sidelines.

His view of white racism turned increasingly critical, and in *The Church and the Black Man* he advocates Black Power without forsaking nonviolence.

> For approximately a decade, black Americans persevered in the dream of non-violent resistance. But its success always depends on the conversion of the hostile white force. An indication of the dehumanizing character of racism on racists themselves is surely found in this failure of love and redemptive suffering to cure the wounds of racism. Non-violent resistance appeared to have failed. In fact, racists redoubled their efforts in the name of patriotism and Christianity, to suppress not only black people but all non-racists.

"However, nonviolence did make profound changes in that it did touch and move many individuals; but these changes were intimate, surrounded by confusion, filled with fears of reprisals and character assassination." Griffin regretted that the "racist attitudes have finally driven black men to abandon many of the old dreams we shared, dreams that were good; and to embark into this period of transition that so bewilders men, but in which we are beginning to see our first real hope." Only by giving up the dream of desegregation could black thinkers move toward their own philosophy, developing black consciousness as opposed to the fragmented individualism that denied their identity in the pursuit of white goals. Blackness was transformed into a sign of beauty and dignity, rather than internalized as negative images. There was a return to the celebration of sisterhood and brotherhood, based on self-determination, turning the community from a ghetto of white-imposed separation into a communal space of unity. Griffin discussed this in lectures to northern whites.

> Black thinkers—usually unknown to white America—began to structure and analyze the weakness of black America, and since their philosophical analyses conformed to their lived experience, much of it was immediately understood. This did not mean relinquishing the struggle for equal rights and justice, but perceiving it as a form of political desegregation rather than as a form of social integration with whites.
>
> Black Power rose to the surface at a time when this land faced a confrontation that appeared inevitably to lead to violence and to genocidal suppression of black people. Black Power rose, if men could only perceive it, as almost *a stroke of genius* that could avoid violence, that could turn the burning resentments and the energies they engendered, into healthful and constructive channels. Black Power implied *not* the

advocacy of violence—as so many white believed—but the alternative to that kind of fruitless confrontation.

The common criticism of Black Power was that it was a form of reverse racism. This was a false analogy, since black people had not lynched whites or burned down their churches. Racism, hate stares, and epithets were capable of causing emotional pain, but without the power to cause injury or to kill another with impunity. Many segregated areas of the South during the 1960s were police states where racist Jim Crow statutes were codified as law. The Black Liberation Movement must be viewed not as "progress" from the white perspective, but as a process of revolutionary consciousness-raising that lighted the cause of justice in a white supremacist system that denied the democratic principals and religious ideals it claimed to espouse. Black Power could *not* change the culture's deeply entrenched institutions in the short term, but it did move the discourse toward a dialogue beyond nonviolence. Nonviolence had succeeded against the racist rule of segregation, yet it had failed to unite the races after unjust laws were erased.

Griffin wrote 229 pages in the 1970 *Journal*—184 pages typed at the hermitage, plus a twenty-two-page handwritten notebook kept in Europe. He had "time for just a few notes" on January 5, outlining his upcoming schedule. He lectured in a few cities, but was due to work on *A Hidden Wholeness* with the book designers at Houghton Mifflin on January 12. He planned on returning to the Abbey of Gethsemani in mid-January, but was scheduled for the *Today* show in New York on January 20, to be interviewed about *The Church and the Black Man*.

Griffin arrived at the hermitage for his sixth visit on January 15. "How I have longed for these first moments alone in this cottage—now more isolated than before by heavy snows." Intending to rise early on January 16, he slept through the alarm. It was a day when "nothing much gets done," but Griffin reveled in those "moments of early dawn and late dusk" that "are similar in the qualities of silence they evoke, and everything in me defers to them." On January 17, he was up at four and worked well. With the dawn he made photographs of the hermitage (several are in *The Hermitage Journals*). He remained isolated by snow and temperatures in the teens through January 18, hours of "wonderful contentment in the work." The next day, he departed for the TV appearance, and "the shock of going from this isolated hermitage to New York City is not something I anticipate with any joy."

Griffin noted that the TV appearance went well, and he was preparing for a trip to Europe with daughter Susan. They arrived in Amsterdam January 27, attending an all-Beethoven recital by pianist Annie Fischer at the Concertgebouw.[101] That night he wrote in a spiral notebook. "A real glory, one of the finest concerts I ever heard—like Lipatti and Schnabel combined. I photographed quietly. Tremendously moved by the audience's attention and response. I feel more at home here than anywhere in the States." He spoke with Annie Fischer afterwards.

Next morning they toured the Rijks Museum, viewing the Rembrandts and Vermeers, and visiting the Van Gogh Gallery in the afternoon. During the next few days they were in Brussels, then on to the Kolbsheim chateau of Antionette and Lexi Grunelius, where he had worked with Jacques Maritain earlier.

After a few days, they visited Maritain at Toulouse, France, at the convent of the Little Brothers and Little Sisters. "Jacques seems splendid, is working hard to finish his books and fears he may die before he gets it done. Now 87 and physically feeble, but marvelously clear and strong in his mind."

They drove a rented car through the Pyrenees on February 11, reaching Prades, Merton's birthplace, the ostensible reason for the research trip. Griffin recognized Merton's birth home from photographs taken fifty-four years prior. "I hardly needed to verify the address. An old photo was there in the reality of stones and plaster, unchanged." The next day he photographed in Montauban, the Lycée Ingres that Merton attended for two years, then on to St. Antonin where Owen Merton, the monk's father ("a fine painter"), had built a house matching the medieval village.

Returning to Toulouse for final visits with Maritain on February 13, he received a gift copy of Raïssa Maritain's book on Marc Chagall. "Feel this may be my last visit with Jacques. But who knows?" Not only would it be the last time he saw Maritain, but also it was Griffin's final voyage to Europe. Their twenty-day excursion ended with two frigid days in Paris, where the highlight was meeting Stanislas Fumet, who had directed editions of Bloy, Baudelaire, Braque, Maritain, and Reverdy. They conversed for hours in French while Griffin made photographic portraits.

Griffin spent a week at home thoroughly exhausted. But the publication of *The Church and the Black Man* and the *Today* appearance resulted in a new batch of hate mail. He admitted in the *Journal*: "It is painful to be in the written presence of people who judge so surely and with vast self-delusion of comprehension—who condemn a book without condescending to read it. I have had too much of all this, and it is too great a change from the wonderful trip to Europe and the warm homecoming. I have no elasticity toward this kind of thing anymore."

Arriving for a seventh visit at Gethsemani and anticipating a longer stay—up to ten days—Griffin confessed on February 24: "It is terrible to say but there are only two places where I am truly at home, where I want to be, where I am completely happy and right: within the rooms of my own home with my wife and children, and here in the solitude of this hermitage. In all others, no matter how pleasant or enjoyable, I am not at home; I am vaguely miserable."

He was up early the next morning, doing "small things that require no thought" and taking Merton's "advice and do nothing, just wait for it to tell me what to do . . ." But energy did not come this day or on February 26, when he felt "this strange collapse of energies with no similar collapse of enthusiasm." Yet he believed he had "enough experience with the hermit life now to know that it is part of the initial 'reforming' of force."

Griffin realized he had come to that profound solitude just as Merton had, each arriving *not* to find the fulfillment of a preconceived plan of hermiticism or, least of all, to discover the "self"—but simply to be immersed in solitude. "I am openmouthed with bewilderment that God should flood me with such fine gifts, and I utter prayers of thanksgiving for Tom for being the instrument that brought me here to be where Christ obviously wanted to find me, in the silence of these woods, at this time." He also clarified that he was not some false reincarnation of Merton, "because we are vastly different men, though similar in our love of the silence and solitude."

Several years later, in the 1977 interview with Thurston Smith, he reiterated this point. "When I was doing the biography of Thomas Merton, a student who was writing a doctoral thesis on him said: 'Before I start, I want to tell you I want to be exactly like Merton.' I said, 'Then you don't understand anything about him, because Merton would have tried to help you be exactly like yourself.' Love does not possess but frees the other to be what he or she really is."

Griffin's eighth visit to the hermitage began on April 18. There were several guests, and he did a lot of cooking with the supplies he had bought. When it rained he researched well, but when it was fair he had visitors.

On the morning of April 20, Griffin heard the birds "chant their roulades loudly from the lush vegetation, with a purity and sensuous echo that gave me the startling illusion that I was at the edge of a rain forest. Surely it would melt the heart of even the president of the National Rifle Association." He accomplished less than usual, because "this has been a terribly fragmented visit."

He made only one dispirited *Journal* entry on May 4, during a few days at home. He lectured in Connecticut, allowing for a day each to visit pianists Bridget and Luiz de Moura-Castro and the photographer Nell Dorr.

Back at Gethsemani for a ninth sojourn on May 13, he did not record a word until May 16, when after a promise from the monks that his solitude would *not* be interrupted, he tried to express the inexpressible.

> But finally this place is an authentic hermitage and is true to itself only when it is inhabited as a hermitage. You accept the visits, you even welcome them sometimes, but no matter how good the visits are, they are a blemish to solitude. And the solitude is where one lives that ultimate harmony of all the sights and sounds and silences and prayers and labors in true naturalness, with perfect interior union with all that is; when that interior union is a perpetual alleluia and magnificat and thanksgiving combined without words; when all activity and all repose and even sleep itself enter into the heart of that awareness; and finally there are no words even to attempt to express it because the words and concepts represented by words all melt into the heart of it, dissolve, and cannot say it.

On May 21, Griffin heard that President Nixon had ordered the flag flown at half-mast for the soldiers who died in Vietnam. "Why doesn't he tell the truth? Their lives were taken from them, in most cases at least. There was always an irony to me in this 'giving one's life,' and this is why I never took any of the medals in World War II. It is a peculiar sort of bravery when a man obeys orders, often against his grain, with the knowledge that if he does not, he gets it from his own beloved country—imprisonment, death, or dishonorable discharge." Not only had he refused his medals, Griffin had also refused all military benefits, which put a severe hardship on his family. He seemed to have turned this prideful gesture into a matter of principle, and those who had to take up the slack financially never knew why. Yet he had considered pride to be the worst of sins.

Back home on May 24, he reported in the *Journal* on June 2 that he faced "a dizzying work schedule." He was also preparing for their seventeenth wedding anniversary. "But under all of that there is the peacock in me. Bit by bit, I prepare the mating by shaving carefully, by preparing for a bath, just in case." Later, company arrives, and "my poor little anniversary gestures just get lost in the bustle. It is almost farcical—like some comedy I am in and also watching. Watching a man doing his little peacock dance, thinking romantically about his wife with all this circulation and activity and telephone calls and children yelling—and feeling some small resentment, which is stupid, but feeling it just the same."

The next day Griffin was undecided about which prints to include in a collection that Unicorn Press was to publish. "I am really terribly undecided about the photos. Should I do the musicians, the Montmartre ones, the Tarascan ones?" He decided on twelve portraits of artists—Zara Nelsova, pianists Lili Kraus and Annie Fischer, composer John Jacob Niles, singer Roland Hayes, poets Mark Van Doren, Denise Levertov, Reverdy, and Merton, writers Wendell Berry and Maxwell Geismar, plus Gethsemani painter Brother Lavrans Nielsen.

That same day he had a call from Bradford Daniel, then living in California. "How glad I was to hear from him again after such a long silence. I wish I earned enough really to pay him the salary he deserves because he was marvelous help, and so easy to have around."

On June 8, the family celebrated Amanda's fourth birthday. Griffin wrote several drafts of his introduction for the Unicorn collection. He decided to cancel the Canadian Broadcasting documentary for July.

> Too hectic to bring in a CBC crew. They ran the TV documentary I did in Europe on June 2. I have been getting excellent reports from it. I hope it does not bring in a bunch of mail. Am sick to death of all these things, of seeing my mug on TV and hearing my words. I have a deep craving for silence and solitude, and a day when I can say a prayer without fifty interruptions. Each day brings work requests for at least ten times the amount I can possibly get done. And all of these are

> requests I hate to turn down. Well, I will get a good night's sleep and wonder tomorrow why I bitched so much tonight. Such bad work today. I knew what I wanted to say in that introduction and I have never written more convoluted sentences. Disgusting. I had to go through and weed them out, simplify, make them straight. Tomorrow morning I think it will go better. The groundwork is laid.

Griffin celebrated his fiftieth birthday on June 16, 1970, receiving gifts from the entire family. At midnight he typed in the *Journal*: "I am tired and happy, lingering to hear the rest of the Antonio Soler sonatas by Alicia de la Rocha."

The ninth visit to the hermitage began on June 27, with Griffin bringing along his sons for the first few days. While the boys were in the guesthouse of the monastery, he worked from three until noon on June 28. The next two days, with the boys being commandeered by Brother Maurice, he was exhausted and slept when no one was at the hermitage. By June 30, the boys were gone, having had a great time with Brother Maurice. Griffin began the real work at dawn on July 1. The next day there follow twenty pages of single-spaced type, more than half the passages *not* included in *The Hermitage Journals*. These pages were the basis for a chapter in the biography, extrapolated from a conversation with Father Eudes Bamberger, concerning Merton's brutal sessions with psychologist Gregory Zilboorg during the 1950s.

July 3, 1970 began with predawn work and an unexpected event.

> At that moment I heard something and saw the electric typewriter blaze in my hands and got a huge jolt that brought up an involuntary scream. In a moment I was on the floor with the wheelchair on top of me, utterly bewildered. Lightning had struck that lead-in wire with a crack, gone through and made jolting contact with me. My eyes were blurry when I climbed to my feet, and I was amazed that the shock had deprived me of control over my functions. . . . The clock was still going, now it was raining and blowing outside—hard. My typewriter was buzzing. I cautiously turned it off.
>
> I realize that the wheelchair saved my life. I was in it, with my feet on the footrest, the whole thing insulated from this stone floor by rubber wheels. Even at that I got a great jolt, but at least I wasn't grounded. If I had been in my desk chair with my feet on the floor (I was wearing

> only cloth slippers), the full power of the lightning bolt would have gone through me. Also, the typewriter is metal but the keys are plastic, and I am sure that helped. What continues to surprise me, because I never was actually unconscious, was that I did not realize until later that my bowels had moved.
>
> Fascinating, in a way, that my first involuntary reaction was a loud scream, like the one Tom gave. This makes me feel absolutely certain that the shock killed him, and not that he had a heart attack and fell against the fan. I feel a strange, almost tender union with him now in that moment of the jolt, the scream, the blank-out and death. I returned from the momentary blank-out, but he did not.

Incredibly enough, Griffin met with Amiya Chakravarty that very afternoon for two hours—"an immeasurably moving encounter—this scholar saint, so full of compassion. We talked of his years with Tagore, his long association with Gandhi, his friendship with Schweitzer, and of course, we talked mostly about Thomas Merton. A tremendous communion together. He let me photograph that most beautiful face. He said he had always lived in the shadow of great men, and never wanted to steal their light." Chakravarty spoke to the community about Merton that night. The next day Griffin listened again to a tape of the talk, commenting, "It is a lesson to me in beauty and delicacy—a masterful talk. How I wish *he* could write the biography. I pray for this kind of sensitivity."[102]

July 4 was "lost as far as work is concerned, but a beautiful and recuperative one, and I feel as if I am now getting my mind back from that accident yesterday." He was examined by Father Eudes Bamberger and given medication. The next morning he was groggy from the medication and concerned about lapses in memory. "Why am I ashamed of this memory blank? I am embarrassed. I find myself wasting a lot of time. The simplest things seem overwhelmingly complex."

There are no entries in *The Hermitage Journals* from July 6 through July 8, but there are manuscript pages, including follow-up speculations on Merton's sessions with Dr. Zilboorg. Griffin disputes the notion that the monk was "neurotic" (according to the doctor). He discusses the difference between what is perceived as "normal" and what is merely "average"—a distinction he made often. "If it is 'normal' then, as Aquinas says, 'true normalcy is approaching man's maximum human potential'—then the saints are supremely normal and they are not average; and therefore, when Father Eudes says that Tom was *not* neurotic, while others claim that he was. He differed from the average, but this does not mean that his life and actions and being were outside the framework of normalcy."

The book returns on July 9, with reflections on journals, in particular those by French novelist Julian Green, which fascinated Merton. "Green's journals are written with the foreknowledge that they will be published," maintaining "a polished quality, a studied quality that lacks spontaneity."

> However, Green's encounters are fascinating—it is a splendid history of the Paris and the people of the art and musical and literary worlds who were and are his friends. I also enjoyed (without always admiring) his constant references to music he heard. I found that in the early days of the war we reacted to the tragedy in a similar way: neither of us could bear great music—it made us feel too much. You needed not to feel this deeply. Green could not listen to a single note of Schubert, and the late Beethoven quartets would have shattered him. I remember writing in that period that I could not hear anything serious or moving, but would listen to music that did not get below the surface of the skin. How late I come to these things. How many years of reading I have missed.

While Griffin's books in journal form tend to be "spontaneous"—he had to work for spontaneity in revising them. The *Journal* entries in his books were not as raw as the original manuscripts, since he did not expect it to be published. He notes that "One of the things that tired me with the Green journals is the realization that so many of his encounters (with Gide, etc.) become a kind of peacock's dance in which each man is aware that the other is going to go home and write up his version of the encounter in his journal, which will be published."

> It seems that Merton would have tired of this fact, but I have to realize that—as Father Eudes emphasized—at this time, Tom was living down in community, mostly with men who had no interest whatsoever in the literary life of Paris, and that he was fundamentally lonely in a special way; and the Green journals, so skillfully evocative, really took Merton right out of the roughness of the community life, into Green's carefully appointed apartment, or into the studies of Gide, Francois

> Daudet, or to intimate dinners in Green's quarters with the Maritains—places where the 'French' part of Merton was really at home.
>
> Also Green's quest for solitude in the heart of Paris, perfect quarters perfectly furnished where he could work without distraction. All of this spoke to Tom in a most special way. Why should I question any of this? In my younger days, I burst with the excitement of such visits, such dinners, such concerts (dinners with Maurice Raynal, the Casadesus, Maritains—the whole thing), and would burst with it again.

Before dawn on July 10, Griffin worked well, researching through the day. That evening he "allowed the thought to come and remain a moment before rejecting it. Why did God allow me to live after that electric shock? One should not entertain such speculation, because there is no way whatsoever of thinking with God's mind." But he speculated anyway. "Perhaps all the years when I moved more and more deeply into an almost innate tendency to abandon what I am (or to hold it in suspension) in order 'to become the *other*' was merely a preparation for this work."

Griffin had reached that dangerous crossroads where empathy and transference collide. How to experience the hidden hermit without pretending to become him? Merton was a supremely autobiographical writer, cataloguing his past while at the same time evoking the eternal present of internal spirituality in prose meditations, journals, and poems. Living in the hermitage, following the hermit's orientations, being the first to read Merton's private journals—even experiencing a similar electrical shock—could not transform Griffin into Merton. One cannot become the *other*, for even the deepest human empathy has its physical limits.

Home on July 11, Griffin was making the first notes in the *Journal* on July 14. The story of being struck by lightning was carried in national newspapers and in *Newsweek*, bringing in the kind of correspondence he ignored.

On July 19, he listened to the Bach *Magnificat*, which "tells me what it is to be alive." That day he copied a quote from Heraclitus, without comment: "Bigotry is the disease of religion." Later he wrote of Merton's "great intuitive preoccupation with freedom. He felt, as I do, that it can only exist with any authenticity in a life of great solitude, as detached as possible from institutions." Then he commented on a statement heard on TV: "This is a nation of laws, not of men."

> It is becoming more and more a nation of "laws" and not of "men"—that is the trouble, without ever reflecting on what they mean. They will also endorse "laws for the common good." Of what? Of man or of laws themselves? This is some distance from the ideal of government "for the people."
>
> Was there anything more absurd than the delusion that free men should pay taxes to support a government "of the people and by the people" that in fact becomes more and more tyrannical in its repression of men's freedoms? Oh, not so much openly (though there is plenty of that) but quite especially in the area of man's freedom to be private. The computers end up gathering all the facts and storing them in a computer bank, and then giving out, whenever desired, with a whole computerized composite of everything about man: a world of facts, medical, psychological, spiritual, intellectual, material. At the press of a button they can cough up all the facts, plus a judgment, and you are there not in truth but in computerized fact with all your driving infractions, overdrawn checks, religious practices, prostate surgeries, sexual practices, etc. in a mangled and dehumanized composite for anyone to see. All of this in the guise of "the common good." The totalitarian state is the logical result.

While these remarks are Griffin's view in 1970, and always he wrote against totalitarianism, now decades later they ring prophetic. This was not a call for "smaller government," but a call for the justice of individual freedom and privacy. He never used a computer, but he could foresee where computers might lead us—not only to computerized facts but also to ideological judgments.

On September 14, he was met at the Louisville airport by Tommie and Frank O'Callaghan for dinner with photographer Eugene Meatyard and Guy Davenport.[103] He stayed at a motel in town, driving to Gethsemani the next day.

Back working before dawn on September 16, feeling he could "recuperate here better than anywhere else in the world, certainly much better than in any hospital." That morning he noticed a new sound, "a rooster crows from some great distance. I glance at the clock and see that I got up an hour before he did. Well, his *Matins* are much louder than mine. He must be the Caruso of cocks."

By September 18, reading in bed and not at the desk, Griffin worked steadily at dictating Merton's journals on tapes. The following day, Brother Patrick Hart brought a package containing the first copy of *A Hidden Wholeness*. "We went through it page by page. Beautiful, simple, unornamented. Significantly our first sight of the book is here in the hermitage—the first bound copy lies on the desk of Merton's cabin. The book offers me a unique and quiet sense of satisfaction."

Late that night, he could not sleep, typing out a consequential observation. "The little finger of my left hand and the little and adjoining finger of my right hand, plus the outer sides of the palms are still quite numb. I feel as though they were sticks when I type. They were that way when I regained consciousness from the lightning, and that was 2½ months ago now, so I suppose I am not going to get any feeling back. They don't really bother me, except when I type."

More research followed, reading Merton's journals and dictating passages onto tapes, until he finally typed on September 24: "In his last talk to the community before coming up here to live as a hermit, Tom remarked: 'You don't go into solitude to practice a lot of virtues—if you did, I'd probably be lost.'"

> It is true that in solitude, the whole idea of virtues and vices simply fades. You are here, open, you live with the reality of days and nights and heats and colds and forests and animals, attentive to, abandoned to the "Christ who dwells in the silences," in a place where you do not seek Christ, but where Christ wants to find you. And it is enough just to "be." It doesn't matter if you or clothed or unclothed, well clothed or ill clothed, uttering words or silence. You cannot live it without loving; that would be impossible. If you love, you are not going to have to worry about committing crimes against man or God, and you are not going to have to worry about what is or is not "virtuous," or stop to consider each act to evaluate its virtuousness or sinfulness. You might scandalize men who have their own ideas about the image of a holy life (which usually means a pietistic one), but you have no worries whatsoever about scandalizing or offending God. So the "practice" of virtues is just no consideration. The very nature of your solitude involves you in union with the prayers of the wind in the trees, the movements of the stars, the feeding of birds in the fields,

> the building of anthills. You witness the creator and attend to him in all his creations.
>
> This is not for one moment *mere* pantheism. It is the anagogic way. You do not "worship" the thing, but the creator of the thing. The thing fascinates precisely because it raises your attention through its beauty or interest above itself to the creator, which prevents your fascination from lifting the thing out of the *ordo universali* into some inflated category of its own (which would mask reality). No, you become more deeply attuned to the mystery of reality as it is in the clods of dirt and in the leaves and in the grasses and in the feel of rain or the drink of water. It teaches you things that can hardly be put into words, that can only be hinted by words—to abandon the self-satisfaction of comfortable (and flattering) categories, to accept the unity of opposites (or contradictories) as the natural thing it is in reality, to give up the deeply nurtured need in man for things to be "consistent." This "sleep" of formalism and subjective prejudices that veils the reality, which would seek to separate and therefore suggest "conflicting" opposites, is the most difficult thing to get rid of. True peace, says Herakleitos, is the "hidden attunement of opposite tensions."
>
> If I can work out the above into words and phrases, I will have done much to penetrate what Merton was. Right now it is too rude and raw—because in my mind I divide it into great leaps from Herakleitos to St. Bernard to Merton. All were aware of precisely the same thing: how to uncover in the realm of the spirit what already exists there.

Griffin clarified his passage. "I am tied to the debris of a language that is not true to the truths of solitude, and am aware of this. (This sentence, for example: I should have said 'that is not true to the truths of contemplation'—because solitude is not really it.)" Unlike those who knew how to uncover in the realm of the spirit what already exists there, his passage revealed intellectual recognition, but does not articulate the experiential reality of contemplation beyond words.

The Hermitage Journals make it certain that Griffin had rediscovered solitude in its naturalness, at a depth he had not previously experienced, but he had not reached the monk's realm of spiritual contemplation. Thomas Merton was also an "intellectual," who understood and wrote about the same issues (racism, war, literature, censorship, theological, and philosophical reflection, as well as the essence of solitude). Since Griffin was neither a poet nor a spiritual writer formed by monasticism, he could not be a true contemplative in the sense that Merton was, but Griffin's empathy was near the edge of transference.

Thomas Merton was a contemplative mystic, who abandoned himself to God. Griffin expressed a desire to withdraw from public view and return to the solitude of writing novels, but he never accomplished this return. While his work was usually created in solitude, he did not become a mystic. Merton's contemplation was lived beyond intellect. Contemplation was possible in solitude, but it was not solitude itself. Griffin recognized this, choosing Merton's words about contemplation in the epigraph to *A Hidden Wholeness*, approaching this by way of metaphor.

Merton emphasized in many of his writings that "The only way to find out anything about the joys of contemplation is *by experience*," but one must abandon the "beaten path" in order to travel "by paths that cannot be charted and measured." Thus contemplation "is the work of love and nothing is more effective in increasing our love for God. In fact, infused contemplation is intimately connected with the pure and perfect love of God which is God's greatest gift to the soul." Merton drew on the guidance of St. Thomas Aquinas and St. John of the Cross, describing the gift of contemplation, as beginning with the Last Supper: "Jesus promised the Holy Ghost, with His contemplative gifts. But the promise was accompanied by a denial. The Holy Ghost would be given to those who would receive Him. To those who could not receive Him, He would be denied." Merton continued, "St. Thomas, commenting on the words of St. John's Gospel, explained the difference between the two."

> Contemplation will be denied to a man in proportion as he belongs to the world. The expression "the world" signifies those who love the things of the world. They cannot receive the Holy Spirit Who is the Love of God. As St. John of the Cross says, "Two contraries cannot coexist at the same time in the same subject."

Aquinas explains that "The Holy Ghost does not manifest Himself to worldly men because *they do not desire to know Him*. They are content to occupy their minds with lower things. But desire is the most important thing in the contemplative life. Without desire we will never receive the great gifts of God." Merton wrote:

> St. Thomas says that worldly men have lost that sense of taste for spiritual things. "As the tongue of a sick man cannot taste good things . . . so the soul infected with the corruption of the world has not taste for the joys of heaven."
>
> In what does this taste consist? *It is love.* Jesus Himself made it quite clear that the one thing on which the spiritual life depends is *love.* . . .
>
> It is really this total and uncompromising docility to the will of God that gives a man a taste for spiritual things. It is this delicate instinct to yield to the slightest movement of God's love that makes the true contemplative.
>
> As St. Thomas says: "It is obedience that makes a man fit to see God."

Even at the hermitage there were too many interruptions, preventing Griffin from reaching true contemplation for long. He experienced such moments in prayer or by simply being, but there was work to be done. Yet "work is part of the joy of the day. Instead of saying: 'Now I must get back to work,' I should say, 'Now, I have to return to my joy,' except that I never leave that joy."

Griffin achieved *active contemplation* rather than *infused contemplation* or mysticism, according to Merton's characterization.[104]

> Here the soul, aided by ordinary grace, works in the familiar natural mode. One reasons and uses one's imagination and elicits affections in the will. One makes use of all the resources of theology and philosophy and art and music in order to focus a simple affective gaze on God. All the traditional means and practices of the interior life come under the heading of *active contemplation* to the extent that they help us to know and love God by a simple gaze on Him.
>
> Active contemplation then demands thought and action and acts of will. Its function is to awaken and prepare the mind, to turn the heart towards God, to arouse a desire to know God better and to rest in Him. It introduces the soul to the joys of the spiritual life. It gives him a healthy taste for the things of the supernatural order and weans him away from the satisfactions of the body and of merely natural knowledge.

> Above all, active contemplation prepares the way for love. It teaches obedience and humility. It shows a man how to seek God in His will. It makes the soul attentive to God's presence and His desires. It teaches one to think about God instead of about the world, to desire to please God rather than to enjoy the satisfactions of the world. It shows us how to trust God and leads us on to abandon ourselves more and to Him. . . .
>
> The liturgy teaches active contemplation above all by its rich content of theology and scriptural revelation, which it surrounds with art and music and poetry of chaste and austere power, deeply affecting to any soul that has not had its taste perverted by the artistic fashions of a degenerate age.

Griffin considered the era to be degenerate also, but he was unable to withdraw from "the world" entirely. His writings and lectures on racism were forms of revolt against the segregated system, a revolt guided by faith. He agreed with Merton that "Faith and revolt are inseparable. Faith is the fundamental revolt."

Both felt the need to critique an unjust world, supported by their faith. Although impaired by the consequences of diabetes, Griffin had lectured extensively. Yet he considered this "activist role to be very foreign to my nature."

> I have had a life that I loathe for these past years—I mean the public life. I have had to go in conscience and also because I am under spiritual direction and because we've had one racial crisis after another. I have been able to function in those crises, but all that time I have been away from my desk, away from what my true vocation is.

Now Griffin was where Merton had been, embracing solitary silence, living close to nature, tasting active contemplation in the Mass, and working through words in an attempt to be that *One Word.* Griffin found this simple equation in the hermitage, agreeing with Merton's later observations. "Words stand between silence and silence: between the silence of things and the silence of our own being. Between the silence of the world and the silence of God."

Departing the hermitage on September 24 and relaxing for a few days at home, Griffin returned to lecturing throughout most of October on the East Coast, including Baltimore and Philadelphia, scripting in a notebook that the lectures went well despite his battling diabetes and fatigue.

Home in November, his first *Journal* entry was on November 3, he discussed Nixon's "get tough" message on the television news.

> We watched Nixon's "get tough" message and it was one of the vilest things we have seen. He was melodramatic, almost drooling at the mouth, as he called for suppressive measures under the guise of law and order. His actions, his gestures, his handling of the voice and the audience reaction reminded me sickeningly of Hitler. The reactions remind me of those great mob roars to Hitler's speeches. This was followed immediately by a calm and lucid Edmund Muskie rebuttal that pointed up sharply the hysteria of the Nixon bullying.

Griffin's twelfth visit to the hermitage began on the evening of November 8. He was relieved to learn that a new gas heater had been installed in the sleeping room, always the coolest room in summer but the coldest in winter. He worked through the next day, drifting "into the natural activity that is based not on hours but on sleeping and waking, and the gathering and waning of energies." That evening he had a visit from Father Stanley Murphy (not mentioned in the book), who joined him and the Trappist brothers for Mass and supper at the hermitage.

During the pre-dawn hours on November 10, Griffin was soaking in the heat of the fireplace and the "profound and healing silence."

> Coming awake, coming to life and work in such surroundings is like some musical theme that slowly unfolds itself in fragments—a hint here and another there until hours later the full theme.

On November 11 Griffin was up at three, working on Merton's journals most of the day. That night he revealed an epiphany in words.

> There are moments here when suddenly, even in the calm and silence, the work comes to a temporary pause, and I find myself overwhelmed by a renewal of the silence, the serenity, as though it came in a new wave to flood me with the full perception of it. Sometimes it lasts only a moment, sometimes several moments. Always it is unexpected. It comes to surprise my spirit with a deeper felicity, a sudden glowing wonderment, a focusless love that is intense and without any object or any impediment. It has a distant religious connection beyond thought, though it has no object: no name, no word comes in connection with it.

The passages characterized Griffin's closest brush with mystical contemplation, although this disappeared once he typed his lucid impressions.

> It is as though everything—every tree and leaf and blade of grass and stone—combines into prayer that has no words, no form, and no need for anything of that nature, and sweeps me into it, transforming the quality of my being, like a modulation from one soundless harmony to another. The harmonic silence modulates my body; and an unfelt change takes place from the soles of my feet to the top of my head. I have only had this occasionally at the moment of reception of communion in the past; never at any other time or in any other circumstance. It comes to me here fairly often, especially after I have got my system back into the natural rhythms of this hermit life, when things flow as nature wills, when the clocks have stopped hounding the mind.

"When the clocks have stopped hounding the mind" strikes the silent bell of authentic solitude. "I do not try to understand this. I only know that for quite some time now I have been given a kind of happiness that seems to me to be supreme, beyond which a man cannot go." The point was neither to attempt to understand the bliss nor to attempt to force its reappearance.

> I have never experienced it before in this sustained manner, and never dreamed a man could have it. I realize that it occupies the very center of my being and it grows there, virtually untouched by what happens. It is a pure gift, beyond my volition, incomprehensible to me. I do not touch it, do not attempt to comprehend it, because I feel I should not tamper with it or try to understand anything about it. Always I bite back the question, "Why?"—and I bite back my protests that I do nothing to deserve it. The only thing I do not bite back is my awe and gratitude that it exists. It has nothing really to do with me, and will go on existing or stop existing as God wills.

Lightning had struck twice—first from above and then from within—and Griffin reached the threshold at which he stopped questioning it.

Schools of Humility

> Sickness—what a school of humility! It makes us see that we are poor, naked, and blind. Childlikeness is lost in life and recovered in holiness.
>
> —ALEXANDER YELCHANINOV
> (1881-1934), *FRAGMENTS OF A DIARY*

The 1971 *Journal* recorded only eighty-six pages, most pages composed at the hermitage, and a few typed at home. He begins with a single entry on January 1, mentioning that the doctors suggested canceling his lecture tour to the East Coast, but approving the scheduled ten-day visit to the hermitage as recuperative.

Griffin returned to Gethsemani on the cold evening of January 12. The monks celebrated Mass and fixed a light supper in the hermitage. After they left, he could not sleep, and recorded insights on solitude. "Only in innocence can it be born—only in a state of grace; but in that state, it is perfect happiness. Otherwise, it is only loneliness, something all hermits have understood. You can bear loneliness in guilt during the day but never at dusk, never at the beginning of night. Guilt is the difference, I suspect, between loneliness and solitude."

On January 17, he had a visit from Carolyn Hammer, who brought copies of Boris Pasternak's letters to Merton. Griffin was "so touched by the Pasternak letters" that he writes a few pages about the poet's funeral, considering "the bravery on the part of his friends to come and pay homage as he lay on the bier in the living room of his house; and the bravery of Sviatoslav Richter, who was in the adjoining room, unseen but heard by mourners, playing the last Beethoven sonatas."[105]

During the next several days Griffin read the Merton journals, living in near isolation. The temperatures were freezing outside, but warm enough in the cinderblock cabin, especially near the fireplace. "The weights and balances begin to form in the biography. In any case, a second reading of the journals, now that I have the large picture of what they contain, gives me a great many new insights. I find that I have in a first reading latched onto things that really had no significance; and in the second I am finding very significant clues that I had overlooked."

During February Griffin remained home, except for a week of lecturing in Ohio. He worked constantly on the biography while in the studio, typing only five pages about family matters in the *Journal* between January 23 and March 19. He returned to Gethsemani for his fourteenth visit on March 20.

That evening at the hermitage Abbot Flavian Burns celebrated Mass, joining Brother Hart and Griffin for supper. Griffin described the Abbott as "a marvelous man. And after all the 'prudence' and caution with which other prelates usually speak, his openness, candor, and unguardedness are almost unbelievable."

Griffin was up by 3:30 the next morning with a cedar fire burning, as it was twenty degrees outside. "I take my time. The marvel of having the illusion of endless time, at first deliberately, and then it becomes natural."

On March 22, he was feverish after "leviathan nightmares," but "plunged into the work." That evening he heard the radio news.

> The FBI had counted the sore places on the mules' rumps during the Poor People's March to see if they were mistreating the mules! Another agent was stationed in a tree above the group of protestors to listen for anything unusual "and be especially on the lookout for obscenity." Anything to blackmail the people, especially the poor and black people. And this by an agency of the federal government financed by tax monies.

Griffin awakened at three on March 23, realizing his insight about guilt being the difference between loneliness and solitude felt true.

> I think of yesterday briefly—the kind of distracting aberration that comes sometimes to show the short distance between a blurred view

> when self gets in the way and the other view when self is transparent and lets you get directly to reality. It is a deep aberration because it fools you into attaching more interest to self than to what is. You are experiencing reality through this film, focusing on the film rather than the dirt on your glasses. You fall into that so easily. It is in a place and time of solitude that you become aware that you have fallen into it. You know it because time is filled with the *guilt* of "wasting" it.

In solitude every "piddling" activity (or no activity at all) seemed right. Griffin "judged that a good portion of mystical speculation revolves around techniques of keeping it as whole and intact as possible. I have only the dimmest grasp of it . . . dim, experiential." He had read the mystics' texts and their commentators for decades, realizing that "you can learn it as 'learned knowledge' and never get more than a hint (if that) of the lived experience. You can, and men do, presume to teach it based on the experiences of others, but such teaching is full of holes because the teacher has too often not been transformed himself by his subject, has not experienced it, has only an intellectual grasp but no interior intimacy with it—that kind of intimacy that melts all the crusts within one. The experience liberates." He embraced living in prolonged solitude, but infused contemplation usually arrived in brief flashes, erased by the conscious awareness of his commentaries about it. Yet he seemed satisfied being an active contemplative. Even having experienced what he considered the one sustained instance of infused contemplation, he did not presume to be a mystic.

In notes typed in his original manuscript (but cut from *The Hermitage Journals*), he transcribed the remembrances of Amiya Chakravarty, concerning the sage's 1968 meeting with Merton in Calcutta.

> Our deepest communion would occur in part-silence and in a few spoken words: one such occasion I clearly remember. . . . Apart from the exchange of ideas on meditation, on faith and doubt leading toward deeper spiritual loyalty, he simply looked at me and said—"I am the same Trappist monk you met at Gethsemani and I belong there. I travel to discover reaffirmations, seek witnesses—but the one affirmation, the one witness for me is the revelation of God in Jesus." He was silent for a while, then added that—"I seek to find the true meaning of Nirvana, of the meaning of silence and contemplation in Buddhism and Hin-

> duism. I will be in Buddhist and Hindu monasteries mainly to be with persons whose lives have been inwardly transformed by prayer and pure action. But in the Cross history revealed itself, I mean the whole meaning of human history." He murmured a few words, but he did not finish the sentence. He looked at me with peace: I felt that he had to be with himself. He had been writing: papers were on his desk and a pen. But he was in no hurry. The repose I saw in his face reflected the same light that came to him during Mass. It was the strength of serenity which we see in the Griffin photographs published in *A Hidden Wholeness.*

Griffin intended to draw on Chakravarty's notes for the Merton biography, but decided not to mention the line about *A Hidden Wholeness*. He spent the next several days interviewing many monks who knew Merton ("splendid anecdotal material"). He was impressed "that these men lived in physically close contact and yet in isolation from one another—they knew each other but did not speak," since the vow of silence always remained in force among the Trappists.

On March 26, he remarked that he was "never aware of having dreams and couldn't care less. But here, I suppose because everything is open and unguarded, the dreams are extraordinarily detailed and prolonged and clear."

On March 27, Griffin received alarming news from Elizabeth that son Johnny had been "beaten up by a gang of thugs." He took a late flight out of Louisville for home. The *Journal* entry of March 31 informed: "It appears now that the group who brutalized Johnny and his friend were super patriots, who dress up in cowboy boots and hats and come in to town, cruise around until they find a long-haired youngster and beat him up. In any event Johnny is handling it beautifully—I'm thrilled that he was spontaneously brave in going to his friend's aid."

Griffin worked on the biography through April, making no entries in the *Journal* until May 2—brief notes on suffering from pain in his legs, alternating between enduring it and being "knocked out" by drugs.

On May 17, he hoped to "put in a week of intensive work before leaving for Gethsemani. The legs are better, not the awful pain of the past three weeks, just a reminder that it is there. I judge it by whether it overcomes the work or the work overcomes it, and now I know the work can overcome it." Later that day he was rewriting the Zilboorg chapter, "which is so difficult to handle in justice to Zilboorg. I have done it several times now and without hitting the right tone."

> Very difficult also to keep in the very texture of the work on the truth and the reality, which is simply that no matter how deeply a man penetrates into the habits of high aspiration, no matter how habitually he lives in these heights, the rest remains a constant companion—the needs of the body, the thousands of small sensualities that distract and are the reality. The secret is to fuse them into the whole, something Merton did remarkably well.
>
> But they were always there, and he would not fake it by pretending they were not in order to present a "consistent" picture. He accepted them without too much judging, did not view them as "enemies of the spirit"—but he also refused in his private self to act as though they were *not* there. They were a constant reality to him, which is why he would not play the role of a man who had "risen above them"—an utterly false role, and one that gave the lie to the spiritual life. This is why he would not and could not defile himself by acceding to the demands for a "contemplative mystique."

Griffin's *Journal* entries catalogued daily realities—no matter how mundane or earthy—including scenes with family and friends, discussing what he was cooking, monitoring weather and bodily ills in passages meant for his eyes only. On May 18, he admitted to "very hard days," because he could not "get enough sleep and the least effort exhausts." He was concerned also by the lack of income, because the advance for the Merton biography had been spent. Besides supporting a family of six, there were unanticipated medical bills and travel expenses.

He made a visit to Gethsemani that was not included in *The Hermitage Journals*, recorded in only two typed pages from May 23 to May 25. "Left home under fairly harrowing health conditions, but felt this work has to get done and now I am glad." The next day he felt that "something desperate is going on—something that involves me in the most passive way—as if life and death were battling within me for possession of the terrain. I feel myself tossed between them, helpless to do anything, beyond doing anything, almost as if I were not involved." After six days at the hermitage, he traveled to Iowa to give a commencement talk at Marycrest, visiting with Sister Luke Tobin and other Merton friends. Then he spent two days in South Bend, Indiana, meeting with Thomas Gallagher, publisher of Magi Books.

In the only *Journal* entry for the month (June 8), Griffin noted that he almost went into shock at O'Hare Airport in Chicago. "Arrived back here with a huge abscess on my hip and the diabetes completely out of control. Dr. Irving Raphfogel opened the abscess that evening and it is about healed, but I am so weak I am able to work only a few hours a day. Things are very tight and exhausting. Am still on heavy dosages of antibiotics, and this is draining all my energy."

Griffin's next visit to Gethsemani, as published in *The Hermitage Journals*, began on June 27, but he did not make his first entry until July 1. "Too much work and too little strength, so that when I was not actually working on the book, I was sleeping. I don't like that. I should be keeping these journal notes."

That day Griffin typed a page of from the diary of Alexander Yelchaninov, a Russian Orthodox priest Merton had admired, including one the monk marked: "In dreams we sometimes experience high and intense states of prayer, emotion, joy, such as we are almost incapable of in our waking hours. Cannot this be explained by the passive condition of our body in sleep? It presents no obstacle." This helped to answer Griffin's question about why his dreams tended to be so vivid at the hermitage. That evening, he also realized that he "had forgotten even the inclination to smoke," and that it had been "many years since I have spent an afternoon without smoking." July 3, 1971 was the first anniversary of being struck by lightning.

> This has been one of the happiest and most peace-filled and prayer-filled days I have ever known. The prayer of the heart goes on, no matter what I do. It is a conscious unconscious kind of self-perpetuating thing. Even when I awaken fitfully in the night that is the one thing I am first aware of—that the heart is praying incessantly as a counterpoint.

Despite a vow to write more in *The Hermitage Journals*, Griffin continued to be immersed in research, taping comments for transcription. The day before departing (July 10), he noted, "Lightning struck close, knocking out the lights temporarily, though nothing actually struck the cabin. A good test for all those lightning rods and other safety measures" now atop the hermitage roof.

Back home Griffin made no entries in the *Journal* until August 21, since he had been steadily transcribing tapes. That morning he felt a "distant knowledge that the body is demanding its share and not getting it behind a thick wall of present activity—21 pages done, not including considerable mail. Fourteen straight hours yesterday—now this is the way I like things to go." The work continued apace during the remainder of August and into the first half of September, a month that produced only scant notes in the *Journal.*

Griffin returned to Gethsemani on September 19, working during the ten days there, despite several visits and the return of pain in his left leg, which doctors would determine to be a consequence of the worsening diabetic condition.

The *Journal* of 1972 runs to exactly one hundred pages, including Griffin's entries typed at home and the selections from *The Hermitage Journals.* On January 2 it was clear that "diabetes has conquered all the oral medications, the blood sugar has remained high, and the pain in the leg is constant. I will have to go back on insulin." This gloomy page also reported that P. D. East died on the last day of 1971.

Griffin "was very near diabetic coma" on January 3, when the doctor arrived with the first insulin shot. His blood sugar was high, but vision had cleared. Constant illness and the death of close friends sent him back to the school of humility. The Trappist monastery and the solitude of Merton's hermitage, like his earlier experience with the Benedictines and the Great Silence at Solesmes, had also been profound schools of humility.

On January 21, Griffin returned to Gethsemani, and taking insulin shots again became part of the daily routine, followed by something to eat and several cups of coffee, and by preparing meals for the generous monks.

The next day he received a phone call from Elizabeth—"very distressed, to tell me that Jean Casadesus and a young couple he was traveling with in Canada were killed in a car wreck after a concert." Griffin wrote to the Casadesus family, and Mass was offered for Jean, who was only forty-five years old at his death.

That week in the hermitage was productive; it is apparent that the less Griffin wrote the more research was accomplished. Yet no matter how much he got done, he always felt it was not enough. On January 27, during a steady rainstorm when he knew that solitude was all but guaranteed, he writes one naked line: "Merton would do everything for Truth except lie about it."

The next day he heard again by phone from Elizabeth. "How much I have missed them! We had a long and very pleasant talk. God love her. She knows how to make everything seem right and perfect, and spreads balm to my heart."

Griffin did not write in the *Journal* during February, March, or April of 1972. On May 2, he comments briefly: "No time to write in these journals for a long time and am now so out of the habit it is not really natural to me." Working continuously on the biography meant he could dedicate his waning energies to only one project. He had put aside his cameras and the *Journal*, ceased lecturing, and yet he felt frustrated. "The biography is a torment at this stage—so terribly much that is new comes in and has to be inserted into pages I thought were done."

Fort Worth entries for May 16 and May 29 appear in *The Hermitage Journals*, the earlier one on George Wallace, and the latter a reminiscence of France.

> Wallace was shot, and that is lamentable. But what was disheartening was to see how this unmasked a lot of people. The great hope for white supremacy had been downed. This law-and-order demagogue who himself so contributed to the calluses on this nation's soul. We are willing to leave the door open to unspeakable abuses (including the continuing war in Southeast Asia, the perpetuation of overt racism, the destruction of help to the poor) in order to avoid busing. What else does it really amount to? They can deny it, but the great undertide of Wallacism is a manifestation of racism and nothing else.

Memories of early days in France were evoked by the death of The Duke of Windsor, because Griffin had spent the summer of 1937 "at the Duthoos' Chateau de Belles Ruries, whose properties adjoined those of the Chateau de Cande, where the duke and duchess were married and honeymooned."

The two entries could not be more different, the first expressing his deep disgust with persistent racism, the second his nostalgia for those "halcyon days" in France. Yet both extremes would remain in his consciousness. Since Merton had developed a similar Francophile sensibility, and written trenchantly against racism, even working on the biography kept these realities in close awareness.

Griffin returned to Gethsemani on June 15, celebrating Brother Patrick Hart's silver jubilee, and his own fifty-second birthday the following day. He wrote that the monks' "concern and thoughtfulness—go straight to my heart." He was impressed with the Abbot Burns' remark "that the old Trappist usages, which they did so much to change, were not unlike Zen training and had much the same purpose."

> Certainly the hermit life brings much of this out in its unadorned nakedness, whereas the community life can allow it to remain obscured because in a sense it forces a man to play a role. My experience is that the deepest health comes in this solitude where gradually the roles are abandoned. Here, the realities are simply faced and not hidden.

He believed "what Merton felt when he said that his only regret about dying was the years of this solitude that he would not have." On the final day of retreat, June 24, the last published entry, he wrote, "My feast day, and never was a day more glorious—absolutely still, sunlit, cool." He recalled Merton's translation of the Chinese Zen master Chuang Tzu: "When the shoe fits, the foot is forgotten; when the belt fits, the belly is forgotten." The sage's words caught the morning and Griffin's sense of oneness with it. "It is like that here this morning with everything—everything fits, and the self is forgotten."

Griffin worked from late June through mid-September on the biography and his photographic book about Jacques Maritain. However, September 19 brought more shocking news—Robert Casadesus, his musical mentor and dear friend of 33 years, had died in Paris.

> I have seldom been so immediately and deeply afflicted. Odd, too, that he had been in my thoughts earlier this day when I was working with the portraits of Lili Kraus, and decided the time had come to do a complete photographic archive of Robert. I stood there with the phone in my hand full of the most terrible anguish over the loss, and even more so over the desolation Gaby must feel to have lost a son and a husband within less than a year.
>
> I thought of his death and there was in it a terrible sense of weakness and vulnerability; and the death of that whole group who

> were so profoundly involved in my life: Merton, Reverdy, Casadesus, Dominique Pire, Gerald Vann, and how only Jacques and I remain, and Jacques just barely in life; and I felt the greatest confrontation with the death of my existence, as though the grave were stalking me in the deaths of these friends.
>
> No real somberness in this, except for that crackling counterpoint of conversation at a time of profound grief, there was peace in me—and now that it is over, and I have had time to be alone and have written a letter to Gaby Casadesus, there is only the deep peace of a deep void. I wonder if he died at home. I am haunted by his remark, made every time I visited their home at 54 rue Vaneau in Paris, that this was the place in which he was married, in which he had lived ever since, and in which he hoped to die. He was 73 last April.

The next morning, he learned Casadesus played his last concert in Prades, the French town where Merton was born, performing Mozart's Concerto #27, which was also the last work Jean played before he died. "In looking at the headline: PIANIST CASADESUS DIES—AFTER 3,000 CONCERTS, I realized that it is one I have long dreaded reading. I have to give it time to work out of my system. Now there is an almost hallucinatory obsession with his life and death." On September 27, he wrote more about Robert Casadesus and dying.

> Thinking of his surgery and the kind of pain the pancreas can pour into the nervous system, I cannot suppress the thought of human dignity and the utter sense of its loss when you are so helpless, so stripped of everything except the agony. I realize that this quality is one for which I have always done battle for others.
>
> It is terribly important to accord dignity to all human beings, but ultimately and personally, it is perhaps better to sacrifice it within oneself, for like any value, it can stand between the soul and the soul's perception of truth. I believe this is at the base of my shocking grief over his death. It was the pity, the empathy involved in knowing too well how this kind of illness strips a man of the last visible vestiges of human dignity, not in the nakedness and handling, but in the terrible vulnerability, defenselessness, helplessness. It has been this connection, since I was a teenager, that made Beethoven and Mozart in reality my

> closest friends and transformed their music into the most direct conversation—at least those mysterious passages that you have to hear alone.

He had developed these insights on human dignity and spiritual transcendence in his essay "The Terrain of Physical Pain"—composed as a third-person narrative, but its meaning was drawn from intimate experience with suffering. Its authenticity would be lost without translating it into universal terms. Physical pain and human suffering are as universal as racism and death, but the intensity and duration of pain vary with each person's ability to cope and adapt. In Griffin's words, "New and vague truths begin to emerge, truths difficult to formulate—and the sufferer perceives that much of what he experiences, much that is most profound in his experience, simply lies beyond the realm of ideas." That is precisely why speculations about pain, uttered by those who had not suffered, "sound false, off-key to the sufferer because they rarely conform to his own lived reality." Griffin understood that the stereotypes about suffering were from the same cultural conditioning as the mythology of race. The attitudes about suffering were more damaging to the one in pain than the reality of pain itself. The best that the sufferer could hope for in relation to those around him was "an attitude of union" with the few who had the wisdom to keep silent and to treat the sufferer as an individual and not as a condition. But no matter how insightful or unaware were those nearby, the solution to the problem of pain resides ultimately with the sufferer, who must live on two planes of awareness.

> This faculty to act at once on two planes can be dissipated when it becomes merely an attempt to escape. No, it must be the contrary—an acceptance and an awareness of the reality that exists in pain and that sometimes becomes obsessive in pain, and then the growing ability, from the same root, to stand off and become the observer; and then again, passing on to the observation of other things until at length and in the natural order of things, the observing self comes to the realization that self, even in pain, is less interesting than other objects of contemplation.

If one does not discover a fresh perspective in suffering, one will fixate on the self as victim, blame the body as mortal enemy, and become obsessed with either playing the role of stoic hero (rationalizing oneself into a stereotype that others can admire), or attempting to escape the pain through massive sedation (a form of denial). The critical break begins with moving from self-interest and meaningless subjectivity toward an observing moment of objectivity. The effort to do so will be arduous, but the result—initially brief—opens a wider horizon.

Eventually the sufferer develops the realization "that pain in the body can cure things which are not of the body," and that the observer's fresh view "brings clarity to intuitions, unclouds perceptions and opens up the whole area of intuitive knowledge" that "can replace cultural distortions" and subjective delusions about the nature of suffering. Neither the pain nor awareness of it disappears, but its resonances are not wasted. This radical shift in perspective allows the sufferer "to be used as a sort of filter for experience, to accept the experience imposed without even judging its value, allowing it to enter, allowing it to teach, and then letting it come back out in some form of expression—prayer, silence, music, contemplation, art."

Griffin believed that certain creative masterpieces, like the poetry of St. John of the Cross or the late quartets of Beethoven, "tend to happen despite men rather than because of some purely human initiative." Such masterpieces that cannot be explained by reason evoke "experience, often in the form of intense suffering, that has been accepted, handled, then released."

The sufferer, who becomes intimate with the universal resonances of pain, will recognize intuitively a hidden connection with the infinite mystery at the core of such masterpieces, accepting that this act of contemplation is enough. Perhaps the sufferer "may even learn an ultimate wisdom—not to care about results," but to care only about "submitting to the action and allowing results to take care of themselves, in the knowledge that if God does not allow suffering to evaporate uselessly, then that suffering is being used and how does not matter."

If the sufferer learned this "ultimate wisdom," Griffin believed, the effect of that knowledge "turns the sufferer into a giver, into lover, into consoler," because extended "experience with physical suffering has taught him that he can bear what he has borne," but that "he cannot bear it when others suffer." He perceived this not as guilt, but as a renewal of innocence, a radical transformation of self-pity into a selfless empathy with the suffering of humanity. "It constantly reawakens him to mercy and to an authentic pity which will bring in their wake a melting of the calluses of indifference and unconcern for others."

Griffin had witnessed people "pass through the ultimate human tortures and emerge with everything burned out of them except a limitless capacity to love," which "transformed [them] into luminous human beings." He had seen those who endured interminable suffering, "totally immobilized and locked in pain," to be capable of igniting "an authentic and curative pity that sometimes seems to blaze from them." He was united with them, because he had known equally intense pain, yet he felt even deeper empathy for those loved ones who had eased his suffering.

The final result of this expanding perspective teaches the sufferer "that others fear this unknown, that others suffer his sufferings, perhaps even more tormentedly because they do not know them with any precision." The sufferer becomes the consoler of those spared suffering "but must witness his suffering." This dynamic process transcends psychological syndromes, philosophical proofs, theological speculations—because pain is real and not merely an idea about reality.

"The ultimate and true effects of suffering," Griffin concluded, "can only occur, from the sufferer's viewpoint, in the very silence and solitude from which they spring, beyond the realm of ideas." Each person called to suffering must discover, step by step, an inward path that no cartographer has charted and in a direction that no compass needle has pointed. "These effects—wisdom, giving, mercy, love—produce their own ferment." This ferment reveals the mysterious effects only in silent communion with the infinite. The sufferer "who has allowed these realities to come through the experience of suffering, in their own time and with their own priorities, knows that somehow and without any special action of his own initiative, that the ferment of these effects will be returned to the world in some form which is ultimately redemptive." The redemptive quality of suffering cannot be measured quantitatively, just as faith cannot be proved by tangible results.

Yet Griffin experienced the truth of these effects in the solitude of suffering, believing that any sufferer, "if he has been deeply enough wounded, will remain reawakened to mercy and to that whole mysterious cycle of replenishment in which he has allowed himself to be used, to be an instrument."

He made a final retreat to Gethsemani, beginning on October 2, during which he wrote only one entry in *The Hermitage Journals*. He wrote before dawn.

> I am aware that at home my wife and children sleep still in their rooms and that the greater part of me is there with them. But you cannot divide up parts like that, because more than "just the remainder" is here in this forest, in the profound felicity of this silence, this solitude, these early morning hours. I pray for my family and friends in these hours when nothing seems rushed, particularly this morning for those who have died this year because in this place and time, everything is open and you do not have to dole out this and that in the way of affections, love, prayers. Here, those things that are merely "time consuming" are no longer so—they enter into the whole and become other dimensions of the same freedom. I have never known such ineffable peace.

Such wholeness, felicity, and freedom would be rare for the remainder of life. Never again would Griffin know such solitude or creative energy.

In the *Journal* of December 13, Griffin remembered poet Mark Van Doren, who died on December 10, the exact date of Merton's death. "I did not know Van Doren that well, but I have written about him so much in the biography, and photographed him, and felt that we knew each other." In his *Twelve Photographic Portraits*, he added this note: "It is perhaps appropriate, and this time and with this collection of portraits, to recall that Thomas Merton stated that Mark Van Doren had been a contributing force in finding his vocation, and added that 'For a man to be absolutely sincere with generation after generation of students requires either supernatural simplicity or, in the natural order, a kind of heroic humility.'"[106]

The final entry of December 19 commented on a lecture he gave at TCU, concerning the principle of the *intrinsic other*. He was asked by a female student: "How do you draw a parallel between this *intrinsic other* error as regards those of different cultures and those of different genders?"

> It is one of those questions I have not really faced, and now it intrigues enough to attempt a clarification. The *intrinsic other* concept, inculcated as early learned behavior patterns, and on which all racist structures are based, is also at the base of men's ideas about women. It may be motivated at profound levels by man's inadmissible view of

> woman as intrinsically *other* as one of the expressions of dominating the "other"—a kind of intimate racism.
>
> From the female viewpoint, the *intrinsic other* concept in male-female relationships is a significant injustice (even though it has been rationalized into a virtue by male thinkers). Isn't this the equivalent of our statements about slavery: Blacks need the white man to take care of them, and the delusion that black people *liked* it that way?
>
> One of the deepest resentments in my work has caused many southern white men to realize that the black woman is no longer easy sexual prey. She is doubly "intrinsically *other*" in this case. What recourse did black women have? If she called the "law" she was calling the enemy. White men rationalized all this by suggesting that it was a racial characteristic of black women that they were "just like animals," and so the white man was doing them a favor. Sexual aggressiveness is deeply involved in all this: both in the racism directed at minority cultural groups and that directed against black women by white men.

Griffin had been taught to be a "Southern Gentleman," and only at this late date did he begin to scruple his unconscious paternalism.

By the end of 1972 he faced another affliction—osteomyelitis—the inflammation and eventual deterioration of bone marrow that was insidiously common in severe diabetics. It would continue to ravage internally, and he would undergo operations to reconstruct his jaw, which necessitated growing a beard to cover the facial scars. For the first time he appeared older than his years.

The *Journal* for 1973 held the least number of typed entries (sixty-three pages), because it was a year of surgeries and immobility. Throughout January until mid-February, he worked on the biography in solitude, while his mother helped with the typing. During that period he took trips to Louisville and Gethsemani, followed by two days in Houston on a photographing assignment. The family heard Dick Gregory speak at TCU on February 15, remarking in the *Journal*: "He spoke more brilliantly than I have ever heard him—beautiful and full of sense."

Griffin sent a telegram to President Nixon on March 8. "Justice Department spokesman says Native American demands at Wounded Knee amount to 'intolerable blackmail,' so government issues ultimatum threatening a second Wounded Knee massacre. *Is that less intolerable*? We cannot believe this decision reflects the will of the people and we protest this tyrannical action against Native Americans and urge direct and immediate intervention to stop it." The reasonable demands: First, Amnesty for Native Americans occupying Wounded Knee; second, a Congressional investigation of Indian grievances; third, removal of a local official of the Bureau of Indian Affairs. He expressed relief that the ultimatum was lifted.

> We are thankful the Native Americans did not give in, and faced down the government. Some pretty scabrous interviews this morning. People deploring their "tactics" all in approving of their goals, suggesting that AIM leaders are more interested in publicity and advancing their own careers than the problems of *their people*. These damned opinions come from whites—not a single interview with a Native American.
>
> The same old story, the same old comments people make about black people seeking rights, approving their goals but not their means, implying that if they would just be *nice* the good things would come in time. My God, to say such things about Native Americans after all the years of broken treaties, paternalism, neglect, suffering, misery—and to hear these idiocies from the mouths of white officials.

Griffin and Elizabeth viewed *Sounder* on March 31.

> Even though the film supposedly took place in 1933, it is not that different today. In how many such homes have I stayed. It was a view of black reality that very few whites could have, except by seeing the film. It was beautiful and authentic. The whole thing was a poem, and the essences were all there. I am still haunted by the beauty of that film, by its resonances from my own past and present, too. Some of the critics objected to the name of the film, which was the name of their dog, not realizing the critical importance of this hound in helping provide the family with meat, he was the one who treed the raccoons and opossums.

In the *Journal* of April 3 Griffin remarked, "We are surrounded by the deaths of friends. I learned yesterday of Carl Backman's death (he was my lecture agent, a grand old man to whom I was devoted)." The next day he heard from Charles Rector's mother, saying that his former assistant had died from an overdose of heroin. He felt "a sense of relief that his torture was ended and his mother seemed to feel much the same. My children especially grieve for him."

On April 28, Griffin received news that "our beloved Jacques is dead." He found consolation in the thought that Amanda was one of Maritain's godchildren. "Odd, I realize that the feelings I had for Jacques, particularly in the later years, were identical to those I have for Mandy: a kind of very pure tenderness without any impediments, conditions or restrictions, a tenderness that seeks nothing but simply exists as a privilege to the heart. This is what has erased death in Jacques' case, filling me with such peace instead of the grief I anticipated."

Throughout the next month, Griffin worked on a large photographic archive of the French philosopher, images that would become part of Maritain's legacy. He made notes about their long friendship, recalling a conversation he had not written about. Once he had informed Maritain of being "obedient to you insofar as my actions have consistently been the incarnation of your thought," which Griffin believed to be the work of the Holy Spirit in the philosopher. "I explained that such a vow permitted me to function in a way that helped me overcome my cowardice." *Black Like Me* had been possible, he insisted, because "I could act under obedience without ever thinking of the consequences in a way I could never bring myself to act from any other motive, even love of truth and justice, love of humanity."

"How I miss the hermitage at Gethsemani," Griffin observed on September 11. "How sick I am of this financial struggle that keeps me from returning there. Those visits were among the glories of my life."

The *Journal* for 1974 runs only sixty-four pages of typescript, but he kept scripted notebooks while traveling. In the spring he reentered the public arena, joining the staff of *Sepia* as an editor and feature writer. The job afforded a decent income, but meant traveling again, so the collapsible wheelchair became part of his baggage. He made several trips to the South, updating the magazine's continuous coverage of changing race relations. After eight months at *Sepia*, financial relief came from a few grants, and he left the daily editorial work, continuing to write historical pieces about the civil rights era for the magazine.

Griffin was in Toronto June 6 for interviews on Merton with John Reeves at the CBC. On June 8, he gave a Merton lecture at Massey Hall in Pembroke, Canada. It was also the birthday of his father, age eighty, and Amanda, who turned eight. "How I wish I could be there for the festivities."

He went to Jackson, Mississippi on August 6, to research a story on the Jackson-Hinds Clinic, located in "a rural region of great poverty for blacks." On the way, he took background photographs, and "got quizzed by a sheriff's deputy when I stopped to photograph a shanty. Stopped in a little country store to see if I could find out anything. It was a place right out of *Sounder*, and every black person in the area knew I was there." During the next few days, he visited black communities in Mississippi. One assignment for *Sepia* was to photograph Governor George Wallace at the capitol in Montgomery, Alabama.

> A hell of a day. Had to park three blocks away and carry the heavy equipment in tropical heat. Was melted down and trembling when I arrived. And irony of ironies. Because of television cameras, I had to get very low, on my knees to approach the Governor, like pilgrims in Mexican churches approaching the altar. There were mostly black people there, and some of them old friends, like Floyd McKissick and Charles Evers, and the sight of my approaching Wallace on my knees did not escape them.
>
> Photographed everyone, but in that position and moving constantly about on my knees, I was soon in serious trouble, vision blurring, ready to faint. I was kneeling beside Mrs. Wallace, who was charming and warm until I introduced myself. Then she chilled perceptively, remaining perfectly controlled and courteous. The Governor responded similarly. Anything for a good photo! But no communication between us. We have a deep mutual antipathy that exists from many years back.

Griffin returned home relieved to have finished a few articles for *Sepia*. "Begin these journals again after a long silence," he typed on September 3. "I have spent the year and a little more working desperately to keep from going bankrupt." However through the efforts of James Laughlin of New Directions, he received "some grants, enough to sustain us while I finish the book. I am clearing the calendar of all other activities and going back full time on the biography."

On September 4, he made prints of Mark Van Doren for publication. "Should really print more today, since I have fresh chemicals, but do not want to stay on my feet that long. The tumors are getting better now that I wear only these crocheted wool slippers." The next day he made prints of the black people met during the recent trip through the Deep South.

Griffin turned his attention to the news on September 8.

> Ford granted a full pardon to Nixon for all offenses committed or "that he may have committed" (implying everything we don't know). I promptly wrote President Ford, asking that he extend the same pardon without any strings to the war resisters. His pretext was that Nixon and his family have already "suffered enough." I suggested that the war resisters and their families had already "suffered enough."

The first copy of *Jacques Maritain: Homage in Words and Pictures*, arrived on September 9. Elizabeth "gave me a fierce lecture about not sending it to someone and not lending this copy out." He often passed on first editions to friends, but Elizabeth's warning ended that reflex.

During late September, he had conversations with Lili Kraus. They had dinner on September 17 with Father George Curtsinger, who had become one of Kraus's piano students, along with her assistant Jo Boatright.

> After dinner Father played his "lesson" for Lili—a Mozart sonata. He was too nervous, but it went well, though not as beautifully as I have heard him play the same work before. Lili was masterful in her tact—and in fact he had done so much on it since she last heard him play it that she was thrilled. It was a lovely evening. It is always a joy to talk with Lili. I am going to try to locate my old recordings of her performances.

That evening Kraus asked for a print of the photograph Griffin had made when she played a Schubert sonata in Dallas. It was among his *Twelve Photographic Portraits.* Lili Kraus "felt that it was the best picture ever made of her. I must make really good prints and give them to her." He completed the darkroom work on September 22, sending them along with Father Curtsinger. A few days later Kraus called to thank him for the mounted prints, and also to point out that he had not included a bill. But Griffin would not take any payment for the prints.

The *Journal* of October 1 recorded Griffin's despair of writing on racism. "I think this work on racism gets me down so much because I come out of it to something filled with light, like the Maritain and the Merton, and I do not like to go back to the gutters." He was reading books about Malcolm X.

> When Malcolm spoke from his own experience and meditation, he was often full of gold. When he tried to rationalize all biblical truths to support his views, he was often full of shit, which may be why he broke from Elijah Muhammad (as propagandist) at the end of his life, and tried to undo the tendency to mindless obedience he had instilled in thousands of Muslims, tried to liberated them from that into thought, intelligence (as he called it). The thing that is so difficult in all this is that one becomes a fool in evaluating such a man from one's own orientation—it has to be done from his. Part of his authenticity as a man of religion springs from the fact that he was one of the rare ones—he could evaluate another's argument from the other's orientation—or at least he frequently did."

He reviewed *The Death and Life of Malcolm X* for *Sepia*, pointing out in the *Journal* something that did not appear in the magazine.[107]

> The Goldman book is another example of a "white" writer apologizing for his whiteness. "This is a white book about Malcolm X" is the opening sentence. What incredible hash. Too many whites disqualify themselves defensively in writing on racism for fear some black person (or some dumb white critic) will be critical. It is a sickeningly demeaning stance. If you latch on to a truth, it does not matter in the slightest what color you are. A book's value depends on its truth, not the ethnic, religious or racial qualifications of the author. What the hell is a "white book" in any case?

The Griffins attended a concert by Lili Kraus on October 2 and then a recital by Luiz de Moura-Castro on October 3. Both events at Texas Christian University, where the internationally recognized pianists taught advanced students. TCU was also the home of the Van Cliburn Competitions.

On October 6, Griffin worked in the pre-dawn light, walking in the backyard where flowers bloomed. "Now in my workroom, I begin the long day's work, gently urged into it by the happiness of the Corelli Trio sonatas." Then he listened to a Bach concerto for two violins, "with its marvelous slow movement that is a love dialogue, and which I am sure was so conceived by Bach." This "so nourished my affections that I went back to bed and relived that slow movement with my wife."

He expressed concern about his blood sugar level on October 7.

> Either the insulin is no good or there is something drastically amiss with the diabetes. I believe the insulin has been poor, which really makes me angry, since there is no excuse for that. I have been feeling so bad that I started testing myself again, 4 to 5 times a day, increased the dosage, but nothing would bring it down. I will know in a few hours if I am in trouble or if I have just got a batch of bad insulin. All of this is crowding me. I have no time left to get things repaired, since I leave for Denver to teach day after tomorrow. I am uneasy about leaving and plunging into that heavy lecture and teaching schedule.

Griffin wrote in a spiral notebook while at Loretto Heights in Denver, October 10-22, recording time alone rather than the classes on racism, briefly mentioning the people he met, meals prepared or eaten, and the slow deterioration of the foot that would not heal because of the diabetes. On November 1, he was back home, hobbling around on crutches and typing in the *Journal.*

> I realize I am just typing to be typing. No thought behind any of this. It is a dead time, a time when the imagination does its work alone, and then dries up when the time comes to put it down on paper. Lying in bed, the thoughts are rich, the imagery full. But the task of getting that onto paper is more and more difficult. This comes from grazing at the edges of reality too long, being too long among people, and too little alone where all of these things have time to develop and to solidify into some form of expression.

On November 2, they visited with Reverend Sherwood Clayton, the Episcopal priest who had known Griffin as an altar boy. The last time they were together had been during the *Black Like Me* journey when Reverend Clayton provided him with a few days respite in New Orleans. "We reminisced that it was 40 years ago today that he first arrived at St. John's in Fort Worth, and my brother and I served his first Mass. He left here for New Orleans, 28 years ago."

> Then he started in on black people. They had moved into his old neighborhood. He was bitter about that and cited statistics about the high crime rate. We fell silent. My mother was about ready to light into him. In that sweet and innocent voice he went on with his nasty little racist figures. We all got sick. I started to tell him, "You need to come

> take my course." But what's the use? He left, and we did not insist he stay a minute longer. He went back to his lily white circle, where he is undoubtedly revered by all those who lament the growth of black people as though it were a tumor. Why do people like that even bother to visit? Why do they throw this kind of trash in our house? These people who cannot open their mouths without spewing their racism, thinking they do not have any prejudices. That is the sad part. That is why they are so open about it, so open about their abysmal ignorance.

The next day Griffin felt "strangely let down about the visit with Father Clayton. I was too hard on him (in my own reaction, I mean, not in anything I said). I have never had a better or more generous friend, and I should not judge his attitudes." But he had work to finish. "I did not take the sedation this morning deliberately, so that I would have a clear mind, but without the sedation, my mind is glued to my sore foot, which is not worth a damn as a solution." After a full night's sleep, he felt better on the morning of November 5. "Very little pain. Got into work immediately—the first time I have worked well in a long time."

On December 9, Griffin delivered a lecture on Gregorian Chant at Brandeis to "a very responsive and large audience. Rather than offer money, for fear it would insult me, they gave my check to their library as a gift. How funny. This does not buy a hell of a lot of groceries." He returned home exhausted, vowing not to lecture again until the foot healed. Next day he had a visit from pianist Luiz de Moura-Castro, who was departing on a two-month tour.

> There is a great joy for me in these short visits, because we talk music. He knows French music thoroughly, especially what is little known, like the Gabriel Fauré piano works. We both lament the death of a certain esthetic in French musical tradition. Both of us latched on to the end of it, and now with the deaths of Marguerite Long and Robert Casadesus, there are really no practitioners of that marvelous tradition, except for people like Elena Costa. He and Elena are going to play the Poulenc sonata for two pianos in Rio in a few weeks.

While rummaging through Christmas cards on December 16, Griffin found an old box of letters and photographs. "It had photos of me in the Pacific; of my first trip to Mexico City in 1940 with Robert and Gaby Casadesus. Then photos I had taken in the 1930s of Chartres and Rouen.

And later photos of my house in Solesmes, and many others that I can no longer identify; letters from Joseph Szigeti and Lotte Lehmann; also, my preface to Gabriel Cousin's *L'Opera Noir*—that extraordinary French opera based on the life of Billie Holiday."

The sore foot continued to plague Griffin for the rest of the year and into the next. The osteomyelitis was not healing, due to the diabetic condition. Either constant pain or heavy sedation would be Griffin's alternating realities in the school of humility for the remainder of his life.

Against All Odds

There are over two hundred single-spaced typed pages in the *Journal* for 1975, beginning with pages written while the family slept late on the first day of the year. He felt uneasy from the heavy pork and black-eyed peas on New Year's Eve, vowing to cut pork from his diet, as he had eliminated sugar and alcohol.

In the solitude of that cold dawning, Griffin listened to Monteverdi, while imagining the details of a short novel he hoped to write.

> One thought keeps recurring of that marvelous little church near Kolbsheim, out in the country in the middle of tobacco fields, but in an oasis of ancient trees, an exquisite ancient church dating back to the ninth century. A short novel works on me about this. A man who lives in a stone house nearby with his wife and children and who is the sacristan of the church, having a great love for it, a connoisseur's love that causes him to lavish a connoisseur's care on the building, the baptismal font, the windows and stone floors—and all of this small-scaled (in contrast to Chartres, which is too full of details for one to encompass).
>
> What could one make of this? Something beautifully simple—the foods they prepare, the quietness, the counterpoint of contemporary life played against constant and devoted contact with that little masterpiece, the continuum that could come from old records. Well, if it is valid it will continue to work on me until I write it. This man need not be an overly simple kind of man. It could even be in the form of his own journals. I will find my photograph of that church to refresh my memory.

Later that morning, he found his photograph of the old church. "In dreams I have been in that rectory where I never really visited." A novel in the form of a journal, which had been his natural form, but it was never composed.

Griffin paid the bills on January 4, complaining that when he had earned extra money, expenses escalated. "At least we manage not to get in debt, just barely able to stay on top of the bills, but with nothing left over for unexpected (now inevitably expected) surprise expenses, like medical bills."

From mid-January to mid-February, he was immersed in working on the Merton biography in the library at the home of Win Hooper, a prominent Fort Worth attorney and family friend. Even though traveling between home and Hooper's house caused some inconveniences, no visitors, phone calls, or mail deliveries reached the secluded author. Throughout these weeks, he typed detailed passages in the *Journal* about everything else *except* the actual progress on the biography, which had passed into its sixth year. He was plagued continually by poor health and financial struggles, demanding that he write articles and travel on lecture tours.

On February 18, he had a phone call from Jonathan Kozol.

> Jonathan has been through hell this winter in Boston, one of the few whites there to battle racial injustice; and having done it on his own home ground, he received all the fury, harassment, and hatred whites could throw at him, until finally he needed police protection. All of this has resulted in hypertension so serious the doctor has ordered him to bed for three months. He did not call to discuss that, but to ask if I would read galleys on his new book. Of course I said yes. But he needed to talk about the recent troubles, and as I told him, it sounded the *deja-vu* theme, like reliving those bad days of the early 60s when the same kinds of things were happening to me.
>
> Being hunted is a fairly rare experience, and it is a devastating one, and I particularly hate it that a man like Jonathan should have to live through it. He has seen unmasked evil, all its inhumanity, and that breaks men in health and in spirit. He has seen ignorant and stupid men hate him, just as Cesar Chavez has, just as so many have. Ultimately, this teaches its incomparable lessons, but it damages so terribly at the outset.

> There is a great difference in knowing about this, even expecting the repercussions and actually experiencing them. It is the experiencing, no matter how well one has been prepared, that finally breaks a man. And this wound is not in what men do to you, it is in witnessing the profound obscenity of the hatred that so disfigures and dehumanizes them, as though one were looking into the heart of their monstrous illness and seeing evil incarnate.
>
> Yet this experience liberates, and that alone is perhaps worth all the ravages. It teaches a man to go his own way and trust that it is the right way, and not to rely ever again on the opinions of those who have *not* had such an experience. This kind of experience teaches you that once you find your own truth, your own vision of justice and humanity, you are not going to fit anyone else's mystique. This may give the illusion of isolating oneself—rarely a comforting illusion—but it does not really isolate. More often it serves as a magnet to draw people to you because they hunger for any evidence of this kind of liberation from intellectual and moral fads of any group or time.

In March, Griffin made a series of audio tapes with John Reeves, covering his life as artist and activist. For three days the Canadian crew worked at the house. Later, readings of his books by actors were combined masterfully into a five-part radio program that aired several times over the Canadian Broadcasting Company and later over National Public Radio affiliates in the States. It was the most comprehensive "oral history" ever done on Griffin.

By late April the grant money had run out, but Griffin managed to stay afloat by doing Merton lectures and *Sepia* articles, including an excellent historical piece on the murder of NAACP activist Vernon Dahmer, tying the 1965 killing to the release of the KKK members who had burned down Dahmer's home. He also wrote about the current situation in race relations for European readers, and, in his editorial for the Dominique Pire Foundation, he is critical of the "benign neglect" of the Nixon administration. "With the 'law and order' politics of Nixon, we soon became aware that almost all of the programs for inner city help were to be killed," citing the impounding of funds "to sabotage the inner city special schools, the scholarship funds for American Indians and a great many other programs that had given minority people hope. Few realize that one of the reasons for the eruption at Wounded Knee was the cut-off of 22 million dollars in scholarship funds."

On April 27, he traveled to give Merton lectures in Denver and Bozeman, his "first attempt to go out and make public appearances in six months." He returned on May 1, commenting on a meeting with Ramsey Clark, "who gave one of the finest lectures I have ever heard, and without any notes."

Griffin visited the doctor on May 8. "The foot is bad, the infection into the joint. The doctor has taken me off of antibiotics and next week they will do a culture and then try to design an antibiotic specifically for what that reveals." He lectured that night at TCU, and "came home dead on my feet."

The following day he received a literary magazine that included his portrait of poet Denise Levertov. The mail on May 9 included a "packet describing a concert in Washington for the President of Zambia by the Pritchard Concert Ensemble. The thing that astonished was a composition sung by Afrika Hayes (Roland Hayes' daughter) and 'Dedicated to Clyde Kennard, John Howard Griffin, Dick Gregory, and the Congressional Black Caucus of the 94th Congress.'"

Griffin realized on the morning of May 14 that "I am putting too many details in the last chapter of the Merton biography, which is packed. I must restrict myself only to the big movements of his last year." Since he had written the second half of the authorized biography first, he was actually only nearing the mid-point of completion. That afternoon he realized that "the work is extremely taxing. I concentrate well until early afternoon and then just completely play out. If I could devise almost any form of exercise, it would be a great help. But I cannot walk." The doctors had isolated the virus in the infected foot, ordering him to stay off of it. For the next week he worked in bed, while reading "almost gluttonously" several books on music.

On May 22, he was "astonished to learn" that he had won the Catholic Press Association's 1975 Journalism Award for the best four-color cover (with one of his portraits of Thomas Merton). The *Journal* maps out a typical Saturday morning at home on May 31. "A great day's work yesterday, and I am hoping for another today. Up early, while everyone else sleeps, doing what I must do each morning: medications, coffee, after a half hour, insulin, making these notes, then breakfast, and in between washing up in the bathroom. It is a beautiful, cool morning, the kind that makes me long for the country: I dream of a place of true quietness and solitude, where I could have a small garden."

On June 4, after hearing a TV special about the government's dossiers on anyone in the country, Griffin warned in the *Journal.*

> Such values once held very dear by Americans as privacy of conscience seem to have vanished. "If you have nothing to hide, why worry?" certain dumb asses are quoted as saying. How damned naïve people get. But how do you combat it if you have to fill out income tax forms, social security information, and medical insurance claims? This drives me into a mood of outraged disgust. The Gestapo was big brother, too. It is precisely the men who worked on this "highly secret" decoding device that became so alarmed about its possible use they leaked it. The White House is denying that such as system exists, but it is a weak denial in view of the fact that NBC now has the information, including the cost of three billion dollars to set it up. Once again the public is required to pay for the very instruments that erode our alleged freedoms. Soon our acts will be computerized.
>
> Freedom in such a context becomes the most blatant of clichés spouted by a chamber of commerce, rationalizing themselves into the delusion they are free men. As long as I do not act in a way damaging to the common good, I do not think big brother has any right sticking his nose in my business, my life, my actions. I've got plenty to hide—all those things that are nobody else's business, which I consider just about everything. I am one of the few who has resisted all of these things out of my old training against the Nazis. I will therefore end up (having fought for fundamental values) being computerized as an utterly suspicious non-cooperator. Of course, my work in Civil Rights (irony of ironies) undoubtedly got me fully investigated by the FBI, and no doubt the CIA has its own dossier, since I have spoken so frankly about our racism when in foreign countries.

Griffin visited the doctor on June 8. "The virus appears to have been slain at last by the medication, though the foot must still drain for a couple of weeks. This is wonderful news. Now, I have to be very careful."

Three weeks later, he received a letter from editor Austin Olney at Houghton Mifflin, suggesting they spend a few days going through the manuscript. "They might consider letting me do it in two volumes, the first being the later years. That could work almost immediately." He had written the book in reverse order, writing about the monk's final years, while memories of Merton's friends were sharp.

Griffin noted in the *Journal* of July 10 that paying the bills had been complicated by not receiving payment for lectures. He bought a roast, describing his meticulous attention to its preparation and, as always, drawing a moral from it.

> Here again, the kind of festive atmosphere in the house which is something to do in poor times, or more exactly with the exorbitant cost of good beef. My parents, who will not take help, and who live on what used to be a good fixed income, and who are managers of the first order, simply do without beef. I invited them to supper, and they were excited. What we used to take for granted is now festive. I learned cooking in France, where you don't waste anything. I am glad for a situation that deepens perceptions, allowing a simple roast to become a grand occasion for the family.

On July 14, he wrote that "We celebrated yesterday with a visit from our old Carmelite friend Father Augustine Healy. Gus has been transferred back to Dallas after many years away, and it was the grandest kind of happiness to have him here again. We will see him often now. He is a wonderful friend."

During the intervening week before returning to the *Journal* on July 23, Griffin worked on the biography. Up before dawn, he reported that "these are the great hours, the hours of true sanity. To awaken later is simply to be in the midst of the mob of hustlers and connivers and people who have to do things." Despite health problems, Griffin managed to carry on a funny campaign along with cartoonist Joe Noonan of *Way* magazine. In response to the Annual Sackbut Week at the New England Conservatory, he created a humorous flyer for his fictional tour.

Writing briefly in the *Journal* during August, Griffin often remembered his friend Robert Casadesus. "Listening again to Robert's version of the Schumann *Fantasy*—a profound experience. How impossible to think of that magnificent musicianship now stilled in a grave near Fontainebleau. I do not get over mourning him."

Responding to a new theology commission to overhaul Catholicism, he swiped at conservatives. "The main problem with right-wingers is that they are so damned sure. They never have doubts. In religion they out-think God. At base they have the delusion that they are sinless and their contempt for our sinfulness is gigantic. Their judgments on us are the projection of their mire."

On August 13, Griffin mentioned *Akwesasne Notes*, including "highly detailed accounts of the FBI at Pine Ridge and of Dennis Banks's trial."

> Maddening to see the distortions that have consistently appeared in the "white media," and to see how we outrage justice and decency in regard to the native peoples and then haul them before "the bar of justice" when they explode. A white man murders a Native American. The local courts decide to try him on a minor charge. The man's mother protests with a group of supporters. She gets arrested and sentenced to 25 years. I can't begin to list the outrages—it would take forever. Like the atrocities committed against black people, these things remain unknown, are never mentioned in the news. *Akwesasne Notes* keeps us informed, and with an objectivity and dignity that put most newspapers to shame.

Griffin read Jonathan Kozol's *The Night Is Dark and I Am Far From Home*, which was sent for a blurb by Houghton Mifflin. "It is a remarkable work," he said in the *Journal* on August 14, "and he is one of the few really first class thinkers who bases his conclusions on lived reality before using them as a basis for speculation. And he has the guts not to equivocate."[108] Later that day he completed their income tax returns—"the most grindingly unpleasant thing I ever do."

> We felt like two lepers trying to console each other, signed it and I attached the check quickly without thinking about it, and she mailed the damned thing before the deadline. I scrupled to make it honest, but I always feel totally dishonest anyway, even though I keep good books. I went back over it a couple of times to see if there was any way I could reduce it, but could not find any. Nevertheless, I always have the feeling that I will soon be in a federal prison. Elizabeth consoled me by saying that if that happened, perhaps I could find a way to get put in solitary where I could work undisturbed!

Griffin read a magazine article, "to my astonishment and delight," about painter Abraham Rattner at the doctor's office on August 20. "I asked Dr. Kyger if I could borrow it, and he said just keep it. Abe has lost a great deal of weight, has grown a beard, and looks splendid. He is now 80, and has been having a retrospective at the Kennedy Galleries. It was through him that I met Reverdy, and through Reverdy the Maritains. What a great artist and a generous man."

He had a "good long day's work" on August 26—"much easier to work now that the children are in school. Father George has brought communion just about every day this year, stays only briefly, although we have had wonderful conversations. What a joyful, tactful friend he has been to the family all these years."

The next day, after reading articles by Irving and Cornelia Sussman, Griffin wrote that "Both are writers with intellectual passion and the insights that come from lives of prayer. These clarifications are filled with a kind of joy that comes from inner energies. A great kind of spiritual vitality, which are the overflow of the marvelous feeding of the mind from the spirit."

> I recognize in that many echoes of myself in the past. All of that has faded though, and I no longer have it. I do not know why. Perhaps it is only the attrition of medication and illness. I find that more and more I take myself out of my writing. Even though I write incessantly, the intellectual passion for finding out why has almost vanished.
>
> Another passion has replaced it and virtually obliterated it. I say all this tentatively, because I really do not know anything and do not know if I am in the right or in the wrong or in delusion: but I do now that now, greatly weakened by a year's treatment with antibiotics, under the surface of events there is an awareness that centers around one thing: communion—either a waiting in anticipation for that moment; or the profound gratitude that colors the hours after reception. This is the foreground of my being right now. All other things remain blurred in the background. I don't evaluate this, or even question it.

"Hard work all day, on the manuscript," he reported in the *Journal* on August 28. "It requires such attention and care. A phone call this afternoon to say that Dan Walsh had died in the hospital in Louisville, a merciful death. Odd, I was at the point in the book where Merton heard of the death of his friend, Sy Freedgood. Now another key link in Merton's life is gone."

On August 31, Griffin laments that Merton's last year, 1968, was like his own situation. "The poor man had so many people just coming up to the hermitage uninvited and unexpected. Then when the temperature dropped to zero, the visits were cut off, and his sense of relief and liberation are palpable in me."

The Griffins had a welcome visit from Father Stanley Murphy for a few days in early September, the guest who never expected to be entertained. "I got up enough courage to ask him to read the 1967 chapter on Merton. No one else has seen anything in the book." Father Murphy considered it an excellent chapter.

During September, Griffin listened each morning to the *Well-Tempered Clavier* by Bach, performed by pianist Sviatoslav Richter; he wrote that it "remains always fresh and nourishing." The September 29 entry looked "at the amount of work stacked here, and my heart sinks. Will I ever make a real dent in it? Well, I won't do it if I sit here and stare at it. I pray for a time of quiet and energy." That did not prevent him from committing a characteristic bit of foolishness. As Elizabeth was giving him a haircut, "Greg put a pair of Civil War glasses on me and photographed while she was trimming my hair on the patio. He got one photo with a highlight turning one of the lenses completely white, which gives it a sinister tone."

Griffin created a press release under the headline

> SECRET CIA TAPES REVEAL RADICAL AUTHOR SHARES LOVE NEST WITH HIS HAIR STYLIST.
>
> AP—Fort Worth, TX. In another leak of CIA information today it was revealed that radical author John Howard Griffin has for years shared a love nest with a woman known only as Elizabeth, owner of The Patio Barber Shop. "I guess this will ruin me with my radical friends," Griffin commented glumly. "They won't tolerate this kind of weakness. They view such things as sinister. Well, I'm sorry. I don't think any man could have a beautiful woman fooling around with his hair and beard and not be overcome." Griffin deeply resented the CIA's illegal taping of his private life. "They're nothing but a bunch of sick *ecouteurs* practicing their perversion in the guise of 'internal security,'" the author said.

The October 2 *Journal* mentioned that the Griffins watched a CBS documentary on the blacklisting of John Henry Faulk.[109] "I remember visiting with him during the frightful days of the McCarthy era (not that we are out of them), when there was murderous character-assassination and you could count on the establishment to be utterly cowardly and cave in to the extreme right."

He did not return to the *Journal* until October 21. "The time has been jammed with a blur of guests and activity, nearly all of which seems pretty meaningless. So many letters, and I do not even recall what they were about, which proves that I waste time with things that would not be greatly altered if I simply ignored them."

The next week Griffin researched the life of Roland Hayes, for an essay in *Sepia* and in preparation for an interview on CBC radio. He had not seen the tenor since photographing him in 1969. He telephoned him on October 25.

> On an impulse I decided just to call Roland Hayes. That blessed old man no longer hears well. He said he is living "very quietly" now. We talked about his 88th birthday and about the documentary. He said he really did not know what to talk about. I said we would be talking about music. "I've already said so much about that. I don't have anything new to say."
>
> I reminded him that we could talk about his performance with pianist Dame Myra Hess. He hesitated a long moment, as though he had forgotten about those glories, and then said, "Oh, yes . . ." I was extremely touched, because he appeared eager to talk, and even appeared pleased to be remembered.
>
> I asked him about his daughter, Africa, whom I met in New York. He hesitated again, searching his memory, and finally said, "I don't know. I have not seen her lately." But I know that he has. This seems to indicate that what I have heard is correct: his memory for the past is excellent, but his memory of the present is faulty. I do hope that we have not waited too long to do the documentary.

Griffin listened to records of Hayes singing "the Italian songs, the arias and spirituals, and also an unexpected treasure of Beethoven's *Missa Solemnis* with Hayes doing the tenor solo with an orchestra conducted by Bruno Walter.[110] I have to do a lot of research, because the man is so flawlessly modest and reticent. I recall my visit to his house to photograph him as one of the great moments of my life."

> All of this familiar from when I was studying repertoire with Pierre Bernac in the 40s—and all of it better than I ever remembered. I am astonished to find the quality of the voice so true, though the originals from which this tape was taken were from 1939-41. The spirituals, which Hayes sang entirely as he had learned them as a child, are immensely moving, and I appreciate them now more than I did as a student. He treats them properly, as great art works, and he sings them incomparably. A Viennese teacher with whom he worked on Lieder and for whom he sang some of these spirituals, compared them to Bach; and on this tape Hayes sings Bach's *Bist du bei mir* heart-meltingly well.

After writing this on October 31, Griffin fulfilled a promise "to bring some order into this studio, which is a disgrace even by my slovenly standards." Over the next days, he was "shocked by the studio's propriety and neatness." On All Souls Day, November 2, he remembered "all the souls dear to me—a long list as I grow older." Then he listened again to Roland Hayes singing *Bist du bei mir*—"a blessed way to slip into the life of the day. Now, 35 years after he made this recording, one man thanks God that Hayes persisted despite frightful frustrations in bringing his art to this high level. I remember Atlanta's response, even after Hayes had become world famous and revered: 'We're not interested in niggers.' Well, Hayes' singing of this Bach erases all of that, wipes such stupidity out, nullifies it."

Griffin returned to the *Journal* on November 19. "Nothing much has happened except work on the biography from morning till night." He mailed the typescript carbon of his unpublished novel, *Street of the Seven Angels* (the original manuscript had been lost by Houghton Mifflin)—to Bradford Daniel, who had interested a producer in making a "quality" film of it. No film was ever produced.

He endured another oral surgery on November 24, reporting in the *Journal* the next day that it had been much more complicated than the x-rays had indicated. He was in surgery nearly two hours, and put on a cold liquid diet.

On Thanksgiving the family was preparing for their annual trip to the Mansfield farm to have dinner with Elizabeth's mother. Griffin felt "pretty miserable, but am trying to build enthusiasm: an enormous sense of exhaustion and discomfort, which I tell myself is from the trauma of the surgery. I wish I could simply remain still today. Yet I long for the country, away from the city, to be in some isolated place. I hope that I may live long enough to have that someday. Gregory is going to photograph the creek bottom at the farm today—and I envy him being out there in the woods alone with a camera. If I could wear shoes I would be out there with him." Then he caught himself in his melancholia, realizing the mood was dictated by the medication. "Why do you have to take stuff that half kills you in order to get well?"

Griffin did not write in the *Journal* again until December 11, because his father had been hospitalized with congestive heart failure. "Everything went wrong with me, too, as a result of walking too much at the hospital and not sleeping. Well, things are better now and I am back at work and off the pain medications that so stupefy." His mother's seventy-fifth birthday was on December 13, but he was unable to visit her and his father (recovering at home). He thought he would go, then realized that "I am acting like a fool. What they need is calm and cheer." Instead he decided to bake them a loaf of salt- and sugar-free bread that Elizabeth delivered the next day.

On Christmas Eve, Griffin returned to the *Journal*, recording a few facts from the previous ten days, because he knew that he would forget them otherwise. "The trip to the doctor's yesterday knocked me out for the whole day. Nothing done, and no great memory of the day. Better this morning though still painful." The entry continues in great detail about the buffet he was preparing for close friends, while the entire family cleaned the house. On Christmas morning, Father George Curtsinger not only brought communion, but also said Mass. That evening they watched Artur Rubenstein play piano works of Chopin and Brahms on TV. "At 89 he plays better than he ever has in his life, and we were overwhelmed by such transcendental playing."

On the final day of 1975, the *Journal* reported that "I had 12 hours of solid work yesterday, but I could not sleep last night because I could not stop working mentally. How I wish I could do this everyday for a long time."

But 1975 would bring more health problems—both the osteomyelitis affecting the bone marrow in the foot and jaw and the diabetes that made any healing difficult. He did not see much healing in race-relations either.

One controversial debate he did *not* want to become involved in during the mid-1970s was what he characterized as "academic racism," rebutting white scholars who claimed black people were genetically inferior. Dr. William Shockley, a Nobel Prize winner in the field of physics, tried to solicit the author's help in recruiting blacks to submit to blood tests and intelligence exams in order to "prove" his racist premise. Griffin refused to cooperate with the scientist because "you are expressing highly inflammatory unproved theories that can result in overwhelming grief to too many people. Also, you have made a historical error in comparing your situation to the silencing of scientists in Nazi Germany. I heard them. No scientist advocating theories of racial superiority was ever silenced by the Nazis. It was those who protested against such theories who were silenced."

Griffin would revisit this debate—from his early exposure to the Nazis to recent exchanges with scientists during the mid-1970s—in a project proposed by an editor at Macmillan. David Reuther invited him to write a personal overview of racism as a book for young adults. He agreed because he was impressed with Reuther's editing on the young adult biography of Merton, written by Cornelia and Irving Sussman. But he could take on the project only if an advance upon signing could be made in time to relieve financial stress. Agreement was reached, and he began to work on the project that would become his final book on racism.

There are less than fifty typed pages in the 1976 *Journal*, along with several spiral notebooks Griffin kept while traveling. The main reason for *not* keeping daily notes was steady work on the new book, *A Time To Be Human*, published at 122 pages.[111] "Typing and editing the final draft for Macmillan," he noted on January 20, "and it consumes all my energies and thoughts. The advance came in this morning (special delivery), but very delayed. I paid off the most distressing debts, and feel relieved. I will be glad to have this little book completed and in the mail."

Griffin confided in the *Journal* on January 27.

> One of the things that distresses is that I cannot detach myself from the kind of work I do. I know that the only thing I can do is write about it, try to alleviate that kind of suffering by making it known and understood, when what I would like to do is act. I suppose God makes it clear that I am not to do that, that I am to remain tethered to the

> typewriter, working to lessen the suffering of others. I have to learn to accept that, to sacrifice the satisfactions of ever seeing anything actually accomplished through my direct actions, since I am physically unable to do much. Sometimes I wonder why it always seems to be my vocation to deal with inhumanity and human misery?
>
> Ever since I was 19, struggling to smuggle Jewish people away from the Nazis, through the years of working to lessen the burdens of racism, and now studies on the problems of the elderly poor. Always I think I can finish and do something beautiful but always new and grave problems are placed in my path. I cannot turn aside or ignore the problems. Nor can I solve them. I can only analyze them, making them known in the hope that world opinion and understanding will bring decent humane solutions. I cannot even work "officially" for anyone at a decent salary, because that would mean giving up the independence that is required to tell these things truthfully, and that would probably mean criticizing the very agencies that want to hire me, and nearly all agencies fear that.
>
> We are seeing now an amazing recrudescence of racism in the sense that people are impervious to data. The worse thing is the acceptance now of an utterly callous attitude in regard to injustices that senselessly wreck lives. Many of the elderly poor of all races can no longer afford to live with even the minimum requirements. It is a new kind of slavery, which seems to disturb no one except the victims.
>
> We cannot hear the groans because they are drowned out by the shouting about "America's Impact On the World" and other such bicentennial nonsense. The whole cause-effect chain has faded from view. The intellectual sell-outs in the journals and magazines are heart-breaking. Self-serving rationalizations have replaced reason.

"Too long without making notes in this *Journal*," Griffin lamented on March 8, while recalling in detail two musical events—a piano concert by Helena Costa at TCU, playing Mozart, Beethoven, Schubert, Schumann, and Chopin, followed by a musical evening with Costa at the two-piano home of the Moura-Castros. Costa played pieces they had not heard, early works by Portuguese pupils of Scarlatti. Then string players from the symphony arrived to perform the Schubert *Trio in B-flat* with Helena, who had played the trio with such legends as Pablo Casals and

Joseph Szigeti. And then Luiz de Moura-Castro lured Costa into playing concerti, going to the second piano and beginning the orchestral *tuti* for the Mozart *Coronation.*

A different musical evening took place at the Moura-Castros on March 14, and Griffin's mother was able to attend. "Helena played a fantastic repertoire, including a Handel *Suite* that knocked me for a loop. Glorious. Surely no one plays like this any more. My mother said that such an evening could last six months and she would be content to never leave."

The magnificent music continued on March 26, when Bridget de Moura-Castro gave a piano concert at TCU. Griffin remarked in the *Journal* the next day that "I had not heard Bridget at concert level before and I was astounded. She played Mozart, Beethoven, Chopin, and Bartók with great beauty and virtuosity—and a quality of noble music making that recalled Dame Myra Hess, particularly in the Mozart and Beethoven. It was simply magnificent playing."

After the concert, they gathered again at the Moura-Castro's home. "Clever Luiz lured Lili Kraus to their Steinway and she tried it—playing a Schubert *Impromptu.* We discussed Beethoven's *Eroica Variations.* Luiz is remarkable in his ability to talk of music in a way that makes people want to illustrate their points. Then Lili played some Beethoven. We were spellbound. She was into the music, sometimes stopping to repeat particularly beautiful passages. It was magical."

Following another "long silence in this journal," Griffin wrote on April 20, "due largely to my preoccupation with my Dad's final illness. He died mercifully in his sleep on April 13. I immediately notified the family and went to Mother's house. My great fear was that after 59 years of marriage, and with her blood-pressure problems that she might have a stroke. I made the funeral arrangements, stipulating that Dad's coffin be sealed. My brother Edgar took over all of the financial and business arrangements. We have spent most of this week close to Mother, to help ease her life without Dad's presence. She is handling it magnificently. She wants to resume teaching piano next week. It is very difficult to write all of this. At unguarded moments I am still flooded with sudden overwhelming grief and tears."

Ping Ferry, a longtime friend of Thomas Merton, sent a check for $5,000 as a gift, and an additional check for the same amount as a no-interest loan. The checks were received and deposited on May 10. Griffin did not mention this in the *Journal*. He did not return to making typed entries until June 16, his fifty-sixth birthday. "Have not kept notes in a long time. An overwhelming correspondence and an attempt to get as much work done as possible. I stay back here, ducking the immense activities involved in Susan's wedding preparations. The best way to celebrate this birthday is to get into the work." The next day he remarked: "I waste too much energy trying to keep up with the mail. This is the problem—the work brings in the mail, and then the mail keeps me from doing the work that brought it in."

On July 4, the *Journal* reported that he worked well before everyone awakened. "Now Mandy is at the piano in her nightgown, practicing like an angel. She has such a wonderful musical intelligence and does something no one else does to these works by Bach, Mozart, Haydn, and Rameau—she communicates a joy that is in the music, and in her own response to the music." While all four children showed talent at the piano, none of them became pianists.

Griffin was in Bemidji, Minnesota, at the eighth annual Upper Midwest Writers' Conference from July 9 through July 13, teaching fiction and giving a lecture. He enjoyed conversations with the other teachers, and thought the story manuscripts by the women were far superior to those by the men.

On July 31, he worked on revisions of *A Time To Be Human*, and then the *Journal* goes blank until September 26, when he reported that his workroom is a "nightmare of piled up work and research and photos—a total chaos in which I spend too much time looking for things."

There is not another word in the *Journal* until his scripted notes of November 27. "Much has happened since I last made notes. A tour (October 20-November 20) in Toronto, London, Detroit, Toronto again, Montreal, Rochester." The trip damaged him, and the diagnosis by Dr. Ross Kyger was congestive heart failure. When Griffin arrived home, the doctor ordered bed rest until January, putting him on digitalis and diuretics, prohibiting all exertion.

Griffin wrote sparingly in a spiral notebook throughout the remainder of the year. "Elizabeth got me a bed desk, so I have written a few short letters. Everyone is helping. Father George has brought communion each day. Force myself to make these notes. Write a line and then rest—no mental activity—a kind of physical and mental numbness, but listening to music."

The final page of the 1976 *Journal* was written December 3. "Much activity, but I have not been involved. The Ellises have been here, but aside from brief visit, they have stayed in the other part of the house, and it was pleasant simply to know they were here. They left for New Mexico this morning. Feel fairly comfortable but weak. Don't feel like doing anything, even reading."

Griffin returned to the typewriter on January 1, 1977, writing several paragraphs about the passing of Roland Hayes. The *Journal* for the year contains only seventy-two typed pages. He made "hasty notes" at the typewriter on January 13.

> Long careful examination by Dr. Kyger yesterday. The wound is healing slowly but the congestive heart failure it produced has left the heart permanently damaged, so I am going to have to learn to live a new way. Everything is working against everything else. The immediate danger is high blood pressure, which increases the danger of stroke or heart attack. Must be very cautious, must have stress and tension minimized. My family was shocked at this news. I do not feel like a dying man, but only one who is aware of the danger. Strange, in this kind of reduced life, how temporarily significant the insignificant things become.

Father Tom McKillop visited for ten days in late January. The Toronto priest helped put his studio in order, "with Father doing all the work." Griffin's heartbeat alternated between erratic and normal. On January 31, Griffin made a full confession to the priest. "The greatest blessing was that he got me through as complete a general confession anyone could make. It took us three days! I have felt wonderfully happy ever since. All of this has been healing to my physical, spiritual, and affective nature. It is good not to have to be anything but what you are, and right now I am a very weak and vulnerable human being in all of these realms."

Griffin typed 12 pages in February, reflecting on his new reality.

> How strange that I should have the will to make these notes. That is the writer deeper in my blood than the fatigue in my heart. Values get tested. I put it down because it is not the way I had ever imagined it. I have always feared this time, fought even the thought of it, and now I wonder why. It is much sweeter in many ways than I could ever have believed. I do not *try* to detach from life. But it seems as natural

> and inevitable as living itself. It is not somber or morbid, except to those in full living. Perhaps I make these notes not because I am a writer and cannot do otherwise, but for those I love more tenderly now than ever before. I do not mind the thought of leaving them, but I mind dreadfully the thought of their grief. I weep very easily now, but I don't let them see it. These are not tears of sorrow but an overwhelming tenderness, which is tied in deeply with my love of God, the relief to have been given the privilege of sweeping my soul clean. These are areas of my being that I could never discuss, and I still cannot, because words cheapen everything at this depth.
>
> What has grown in importance is music. I hear music these days as the most direct language that speaks to me, that reveals something very nearly sublime. I learn more about sanity, order, love, more about theology and psychology from great music than I ever do from words. The music shows me exactly where I am and where I ought to be. When I hear such sanity, such felicity of heart, such jubilance and tenderness combined—it begins to create those things in my depths.

Griffin received a registered letter on February 11, from Ford and Klapheke, attorneys for the Merton Legacy Trust, demanding that the completed manuscript of the biography of Merton be delivered to Houghton Mifflin within sixty days. "Should you fail to comply with this demand, you are hereby notified you will be removed as of the time set forth above as the official biographer for the Merton Legacy Trust." He replied on February 13. "If I had any strength at all, I could do the work in 60-90 days, but the chances are that I cannot even begin to resume work before 30-60 days. My editor, Austin Olney, knowing of my condition, had already made arrangements to come here to see what the situation is, and how we might work it out, possibly getting some kind of professional help from another writer."

But after the continuous physical setbacks and precipitous decline in health, the project was turned over to Michael Mott, at the insistence of the Merton Legacy Trust.[112]

At first Griffin was devastated because he felt the Merton biography was his calling—a calling he wanted to answer from the ground of his being. But it was not to be. He accepted this worldly fate, but openly wondered about the consequences.

In a June 16 letter to Houghton Mifflin, Griffin wrote: "I have many questions of course. What happens to my family and the work and the expense I have been to all these years? I will simply trust you to see that the right arrangements are made." Even as "arrangements" were made they seemed inequitable to him.

Griffin kept his deep disappointment private, turning energies toward completing *The Hermitage Journals: A Diary Kept While Working on the Biography of Thomas Merton*, marking his existential passage through the deceptive veils of human consciousness toward a spiritual ecstasy. The journal of solitude reflects his dialogue with Merton during those sojourns at the hermitage. "No seeking, because there in the surrounding silence all that would otherwise be loneliness is filled with Christ, filled with the ravishment," which permeated all the human registers.

The new medication schedule is duly noted in the *Journal* of February 19. Upon awakening, he took Lanoxin (digitalis), Lasix (diuretic), Salutension (blood pressure), and Pronestyl, to regularize heartbeat. A half hour later, insulin. Then breakfast some thirty minutes later. More Pronestyl before lunch and supper. Potassium chloride in the afternoon and a repeat of Pronestyl and Lonoxin at bedtime. "Medical problems in my case are almost overwhelming: I have heart disease, the enlarged heart is impinging on the liver and the kidneys are affected; the diabetes complicates everything as does the osteomyelitis. Literally being kept alive chemically. Most of these things can only be contained, not cured. They are irreversible."

Griffin had another attack on March 16. "Myocardial infarction, and I have been virtually dead to everything, all feeling (except anguish), all life, all mind. Struggling against this, now, for the first time, despite enormous fatigue. If you are a writer you can write regardless. Three things are healing to me: love, work, music. If I am forlorn in everything else, I am rich in love. In this realm of near-death, it is good to learn these things, but not always good to share with the family."

From June 10 through June 25, Griffin was in Canada, keeping handwritten notes about days in Toronto to lecture and a retreat in Sharon, both organized by Father Tom McKillop.

On June 11, he first met psychiatrist Dr. Viktor Frankl, author of twenty books, including the extremely popular *Man's Search for Meaning*.[113] "Yesterday a great interview with Frankl. I have never met a man whose thoughts and conclusions so nearly match my own. Everything he says about suffering and dying strikes my deepest beliefs. I detect no false notes in his statements."

Throughout this time, he struggled to overcome the despair brought on by pain, exhaustion, and spiritual aridity. When Father McKillop took him out each day in a wheelchair, he remained calm, conversing with everyone, taking photographs. When alone he scripted thirty-five pages about internal struggles, racked with unworthiness, analyzing his views on unconditional love and innocence.

"Extremely difficult days," he reported on July 4, after returning from Canada. "Worked eight hours on Tuesday, about four on Wednesday, woke up hardly able to move on Thursday. Friday could not leave the bed and slept most of the day." Then came "days and nights of helplessness, blending into a sameness of struggle. I do not remember the sequences: the doctor cutting into the foot, then another heart attack, then sudden overwhelming weakness. Elizabeth stays cheerful and busy, keeps the house alive, and is very attentive without crowding."

Griffin typed on July 10 that "I force myself to make these notes."

> Never have I felt closer to death. Work usually helps. I try not to give in to this darkness. But today I cannot breathe well enough to work. I listen for the beloved, and hear no voice. That is part of this condition—waiting, waiting. I have not reconciled myself to the feeling of physical ruin. I had rather die trying to do something than just vegetate. I am a man dead on his feet and still passionately I love. The only words that break through in their full meaning at such times are 'love' and 'innocence'—those two words in conjunction with each other—innocent love that is nevertheless total. Innocence is difficult for me, as it always has been. Innocent love is the supreme love. I have tried to be obedient to it with many failures.

During supper with Father Augustine Healey, Griffin (in the wheel chair) experienced violent chest pains and fell forward on the table. Johnny sprinted to get the nitroglycerin and Elizabeth slipped one under his tongue, then wheeled him to the sofa, where Johnny pressed hard against the left side, holding him half-upright, in order to keep his lungs from drowning in liquid.

Yet a few days later, Griffin taught a seminar on Merton at TCU. He admitted in the *Journal* of July 24: "It was insane and too deep a physical torture. That kind of risk is foolhardy, and yet the students were irresistible, delaying me after each lecture to autograph books. They seemed to find what I said a revelation about which they had never thought before."

In the *Journal* of August 8, Griffin wrote that the "medical examination and tests yesterday were pretty terrible—the worst yet."

> I put this down not to complain but to keep a kind of record. The only thing that really holds me is trying to live and to understand this experience. It is not in the result, but in the value, the rightness, the truth of the experience. I am sure the rest takes care of itself in direct ratio as this orientation becomes our way of thinking and being. This is why I remained aloof to causes, organizations, slogans, and myths. At the end of my life, there are only two words which express meaning—Love and Innocence.

In the *Journal* he reported new health problems on September 22.

> I have lost almost all use of my right hand, but I am learning to type again in bed. I can get the fingers to work pretty well, but they have no sensation. This has been a month of rapid degeneration in heart function. Also I'm having hearing difficulties—over-amplification and harshness of sounds, especially music, so that I can no longer listen without great nervousness. I read a little, but have been unable to do any work. These journal notes for example. I lie here wanting to make them. Then when I begin to type, all strength goes. I do not find the energy to put down what I am really thinking and feeling.

Two days later, after a visit with Dr. Kyger, Griffin learned that the hearing and right hand problems were related, caused by plaquettes breaking off from the carotid and washing up into the brain because of high blood pressure. On September 25, Griffin lamented that "all of the truly stratospheric music, those expressions of great eternal and transcendent beauty are not bearable now, not because of the hearing problem, but because the slow movement from Beethoven's *Opus 132 Quartet*, for example; or the Mozart *Quintet in G minor*, simply hurt too deeply. They make you face things that are already too near. A profound instinct to struggle, even when no strength remains. I sit up and type even though thoughts are too difficult to express. I keep on even when I can't keep on. I learn to count on nothing but mercy."

Griffin suffered another attack on October 8. "This time I really thought I would not survive." It took three nitroglycerin tablets to bring him back. Three days later he received calls from Studs Terkel, Joe Noonan, and Viktor Frankl (from Vienna), that turned out to be "marvelous conversations that touched me deeply."

On October 23, he had phone calls from three priests (Daniel Berrigan, Stan Murphy, and Tom McKillop), during which he almost confessed to considering *not* taking nitroglycerin the next time he had a heart attack. But he rejected suicide: "I believe that I am called on to go through this for some reason; and to end it by an act of commission or omission would be simply to refuse to make the whole sacrifice." Reading Ernest Becker's *The Denial of Death* stirred connections and clarifications during late October into November.[114]

> I think of Frankl's transliteration of Goethe: "If we take man as he is, we only make him worse. But if we take him as he could be, we help him to become that."
>
> From Becker: ". . . psychology has limited its understanding of human unhappiness to the personal life-story of the individual and has not understood how much human happiness is itself a historical problem in the larger sense, a problem of the eclipse of secure communal ideologies of redemption." And also from Becker: "When you narrow down the soul to the self, and the self to early conditioning, what do you have left? You have individual man and you are stuck with him." And you have these attitudes that make a virtue of this situation. This gives no individuality and it certainly gives no reason to become what we could be. It merely produces a conformity that glorifies the lowest horizons.
>
> All of these things haunt me in this darkness. It is though I were hidden from what I know could be by some high wall of pain and weakness, of physical, moral, and spiritual poverty. Inside, the struggle to climb that wall somehow fails. I keep trying and keep getting beaten back. And each time it seems to take longer to start climbing again.
>
> This was Merton's great intention—his determination not to fall into the traps of a kind of sanity of consensus, which is really an escape

> from the loneliness of our individual normalcy into the "averageness" of comfortable mediocrity. Merton was determined not to do this, not to live incognito to himself. For him the solution was to move into deeper contemplation and solitude; only alone, he felt, could he get away from that "codification of sanity" into his own freedom and truth, into harmony with reality that would allow the needs to conform to that incognito existence to vanish—regardless of the tremendous risks.
>
> Again from Becker: "From childhood we learn to subdue our sense of ecstasy and awe. . . . We codify our madness, socialize it, and call it sanity. This is the tragedy of our lives. We are condemned to live incognito, even to ourselves."
>
> When I was blind, I knew I could handle it only in solitude, away from the "codified sanity" of public attitudes and indeed official attitudes about "adjustment to blindness" (attitudes now largely discredited). To some extent, the same holds in my present illness, where others seek always to impose on me the "codified sanity" of their own unreal attitudes about extreme illness (though my friends do not)—in effect asking that I do things that the condition make it impossible to do, and therefore to live this condition "incognito" in relation to its reality. The people who try to force the placebo of ignorance, mindless optimism or pietism down my gullet, become quickly unendurable.
>
> Becker regards the "fear of death" as our driving force, and the frustration of heroism as the clue to our frustrations in our attempt to transcend the fear of death. Frankl regards the "search for meaning" as our driving force, which is another aspect of the same thing.
>
> How poorly I express myself in all of these things. I throw these notes down to clarify them for myself. It is distressing now, because before I could tell myself—"Someday I'll go back and straighten all this out," but now I know I never will.

On All Saints Day, November 2, Griffins watched Marian Anderson interviewed on TV. "Now an elderly lady of imperishable beauty, she spoke about Roland Hayes. One great disappointment was that I fell ill on my way to photograph Ms. Anderson after I had photographed Mr. Hayes."

He typed two pages on November 9. "I try to build a world around this bed, in this room. The typewriter and cassette player are nearby, but little used. I know there is a way out, but these attacks floor me, and they keep coming."

Griffin did not return to the *Journal* until December 5, quoting from a hate letter he had received. The final entry for 1977 was made on December 6. "Days of unbelievable fluctuation in this condition. Yesterday I seemed to have energy, and life was nearly comfortable. It seemed a turning point. Everyone was happy, a sudden change for the better after the low point on Sunday, when nearly all the family came because it looked as though I could not hang on. Then last night, this attack came suddenly. It took an hour on the oxygen and three nitros to get me through it. Now, with all the medication, and more oxygen, I begin to stir back into life. These apparent rallies are terribly misleading and my disappointment to wake up during that violent attack was very great."

Against all odds, Griffin had made it this far.

His last typed words of 1977 return to the hate letter that had reanimated his nightmares. "The 'civilized' white mob converging mercilessly, to lynch me as a protest against my work, which they say encourages 'Negro savagery.' My God, could any savagery equal the desires expressed in that hate letter? I don't pay conscious attention to it, but apparently my nightmares do—and not without cause—since I have viewed too many mutilated bodies that were the victims of savagery and the sadism that accompanies it. And of course, the sickness of suggesting that any bad act by black people is 'savagery,' whereas the cruel, merciless, sadistic acts by whites are protection of 'white civilization.' Finally it is unspeakable."

Final Years

The *Journal* entries of Griffin's final years are less than one hundred pages—observations typed in the bedroom or handwritten impressions in spiral notebooks—usually multiple pages separated by weeks of silence. He was mailing carbons of his entries to several friends.

Father Murphy visited a few days before Christmas, and Father McKillop stayed during the holidays, helping during two severe heart attacks. In the *Journal*, Griffin attempted to describe the attacks in one long sentence.

> I wish I could describe the attacks accurately—the fading, the reality of pain and suffocation, the absolute certainty that I was dying, the loss of pulse and heartbeat and the inability to breathe even when the oxygen was pouring in through the mask, the sadness and release of tears, the terrifying loss of focus, searching faces, certain that when I could not see expression in their eyes I was gone, but as long as I could focus on that, I had some chance.

While Father McKillop was in Fort Worth, they did a brief interview that was published in *Catholic New Times* of Toronto. Griffin considered it "the highlight of his stay." He typed three pages on January 16 and two more on January 18, describing a snowstorm that was "a good excuse to beg off going to the doctor."

Griffin did not return to the *Journal* until January 31, celebrating the birth date of Thomas Merton and Father Tom McKillop. "I pray for these two friends, so similar in their craving for truth." He quoted a statement by Merton. "In the whole world, Christ suffers dismemberment. His Mystical Body is drawn and quartered from age to age. As long as we are on earth the love that unites us will bring us suffering by our very contact with one another, because this love is the resetting of a Body of broken bones." Griffin's response: "How deeply I feel the truth of that statement."

He kept the quotation, printed on a piece of newsprint, in his wallet. After "extreme killing pain," Griffin wrote on February 3.

> The only escape from those burning pains comes in flashes of temptations to put an end to it. The thing gnaws at my entrails like a buzzard. Fish bones in the throat.
>
> Finally, unable to bear it any longer I got up to water the plants in front of the window. Sunlight poured in. Then I transplanted three cuttings into containers with potting soil. Something to do with life. My hands and lower body like ice, my chest constricted, giving lie to the activity of life. I have not lost my faith. I am just not sure the faith can come along with me into harshness. I pray it can, because it is too lonely in this darkness. I write down what comes. I dare not read back over it.

On February 11, Griffin commented on a Christmas gift from Father McKillop, *Encounters With Silence*, by Jesuit theologian Karl Rahner.[115]

> How directly and simply this speaks to my heart and present experience. It is a book of the deepest sustenance and companionship. Rahner notes that God is as silent as his own dead beloved friends. I recall that Merton, facing his own possible death at the time of his surgery in 1966, spent an afternoon trying to prepare himself to meet God, and he concluded, "I honestly don't have a clue how to go about this."
>
> The theologian faces this and says, "You are the answer, even though incomprehensible, silent: Your silence is the framework of my faith, the boundless space where my love finds the strength to believe in Your Love. Your love has hidden itself in silence so that my love can reveal itself in faith."
>
> I believe this is a truth, much as our human hearts would like something easier. God has sent a great richness of friends so that the emptiness is mitigated by the fullness of that love, which seems a direct and real expression of God's love. These are friends who see me as a struggling, grossly diminished wreck, and who love me despite that.

After a few days of rest Griffin awakened on February 15 to another snowfall, "as a moment of marvelous contentment, lying there in the early dawn, alone while the family slept, giving myself to the beauty of that snow on the trees and bushes. It is always a blessed astonishment not to feel pain, realizing what a great liberation to mind and soul the simple gift of physical comfort could be, and how pain can have such dreadful and drastic effects on intelligence and spirit."

Three weeks later, Griffin wrote on March 5, "spending the happiest moments in the wheel chair, watering the indoor plants—caring for them has become my principle job, and there is something akin to peace and joy in that."

Griffin related a memory of researching the chants on March 12. "It was at the Abbey of Solesmes where I truly felt my vocation, in tune with the Divine. I heard in those musty scores, a return to worship, perfect communication, without blemish. I felt truly at home there but I had to leave because obedience called me elsewhere. It was the only home where I have ever felt truly myself."

He meditated on Palm Sunday, March 19, about the profound separation of the dying from the living. "Perhaps the most desolating thing that occurs in those who die slowly is the attrition of affections in those who love them. Slowly, tangibly, you feel yourself being shifted from the loving centers of people's hearts to places on their duty rosters. This is the central agony of dying slowly. I realize that for some this is almost unbearable. From my viewpoint, it is the truth."

Griffin did not type again in the *Journal* until April 21. "Nothing much happens during these interminable days and nights, but I am learning to adjust, and have less sense of desperation except during the attacks. But I have rediscovered the patio outside the bedroom window, ignored all these years. I sometimes sit in the sun and gradually have had all the potted plants moved out there. I am able to do so terribly little, but anything is better than nothing and lifts my spirits."

Nearly two months later, on his fifty-eighth birthday (June 16), he wrote of his "astonishment to have reached it. On my last birthday, celebrated in Toronto, there seemed little chance of living another year." He wrote a "confidential" letter to the Sussmans on July 17 (with his typical salutation of "Beloveds").

> We have been concerned about the same thing, the Merton biography, on which I have worked for ten years now. This has been almost an unendurable burden in the last two years of growing helplessness, especially since I constantly receive pressuring mail about it. I will not be able to work any more, and I have finally decided with Houghton Mifflin and the Merton Legacy Trust that it is no longer reasonable for me to hold up this work.
>
> Another author has been found, apparently very fine. He will do the work, but wants to research from scratch, and I cannot but admire that. Perhaps my own work may appear, but I cannot think about that now, nor am I able to work with anyone else, as I had hoped. I cannot bear the continued responsibility for anything to do with a work so massive.
>
> So, although all of my materials have been made available to the new biographer, the work is really out of my hands now, and I have no inclination to grieve over this. It is so transparently God's will. Even though it may seem an inexplicable waste in human terms, I am no longer able to feel it is. Nothing is lost as far as I am concerned, except the satisfaction of having completed a work of my heart. It is not a question of giving up, but of recognizing the truth as it is.

Only a fraction of Griffin's projects ever reached conclusion, and the archives at Columbia University contain unfinished manuscripts and notes about abandoned projects. Yet considering that during his life he was a serious writer for less than thirty years and an accomplished photographer for only twenty years, the body of finished work is staggering. His official biography of Merton was left unfinished. What remained in complete form—the sensitive, detailed chapters about Merton's last years, 1965-1968, became *Follow the Ecstasy: The Hermitage Years of Thomas Merton*. These years, when the monk became a hermit, fascinated Griffin most deeply. There are other finished chapters and a rich lode of notes and documents.

After surviving several attacks and surgeries, Griffin typed on August 2: "During an attack last week, I muttered 'Check on the beans.' Apparently in a coma I was preoccupied that the beans not be allowed to scorch."

The August 10 *Journal* entry discussed reading art books, letters, and reflections. "Great happiness in reading these things, so intimately connected with my formation in France—like meeting the friends of one's youth, almost forgotten in old age. It is true that having very little life of my own, I live largely in the lives of others, which is why I can almost not read fiction any more but turn toward biography, spending many hours with my friends from the past."

Two weeks in Toronto (September 4-18) with Father McKillop resulted in five pages scribbled in a notebook. Griffin looked back on that time in two typed pages on September 21. "Two magnificent weeks when we managed, in spite of heart attacks, to accomplish things I could not think of accomplishing alone."

Since returning home, Griffin was on massive dosages of antibiotics to prevent peritonitis. "Days and nights in a haze, fighting off the danger of peritonitis and the osteomylitis, which now threatens the right foot," he typed on September 25. The infections and antibiotics left him depleted of energy, although he continued to have occasional short visits from friends, calls from Father McKillop and Father Murphy, and letters from the Sussmans and Joe Noonan.

Griffin made two final entries in 1978. On October 12, he wrote, "sleeping almost incessantly, day and night, for a long time now. I awakened in the darkness before dawn and lay here remembering how those hours used to be so precious. At such times a deep contentment is interlaced with unbidden prayers."

On October 16, he lamented: "These notes are obsolete almost before they are made. This page has remained in the typewriter since October 12, because everything fell to pieces, and I have been unable to write, read or do anything else. Strange—I still enjoy reading good cookbooks, but can hardly bear to eat anything. I live mostly on milk, cheeses, soup—and I can take only the tiniest portions. Left to my own devices, I have the impression that I would simply stop eating." The question of suicide never remained in his thoughts, but he would have been dishonest if he had not answered that possibility by staying alive.

1979

Griffin did not type another page until April 24, 1979, more than six months later. He was taken to the hospital in mid-February, where the inability of his right leg to heal from the underlying diabetic condition led to infections of the bone. The right leg was severed just below the knee. He went into the hospital weighing 190 pounds, leaving eight weeks later at 158 pounds. He was practicing with a walker, taking dialysis and physical therapy twice a week, "and learning how to take a bath in a tub." While he was in the hospital, one of the Griffins' dearest friends, painter Robert C. Ellis, died from an unexpected heart attack. Ellis was just fifty-nine.

Father McKillop was the only visitor at the house until the day Griffin entered the hospital. "We have pretty well weeded out the real pests." Close friends were handling his important correspondence.

On April 27, he noted that "Already it is late April, and I have passed through all of it, either semi-conscious or unconscious. I do not feel fully conscious today, and I am exhausted from sitting in this wheel chair. I tried to practice with the walker, but kept veering to the left and had to give it up. Got a call from Tom and another from the Sussmans last evening, and for some reason I was filled with a sorrow, because I felt I would not see any of them again."

Since he now used earphones for music, Griffin was able to take some solace in a "splendid performance of a Mozart piano concerto by Annie Fischer" on May 3, typing fragmented remarks, but leaving the unfinished page in the typewriter.

The next day he practiced typing "to get some speed and skill back in my hands, to keep the mind occupied in harmless things." Griffin's one line that day: "Last night, one of the kittens tore up my finest begonia."

A few fragments of type followed. On May 6: "Everything is dry today. No ideas flow. A terrible loneliness."

May 7: "Blood tests and therapy this morning. Father George brings communion nearly every day."

May 8: "Can only read with the aid of a large magnifying glass."

May 9: "Received *Profiles in Hope* by Cornelia Jessey Sussman—a total surprise. The book contains chapters on Schweitzer, Buber, Edith Stein, Bonhoeffer, Dr. King, Dorothy Day, myself, and others. I have not been able to read it yet, but she certainly has placed me among magnificent company."[116]

The Griffins were expecting a visit from Rosa Ellis on the afternoon of May 10. "Later I was awakened by Father George, who brought communion and also some dried apricots, crème fraiche and some soup—a great treat."

Rosa Ellis left the following morning, May 11. "Elizabeth and Rosa talked until very late. It was a delight to see her again. She looks very beautiful. Apparently she is going to stay in country, though her family lives in Toluca, Mexico."

On Mother's Day the family celebrated with an outdoor cookout. The following day, May 15, he was down with the flu, eating only yogurt.

May 16: "We're all sick as dogs, flu spreads all over town."

May 17: "Continue very sick, eat little, sleep the remainder of the time. How is this possible?"

Griffin was returned to the hospital on May 23. The next day he was uncertain about the date, deciding, "it must be Friday since I spent Wednesday and Thursday at the hospital." He typed a half page each on May 27 and Memorial Day, but did not type further notes throughout the next four months.

On October 10, he stated briefly in the *Journal*: "Not much to write about these days when I am so sedated from the infection in the stump and the prognosis that I may lose my other leg." It did not become necessary to amputate the left leg. He began having a therapist visit three times a week on October 15, in an attempt to build up the arm and shoulder muscles, "but they are in poor shape and I don't see how they can be built sufficiently at my age to do much good. Anyway, I can handle the wheel chair, getting in and out with no help."

An appointment with the bone surgeon on October 16 had been moved back a day. "I am deeply fearful, sedated, and in the kind of pain that makes me feel that I'm losing sanity. About all I can do is look at art books. Elizabeth brings them home from the TCU library by the armload."

Griffin spent most of the day with doctors and nurses on October 18. "The pulse is very low, and they will try another month of antibiotics for the legs, since the heart cannot stand surgery. Any way you look at it, the report is dismal, but at least I escape surgery for a while."

Five days later, he learned that Nadia Boulanger had died at 92, after a long coma. "So my great influences in music are gone: Casadesus and Boulanger."

The next day, October 24, Elizabeth bought an electric blanket, which "is a real comfort during these cold nights." While he did not listen to music, because he did not "have the strength to play it," he did hear a 1950 recording on the radio, of Boulanger and Dino Lipatti playing the Brahms Waltzes—"gorgeously done."

Griffin had a long session with Dr. Kyger at home. "Like the bone surgeon, he sees no way out. How bizarre it is to know that you have very little chance of surviving—that in a sense you have been condemned. We all have one way or another, but usually we have no idea when it will be. I do not consider myself lucky to know that mine will be very shortly."

Father Tom McKillop visited in early November. "We resolved some of the problems of my unfinished works. He will edit the final years of Thomas Merton and the personal journals I kept at Merton's hermitage, if I die or become totally disabled. That is a relief. He heard my confession and generally took care of me. There were times when I was very sick, but I felt a great happiness to have him here, and we both realized there is little chance I will see him again in this life."

On November 5, Elizabeth called Austin Olney at Houghton Mifflin, who said they "would be delighted to publish the final years of Merton or anything else." But the book that became *The Hermitage Journals* was rejected as "too spiritual," and the Boston firm never published another Griffin title.

"I am becoming a skeleton," he typed on November 7. "I was shocked a moment ago when I took a bath." That evening he worked with the therapist, and "I hurt so badly I could only sleep on my right side or sit up all night."

On November 9, Griffin typed a half page. "I type a line, wait a long time before another comes, try to pray, forget where I am. Severe phantom pains in the amputated leg and real pain in the other."

The next day Griffin sat in the wheelchair beside a heat vent, "drifting in and out of sleep, mumbling prayers, begging mercy for those I love, but mostly in a drowse. Sometimes I weep from the pain, but then hear a voice saying, 'You can do better than that.' And so the hours pass. I type a few lines and fall into exhaustion."

Griffin visited the doctors on November 11. "The vital signs are so poor they can do no more surgery." He spoke with Father McKillop. "He may get to visit again, especially if I can live until Christmas." A week later, he wondered, "Very difficult to make these notes. I don't really know why I make them."

The last *Journal* entry of 1979 was typed on November 27, after he was moved from the north bedroom to the front bedroom facing south, which was considerably warmer. Friends helped to move the furniture, including the big refectory table he had used as a desk in the studio.

> Something about the light in this new room reminds of the days when I would take long walks from Tours to Parc de Grammont, always and especially to visit the small home of Balzac—his workroom upstairs, the kitchen and sitting room downstairs—a real country stone house. I would talk endlessly with the caretaker—an old man—and help him scrub the stone floor downstairs and wax the wooden one upstairs, and we would have us a fine gentle time, always aware that Balzac's presence lingered in those rooms where he would do intensive work and where he seldom received anyone. If we got thirsty, we drank the red *vin ordinarie* of the district, which was probably cheaper than water. We drank it so slowly we never felt its alcoholic effects.
>
> I write this because it represents memories of an experience that never lost its savor—and because it keeps my attention away from this terrible pain in my leg.

He did not mention that literary historian Maxwell Geismar had called Griffin a "Texas Balzac" in his essay about *The Devil Rides Outside* and *Nuni*. But he does mention that the bedroom had been daughter Susan's, and it had one of Robert Ellis's works on the wall—"a large color drawing—very beautiful."

1980

Griffin continued the fragmented *Journal* entries on January 6. Father McKillop had visited from the day after Christmas until January 4. "Having him here made me feel better. He worked almost constantly editing and getting one book—the diaries of my stay at Gethsemani ready for publication. Tom took back 20 volumes of journals to edit." The ailing author composed his very last piece of published prose, the preface to *The Hermitage Journals*, on January 3.

He typed only brief comments in the *Journal* throughout the first month of 1980. On January 11, he wrote about hearing Leontyne Price sing with the New York Philharmonic, "especially a Mozart aria with violinist Pinchas Zuckerman."

Griffin learned about the death of critic Lon Tinkle on January 13. "I had talked with him a couple of weeks ago. His latest book was about J. Frank Dobie. Without ever being close, he was a good friend"

January 23: Griffin noted that his work was discussed by Phil Donohue on NBC, but he did not hear about it in time to watch the program.

January 24: "I believe the truth of Saint Teresa of Avila, who said that if a man had five minutes to die he would spend four of them trying to get comfortable. That sounds almost sardonic, but it becomes a truth with me."

The *Journal* listed painful observations on February 3. "Much edema in the leg. Unable to sleep or to retain food. Even the stump has opened up again. A kind of crisis occurred last night. From some dim memory came the phrase 'God knows best.' And then the answering question: 'Is this really the best?' From a depth within me I made an act of faith, far more profound than those I have habitually made. I got up into the wheel chair, went into the bathroom and shaved—at two in the morning! Why, I don't know. I stay cold nearly all the time and all the color has gone from my hands."

The same despairing tone continues the next day. "I think of my jail as my own flesh. There are no locks on the doors, but there need not be for where can you go with only one leg that will not work and a stump that will not heal?"

On February 5 Griffin typed a preface to the collected journals, under the assumption that those volumes would be published posthumously. The journals remain unpublished. The preface was the last work he composed.

> In my teens, when I was a student at the Lycée Descartes, in Tours, France, a teacher whom I greatly admired suggested that I begin keeping a journal. He said it was one way of learning to know myself, provided I let no one else see it, wrote it honestly, and wrote in it even when I felt I had nothing to say.
>
> From the age of 16, I wrote faithfully in the notebooks. Those were days without the distractions of TV or radio when we had plenty of time for studies and for writing. When the war came, I remained in France and worked with the resistance, smuggling Jewish people to

> safety. I was then in medical school, a research assistant in psychiatry to Dr. Pierre Fromenty at the Asylum of Tours. When he was conscripted into the French army I was left in charge of the women's sector of the asylum with only eight nuns to help care for 120 patients. At night I would be called out frequently to dress the wounds of our soldiers who were being shipped back to hospitals—when the public was being told fighting had not even begun.
>
> Always I kept my journals. When finally France was about to fall, I gave the journals to a schoolmate to keep for me, and I returned to the United States.
>
> Years later when I returned to France, I retrieved the journals, which had been buried on my friend's family farm during the war, and began to read them. It was a sickening experience. Pages were filled with literary analyses, musical analysis, food we ate, with scarcely a word about the supreme reality of the war which preoccupied us day and night. It was pure escape from that reality, rather than any attempt to handle it. I was heartsick to find myself so false. What I remembered was sitting beside a poor woman in a straight jacket, brushing the flies from her face, searching for a better food for her than the bread and wine that was all we had left at the asylum. But what I read through the faded ink of my handwriting were accounts of my reading of Gide and Sartre.
>
> I burned those pages, and did not resume my journals until some years later, when I was blind and had learned to use the typewriter. I moved with my parents to a farm near Mansfield, Texas, where I worked in a concrete tile barn. My mother had learned to read to me in both French and Latin. At a party, I spoke with John Mason Brown. After a long talk he told me I must write, that I talked like a writer.
>
> I called the local Lighthouse for the Blind, asked if anyone there could teach me to type, and was soon able to make notes and then write books with the aid of the typewriter and a wire-recorder, which was later updated to a tape recorder. These journals are from the long series I kept through the years (1950-1980).

Later that day "the therapist came with the sad news that the doctors had decided to give up the therapy, since it had become too dangerous for the 'good' leg. He seemed genuinely affected and it was a considerable blow to us since it was a source of hope that eventually I might walk some with a prosthesis. So that is that. How we cling to such hope, even when it is unrealistic."

During the following dozen days of cold weather, Griffin rarely left the bed. "Yesterday awakened to the brilliance of snow," he wrote on February 17, "but today the snow is mostly gone. Read the gospel of the Beatitudes—beautiful and reassuring. I lay in bed, covered up, reading with the magnifying glass. I look at the wheel chair and wonder where I would find the strength to get into it."

The next day he thought about a request by Tony Simon that he record a tape about the spirituality of Jacques Maritain and Thomas Merton for the forthcoming September conference in Louisville. Five days later he got a call from Simon, asking to borrow photographic portraits of Maritain and Merton. Normally this would have been commonplace, since he had often mailed out photographs (as gifts to friends or for sale to magazines or as cover art for publishers). But this time Elizabeth sent the package from a supply of back-up prints made during earlier years.

Three days later, on February 28, he wrote that "I struggle to do a little work, but these are bad moments. It is very difficult to get out of bed. My leg aches from the hip down, and my mind is a blank of premonition of death. It is not something to give in to, but it becomes more difficult not to."

Griffin made only scant notes in early March. On the first day of that month, he wrote of the "Beautiful antiphon today: 'The law of the Lord is perfect, reviving the soul; his commandments are the wisdom of the simple.' They are also the happiness of the simple. Without them there is no happiness."

March 3: "High winds this afternoon deepen the silence of this house. I sit up in the wheel chair while my body begs to return to bed. Many of the Mass readings these days beg for forgiveness and mercy."

March 4: "Oxygen and nitro at three this morning. A kind of lonely battle because I could not awaken anyone to help me. At the height of it, when it no longer seemed bearable, a fragment from Samuel Beckett's *Waiting for Godot* splashed into consciousness: Estragon saying, 'I can't go on like this.' Vladimir responding, 'That's what you think.' And in that greatest misery I felt the anodyne of silent laughter throughout my body."

Four days later he reminded himself to write short bridge passages for portions of his journals, but never wrote them. On March 10, he comments briefly on the death of John Jacob Niles, who died on March 1, at age 87. "He was a man of great gifts." Nothing more until March 17, after "Days and nights of nearly unbearable suffering. I put down what I can. No desire to eat or drink. I have to force myself. I usually read the Mass because the texts speak so directly to me."

"After a long silence," Griffin wrote on May 17, "I have grown almost too weak to get from the bed to the wheel chair without help. A nurse now comes twice a week to dress the wounds. With very little vision left, I cannot enjoy reading any more. Fortunately, I pray without effort, and for much of the time when I am awake. It is now something so natural that it is almost continuous." He learned of the death of poet John Beecher, another artist he had photographed. "Beecher once said he was looking forward to meeting Chaucer. I continue to get the most wonderful letters. Those, with frequent calls from Father Tom, keep me filled with gratitude."

The next day, Elizabeth helped him into the wheelchair and they had a long conversation about "the wonderful black people we know and have known. Very pleasant talk." Griffin learned from the nurse on May 19 that she thought the "good leg" could not be saved, though it could not be amputated because of the heart. "I feel utterly miserable, and sit up in the wheel chair to give the hips a rest from constant lying in bed."

Two days later, Griffin had a phone conversation with an unnamed friend, who told him that the Maritain symposium was to convene at the Ramada Inn rather than at the Merton Center at Bellarmine, "because the people at the Center thought we were trying to use Merton's name to promote Maritain. This represents such abysmal ignorance, I cannot believe it, especially in view of Merton's own written comment that he came to the Faith through reading Maritain and Gilson."

Griffin signed a contract with Andrews & McMeel for *The Hermitage Journals,* calling for a $5,000 advance (with 10 percent editorial fee to Father McKillop). Elizabeth sent a package of ready prints to illustrate the book.

During the early days of June, Griffin wrote a piece in longhand, then revised it as a brief typescript ("A View of Changing Colors").

> We have to view these advances in altering skin color clearly. They are important certainly in the treatment of diseases such as vitiligo,

> which cause suffering, but some will see them as a cure for racism, and to view them as such is to fool ourselves. Perhaps the most devastating shock of my own transformation from white to black lay in the relentlessness of the open distaste of perfect strangers, and the fact that simply living was so much more difficult. The cure does not lie in changing color, but in the search for justice.
>
> Often I have been asked if this process can be reversed. I was asked this once by a figure of world importance. When I told him it was possible, he said: "Then why not make all blacks white and solve this racial problem for good." He was serious. I said: "Since three-fourths of the world's population is non-white, why not darken the one-fourth of us who are white?" He quickly lost enthusiasm, and of course the whole idea of some of us making such decisions for others is a profound arrogance. Another error in his question is the idea, racist to the core, that all blacks want to be white. I never once met a black person who wanted such a thing. Above all, a great many white people will see this development as a cure, perhaps compulsory, for racial injustice. This would be the greatest injustice of all.

Griffin's final *Journal* entries were scripted in a spiral notebook, beginning on the hottest June 23 ever recorded in Fort Worth (104 degrees). "Desire to write but I am weaker and weaker. Will try to continue in this tablet."

Father George Curtsinger brought communion every day, which Griffin noted along with the rising temperatures on June 26. "All heat records are being broken here. 114 degrees today." The next day it was 111 degrees.

On June 28, he wrote: "Heat is the obsession: 113 today, 13 deaths locally. My heart pounds at the slightest movement."

The scribbled notes continued for the next month.

July 2. "Everyone in this house sleeps under air conditioning. I think of those people, particularly the elderly, who swelter, suffer, and die from the heat this night. This stops being poverty and becomes misery. I try to think what I can do. I have no legs, no strength, no money—only prayers. Yet I ache to do more. How desperately we need saints who are strong enough to dedicate their lives to the helpless, who have a right to live decently and with dignity."

On July 3, Griffin learned he would receive a Pan African Humanitarian Award to be conferred in a ceremony at the United Nations. "A great surprise. I would like to go to be with the other awardees—Andrew Young, Jesse Jackson, Muhammad Ali, and Ramsey Clark. Of course that will be impossible."

Blistering heat on July 6: "Fragmentary sleep. In the long hours of wakefulness at night, I think of the untouched islands of the Pacific, places to live simply, lying there listening to perpetual wash of the waves. At such moments one glimpses a quality of eternity. I detest what we have done to cities—and what cities have done to us (really what we've done to ourselves in these dehumanized times)."

During the predawn hours of July 7, Johnny arrived from the oil fields of East Texas. "We had a long, very touching talk. It was a blessed one for me."

By July 11, Griffin felt that the "Days are all alike—days of intense heat." The following day, he observes that "the prolonged heat and lack of water are destroying farm life, livestock, and wildlife. Often I think of writing a beautiful story of country life, one without killers or thieves."

On the night of July 12, Griffin watched an NBC show about the forthcoming Republican Convention.

> A general lemming stampede seems to be taking place for Reagan. The man's ignorance, ineptitude, and abysmal mediocrity are terrifying. Why do I feel such a sense of rage over this? I felt the same rage about Nixon. It is that the poor, the elderly, the minority peoples are going to suffer even more, while the rich play the "fastest guns in the West."

Griffin made scant scribbled notes in the *Journal* during the next week.

July 16: "I have to go back to the hospital for a couple of weeks."

July 17: "108 again today. It is a little past midnight. Trouble sleeping—too much pain in hips and leg. Slept much of the day. Extreme pain."

July 20: "Trouble sleeping. Still very hot."

Griffin's last remarks in the spiral notebook on July 21: "No way to sleep. I nap. Then the pain awakens me. I go to the hospital later today to see what we can do. Impossible to go on this way." He was taken to the Medical Plaza Hospital in Fort Worth later that day, remaining there for nine weeks. As he had feared, he would never return home.

In the *Catholic New Times*, Father McKillop writes about his last visit with Griffin, just a week before the author died.

> John Howard was very sick and extremely fragile. When the parish priest asked him if he would like to receive Holy Commnion, he gave him a small portion of the Host. Then he took a plastic cup of water and he held it six inches from his mouth and it seemed to take a long time for him to be able to sip water. He looked down and prayed for a short while, and with all the pain that he was feeling, he said, "Father, would you like a cup of coffee?" To me that was John Howard Griffin!
>
> Shortly afterward, when the priest had left, he said, "It's so hard to be reduced to nothing! All I have left now is the pure silence of love."

Griffin died in the hospital on Tuesday, September 9, with Elizabeth at bedside. A nurse said he could not comprehend her presence, but she held his hand anyway. Soon he pressed his hand against hers, and "a beatific smile graced his lips."

Hundreds of obituaries and articles were published worldwide. An extensive obituary by Doug Clark appeared on the front page of the Tuesday evening edition of the *Fort Worth Star-Telegram*. On the front page of that paper's Wednesday morning edition there was a follow-up article by Jon McConal, in which Elizabeth was quoted extensively. "I don't think anyone knows how much he suffered the last two years. During this period, there was nothing but support, prayers, and how much people admired him. He had great hopes and a great love for humanity. I don't think he ever felt discouraged by the events of the past. He always felt people would rise to a challenge and would do in their hearts what they knew to be right. He was optimistic about that, and fought for equality and understanding to the end."

The funeral Mass was celebrated at St. Anthony's Catholic Church on Thursday, September 11. There was an extended homily and many friends were there to speak and to listen. Father McKillop was the moderator and main speaker.

The first reader was Father Tarcisius Conner, a monk from Gethsemani, who had been immensely helpful when Griffin was researching the biography at Merton's hermitage. He read from the first letter of John.

> You must not be surprised, brothers, when the world hates you; we have passed out of death and into life, and of this we can be sure because we love our brothers. If you refuse to love, you must remain dead; to hate your brother is to be a murderer, and murderers, as you know, do not have eternal life in this. This has taught us to love—that

> he gave up his life for us; and we, too, ought to give up our lives for our brothers. If a man who was rich enough in this world's goods saw that one of his brothers was in need, but closed his heart to him, how could the love of God be living in him? My children, our love is not to be just words or mere talk, but something real and active.

The second reading was *Psalm 18* read by Wilenne Berbér, wife of Luis Berbér, which carries the lines that were particularly relevant to Griffin. "I take shelter in him, my rock,/my shield, my horn of salvation, my stronghold and my refuge./From violence you rescue me."

Father August Thompson read from the Gospel according to Luke, about the great banquet, when all the elite who had been invited did not appear. So the host sent his servant out to gather "the poor, the crippled, the blind, and the lame," a passage with which Griffin had identified.

Father McKillop ended the homily with these words: "There is one great saying that John used in his talks in the 1960s and it is a phrase from Edmund Burke: 'All that is necessary for the triumph of evil is that good men do nothing.'"

> Two years ago, when he was very ill, John thought over those words and wanted to say something positive, something encouraging, and these are the words: "All that is necessary to triumph over evil is that good men and women with integrity, living in the Beloved, do good over and over, again and again, together."

John Howard Griffin was buried that day, as the long funeral cortège made its way from Fort Worth to Mansfield. He was laid to rest in the Holland family plot at the Mansfield cemetery next to Elizabeth's father, Clyde Parker Holland, who had been Griffin's closest friend during the decade of blindness.

When asked by many what her husband had died from, although knowing intimately that he had died of uncountable heart attacks brought on by the years of diabetic complications, Elizabeth simply said: "He died of everything."

A long wave of recognitions washed over the deceased artist like other waves he had described in the *Journal*, his oceanic text of hurricanes and calm seas, of brutal undertows and edifying eddies, of blind plunges into unfathomable depths. Except now there was a sea change, as his words set sail for other shores.

The Griffin Legacy

Among John Howard Griffin's accolades are the *Journey Into Shame* series in *Sepia*, which was recognized in 1960 by the National Council of Negro Women; the 1962 Ainsfield-Wolf Award from *Saturday Review* that went to *Black Like Me*; the Pope John XXIII *Pacem in Terris* (Peace and Freedom Award) he shared with President John F. Kennedy, in 1963; the 1968 Christian Culture Award, Assumption University of Windsor, Ontario; and in 1980 the Kenneth David Kaunda Award for Humanism from the Pan African Association.

Griffin was a member of both the American Society of Magazine Photographers and the Royal Academy of Photographers (UK), and the music fraternity of the Conservatoire de Fontainebleau, France, where he earned certificates of musical study. Also he received a certificate in medieval music from the Abbey of Solesmes.

Griffin's legacy was advanced first and foremost by the author's widow, Elizabeth Griffin-Bonazzi, and also by Father Tom McKillop, who worked with Griffin on the first posthumously published book, *The Hermitage Journals* (1982). Elizabeth established the Estate in 1982, wrote the first biographical sketch for *The Handbook of Texas*, and compiled the first bibliography for *Kairos*. She established JHG Editions for Latitudes Press, which published the posthumous titles, *Follow the Ecstasy* (1983), *Pilgrimage* (1985), and *Encounters With the Other: A Personal Journey* (1997).

Follow the Ecstasy, the most important of the titles from Latitudes, was somewhat ignored by the more conservative Mertonians, because it tells the story of Thomas Merton's love affair with Margie Smith, the young nurse he met in the Louisville hospital. Before Griffin wrote about Margie Smith, he exchanged letters with her, getting permission to use her name.

Thomas P. McDonnell remarked that the book "contains a stunning revelation which sooner or later must be taken into full account. Though the love affair ended in a whimper of sensible resignation, Griffin's is the only book that dares to mention the woman by name." In his review of *Follow the Ecstasy* ("A Life of Radical Absurdity" in *This World,* Autumn, 1984), McDonnell wrote: "Before getting into the subject matter of that book, it is important to reach a clear understanding of Griffin's quintessential sense of integrity. With *Follow the Ecstasy*, in fact, he does not come fresh and untested to the problem of Merton, if one may put it that way, but had already achieved something of a contemporary Christian classic in *The Hermitage Journals* (1981), a diary he kept while working on the biography of the monk and living for months at a time, between August 1969 and September 1972, in Merton's hermitage on the grounds of the Abbey of Gethsemani in Kentucky. It is a beautiful book which ought to be read in conjunction with *Follow the Ecstasy*. Since the death of Thomas Merton by a bizarre accident in Bangkok, the Merton commentary business is flourishing and promises more to come; but the real reputation is still very much in the process of evolvement. The protective cocoon that had been wrapped around the poetic Young Monk of the Western World has now been unloosed for good or ill, as the case may be, but we shall no doubt come to know him better and more authentically than we ever had before in the days of mere adulation. Credit for the possibility, if not the necessity, of fresh but increasingly mature appraisals must go, in appreciable measure, to the last works of John Howard Griffin."

Robert Ellsberg at Orbis Books published a revised edition of *Follow the Ecstasy: The Hermitage Years of Thomas Merton* (1993); *Scattered Shadows: A Memoir of Blindness and Vision* (2004); and the first biography, *Man in the Mirror: John Howard Griffin and the Story of Black Like Me* in 1997 (by Robert Bonazzi, now Executor for the Estate of John Howard Griffin).

Bryce Milligan's Wings Press published hardbacks of *Street of the Seven Angels* (2003) and *Black Like Me* (2004, 2006, and the 50th Anniversary Estate Edition in 2011). Wings brought out trade paperbacks of *Available Light: Exile in Mexico* (2008), and Griffin's essays on racism and spirituality, *Prison of Culture: Beyond Black Like Me* in 2011, as well as e-books of *The Devil Rides Outside*, *Nuni*, *Follow the Ecstasy*, and the aforementioned titles, plus *Man in the Mirror*.

Black Like Me has remained in print in English since 1961. It has been translated into sixteen languages, as well as being an audiobook and appearing in Braille and in large print editions in English, selling more than 16 million copies worldwide. *Black Like Me* in the United Kingdom and in all translations has been represented by the Rosica Colin Agency since 1961. Under the directorship of Colin's niece, Joanna Marston, the agency represents the Griffin Estate.

Documentary filmmaker Morgan Atkinson produced *Uncommon Vision: The Life and Times of John Howard Griffin*, as a DVD in 2010, viewed on many PBS affiliates. The documentary was included with the 1964 film version of *Black Like Me*, in a package arranged by Barry Griffin, for Video Services Corporation.

In honor of Griffin's accomplishments, Mansfield, Texas—the town where he was hanged in effigy—was named as a National Literary Landmark in 2011 by the Association of Library Trustees, Advocates, Friends and Foundation, a division of the American Library Association. A bronze plaque was dedicated in Griffin's honor by former First Lady Laura Bush at the Mansfield Public Library's celebration. Both Mrs. Bush and Robert Bonazzi spoke at the event, and all four of Griffin's children—Susan, John, Gregory, Amanda—were in attendance, all quoted pertinently in several *Mansfield News-Mirror* pieces by Amanda Rogers. The film of *Uncommon Vision* was shown downtown, presented by producer Morgan Atkinson.

Other celebrations were held in honor of the fiftieth anniversary of *Black Like Me*. In 2011 Grassroots Economic Organizing (GEO)[117] published a collection of articles and the University of Texas-Pan American (at their annual FESTIBA)[118] included a panel discussion of *Black Like Me* and a presentation of Morgan Atkinson's *Uncommon Vision* documentary. Gemini Ink and Trinity University sponsored a panel discussion on Griffin's classic and the University of Texas at San Antonio presented a viewing of the Atkinson documentary.

Articles about *Black Like Me* at fifty appeared in *Smithsonian*, the *Washington Post*, the *Times of London*, the *Guardian*, *Christian Science Monitor*, *BBC News*, *Chicago Reader*, *Catholic New Times*, the *Jewish News of New York*, *San Francisco Chronicle*, *Humanities Texas*, *Texas Observer*,

Texas Monthly, Fort Worth Star-Telegram, Dallas Morning News, Houston Chronicle, and *San Antonio Express-News.* Radio interviews with Robert Bonazzi were on 32 PBS affiliates and via the BBC in 176 countries.

Clémentine Célarié took *Black Like Me* to the stage all over France, playing all the parts—male and female, black and white, opening her version in Avignon in July of 2012.[119] She was born and raised in Dakar in sub-Saharan Africa. Living there for twelve years, she says she feels African. "This show depicts the adventure of the man I incarnate, white and black with courage and humanity. His testimony is a universal cry of alarm and, at the same time, a call to respect the other and their differences."

Griffin completed only one piece of fiction after regaining eyesight in 1957—the satirical story "Pilgrimage" that was a posthumous chapbook produced by the late Elizabeth Griffin-Bonazzi and Latitudes Press in 1985. Like Griffin's two published novels—*The Devil Rides Outside* (Smiths, 1952) and *Nuni* (Houghton Mifflin, 1956)—his third novel, *Street of the Seven Angels*, was composed during a decade of sightlessness. All three novels (as well as incomplete fourth novel, *Passacaglia*) draw upon classical music for their forms. *Street of the Seven Angels* takes its shape from Mozart. Except for Geismar's *American Moderns* and studies by Eugene McNamara (in Canada), Griffin's novels received only reviews in the local and national press, although the published articles about *Black Like Me* have been voluminous.

Perhaps the most controversial reaction was registered in the essay by popular Texas novelist Larry McMurtry, "Ever A Bridegroom: Reflections on the Failure of Texas Literature."[120] He included *The Devil Rides Outside* along with *Goodbye to a River* by John Graves, *The Ordways* by William Humphrey, and William Goyen's *The House of Breath*—as being "among our very best books." About *The Devil Rides Outside,* McMurtry wrote: "It is a strange, strong book whose verbal energy—a quality very rare in our fiction—still seems remarkable. In the mostly all-too-healthy and sunlit world of Texas fiction, the book remains an anomaly, dark, feverish, introverted, claustrophobic, tortured." He also quipped that "*The Devil Rides Outside* has the lonely distinction of being the best French novel ever published in Fort Worth." This was a reference that the novel set in France was published in Fort Worth by Smiths, Inc. These were *not* the "coughdrop kings," as Maxwell Geismar joked, but Gordon and J. Hulbert Smith.

Then McMurtry goes on to dismiss Griffin's work in a series of unenlightened opinions: "It [*The Devil Rides Outside*] was so complete and so explosive an outpouring of intellectualized emotion that Griffin seemed, from then on, a sort of emptied man. His second novel, *Nuni*, had neither energy nor force. He then wrote a history of a Midland bank, and finally, perhaps in desperation, turned himself black, in a last effort to find something strong to write about."

What might "intellectualized emotion" be—projecting emotion with one's head but not feeling it in one's heart? How could McMurtry know that Griffin was "a sort of emptied man," merely by cataloging the late author's books that he seemed not to have read carefully—or perhaps not at all? *Nuni* has force that cannot be denied, even if one is not drawn to the dark allegory or if one misunderstands its spiritual subtext. Griffin never wrote "a history of a Midland bank," but an engaging history of the staked plains region of West Texas, *Land of the High Sky* (1959), which was produced by a Midland bank in an edition as a gift to new customers.

No indication emerges to suggest that Griffin had embarked "in desperation" upon the *Black Like Me* journey "in a last effort to find something strong to write about." He had decided to risk the experiment because he felt under obedience to the sacredness of human life as a devout Catholic, and he was moved by the ethical challenge of his spiritual mentor, Jacques Maritain, who had called on fellow Catholics to make personal sacrifices in the human rights struggle.

A starkly contrasting view and tone are evident in Decherd Turner's essay about *The John Howard Griffin Reader*.[121] "My claims for the work of Griffin are not extravagant. They're just universal," writes Turner. "Griffin has the poetic gifts and graces to capture the eternal struggle of a man to know his own soul. He has ranged with the skill of a master-confessor who, with exquisite casuistry, elicits the intertwined skeins of slave and saint in everyman. No living artist has drawn such classic and extensive contours around his work."

McMurtry's assertion that Griffin had "an odd, lop-sided career" as a novelist is true, but not because he had "been pressed into fiction by the force of one compelling traumatic experience," or that he had "the always serious, usually fatal misfortune to write his best book first." Instead his "misfortune" had been due to the unexpected success of *Black Like Me*, which provided a platform to speak out against white racism, segregation, and human rights abuses. That reluctant activist career made it possible to support a large family and to pay the astronomical medical expenses of his battle against the ravaging complications of diabetes, but the extensive lecture tours kept him from the solitude necessary to compose novels of significance.

"My fiction is permeated with the profoundest belief," Griffin wrote to novelist Lillian Smith in a 1961 letter, "that art and man's gift to his daemon, no matter what his superficial personal life and beliefs, restores to him the innocence of mystery; and restores it also to the world, in that it allows, in Heraclitis' phrase, humanity to look into the essences of things and to encounter the mystery. It seeks, by implication only, to show how art and the artist re-establish, in the subtlest way, a hierarchy of values that the world is always losing, restores the clarity of the *ordo universali* from which we are always skittering toward our suicide; and within this, reveals the basic obscenity of our standards of modesty and delusion."

Griffin meant the universal order that remains a mystery when we contemplate its essence rather than presume to know it by appearance. He was appalled by the politico-economic notion of The New World Order—a global creed of greed that remains insensitive to human rights and also "reveals the basic obscenity of our standards," controlled by wealth and power but without stringent ethics. His literary vision in this new millennium exposes the ugly while exalting the humane. He brings to the library of the living the neglected works of a dynamic, original, and deeply spiritual twentieth century writer, who transcended the hatred of his attackers with the wisdom of fraternal love and genuine humility. And now he laughs with the angels.

Acknowledgments

I cannot acknowledge anyone more significant in helping me to complete this work than my late wife Elizabeth Griffin-Bonazzi (1935-2000)—for her memorable witness and incredible work accomplished on behalf of the John Howard Griffin legacy.

Thanks to Estate members: Susan Griffin Woods, John Howard Griffin Jr., Amanda Fenton, and the late Gregory Parker Griffin (1960-2013).

To friend Bryce Milligan for keeping Griffin's titles in print through Wings Press editions and e-books, distributed by Independent Publishers Group.

An early version of a chapter is in a package produced by Video Services Corporation (2012), including the 1964 film version of *Black Like Me* (owned by Barry Griffin) and *Uncommon Vision,* produced by Morgan Atkinson (2010).

To Morgan Atkinson for *Uncommon Vision: The Life and Times of John Howard Griffin.*

To Poppy Simpson and Tansy Simpson for their BBC documentary film work.

To Chloe Hadjimatheou for her interview on BBC in 2012.

And to Don Rutledge for timeless *Black Like Me* photographs.

To Studs Terkel, Robert Ellsberg, Jonathan Kozol, Michael Power, Thomas D. McDonnel, Jonathan Yardley, Julius Lester, John Reeves, Bob

Ray Sanders, Bruce Watson, Jerry Harp, Richard Fricker, Rudolph Rau, Thomas Fench, Kevin Connolly, Amanda Rogers, Michael Swellander, Steve Lipman, Chris Vognar, Ajiwa Nzinga Ifateyo, Jay Copp, Michael Johnson, Steve Bennett, Beverly Frank, and Daniel L. Robertson—all of whom have written about the life and work of John Howard Griffin.

And to Michael Nye, Naomi Shihab Nye, Violet O'Valle, Cary Clack, H.C. Nash, and Lucia and Jim LaVilla-Havelin, who have been supportive of this project.

Notes

Throughout the biography I refer to John Howard Griffin's journals as the *Journal*, even though this massive text has not been published in its entirety. While it is customary to italicize only published works, I italicize the *Journal* because entries appear in Griffin's many books, but also to emphasize this primary source. Any Griffin quotations that are not annotated are from the *Journal*, including several epigraphs to chapters.

The original single-spaced typescript (2800 pages) and several scripted notebooks are in the Butler Library at Columbia University in New York City, where the core of Griffin's papers and photographs reside. Elizabeth Griffin-Bonazzi (1935-2000), first Executor of the Estate, made his archives available to scholars in 1992. Other archives are in The Harry Ransom Humanities Research Center, University of Texas at Austin; the Thomas Merton Center at Bellarmine College (Louisville); Baylor University; and Boston University.

Robert Bonazzi became Executor of The Estate of John Howard Griffin and Elizabeth Griffin-Bonazzi in 2000.

1. First quote: *Notebooks 1935-1942*, translated by Philip Thody (Alfred A. Knopf, 1963); second quote: *Notebooks 1942-1951*, translated by Justin O'Brien (Knopf, 1965).
2. *The Devil Rides Outside* (596 pages, Smiths, 1952) was published in the UK by Collins (1953), and translated into French and German. Griffin fought a contractual battle with the Fort Worth publishers to regain the rights to his first novel. He preferred the Collins version, which he had revised, including correcting the typographical errors in the Smiths' publication. The Collins edition is 511 pages, but the difference in pagination is due to the smaller point size and the different font. The Pocket Books edition of 1954 ("Giant Cardinal" paperback of 579 pages) was based on the Collins version. It was involved in a censorship case adjudicated by the US Supreme Court in 1957. *Nuni* (Houghton Mifflin, 1956) was

translated into German. *Black Like Me* (Houghton Mifflin, 1961) has appeared in sixteen languages. Paperback editions have been in print from Penguin since 1962. Audio Bookshelf (via Penguin) produced an audio book in 2004. A Braille edition appeared in 1967 (via Collins). Wings Press published the 50th Anniversary cloth edition of *Black Like Me* in 2011, following hardback editions in 2004, 2006, 2011. Wings Press has also issued e-books of *Black Like Me, Nuni, The Devil Rides Outside*, and other Griffin titles. *The John Howard Griffin Reader* (Bradford Daniel, editor, Houghton Mifflin, 1968).

3. Studs Terkel (1912-2008). Griffin's first interview with Terkel was aired on radio by WFMT (Chicago) in 1960. "I wasn't drawn to the monastic life—the music had drawn me there (in terms of psychiatric therapy)," Griffin told Terkel. "I went there actually quite antagonistic to the monastic system, purely as a scientist."
4. *A Time To Be Human* (Macmillan, 1977).
5. *Latitudes* interviews with Robert Bonazzi in 1966 and 1967.
6. Radio interview with Studs Terkel on WFMT in 1975.
7. Radio interview with Studs Terkel in 1978. This last interview was in Terkel's *American Dreams: Lost and Found* (Pantheon Books, 1980).
8. *Scattered Shadows: A Memoir of Blindness and Vision* (Orbis Books, 2004). E-books of the memoir and *Prison of Culture: Beyond Black Like Me* (2011) are from Wings Press.
9. "A Different Species" (1954) appeared in *Encounters With the Other: A Personal Journey* (Latitudes Press, 1997).
10. Interview with Thurston Smith was published in *U.S. Catholic* (1977).
11. Griffin's unpublished "Epilogue" to *The Devil Rides Outside* was added to the Wings Press e-book, revealing that the narrator did *not* convert to Catholicism.
12. "The Terrain of Physical Pain" appeared in *Creative Suffering* (Pilgrim Press, 1970), and was reprinted in *Encounters with the Other* and *Prison of Culture.*
13. *Man in the Mirror: John Howard Griffin and the Story of Black Like Me* (Orbis Books, 1997), which is now an e-book from Wings Press. Portions of *Man in the Mirror* are included in *Social Issues in Literature: Race in Black Like Me* (Greenhaven/Gale, 2013).
14. Griffin on journaling is in "The Men From the Boys," which first appeared in *Basilian Teacher* in 1961, and was reprinted in *The Griffin Reader.*
15. Thomas Merton (1915-1968). *The Hermitage Journals: A Diary Kept While Working on the Biography of Thomas Merton* was the first posthumous title under Elizabeth Griffin-Bonazzi's direction as executor of the estate. The

cloth edition was from Andrews and McMeel in 1981 and Doubleday/Image reprinted it as a trade paperback in 1983. The correspondence of Merton and Griffin is at the Thomas Merton Center.

16. Griffin mentions in the 1966 *Latitudes* and the 1960 Terkel interviews that he wanted a "classical education" and had there been a newspaper advertisement for a school anywhere in Europe, he would have written to them. The Lycée Descartes in Tours was the only advertised school that he happened to see. The comments by Lena Griffin are from interviews with Beverly Frank, when she was researching her master's thesis on Griffin.
17. Griffin's passages are in "From Boy to Writer in One Night" (1957), first published in *Handbook of Short Story Writing* from *The Writer's Digest* in 1970. The complete text of this essay is the *Prologue* ("Adventure-Prone") to *Scattered Shadows.*
18. The musicological monograph coauthored by Father Pierre Froger and Griffin, *Interpretation of the Ornaments of the Music for Keyboard Instruments of the 17th and 18th Centuries*, was privately printed in Tours, France, in 1939.
19. Under the pro-Nazi Vichy government led by Philippe Petain, French racial laws were stricter than Germany's, leading to systematic persecution. The General Office of Jewish Affairs established that approximately 75,000 Jews, including 12,000 children, were deported from France to Nazi death camps between 1941 and 1944 (only about 2,500 survived). Griffin wrote a forty-page short story ("Roadblock") about the French underground, but the story remained unfinished. He mentions it in the *Journal*, indicating he was not pleased with the effort. The typescript is at Columbia University.
20. Griffin compiled a glossary of the oral Floridian dialect that he translated into English, while living on the Solomon Islands during World War II. Griffin's personal essay about Chief Vutha ("A Hero's Silence") was published only in *Encounters with the Other.*
21. The passage about listening to the Beethoven string quartet is from *Scattered Shadows.* The Opus 132 quartet was composed between 1824 and 1825, *before* the Opus 131 quartet composed between 1825 and 1826, and upon which *The Devil Rides Outside* is based. Beethoven considered the Opus 131 to be his finest string quartet, but since it was not published or performed during the composer's lifetime (as had been the Opus 132 in 1825), the quartet was miscataloged as an earlier work.
22. Robert Casadesus (1899-1972), considered among the great pianists of the last century, met Griffin through the Duthoo family, when the American student was studying at the University of Poitiers in Tours. He

became close to the "first musical family of France"—composer Robert, wife Gaby, and son Jean, all superb concert pianists. Their correspondence from 1941 to 1972 is at Columbia University. Nadia Boulanger (1887-1979) was considered the greatest teacher of composition in the twentieth century. Her famous alumni included Aaron Copeland, Walter Piston, Elliott Carter, Philip Glass, Virgil Thompson, and David Diamond. French baritone Pierre Bernac (1899-1979) was the most renowned interpreter of French art song, especially the compositions of Francis Poulenc.

23. Griffin's observations are from *Scattered Shadows.*

24. Friar Marie-Bruno, formerly André Hussar (1911-1996), His correspondence (in French) is at Columbia University.

25. The Dominican Saint Thomas Aquinas (1225-1274) and the Franciscan mystic Saint Giovanni Bonaventura (1221-1274) lectured there in the eleventh century. Founded by Saint Dominic (1170-1221) as the first priory of the Dominican Order of Friars-Preachers, they assumed St. Augustine's Rule and were confirmed by Rome in 1216. "The Apples of God" is a brief, unpublished text by Griffin and two photographs of apples on a foldout (one glowing radiantly, the other seeming to emit an interior light)—it remains in the Estate of John Howard Griffin and Elizabeth Griffin-Bonazzi.

26. The Divine Offices are *Matins*, *Lauds*, *Prime*, *Sext*, *None*, *Vespers*, and *Compline*. Griffin's passages are from *Scattered Shadows.*

27. American expressionist painter Abraham Rattner (1893-1978) was a close friend of Picasso, Braque, Miró, Giacometti, Rouault, Soutine, Gris, and Dali in Paris. Rattner's core credo, that "the work becomes a created one as the artist forgets himself, and the good work of art must not be subordinated to the personal good of the artist," influenced Griffin early on. Their correspondence began in 1940, ending with Rattner's death. Their correspondence is in the archives of Columbia University. French poet Pierre Reverdy (1889-1960): His letters to Griffin (in French) reside at the University of Texas. This *Journal* entry was developed into "My Neighbor, Reverdy" in *Southwest Review*, then expanded into chapters of *Scattered Shadows*. Jacques Duthoo (1920-1960) was a second generation Cubist. One of his paintings is the cover art for the Wings e-book of *The Devil Rides Outside.*

28. French theologian Léon Bloy (1846-1917).

29. Jacques Maritain (1882-1973). His *Art and Scholasticism* appeared in French in 1935. The English translation was by Joseph W. Evans (Scribner's, 1962). Griffin considered Maritain to be a mentor; Maritain's letters to him (in French) are at the University of Texas.

30. Griffin's unpublished lectures are at Columbia University.
31. The typescript of *The Devil Rides Outside* varies from the final published version in relatively minor ways. It does not open with the musicologist being driven to the monastery by the cab driver Salesky, but begins with the anonymous narrator in a monastic cell. Otherwise, the typed manuscript runs close to the published book. This does *not* suggest that Griffin had to make several complete drafts from 1949 to the finished manuscript of 1951. The "typescript of 800 pages" is a tall tale perpetrated by the publishers. Rather he made minor cuts, like changing the real name of Dr. Carrazo to Dr. Castelar in the final draft. Also in the manuscript he mentions several famous friends, but their names were struck from the published novel, along with the references to military years in the tropics. This back-story went national when *Look* did a magazine feature on Griffin, along with an interview with Gordon Smith, one of the publishers. There was a second tall tale circulating in 1952 press accounts. Several local papers reported that he had lost his vision as a result of injuries suffered in a crash-landing of a B-24 in the Pacific when, in fact, he had been injured in a Japanese bombing raid. The irony is that Griffin used the idea of a crash-landing in *Nuni*, with his narrator Professor Harper being the only survivor.
32. "Approached to do a Casadesus biography, and face this immense temptation. But the task of presenting a true, whole picture requires a great deal of work. I would like to write it, someday I may. I can characterize him, tell stories no one else could know, but whether I can evaluate him is another question—I love him too much to be objective or impartial. I know his faults, accept them, and even have affection for them."
33. Griffin's reflections on blindness in this *Journal* passage are more detailed in his book, *Handbook for Darkness: Designed for Those Who See*, published by The Lighthouse for the Blind (1949), which also produced the monograph in Braille.
34. From an interview with Thomas D. McDonnell (*Ramparts*, 1963).
35. "The Intrinsic *Other*, originally written in French, appeared in *Building Peace*, edited by Dominique Pire (Gerard, Belgium, 1961). The anthology was issued in France, Switzerland, and Canada. Griffin's translation into English was first published in *The Griffin Reader* and reprinted in *Encounters With the Other* and *Prison of Culture*. Pire's letters to Griffin (in French) are at the University of Texas.
36. Griffin preferred the Collins edition of 1953, which corrected typographical errors in the original Smith's 1952 printing.
37. *American Moderns: From Rebellion to Conformity* (Hill and Wang, 1958). Geismar's essay on Griffin ("The Devil in Texas") ends the final section,

with Norman Mailer, John Hersey, Nelson Algren, J.D. Salinger, Saul Bellow, James Jones, and William Styron. His essay (plus postscript) became the introduction to *The Griffin Reader*.

38. The 1946 study by Father Reginald Garrigou-Lagrange is *Christian Perfection and Contemplation: According to St. Thomas Aquinas and St. John of the Cross.*

39. Clyde Parker Holland, a descendant of Comanche Chief Quanah Parker, is featured in two chapters of *Scattered Shadows*.

40. Only one chapter from *Street of the Seven Angels* was published in Griffin's lifetime, the story "Chez Durand" in the *New World Writing* anthology of 1957. Wings Press published a cloth edition of *Street of the Seven Angels* in 2003, and the novel is now a Wings e-book. The title is based on the location of the Dominican Convent St. Jacques in Paris, at the corner of Boulevard St. Jacques and Street of the Seven Angels. The cover art is by Abraham Rattner.

41. Geismar's letters are at the University of Texas. Griffin letters to Geismar (1909-1979) are at Boston University. Griffin's portraits of Geismar appear in *Twelve Photographic Portraits* and in *The John Howard Griffin Reader*.

42. "Incarnation and Pseudo-Incarnation" is from the collection, *Conflict and Light: Studies in Psychological Disturbance and Readjustment* (Sheed and Ward, 1952).

43. Georges Braque's cover to *La Liberté des mers* (*Freedom of the Seas*, 1960), the last book of poems by Pierre Reverdy, was published in a series of three thousand lithographs. Madame Braque sent the original painting to Griffin, which is in the Estate archives.

44. *Sex, Pornography and Justice* by Albert B. Gerber (Lyle Stuart, 1965).

45. The Anti-Defamation League of B'nai B'rith published the monograph in 1956. Written by Griffin and Theodore Freedman, it was one of five Field Reports on Desegregation in the South, entitled *What Happened in Mansfield: A Report on the Crisis Situation in Mansfield, Texas, resulting from efforts to desegregate its school system in 1956.* Griffin transformed these experiences into a short story about the lynching of a black man in a small town. "The Cause" is a nightmarish tale told from the viewpoints of the white killers. The story appears only in *The John Howard Griffin Reader*.

46. Whit Burnett edited *The Spirit of Man* (Hawthorne, 1958), which included work by Thomas Wolfe, D.H. Lawrence, Sherwood Anderson, Etienne Gilson, Thomas Merton, Katherine Mansfield, William James, George Santayana, Paul Tillich, Gabriel Marcel, Somerset Maugham, Albert Schweitzer, Graham Greene, and others.

47. The first draft was alternately titled *Country Full of Sky* or *Land Full of Sky*, exceeding 1300 manuscript pages. Neither this draft nor the final 212-page manuscript survives. Portions of this *rare* book—the *Preface*, two chapters, and a story *not* in the final text ("The Love Letters of Bessie Love") were in *The Griffin Reader*. "Eighteen Covered Wagons" was in *A Part of Space: Ten Texas Writers*, edited by Betsy Colquitt (TCU Press, 1969).

48. *Scattered Shadows* was entitled *The Scattered Shadows* and Griffin always referred to the book as an autobiography. *Scattered Shadows* was first mentioned in *Journal* entries of 1954. The title was based on a Latin text for Holy Saturday, which says, "the light of Christ dissipates the shadows of men's minds." Chapters appeared in *Ramparts*, *Southwest Review*, and *The Griffin Reader*. The Orbis Books *Scattered Shadows: A Memoir of Blindness and Vision* (2004) did *not* include Robert C. Ellis's painting as cover art, but the e-book from Wings features the painting as its cover.

49. Good Publishing of Fort Worth was owned by George Levitan (1905-1976). *Sepia* debuted in 1947 as *Negro Achievements* and was discontinued in 1983.

50. Miss Sadie Jacobs and Harold Levy were *not* named in *Black Like Me* to protect them from reprisals, and Griffin never named the white dermatologist. The passages are from *Black Like Me*, unless otherwise noted.

51. *The Silent Language* by Dr. Edward T. Hall (Doubleday, 1959). Hall's book clarifies a related aspect. "It is essential," he writes in a new introduction to the 1973 edition, "that we understand how other people read our behavior (not our words, but our behavior)."

52. P. D. East (1921-1971) was the only white person near Hattiesburg Griffin trusted. They knew of each other through mutual friend Maxwell Geismar. East ran *The Petal Paper* (1957-1971), a newspaper considered "communist-inspired" because it advocated justice. East's *The Magnolia Jungle* (Simon and Schuster, 1960).

53. "Dream Variations" by Langston Hughes (1902-1967). The *Black Like Me* title comes from the second variation of the poem, and the last four lines are quoted as the epigraph to the book. In the text, the last two lines are quoted again.

54. Don Rutledge (1931-2013). Photographer for Black Star, author of *Light: The Photojournalism of Don Rutledge* (Baptist History & Heritage Society/Fields Publishing, 2006). The Rutledge book includes photographs from *Black Like Me*.

55. "Journey Into Shame" was published in six consecutive monthly issues of *Sepia*, from April through September of 1960. An international newspaper serial was also published by King Features Syndicate in 1960.

56. Dave Garroway (1913-1982), host of the *Today* show on NBC.
57. Mike Wallace (1918-2012), host of his interview show on CBS.
58. The "magnificent volumes" of *Paléographie Musical* (bound scores of Gregorian Chant) had been brought from the Abbey of St. Pierre de Solesmes. These were leather-bound collections with texts in Latin, title pages and prefaces in French, and printed on heavy, semi-gloss stock with gold-leafed edges. According to the dates written in the French-language paperbacks, they had been purchased in 1936.
59. The complete story of the Griffin's time in Mexico was published in a deluxe edition, *Available Light: Exile in Mexico* (Wings, 2008), and as a Wings e-book. This chance meeting began a lasting friendship between the Griffins and the Bebérs, as both families eventually lived in Fort Worth and visited often. Griffin wrote an introductory essay for *The Singing Boys of Mexico*, a booklet published in 1962. The choir sang at Carnegie Hall in 1958. A portrait of Luis Berbér appears in *The Griffin Reader*.
60. "Notes on Photography" was first published in *Available Light*.
61. "The Watch of the Dead" first appeared in *Encounters with the Other* and was reprinted in *Available Light: Exile in Mexico*. The Purépecha tribe, ancestors of the native people known as the Tarascans, came to prominence in western Mexico during the thirteenth century. The once-nomadic tribe migrated to Michoácan, growing equal in size to the Aztec empire. The civilization achieved its zenith in the sixteenth century, just before the arrival of the Spanish. The name "Tarascan" was given to the Purépeches by the Spaniards, meaning "son-in-law" (*tarasco* in Purépecha). To avoid war, the Tarascans offered daughters of the court to the conquistadors as gifts of friendship. Since the Spaniards heard this word constantly, they mistook it for the name of the tribe. The Spanish chroniclers called the Tarascans "the most beautiful of the Mexican Indians."
62. Griffin's description of the Santa María hacienda appears in *Available Light: Exile in Mexico*, as follows: The U-shaped structure, restored from the ruins of a hacienda built two hundred years earlier, had taken nearly five months to complete. The large house was a traditional whitewashed adobe, its ceiling supported throughout by exposed split-cedar logs, with a red brick floor and a red tile roof.

    There were three bedrooms plus a private alcove that became his studio and the second bathroom became his darkroom. The living and dining areas were one enormous space, naturally lighted. The flagstone courtyard was an open-air garden that was surrounded by windows, filled with lemon and lime trees and a lush array of flowers. It was furnished by the Shoemakers, who loaned a houseful of originally designed wooden pieces. They would eat around a huge refectory table, with matching chairs purchased from the local Benedictine monastery. The front door opened on to the sidewalk, across the street from the church and the village water well.

63. "Passion at Tzintzuntzan" was first in *The Griffin Reader* and then reprinted in *Encounters with the Other* and *Available Light: Exile in Mexico.*
64. Lillian Smith (1897-1966). *Killers of the Dream* (W.W. Norton, 1949) was expanded in 1961. Griffin's assessment appeared in *Southwest Review* in 1962. It is reprinted, along with excerpts from their eighty-page correspondence, in *Prison of Culture.* Smith's letters are at Columbia University.
65. Charles de Foucauld (1858-1916) was canonized in 2005. The Little Brothers and the Little Sisters of Jesus "represented the nearest thing to the unspoiled early Christian that existed long ago," writes Griffin in a 1965 *Ramparts* article, stating that this was the reason Jacques Maritain retired at the order's motherhouse in Toulouse, France. This essay was reprinted in *Prison of Culture.*
66. Decherd Turner (1922-2002). Turner was the director of the Bridwell Library at Southern Methodist University from 1950-1980. He became director of the HRC/UT in 1980, retiring in 1988. He was a legendary bibliophile and author, who brought famous collections to both SMU and UT. Turner was Griffin's first literary executor and arranged the sales of his papers to Columbia University and University of Texas.
67. Martin Luther King's "Letter from a Birmingham Jail" was written in April 1963, in response to a statement by white Alabama clergymen, calling for a cessation to demonstrations in Birmingham. It has been translated into 40 languages.
68. The Mohandas Gandhi quotes are from *Gandhi on Non-Violence*, edited by Thomas Merton (New Directions, 1965). New Directions published many Merton titles under publisher James Laughlin (1914-1997).
69. "Martin Luther King's Movement" was in *The Sign* (1963).
70. "The Cultivated Mind—Guardian Genius of Democracy" (University of Dallas, 1962) is a monograph on religious institutions that established private education in Texas, from 1689. The University of Dallas is a Catholic college in Irving, Texas.
71. Griffin kept a file of note cards containing quotations by world-class thinkers, including several by Rabbi Olan. This one appears in the essay "Life has become a matter of adjustment instead of a matter of right." The Dallas rabbi had been one of the few profound voices against censorship and racism from the Jewish perspective, whereas Turner and Griffin had been the most critical Protestant and Catholic voices in the discourse. They kept in touch with each other on the issues, contributing greatly to the battle

against censorship that was sweeping Texas during the early 1960s.

72. Anne Fremantle's *Pilgrimage to People* (McKay, 1967). Her portrait is in *The Griffin Reader* and her letters are at the University of Texas.

73. "Current Trends in Censorship" appeared in *Southwest Review* in 1962. The Griffin quotes from that article are on pages 227-231.

74. "Prude and the Lewd" appeared in *The Nation* in 1965.

75. "Notes on Smut-Hunters" first appeared in *The Griffin Reader.*

76. Further coverage on Dick Gregory is in *The Church and the Black Man* (Pflaum, 1969; French translation, Desclée de Brouwer, 1970) and in *Uncommon Vision*. The book includes Griffin's text and photographs, a manifesto by the Black Priests Caucus, and a diskette of talks by Reverend Albert B. Cleage and Father James Groppi.

77. The Second Edition of *Black Like Me* (Houghton Mifflin, 1977) includes a thirty-page *Epilogue*, which has been included in all subsequent printings.

78. Griffin's books of photographs and texts are *A Hidden Wholeness: The Visual World of Thomas Merton* (Houghton Mifflin, 1970) and *Jacques Maritain: Homage in Words and Pictures* (Magi Books, 1974).

79. Griffin's portraits of cellist Zara Nelsova (1918-2002) are in *The Griffin Reader* and *Twelve Photographic Portraits.* Nelsova's letters to Griffin are at Columbia University.

80. J. Frank Dobie (1888-1964). To this day writers take refuge at the Dobie ranch for six months at a time with a stipend from the Texas Institute of Letters. Dobie's letters to Griffin are at Columbia University.

81. Griffin's essay "Journal of a Trip South" and the interview with Father Thompson appeared in *Ramparts* in 1963. The essay (entitled "A Visit with Klansmen") and the dialogue with Father Thomson were reprinted in *Encounters With the Other.* The Latitudes collection was dedicated to Father August Thompson. The Thompson-Griffin dialogue also appeared in *Black, White and Gray: Twenty-one Points of View on the Race Question*, edited by Bradford Daniel (Sheed and Ward, 1964), who also edited *The Griffin Reader.*

82. "Racist Sins of Christians" was published as the cover story in *The Sign* in 1963, reprinted in *The Griffin Reader*, and included in *Prison of Culture.*

83. The all-white-male juries failed to reach a verdict in two trials of Beckwith. In 1994 the assassin was convicted based on new evidence. Medgar Evers's legacy reached awareness through the writings of James Baldwin, Eudora Welty, Ann Moody, and Margaret Walker; in protest songs by Nina Simone, Bob Dylan, and Phil Ochs; and in a TV movie (*For Us the Living* in 1983) and a feature film (*Ghosts of Mississippi* in 1996). His

widow, Merlie Evers, became a noted activist, serving as national Chair of the NAACP. Charles Evers, the slain activist's brother, became the NAACP field secretary for Mississippi.

84. Griffin spoke about Clyde Kennard in an interview with Bradford Daniel, "Why They Can't Wait," which was published in *The Progressive* in 1964. The interview was edited into an article, "Requiem for a Martyr," and appeared in *Encounters With the Other*. The article was reprinted in *Prison of Culture*.

85. Griffin's article on the trip was published in *Ramparts* ("A Visit to Huy") in 1965. It was reprinted in *The Griffin Reader* and *Prison of Culture* (as "Fraternal Dialogue"). Nobel Peace Prize winner Dominique Pire's letters to Griffin are at Columbia University.

86. *The Bare Feet* (New York Graphic Society, 1962) by Nell Dorr (1893-1988). Her letters to Griffin are at Columbia University.

87. The first Christian Culture medal was awarded to Sigrid Undset in 1941. Among other winners were Jacques Maritain (1942), Etienne Gilson (1949), Benjamin Mays (1962), Mircea Eliade (1968), Dorothy Day (1970), Marshall McLuhan (1971), Jean Vanier (1973), Malcolm Muggeridge (1979), and Robert Coles (1989). Historian Michael Power writes about the winners in *The Christian Culture Award* (Assumption University, 2001).

88. *The Eagle's Word* (Collins, 1961) by Gerald Vann (1906-1953). Vann's letters to Griffin are at Columbia University.

89. James Meredith (born 1933) was the first African American student to attend the University of Mississippi in 1962.

90. John Oliver Killens (1916-1987). Griffin reviewed Killen's novel, *And Then We Heard the Thunder* (Howard University Press, 1962), in *Saturday Review*.

91. John Beecher (1904-1980), *Collected Poems, 1924-1974* (Macmillan, 1974). Griffin's portrait of Beecher is in *The Griffin Reader*.

92. Penn Jones, Jr. (1914-1998), *Forgive My Grief, Volume I* (*Midlothian Mirror*, 1966), with a Preface by Griffin. Jones was one of the earliest critics of the *Warren Report* and wrote four volumes of the book and a cover story for *Ramparts*. He is the subject of *Citizen's Arrest* by H.C. Nash (Latitudes, 1977), and Jones is the subject of a chapter in *Praise from a Future Generation* by John Kelin (Wings, 2007). Griffin's portrait of Penn Jones is in *The Griffin Reader*, and their correspondence is in the archives of Baylor University.

93. Pianist Lili Kraus (1903-1986). Studied with Bartók, Kodály, and Artur

Schnabel. Considered among the great pianists of the last century. Taught master classes at TCU (1967-1983). Griffin's photograph of Kraus appears in *Twelve Photographic Portraits.*

94. The cloth edition of *The John Howard Griffin Reader* sold more than 90,000 copies, but it was never translated or published in paperback. The out-of-print book is the most comprehensive collection of Griffin's writing and photography.
95. Grace Halsell (1923-2000) was a Fort Worth native, but they had not known each other. *Soul Sister* appeared from World Publishers in 1969.
96. Griffin's essay in *Continuum* (1969) became the introduction to *Follow the Ecstasy*, first published by Latitudes in 1983. Orbis Books published a revised edition in 1993, and it is now an e-book from Wings Press. These separate editions have three different Griffin portraits of Merton as cover art.
97. Father Bamberger was a psychologist and Merton's first confessor during their early years at the Abbey of Gethsemani. He was Abbot of the Abbey of Genesee from 1971 to 2001, and the author of *Thomas Merton: Prophet of Renewal* (Monastic Wisdom Series, 2005).
98. Dom Jean Leclercq (1911-1993), French theologian. Merton's last journal became *The Asian Journal of Thomas Merton* (New Directions, 1973).
99. Jim Andrews (1936-1980) edited *National Catholic Reporter* and also cofounded the publishing house Andrews-McMeel.
100. Folk singer and composer John Jacob Niles (1892-1980). Griffin's photograph of Niles is in *Twelve Photographic Portraits.*
101. Pianist Annie Fischer (1914-1995). Griffin's photograph of Fischer playing at the Concertgebouw is in *Twelve Photographic Portraits.*
102. Amiya Chakravarty (1901-1986), Bengali poet. Merton's *Zen and the Birds of Appetite* (New Directions, 1968) is dedicated to Chakravarty.
103. Photographer Eugene Meatyard (1925-1972) and author Guy Davenport (1927-2000) were Merton friends in Louisville.
104. *What is Contemplation*? (Templegate, 1950). Merton's insights were expanded in later books, including *New Seeds of Contemplation* (New Directions, 1962). The old term *Holy Ghost* references what we now call the *Holy Spirit.*
105. Pianist Sviatoslav Richter (1915-1997), born of a Russian mother and a German father, is considered among the great pianists of the last century. Poet and novelist Boris Pasternak (1890-1960) won the Nobel Prize for Literature in 1958.

106. Mark Van Doren (1894-1972) was a close friend to Thomas Merton and one of his professors at Columbia University. Van Doren won the Pulitzer Prize for poetry in 1940 for *Collected Poems, 1922-1938* (Holt, 1939). Griffin's portrait of Van Doren is in *Twelve Photographic Portraits.*

107. Peter Goldman, *The Death and Life of Malcolm X* (University of Illinois Press, 1973). Griffin's review first appeared in *Sepia* and was reprinted in *Prison of Culture.*

108. *The Night Is Dark and I am Far From Home* (Houghton Mifflin, 1975)

109. John Henry Faulk (1913-1990). *Fear on Trial* (University of Texas Press).

110. Roland Hayes's letters to Griffin are at Columbia University. Griffin reminisces about Hayes (1887-1977) in the *Journal.* "Robert Pritchard called this morning to tell me that Roland Hayes had just died—another of our great cultural heroes gone. The morning turned quiet, the brightness and stillness of this frigid weather somehow fitting. A great sense of personal loss and cosmic loss. The news threw many images into focus—my student days in France when we idolized this great artist and memorized every nuance of his interpretations of art songs, my visit with him a few years back in his home in Brookline, Massachusetts, and the happiness of sitting throughout the afternoon with him, and the photos I made of Hayes, one in *Twelve Photographic Portraits,* and copies sent to his admirers.

"I hear Roland Hayes' voice singing the spiritual 'Plenty good room, plenty good room, good room in the Promised Land . . .' Yet words on paper give no hint of the magic of his interpretation of that spiritual, but those who heard it will know exactly how consoling it was. I was astonished that this particular spiritual came to mind. Usually, I carry in memory the Italian songs that were such a revelation to us in his interpretation. As Pritchard said on the phone—this is the end of an era, the death of one who helped form us, who gave an example of greatness both as an artist and as a human being—a simple, magnanimous man without a trace of vanity. The house begins to smell of black-eyed peas simmering in ham hocks—our traditional New Year's dinner. And I remember when he was living in France, and spoke of longing for some of his mother's black-eyed peas cooked in fatback, with some cornbread.

"I always viewed Roland Hayes as the gentlest and most courteous of men, but he was also tough. You had to be tough not to compromise on the quality of concert programs in those days, and he absolutely refused to compromise. He was tough, yes, but not vindictive. What I find most touching was his return to Georgia, after he became famous and wealthy, to buy the land on which his mother had lived as a slave."

111. *A Time to Be Human* was published by Macmillan (US/Canada, 1977, and by Collier in the UK that same year). Griffin dedicated the book to Roland Hayes, taking his title from Merton's translation of Chuang Tzu's words that became the book's epigraph. He chose the ancient sage's lines because they were profound and sounded aptly modern. "When men do not get twisted and maimed beyond recognition, when they are allowed to live—the purpose of government is achieved. From the time of the Three Dynasties men have been running in all directions. How can they find time to be human?"

112. Michael Mott's official biography, *The Seven Mountains of Thomas Merton*, was published by Houghton Mifflin in 1984.

113. *Man's Search for Meaning* (1959) by Viktor Frankl (1905-1997) has been translated into 40 languages. Originally entitled *From Death Camp to Existentialism*, it was his first book and the introduction to Logotherapy.

114. *The Denial of Death* (The Free Press, 1973) by Ernest Becker (1924-1974) won the Pulitzer Prize for Nonfiction in 1974.

115. *Encounters with Silence* (Newman Press, 1960) by Karl Rahner (1904-1984).

116. *Profiles in Hope* (Veritas, 1978). Cornelia and Irving Sussman were loyal friends, and their letters to Griffin are at Columbia University.

117. The GEO collection was edited by Ajowa Nzinga Ifateyo, including her preface and an essay on unconscious racism. Dan Robertson's "Fifty Years with *Black Like Me*" evoked meetings with Griffin and an insightful discussion of the segregated world of Houston where he grew up that was parallel to Griffin's "Southern background" in Dallas. Robert Bonazzi's "Encountering John Howard Griffin"—a remembrance of a mentor—talks about the first *Latitudes* interview with Griffin (accompanied by Robertson) and subsequent visits. This Bonazzi piece on Griffin also appeared in *Voices de la Luna*.

118. The FESTIBA panel included Bryce Milligan, Dr. Francisco Jiménez of Santa Clara University, Chicana poet Lorna Dee Cervantes, and Robert Bonazzi. The Trinity panel included talks by columnist Cary Clack, Gary W. Houston, poet Carmen Tafolla, artist Anne Wallace, photographer Michael Nye, and Robert Bonazzi.

119. French actress Clémentine Célarié (born 1957) has appeared in more than fifty films, winning awards for *I'm Afraid of Forgetting* (2012) and other roles. She has appeared all over France and, in May of 2014, took her one-woman show to San Francisco.

120. "Ever A Bridegroom" appeared in *The Texas Observer* in 1981. *Goodbye to a River* (1960) by John Graves, *The Ordways* (1965) by William Humphrey, and *The House of Breath* (1950) by William Goyen.

121. Turner's essay appeared in the *Dallas Times-Herald* in 1968.

About the Author

Photo by Elizabeth Griffin-Bonazzi

Robert Bonazzi is the executor for the estate of John Howard Griffin and has edited many of Griffin's works. Bonazzi also authored the critically acclaimed *Man in the Mirror: John Howard Griffin and the Story of Black Like Me*. His most recent books include *Awakened by Surprise*, *Outside the Margins*, and *The Scribbling Cure*. His book *Maestro of Solitude: Poems & Poetics* was a finalist for the Texas Institute of Letters Poetry Award. Bonazzi now lives in San Antonio and writes a column, *Poetic Diversity*, for the *San Antonio Express-News*, and reviews for *World Literature Today*.